The
Christian Gospel
for Americans

The
Christian Gospel
for Americans

A Systematic Theology

David Ray Griffin

PROCESS
CENTURY
PRESS
ANOKA, MINNESOTA 2019

The Christian Gospel for Americans: A Systematic Theology

Process Century Press
RiverHouse LLC
802 River Lane
Anoka, MN 55303

Process Century Press books are published in association with the International Process Network.

Cover: Susanna Mennicke

VOLUME V: THEOLOGICAL EXPLORATIONS SERIES
JEANYNE B. SLETTOM, GENERAL EDITOR

ISBN 978-1-940447-42-1
Printed in the United States of America

Series Preface: Theological Explorations

This series aims to explore the implications of Whiteheadian philosophy and theology for religious belief and practice. It also proposes that process religious thinkers, working from within many different traditions — Buddhist, Confucian, Christian, Hindu, Indigenous, Jewish, Muslim, and others — have unique insights pertinent to the critical issues of our day.

In 1976, we published a book, *Process Theology: An Introductory Exposition,* in which we aimed to "show the creative potentiality of a process perspective in theology." In addition to its explanation of process concepts and their application to Christian doctrine, the book noted the contribution of Whiteheadian thought toward "intercultural and interreligious understanding" and took an early stance on the ecological threat, claiming that process theology was prepared to "make a distinctive contribution" to this challenge.

Since the publication of that book, we have seen many others explore these and other themes in articles, books, and conferences. At the same time, the threat to planetary health and the need for "intercultural and interreligious understanding" has only accelerated. This series is an effort to support theologians and religious philosophers in their ongoing exposition of possible Whiteheadian solutions.

John B. Cobb, Jr.
David Ray Griffin

CONTENTS

Salvation
and the Reign of God

Morality
and the Christian Community

ACKNOWLEDGEMENTS

I am grateful to several people for help with this book.

Daniel Ahearn and Elizabeth Woodworth kindly read the chapters, offering valuable suggestions.

I obtained much help from a small "Process Group" that met every other week to critique the chapters. This group was comprised of the Rev. Mark Asman, Mary Becker, the Rev. Tim Burnette, Karen Carlander, Kent Carlander, Anne Heck, Thomas Heck, Ann Jaqua, and Ernie Tamminga.

I remain grateful to Gary Becker, who organized the group several years ago, who was with us for a couple years before he died from a stroke.

I am also grateful to Jeanyne Slettom, the editor of Process Century Press, for putting the book together in an attractive way.

Finally, I am most grateful to my wife, Ann Jaqua (who was part of the group). If it were not for Ann, I would not have been able to write this book, because I would surely have been dead long ago.

~David Ray Griffin, Isla Vista, California, June 2019

Introduction

THE CHURCH IN AMERICA needs a new theology for the twenty-first century. The new theology must differ from *traditional* theologies, which presuppose supernaturalism—the view that God can perform miracles, in the sense of events that violate the laws of nature. The new theology must also differ from modern *liberal* theologies, because their commitment to modernity leaves them with theologies too thin to support robust Christian life.

The theology articulated in this book belongs to the kind of approach that is known as "progressive Christianity."[1] But it differs in many respects from most other types of progressive Christianity. While this book is liberal in method, it is conservative in content, affirming several doctrines that had wrongly been rejected as necessarily entailing supernaturalism—such as the resurrection of Jesus and the reality of demonic power (discussed in Chapters 7 and 9, respectively).

AMERICAN EMPIRE

This theology emphasizes the extent to which the American Empire has become a threat to other countries, to the planet's life, and hence

1

to the survival of the human race. Because of the overriding issue of survival, this book's discussion of sin and the demonic focuses on America's foreign policy, its role in the development of nuclear weapons, and its responsibility for the climate crisis.

The title of this book, *The Christian Gospel for Americans*, might easily be misunderstood. To paraphrase William Stringfellow, the purpose is to understand America in light of the gospel, *not* to interpret the gospel Americanly—not to interpret the gospel for the convenience of America.[2]

Because of its focus on American imperialism and America's nuclear and environmental policies, this book presents a dark picture of America. The tendency of many commentators, especially political leaders, has been to exaggerate America's goodness, praising "American Exceptionalism" and even calling America "the greatest nation on the face of the planet."

The history of American foreign policy contradicts the claims of American Exceptionalism, according to which America has been—in the words of former Vice President Cheney—"the greatest force for good the world has even known."[3] Such exaggerations aside, there are many reasons for Americans to take pride in their country's history: its civil rights movement; its long leadership in science and technology; its films and other forms of entertainment; its acceptance (at least until recently) of immigrants; and—most important—its ability to retain a somewhat democratic form of government for 200 years.

But if a theology for America is to have any chance of being truthful and worthwhile, it must deal with the darker side of America, especially its imperialism, its racism, and its nuclear and climate policies. The new theology must point out ways in which the American Empire is similar to the Roman Empire, which crucified Jesus.

CENTRAL THEMES

The remainder of the introduction lays out a number of themes that characterize this theology—themes that together summarize the distinctiveness of this effort to develop a theology appropriate for Americans in the twenty-first century.

Both Universal and Local

Most theologies have intended to be *universal,* stating the Christian message as relevant to peoples in all times and places. But every theology is also inevitably *local,* being written for people of a particular time and place. Such theologies seek to formulate the gospel so as to be credible and relevant to the major issues confronting Christian faith at the time.

However much theologies intend to be both, they can differ greatly with respect to their emphases. Traditionally, theologies sought primarily to be universal, intending to address Christians as such. More recently, many theologians have shifted toward the local. That is, they have made little attempt to speak of Christian faith as such, focusing instead on addressing current and local issues.

By virtue of being written for contemporary Americans, this theology, while seeking to articulate the Christian gospel as such, seeks to address issues that are central, or at least should be central, to Christian churches and people in the United States of America. Writing a theology for Americans is justified by the overwhelming power of America—economically, militarily, and culturally—for good or ill, and also by the tensions that exist between the American image of itself as a moral and Christian nation and its actual behavior.

A list of respects in which this book's theological stance is different from the kinds of theology that have thus far been dominant in American churches would include the following points.

Primary Doctrines

This theology attempts always to keep in mind the meaning of "gospel"—good news. Insofar as the attempt is successful, this theology focuses on the *primary* doctrines of Christian faith, which are unqualifiedly good news, as distinct from secondary and tertiary doctrines, some of which have delivered bad—sometimes horrible—news. The primary doctrines are rooted in the Bible, especially the teachings and presuppositions of Jesus of Nazareth. These primary doctrines include the following points:

- Our world was created by a good, loving, wise, and purposive God, one who loves the world and all creatures, great and small, unreservedly.

- Loving all of us, God desires that we treat each other with justice and compassion; this implies that, as Luke 4:8 indicated, the Christian message is first of all supposed to be "good news to the poor" (as liberation theologians have emphasized).

- Although anthropocentrism is to be avoided in favor of the idea that God loves all sentient beings, human beings are still to be considered the crown of creation, at least on this planet.

- Our world is essentially good, although it is now full of evil.

- God is uniquely powerful, being alone capable of creating a universe.

- As the Book of Genesis suggested, God created the universe not out of nothing but out of chaos—out of materials having their own power, so God cannot unilaterally determine all events. The world's evils do not, therefore, imply that God is evil or indifferent.[4]

- God's love, purpose, and concern for justice, having been expressed in the biblical tradition through a series of prophets and sages, were revealed in a decisive way through Jesus of Nazareth.

- The divine purpose, thus revealed, is to overcome evil by bringing about a Reign of Divine Values (traditionally called Kingdom of God) on earth, in which the present subjugation of life to demonic values—lies, ugliness, greed, destructiveness, injustice, hate, and indifference—will be replaced by a mode of life based on divine values—truth, love, beauty, goodness, justice, and compassion.

- Christian theology is necessarily at once theological and political, to use the words of William Stringfellow, because "the theology of the Bible concerns politics in its most rudimentary meaning. ... The Bible is about the politics of fallen creation ...; the politics of the Kingdom of God ...; [and] the politics of the demonic powers and principalities."[5]

- In a Reign of Divine Values, the rich and powerful will not oppress the poor and the weak, but will enable them to have sufficient food, water, and other necessities of a good life.

- Salvation can be enjoyed here and now, at least in a partial way, through direct experience of, and empowerment by, God as Holy Spirit, and by the faith that our lives have ultimate meaning, because nothing can separate us from the love of God.

- The divine purpose is also to bring about an even more complete salvation in a life beyond bodily death.

- Although God as Holy Spirit is present in all human beings, God was especially incarnate in Jesus of Nazareth, and in a way making it appropriate for Christians to regard him as the decisive revelation of the nature and purpose of God.

- Jesus called on people to live with fidelity *(fides)* to God (rather than to the emperor). Living with fidelity to God involves obeying the Golden Rule—do to others what you would want them to do to you—or at least the Silver Rule: Do not do to others what you would not like done to you.

- The Christian church is ideally comprised of communities that seek to imitate Jesus's own fidelity to God.

- Central to worship is Communion (the Lord's Supper, the Eucharist), in which we remember that Jesus remained faithful in his opposition to the empire, which led to his death on a Roman cross.

- Affirming the truth and saving value of Christianity does not imply that other religious traditions have less truth and value.

Secondary and Tertiary Doctrines

These primary doctrines should be strongly distinguished from secondary doctrines, which were developed at particular times and places to defend or spell out primary doctrines, and also from tertiary doctrines, which were developed at particular times and places to support or elaborate secondary doctrines.

Although the primary doctrines show Christian faith to be unambiguously good news, these primary doctrines have often been overshadowed by secondary and tertiary doctrines, which may contradict the primary doctrines and thereby announce bad news.

For example, the idea that God is uniquely powerful has widely been understood to mean that God is *omnipotent*, in the sense that creatures cannot resist the divine will. This secondary doctrine led to the problem of evil—why does God cause or at least permit so much evil?—which suggests that God is far from perfectly loving.

The secondary doctrine that God is omnipotent even led to the tertiary doctrine that God, in creating the world, foreordained all events that would occur. This tertiary doctrine led to the most horrible of all traditional Christian doctrines—that some people, perhaps most people, were predestined to hell, where they would suffer everlastingly. The primary doctrine that "God is love" (I John 4:8) was clearly lost.

Another example: In developing the doctrine of God as the supreme being, theologians in the second and third centuries used the idea, derived from Greek philosophy, that God is unchanging and impassive—meaning that God cannot be emotionally moved by the creatures' sufferings. This secondary doctrine of divine "impassibility" was another way in which hymn-writer Charles Wesley's phrase—that God is "pure unbounded love"—was undermined.

One way of responding to this problem was provided by eleventh-century theologian St. Anselm. Facing the question of how the doctrine of divine impassibility could be compatible with the biblical doctrine that God is compassionate, Anselm asked in a prayer:

[H]ow art thou . . . compassionate, and, at the same time, passionless? . . . [I]f thou dost not feel sympathy, thy heart is not wretched from sympathy for the wretched; but this it is to be compassionate.

[Anselm answered]: "Thou art compassionate in terms of our experience, and not compassionate in terms of thy being."[6]

In other words, God is not really compassionate, but only seems so to us. On the basis of this tertiary doctrine, I John 4:8 would need to be rewritten: God may *appear* to be love, but really is not.

For an example of how a tertiary doctrine could be created to support a secondary doctrine: The primary doctrine that Jesus was the supreme revelation of God was expressed metaphorically in the New Testament by referring to Jesus as "the son of God." But soon this metaphor was interpreted literally, resulting in the doctrine that Jesus was literally God's son. The first phase of the development of this doctrine was based on the fact that, if Jesus was literally the son of God, he could not have had a human father: Accordingly, Jesus was said to have been impregnated by the Holy Spirit rather than by Joseph, and Mary had remained a virgin.

The doctrine of the virgin birth of Jesus became central to American Fundamentalism, which was based on the so-called *five fundamentals.* But rather than truly being one of Christian faith's fundamental doctrines, the virgin birth of Jesus was merely a secondary doctrine, which provided one way of expressing how Jesus had a special relationship to God.

The idea that Jesus was literally the son of God soon, through various means, led to the idea that Jesus *was* God—"God the Son." As if Jesus could have had divine attributes, such as omniscience, while being truly human.

While the doctrines identified here as secondary and tertiary were intended to support the primary Christian doctrines, today these doctrines—such as divine omnipotence, divine impassibility, and the virgin birth of Jesus—serve to discredit the gospel. A theology for the twenty-first century needs to express the gospel's primary doctrines without having them undermined and discredited by secondary and tertiary doctrines formulated in bygone days.

Unfortunately, the historic Christian creeds contain many such doctrines. For example, the Nicene Creed, which is probably the creed most often reaffirmed in churches, speaks of Jesus as "the only-begotten Son of God, begotten of the Father before all worlds," who "came down from heaven, and was incarnate by the Holy Spirit of the Virgin Mary."

These historic creeds need to be replaced. More generally, Christian thinking needs to be revised, when necessary, so as to express unambiguously and intelligibly the good news contained in the gospel's primary doctrines.

Doctrines: Literally True, Symbolically True, or Simply False?

Another major theological issue is that of truth: Are Christian doctrines true? And if so, in what sense? The position taken in this theology is that some traditional Christian doctrines are literally true, some can be regarded as symbolically true, and others are simply false.

In modern liberal theology, there has been a tendency to say that, although Christian doctrines are true, they are not true *literally*, but only symbolically. For example, to say that "God created the world" might mean only that the world is both contingent and good. To speak of "the resurrection of Jesus" might mean only that he now lives in our hearts. However, this approach, according to which all Christian doctrines are only symbolically true, is doubly problematic.

On the one hand, there are some historic Christian doctrines that must be called just plain false. To give some examples: the idea that the world was literally created in six days; the idea that heaven is above the earth and hell below; the idea that some people are predestined to hell; the idea that those who go to hell will suffer everlastingly. On the other hand, unless some doctrines are considered literally true, there is no basis for describing the Christian worldview as superior to any other worldview, such as that of mechanistic determinism.

Each of the primary doctrines listed above is portrayed as being literally true. Take, for example, the first one: *Our world was created by a loving God, one who loves the world and all creatures, great and small, unreservedly.* Many modern theologians have asserted that we cannot in any literal sense say that our universe was created by God. There have been many reasons for making this claim, such as:

- If we say that God created the world, then God is responsible for evil so cannot be called good.

- God is by definition infinite, so God cannot be regarded as one being among others. God must instead be being-itself, so we cannot describe God as acting, such as creating things.

- Modern cosmology provides a fully adequate account of how our world, with its stars, planets, and galaxies was formed, and Neo-Darwinism provides a fully adequate account of how life, including human life, evolved. So there is no place for a divine reality to play a causal role.

Likewise, some modern liberal theologians have said that the doctrine of the resurrection of Jesus cannot be described as literally true, because life after death in any literal sense is impossible. Therefore, the language of the "resurrection of Jesus" cannot be given any literal meaning. German New Testament theologian Rudolf Bultmann, for example, said that "Jesus rose into the kerygma"[7] (with *kerygma* meaning the early Christian proclamation).

Demythologizing

Bultmann's statement about the resurrection was made in the context of his program in the 1950s and 60s calling for Christian faith to be "demythologized." Insofar as a "myth" is an idea that cannot be literally true, the call to demythologize the gospel should be accepted. But the idea was controversial because of Bultmann's way of explaining what he meant by *demythologizing* Christian faith.

What was wrong with myth, Bultmann said, was that it objectifies divine action. By this, he meant primarily the interruption of the natural course of affairs by attributing a natural effect to a supernatural cause.[8] Thus defined, to demythologize Christian faith is simply to free it from supernaturalism.

But Bultmann also insisted that the only way to do this is to understand an event from two points of view. On the one hand, we view any event, such as a case of healing, from a fully naturalistic point of view, in which there is no room for God's acting. On the other hand, we can, from the perspective of faith, say that the event is nevertheless an act of God.[9]

But how are we to understand how this could be? One way to understand it would be that the healing was produced partly by natural causes and partly by divine action. But Bultmann rejected this view, saying that it was *wholly* produced by natural (nondivine) causes and *wholly* produced by God. This view, he conceded, was paradoxical.[10] Bultmann's view was influenced by the modernist perspective of Immanuel Kant, according to which there can be no divine influence in the world.[11]

Alfred North Whitehead, however, provided a postmodern way of relating divine and natural causation that does not need to resort to paradox. According to Whitehead's philosophy, divine influence plays a role in every event. In most events, the divine role is trivial; but this role can vary greatly. In some events, such as crucial events in Jesus's life, the divine influence can be great, so those events can be considered "acts of God" in a special sense.

Hence, we can speak of God as active in Jesus without supernaturalism, because God is involved in all events. Language about God as active in Jesus need not be demythologized. In other words, the traditional doctrines, such as those of the incarnation, trinity, and resurrection, need to be demythologized, but not in Bultmann's sense.

From Supernaturalism to Theistic Naturalism

In traditional theology, Christian doctrines were formulated within a supernaturalistic framework, according to which miracles in the traditional sense could occur. In this traditional sense, a miracle was an event that was impossible naturally, but was brought about supernaturally by God.

In the eighteenth century, an approach known as "liberal theology" emerged. This approach accepts a fully naturalistic worldview, according to which miracles cannot occur: There can be no interruption of the web of natural causes and effects.

By contrast, conservative (including fundamentalist) theologians have continued the older approach. They reject liberal theology as vacuous, having lost virtually all Christian substance. For example, conservative theologians portray liberals as not only rejecting the idea of God as creator of the world, but also as rejecting divine inspiration, divine revelation, and the idea that God was incarnate in Jesus.

This criticism is largely true of *modern* liberal theology, which has a mechanistic worldview, according to which all events, including human thought processes, proceed mechanistically and hence deterministically. There is no room for free actions. Our *feeling* of freedom is an illusion.

This modern worldview also accepts the sensationist epistemology, according to which our experience of things beyond ourselves comes entirely through our physical sense organs. Unless an experience comes to us by means of our eyes, our ears, our sense of touch, and so on, it is not considered genuine. Accordingly, putative religious experiences, in which people believe that they have felt the presence of God—or otherwise "experienced the holy"—are automatically ruled out of the category of possibly genuine experiences.

According to this view, even if there is a divine reality, we could not experience it (regardless of what mystics have said). This divine reality could not have become incarnate in Jesus. Indeed, modernity cannot support a religious worldview of any type, let alone a distinctively Christian one. This modern worldview was articulated by philosophers such as David Hume and Immanuel Kant.

To speak more precisely: One must distinguish between the early and the late modern worldviews. The main difference involves the existence of God. Most early modern thinkers, such as Descartes, Locke, and Kant, affirmed the existence of a divine reality, who created the world. But late modern thinkers, anticipated by Hume and pioneered by neo-Darwinism, add atheism to the other characteristics of modern thought

In the twentieth century, however, philosophers such as William James, Henri Bergson, Charles Hartshorne, and Alfred North Whitehead worked out a *postmodern* worldview.[12] Thanks to this view, it is now possible to have a position that, while being philosophically sound, is religious and even distinctively Christian. This worldview, known as *constructive* postmodernism, is completely different from *deconstructive* postmodernism, which emerged in the 1980s.[13]

Given the (constructive) postmodern worldview, we can see that mechanistic and sensationistic naturalism is merely one type of naturalism. *Naturalism as such*, which can be called *generic* naturalism, is simply the doctrine that there are no supernatural violations of the normal laws of nature. Naturalism in this sense simply insists that, if theism is true, divine influence must be understood as part of the normal cause-effect relations, not an exception to them. This is the position of postmodern naturalism.

Because naturalism had for a long time been equated with a mechanistic-sensationist worldview, naturalism has generally been considered anti-religious. But with the rise of this postmodern worldview, we can affirm religious beliefs without affirming supernaturalism.

Science and Theology

Since the nineteenth century, science has presupposed generic naturalism, according to which there are no supernatural violations of the normal laws of nature. However, the ideological leaders of the scientific and philosophical communities have largely equated naturalism as such with the mechanistic-sensationist-atheistic type of naturalism. Because of this equation, it became widely accepted that theology and science are necessarily antithetical to each other.

Given this presupposition, theologians have been faced with an untenable choice. On the one hand, they could continue to affirm Christian faith by adopting a supernaturalist, anti-science position. This position has been taken by most conservative theologians involved in the science-religion discussion. On the other hand, theologians could avoid taking an anti-science position by reinterpreting Christian faith in terms of modernist naturalism, hence giving an anti-religious interpretation of Christian faith. The present theology provides an alternative to both of these options. Thanks to (constructive) postmodernism, there is no need to choose between being fully scientific and being fully religious.

Philosophy and Theology

It has long been assumed that philosophy and theology are radically different enterprises. It is the task of philosophy to articulate a world-view that makes a claim to truth in terms of the normal philosophical and scientific criteria: self-consistency and adequacy to the facts that are relevant to the subject at hand (such as quantum physics or micro-biology). Philosophy differs from science in this respect by needing to treat *all* the facts of experience, because the task is to develop a worldview inclusive of all types of facts. But philosophy and science are identical in insisting on a fully naturalistic worldview. There can be no *miracles,* events that violate the universe's normal cause-and-effect relations.

But it has been widely assumed that theology is different in kind from these two enterprises. According to this view, theology proceeds from revelation based on supernatural events and divine inspiration. A theology is not to be judged by whether it can develop a position that can put the facts of our experience into a self-consistent position. Rather, it is to be judged by how well it can put revealed doctrines into a self-consistent system.

By contrast, the present theology holds that Christian theology is like philosophy in seeking to provide an all-inclusive worldview. It differs from philosophy only by giving special attention to events of Jewish and Christian history, especially the life, teachings, crucifixion, and resurrection of Jesus of Nazareth. Whereas this history includes exceptional events, these events are not interpreted as involving miracles, in the sense of violations of the laws of nature.

Hard-Core Common Sense

Besides avoiding any appeal to supernaturalism, a theology for the twenty-first century should also be like philosophy in taking hard-core common sense as the fundamental criterion for deciding which claims should be accepted as credible. The term "hard-core common sense" is used here to refer to what Whitehead called *inevitable presuppositions of practice*. Agreeing with the tradition known as *commonsense philosophy*, he said that "we must bow to those presumptions, which, in despite of criticism, we still employ for the regulation of our lives."[14]

For example, philosophers have debated the possibility of affirming "solipsism." For one to affirm solipsism, one would say that, for all I know, I might be the only being that exists: I doubt that other people and other things beyond me exist. But if we accept hard-core common sense as the basic criterion for deciding which beliefs are credible, we would not waste time debating solipsism, because it is self-refuting: If I announce to an audience, or write on my computer, that I am a solipsist, doubting the existence of an actual world beyond myself, I show by my act of speaking *to* the audience or writing *on* my computer that I do not doubt this at all.

Whitehead made this point by saying that we need to avoid "negations of what in practice is presupposed,"[15] because in affirming such negations, we contradict ourselves, explicitly denying what we are implicitly affirming.

German philosophers Karl-Otto Apel and Jürgen Habermas made this point in terms of the concept of a "performative contradiction," which occurs, in Martin Jay's words, "when whatever is being claimed is at odds with the presuppositions or implications of the act of claiming it."[16] One is thereby violating the law of noncontradiction, which is the first rule of reason.

The adjective *hard-core* is used here to distinguish such beliefs, which are truly common to all people, from those beliefs that are sometimes described as common sense but are not truly universal. These beliefs, which can be called *soft-core common sense,* can be denied without necessarily contradicting any presuppositions of our practice.

In any case, we will be able to achieve much more unanimity if theologians, along with both philosophers and scientists, avoid making assertions that contradict any of our inevitable presuppositions.

Liberal in Method, Conservative in Content

This theology employs the process philosophy of Alfred North Whitehead as a "natural theology," just as early and medieval Christian theologians used the philosophy of Plato and/or Aristotle. Whitehead's philosophy, however, provides a much better philosophical basis for Christian theology than either Platonic or Aristotelean philosophy.

Process theology is normally categorized as a type of liberal theology. But some liberal theologies in recent decades have become hardly recognizable as Christian, so that conservative theologians rightly criticize them as vacuous. This charge is based on the fact that many modern liberal theologies have rejected the idea of God as creator of the world, of God as a personal being, of ongoing divine activity in the world, of divine revelation and inspiration, and so on. But all of these ideas are reaffirmed in the present theology. So while this theology is liberal in method, it is conservative in content.

"Liberal in method" means that all appeals to authority to establish truth are rejected. Theology, like philosophy, can argue for the truth of its doctrines only on the basis of evidence and reason. So although the reality of revelation can be affirmed, theologians cannot make claims for the truth of events or doctrines by claiming that this truth was revealed.

This theology is "conservative in content" by virtue of employing a constructive postmodern worldview, based on Whitehead's philosophy. Being "conservative in content" cannot, of course, mean affirming the types of conservative theology that allow secondary and tertiary doctrines to distort the gospel's primary doctrines. It means reaffirming primary doctrines of the Christian gospel, such as God's creation of the world, God as actively present in us, and divinely-given life after death.

The Golden Rule

Although doctrines are important, being a Christian is primarily a matter of how an individual or a community *lives*. At the center of Christian morality is the Golden Rule, which is the name that has been given to Jesus's statement in Matthew 7:12: "In everything do to others as you would have them do to you; for this is the law and the prophets." In light of Jesus's statement that this statement summarizes the teachings of the Pentateuch and the Hebrew prophets, one would think that it would have played a much more central role in Christian teaching and piety than it has in fact played.

God, the Bible,
and Humanity

CHAPTER ONE

The Bible and
Theological Method

A<small>LTHOUGH</small> "<small>METHODOLOGY</small>" may sound boring, it is actually the crucial factor in determining the nature and credibility of a theological position.

TRADITIONAL THEOLOGICAL METHOD

One of the major questions about theology today is whether it should continue to presuppose traditional theological methodology, according to which it is different in kind from the methods employed in science and philosophy, or whether theology should employ essentially the same method as those disciplines. This issue, broached in the Introduction, is discussed more fully here.

Revelation

In science and philosophy, theories are judged in terms of two questions: (1) Are they self-consistent? (2) Are they adequate to the facts? Theology traditionally employed a different method. It based itself on revealed doctrines, which were found, at least primarily, in the Bible. Unlike philosophical and scientific doctrines, the theological doctrines were not judged to be true because they are self-consistent and adequate to the facts, but simply because they were revealed. The theological task was to show how various revealed doctrines could be fit together into a coherent position. If some of the doctrines could not be made consistent with the remaining beliefs, so that we could not see how they could possibly be true, they were not necessarily rejected as false, but simply categorized as "mysteries."

However, aside from beliefs classified as mysteries, one could still ask how revelation should be related to other possible sources of religious knowledge: tradition, experience, and reason. There have been four major ways of answering this question.

Four Approaches

According to traditional Roman Catholicism, at least as normally understood, Christian faith and hence theology are based on:

> Scripture plus apostolic tradition, as manifested in the living teaching authority of the Catholic Church, to which were entrusted the oral teachings of Jesus and the apostles, along with the authority to interpret Scripture correctly.[1]

Tradition consisted primarily of "the first seven ecumenical councils, beginning with the First Council of Nicaea in 325 and closing with the Second Council of Nicaea in 787." According to this two-source model of authority, "there are certain divinely revealed truths which are found in the unwritten word of God alone, not in Sacred Scriptures."[2]

By contrast, early leaders of the Protestant Reformation, especially the so-called magisterial reformers—Martin Luther, John Calvin, and Ulrich Zwingli—insisted that faith and hence theology should be based on scripture alone (*sola scriptura*). According to this view, tradition is not to be accepted as an authority alongside of scripture. If some doctrines of the church are not supported by scripture, they should be deleted.

The Anglican Church, by contrast, maintains that faith and theology are to be based on reason as well as scripture and tradition. This idea, which was enunciated by Richard Hooker in the sixteenth century, came to be known as the "three-legged stool." Many Anglicans believe, however, that this is a misleading image, because it suggests that the three components of the triad are of equal authority, whereas Hooker had understood tradition and experience to be subordinate to scripture.[3]

The Methodist Church, which grew out of the Anglican tradition, was based primarily on the ideas of eighteenth-century evangelist John Wesley, who added "experience" as a fourth source. This four-source view came widely to be called the Quadrilateral. But the term has become controversial in conservative Methodist circles, because it has been widely interpreted to mean that the four sources are equal in importance. Conservatives, by contrast, insist that scripture is supreme, with the other three sources helping to interpret it. Another complaint is that some Methodists use "experience" to refer to experiences of various types, whereas Wesley meant specifically an experience in which people are assured that their sins have been forgiven.[4]

Which of these four traditional ways of theologizing is appropriate today? The correct answer is: None of the above. They are all inappropriate because, in their traditional forms, all share a view of scripture that today must be considered incredible.

DIVINE OMNIPOTENCE AND THE SCRIPTURE PRINCIPLE

The incredible view is what theologians Edward Farley and Peter Hodgson called "the scripture principle." In a brilliant essay, simply entitled "Scripture and Tradition," they said that, according to this principle, "the collection of writings called scripture contains a unique deposit of divine revelation—a deposit whose special qualities are due to its inspired origins."[5]

The idea that this deposit is "inspired," moreover, traditionally meant inspiration in a precise sense: that the inspired documents are characterized by "inerrancy, infallibility, and absolute truthfulness." Accordingly, there is an identity "between what is divinely willed and what is humanly asserted."

But how would this be possible? Normally, human beings arrive at their beliefs by means of extremely fallible processes, in which false beliefs can enter in through prejudice, wishful thinking, party spirit, limited information available at the time and place, and countless other factors. The belief that the ideas put forth by some particular human beings are infallible and inerrant, guaranteed to be devoid of error, presupposes that the normal human processes of belief-formation have been supernaturally overruled. This infallibility, said Farley and Hodgson, could only have been "brought by the causal efficacy of God in the form of 'inspiration.'" In other words, God is omnipotent, "the infinitely powerful world sovereign," who "is always able to accomplish the divine will."[6]

This notion—inerrant inspiration based on divine omnipotence—may have seemed credible in the past, but it clearly is not today. Three centuries of biblical criticism have made the idea that the Bible was inerrantly inspired no less incredible than the idea that the Earth was created 4,000 years ago. Below are discussed some of the major reasons why, in light of the modern study of the Bible, theologies based on the idea of the Bible as inerrantly inspired cannot be considered credible.

BIBLICAL CRITICISM

"Biblical criticism" does not mean an approach that is critical, in the sense of hostile to, the Bible. Rather, it means an approach that studies the Bible critically, as opposed to naively.

According to traditional theology, the various books of the Bible were written by men who had been inerrantly inspired to write them. The Pentateuch, consisting of the first five books of the Bible, was said to have been written by Moses (except for the last eight verses of Deuteronomy, which describes Moses's death). Two of the Gospels were said to have been written by two of Jesus's disciples, named Matthew and Luke.

However, starting in the seventeenth century, scholars began engaging in historical criticism of the Pentateuch, the Gospels, and the other biblical books, in order to discover when, why, and by whom the biblical books were written, in order to determine what they meant at the time. One effect of this historical criticism was that it undermined the idea that the Bible is inerrant and thereby the claim that it was omnipotently inspired.

Hebrew Bible

Beginning with the Hebrew Bible, scholars showed that Genesis, along with the rest of the Pentateuch, was based on at least two different documents, which were dubbed J and E, with J standing for a document that referred to God as Jahweh (Jehovah, Yahweh), and E standing for a document that referred to God as Elohim.

These documents sometimes give contradictory accounts. According to the account of creation in Genesis 1, for example, Yahweh created all the plants and animals before creating humans, referred to only as "male and female." But according to Genesis 2, Elohim began by creating a man (Adam), after which Elohim created all the animals. Only at the end was the first woman, named "Eve," created.

Scholars later described two more documents: D, referring to Deuteronomy, and P, referring to a Priestly editor. This four-source view of the writing of the Pentateuch came to be known as the "documentary hypothesis." This hypothesis explains many more of the contradictions in the Hebrew Bible.

Since the original formulation of this hypothesis in the late nineteenth century, it has undergone considerable debate and refinement, but the basic idea stands: The Pentateuch was written by at least four authors (J, E, P, and D), plus a fifth, R, the redactor who combined their writings.[7]

Another source of contradictions is the fact that the history of Israel told in the books of Samuel and Kings is told again in 1 and 2 Chronicles from a different perspective. These two histories contradict each other on many points, far more than could be explained as slips and copyist errors. For example:

- In 2 Kings 24:8, King Jehoiachin was said to have begun his reign when he was 18 years old (24:8), but according to

2 Chronicles, "Jehoiachin was eight years old when he began to reign" (36:9).

- According to 2 Samuel 6:23, "Michal the daughter of Saul had no child unto the day of her death," but the same book spoke earlier of "the five sons of Michal the daughter of Saul" (21:8).

- According to 2 Samuel 24, a census was taken because the Lord told David to "number Israel," but according to 1 Chronicles 21, it was Satan who "provoked David to number Israel."

- According to 1 Kings 4:26, "Solomon had forty thousand stalls of horses for his chariots," whereas 2 Chronicles says that "Solomon had four thousand stalls for horses and chariots" (9:25).

The differences largely reflect the fact that they were written at different times, under different circumstances. Samuel-Kings told the history of Israel up to the destruction of Jerusalem and the exile to Babylon, emphasizing that these disasters resulted from sin—the sins of David, Solomon, and later kings, in particular.

But Chronicles, which was written after the return of Israel from exile, gave a much more optimistic account. Focusing on the rebuilding of Solomon's Temple, the Chronicler presented David and Solomon as virtually without blemish. The Chronicler did not mention David's sin with Bathsheba, including his sin of having her husband killed; it also did not mention the attempted coup against him. Nor did the Chronicler mention Solomon's idolatry, his foreign wives, or the rebellions against his rule.

The New Testament

The scholarly study of the four gospels, which present the history and message of Jesus, has revealed enormous differences between them. One big realization was that the gospels were written 40 to 70 years after the death of Jesus, so that none of the gospels were written by disciples of Jesus, contrary to the traditional view that the books of Matthew and John were.

A second big realization was that, whereas the first three gospels are rather similar to each other (so they are called the "Synoptic Gospels"), the Gospel of John is very different. The scholars also realized that, if they were interested in the historical Jesus, they would find relevant material almost entirely in the Synoptics, not in John.

As for the differences between John and the three Synoptics: Besides portraying Jesus as having a very different speaking style from that of Jesus as portrayed in the Synoptics, John and the Synoptics include many contradictions, such as:

- The Synoptics portray Jesus's ministry as lasting only one year, during which he journeyed to Jerusalem only once, while John has Jesus's ministry lasting three years, with three trips to Jerusalem.

- According to Mark 15:25, "it was the third hour" when Jesus was crucified, but John 19:14-16 says that it was "about the sixth hour."

- According to the Synoptics, the ministry of Jesus began only after the arrest of John the Baptist, whereas the Gospel of John portrayed the two ministries as overlapping.

- According to the Synoptics, the Kingdom of God is coming, whereas John says that it, described as eternal life, is already here.

- The Synoptics portray the Temple incident as occurring a week before Jesus's death, whereas John describes this incident as happening at the beginning of Jesus's ministry.

- According to the Synoptics, Jesus was betrayed, whereas John says that Jesus identified himself to the authorities.

A third discovery was that the similarities between the books of Matthew and Luke reflect the fact that they both used the same two sources—the Gospel of Mark plus a hypothesized source, called Q (from Quelle, the German word for source). Q contained a collection of sayings of Jesus that are not in Mark (or John). This "two-source hypothesis" is now accepted by most New Testament scholars.

A fourth realization was that the authors of the three Synoptic Gospels were not simply historians, but primarily—like the author of the Gospel of John—theologians. This fact is especially clear with regard to Matthew and Luke, because we can compare with each other the frameworks in which they embed the material from Mark and Q.

A fifth discovery was that some of the unique material in Matthew probably came from a distinct source, which scholars call simply "M," whereas some of the unique material in Luke probably came from a source known as "L." As in the Hebrew Bible, some of the material was provided by redactors, who combined the sources. The process of discerning the contributions of each of the redactors is called "redaction criticism," to be discussed later.

A sixth discovery was that Luke and Acts were by the same author, now known as Luke-Acts.

Other Contradictions

In addition to the contradictions already mentioned, there are many other contractions in the Bible. For example:

- According to Matthew 27:5, Judas died after betraying Jesus for pieces of silver because he "went and hanged himself," but Luke-Acts 1:18 reported that Judas "burst asunder in the midst, and all his bowels gushed out."

- According to Psalms 145:9, "The Lord is good to all," showing them "his tender mercies," but Jeremiah 13:14 quotes the Lord as saying about the enemies of Israel, "I will not pity, nor spare, nor have mercy, but destroy them."

- Likewise, whereas Romans 15:33 speaks of "the God of peace," Exodus 15:3 had said, "The Lord is a man of war."

- James 1:13 says that God does not tempt anyone, whereas Genesis 22:1 said that "God did tempt Abraham."

- According to Matthew 19:26, "with God all things are

possible," but "the Lord," reported Judges 1:19, "could not drive out the inhabitants of the valley, because they had chariots of iron."

These contradictions are incompatible with the idea that the Bible was written by an omnipotent deity, one that "is always able to accomplish the divine will."

Solution by Allegory?

The contradictions in the Bible are so obvious that it did not take modern biblical scholarship to detect them. Theologians in the early church, such as the third-century theologian Origen, dealt with these contradictions and other problems by distinguishing the literal meaning of the texts from a more profound, allegorical meaning. As Farley and Hodgson explained:

> Allegory interprets all the details of a story or text as having a figurative meaning different from and encoded within the apparent literal meaning. The task of allegory is to "decode" a text by making explicit the higher meaning of each and every unit.[8]

Perhaps the most famous example of allegorical interpretation by Origen is his explanation of the Parable of the Good Samaritan (Luke 10):

> [T]he man who is robbed is Adam, Jerusalem is paradise, and Jericho is the world. The priest is the Law, and the Levites are the Prophets. The Samaritan is Christ. The donkey is Christ's physical body, which bears the burden of the wounded man (the wounds are his sins), and the inn is the Church. The Samaritan's promise to return is a promise of the second coming of Christ.[9]

Origen often used allegories to deal with texts that contain contradictions and other problems, such as unbelievable claims. For example, referring to the statement about the patriarchs "seeing" God, Origen said: "[T]hey saw him not with the eyes of the body but with a pure heart. In the words of our Jesus, 'blessed are the pure in heart, for they shall see God.'"[10]

By means of the allegorical method of interpreting texts, the medieval church implicitly claimed that the contradictions and other apparent errors in scripture did not contradict its inerrancy and hence the idea that it was written by a perfect and omnipotent deity.

However, leaders of the Protestant Reformation, such as Martin Luther and especially John Calvin, insisted that the Bible had to be interpreted according to its literal meaning, and this idea has become generally accepted. This does not mean that there are no allegorical passages in the Bible. But it does mean that appeal to allegory cannot be used to reconcile all of the Bible's contradictions and false statements with a claim of biblical inerrancy.

Redaction Criticism

It is redaction criticism that has revealed the full extent to which the Synoptic Gospels are theologies. The different theologies of Matthew and Luke can be illustrated by summarizing some of their main features.

The distinctive features of Matthew include the following elements:

- Being addressed to Jewish Christians, the book of Matthew portrayed Jesus as the Messiah, who fulfilled scripture (the Hebrew Bible).

- Jesus is presented as a teacher like Moses, only greater. As with Moses, miracles surrounded the infancy of Jesus, and he survived when babies his age were massacred.

- Matthew and Luke had Jesus give a sermon with very similar material. But whereas Luke portrayed it as a Sermon on the Plain, Matthew's Jesus delivered a Sermon on the Mount— just as Moses had brought the law down from a mountain.

The distinctive features of Luke include the following elements:

- Luke's Jesus presented his message as being for Gentiles; for ordinary people, especially the poor; for outcasts, such as Samaritans and sinners; and for women.

- Whereas Matthew's birth narrative had Magi (rich men from a distant country) coming to worship Jesus, Luke had angels announce the birth of Jesus to ordinary people—"shepherds in the field."

- In his first sermon, Luke's Jesus announced that the Spirit of the Lord had anointed him to "proclaim good news to the poor."

- Whereas Matthew's Jesus said in his Sermon on the Mount, "Blessed are the poor in spirit," Luke's Jesus simply said, "Blessed are the poor."

- With regard to Samaritans, Luke is the only gospel giving the parable of the Good Samaritan and the story of the Ten Lepers, in which only the Samaritan returned to give thanks to Jesus for the healing.

- With regard to tax-collectors and sinners, the parables of the Lost Sheep, the Lost Coin, and the Prodigal Son are unique to Luke.

- With regard to women, they are more prominent in Luke than any other gospel: (a) The child Jesus blessed by prophetess Anna only in Luke; (b) Jesus's mother Mary was given more attention than in other gospels; (c) Jesus healed more women than in other gospels; (d) women were especially presented as good examples, such as the widow who gave a mite and the sinful woman who anointed Jesus; (e) women prepared spices to anoint Jesus's body, found the tomb empty, were told by angels that Jesus had been risen, told other disciples.

Inspiration

Whereas traditional theology portrayed the Bible as ultimately having only one author—God—historical scholarship has shown that the Bible was composed by many authors, who disagreed with each other on numerous issues. It cannot be responsibly said that the Bible was *inerrantly* inspired.

However, the Bible can intelligibly be described as inspired in other senses. For example, it correctly says that our universe was brought about by a loving creator who loves and wishes the highest creatures, who have consciousness and intelligence, to treat each other with compassion and justice (in the sense of fairness). Chapter 7 explains that God's activity, without being supernatural, can result in divine self-manifestation.

CHAPTER TWO

God: Creator
of Heaven and Earth

CENTRAL TO CHRISTIAN FAITH is the conviction that the divine reality that inspired the Jewish prophets and Jesus was the creator of the universe—a conviction that was expressed in early Christian creeds. This fact means that statements of Christian faith for today cannot be divorced from science-based discussions of the nature of the universe. At one time, this need to correlate faith and science was widely regarded to be a problem, because it seemed that science undermined Christian faith.

For example, in a 1903 essay entitled "A Free Man's Worship," Bertrand Russell said that the presuppositions of religious belief and practice are undermined by "the world which Science presents for our belief." Using the term "Man" to represent humanity, Russell said that "his origin, his growth, his hopes and fears, his loves and beliefs, are but the outcome of accidental collocations of atoms." Accordingly, he argued, "all the labours of the ages, all the devotion, all the inspiration, all the noonday brightness of human genius, are destined to extinction in the vast death of the solar system."[1]

Biologist-turned-sociobiologist E. O. Wilson, speaking of "the collision between irresistible scientific materialism and immovable religious faith," wrote in 1979:

> [M]ake no mistake about the power of scientific materialism. It presents the human mind with an alternative mythology that until now has always, point for point in zones of conflict, defeated traditional religion. . . . Every part of existence is considered to be obedient to physical laws requiring no external control. The scientist's devotion to parsimony in explanation excludes the divine spirit and other extraneous agents.[2]

Psychobiologist William Uttal said that a science of the mind requires the assumption that mind is reducible to matter, so that the state of the mind is "totally dependent on the arrangement of the matter." This reductionistic position, Uttal added, "conflicts in a fundamental way with the predominant theologies of our society," including "the nearly universal acceptance of the idea that the mind directly affects the body."[3]

In a book entitled *The Creation,* chemist Peter W. Atkins argued that "the universe can come into existence without intervention, and that there is no need to invoke the idea of a Supreme Being in one of its numerous manifestations."[4] In an article entitled "Professor Says Science Rules out Belief in God," Atkins—after calling religious belief "outmoded and ridiculous"—said:

> To say that "God made the world" is simply a more or less sophisticated way of saying that we don't understand how the universe originated. A god, in so far as it is anything, is an admission of ignorance. Science, on the other hand, gave us the hope of comprehension.[5]

However, more careful discussions of both "science" and "religion" have shown that there is no necessary conflict between science and religion. The present chapter deals with the question of whether science supports or refutes belief in a divine creator of the universe. Although most philosophers and theologians have not caught up with this fact, recent developments in science have shown that it actually supports Christian faith in a divine creator. But it is crucial to understand that science does not support every version of Christian faith. Insofar as classical creeds are no longer undergirded by science, they need to be replaced.

CHRISTIAN CREEDS AND "FATHER ALMIGHTY"

The Apostles Creed and the Nicene Creed are the two most popular Christian statements of faith. The Apostles Creed begins: "I believe in God, the Father almighty, creator of heaven and earth." The Nicene Creed begins: "We believe in one God, the Father, the Almighty, maker of heaven and earth."

Almighty

Accordingly, millions of Christians around the world reaffirm every week the belief that God, the creator of the universe, is "almighty," in the sense of *omnipotent*. Because of these creeds, omnipotence is taken to be God's most important attribute. The Catechism of the Catholic Church says: "Of all the divine attributes, only God's omnipotence is named in the Creed."

It is generally assumed that these affirmations of divine omnipotence are rooted in the Bible. But they are not. The term in the Hebrew Bible translated "God almighty" is El Shaddai, which occurred five times in Genesis, once in Exodus, and once in Ezekiel. After the period of the patriarchs, "the term seems to fade away." The correct translation is uncertain. Shaddai may have meant "mountain dweller," and El Shaddai may have meant "God, the one of the mountain." The term does not seem to mean power, except for generative power: "When God reveals Himself as El Shaddai in Genesis, it is in connection with blessings of fertility." In any case, said the New Jerusalem Bible, "translating 'El Shaddai' as 'Almighty God' is inaccurate."[6]

The reference to God as "almighty" in the creeds is not biblically grounded and is not otherwise appropriate. It is not appropriate because there is no longer any good reason to speak of God as "omnipotent." That description of God was appropriate when it was thought that the world was literally created in six days: In that short period, our universe could have been created only by overwhelming coercive power. But now we know that our world, rather than being created in six days, was created in more like 15 *billion* years. This quantitative difference is so great that is suggests a *qualitative* difference in the nature of God's creative activity. The idea that God spent some 15 billion years creating our world suggests that God's creative power must be persuasive, not coercive or controlling power.[7]

However, although the adjective "almighty" is appropriate to neither the Bible nor our present scientific knowledge, the reference to God as the "creator of heaven and earth" is biblical and, as this chapter argues, otherwise appropriate. Of course, the authors of the Bible and creeds had a very limited understanding of "heaven and earth" compared with what is known today. But there is no reason to consider the statement merely metaphorical or symbolic.

If this creedal statement has a literal core that is true, this fact would be important, because our basic drive is to be in harmony with the essence of the universe. For us to be consciously in harmony with the universe, therefore, means that we need to understand the nature of our universe—what it is most fundamentally. According to one of the primary Christian doctrines: *Our world was created by a loving God, one who loves the world and all its creatures, great and small, unreservedly.*

But is it possible today to say that the universe was literally created by a divine being, whom we can call "God"? That this is so is arguably the most important scientific discovery of the past 100 years (as explained below). It is wrong to think of God as being omnipotent in the sense of being able to do simply anything (except for the self-contradictory). But it *is* appropriate to think of God as uniquely powerful, in the sense of *alone having the power to create a universe.* There could be no comparable power.

Too often, God's unique power has been portrayed as controlling power, even destructive power. But the power of God should most fundamentally be portrayed as creative power, generative power. To praise God as creator of heaven and earth is to praise God's unequaled generative power. No power could be greater than the power to create a universe. The church should quit using "almighty" to refer to the creator of heaven and earth.

Father

However, the term "almighty" is not the only problem with the reference in the creeds to the "Father almighty." The term "father" is also problematic, because it implies that God is male. One reason that this implication is problematic is that there is no good reason to think of God as more like men than women. The creator of the universe surely transcends the male-female contrast.

A second reason is even more important. In her seminal 1973 book *Beyond God the Father,* Mary Daly said: "If God is male, then the male is God."[8] In an earlier and more self-explanatory statement, Daly said: "If God in 'his' heaven is a father ruling 'his' people, then it is in the 'nature' of things and according to divine plan and the order of the universe that society be male dominated."[9]

When people first encounter the idea that it is problematic to refer to God as Father, at least in a context in which exclusively male language is used, they commonly think that this language is *not* problematic, because this has always been the way of speaking of the Divine Reality.

In recent decades, however, several scholars have argued that this is far from the truth. In 1978, Merlin Stone published a book entitled *When God Was a Woman,* which began: "In the beginning, people prayed to the Creatress of Life. . . . At the very dawn of religion, God was a woman. Do you remember?"[10] In commenting on this statement in a 1997 book, Carol Christ, a theologian who was influenced by Stone (as well as Mary Daly), wrote: "Goddess religion is far more ancient than Judaism and Christianity."[11]

With regard to *how much* "more ancient": The Museum of Ancient and Modern Art said: "The Great Goddess, the Divine Ancestress, was worshiped as far back as the Upper Paleolithic about 25,000 BCE."[12] The worship of goddesses started to be suppressed in the Neolithic period, as culture started becoming more patriarchal. Although the "Old Testament" has sometimes been blamed for the emergence of patriarchy, with its male deity and its increased violence, this is an error, Carol Christ wrote:

Neither Jews nor Judaism are responsible for the development of patriarchy. Patriarchy existed in the Near East and
in Europe long before the time of the writing of the Hebrew
Bible. The transformation of the Goddesses to support the
values of ancient Mediterranean warrior cultures happened
independently of the Bible.[13]

It has widely been thought that Goddess religion is wholly antithetical to Judaism and Christianity, largely because of the idea that
it involves the worship of an impersonal deity. That is true of many
of its devotees, but not of all, including Carol Christ. In her jointly
authored *Goddess and God in the World,* she said that she characterized
"Goddess" as "the intelligent embodied love that is the ground of all
being."[14] She elsewhere said that she understands the Goddess as "a
personal presence, a power . . . who cares about my life and the fate
of the world."[15]

In thus speaking, Carol Christ has described Goddess in terms
identical with the view of God in the present theology. Given this
fact, plus that there is no good reason to think of the Divine Reality
as male rather than female, and likewise no good reason to use exclusively female language, she has spoken of the deity as "Goddess or
God."[16]

"IN THE BEGINNING"

The assertion by the creeds that God created heaven and earth was
derived from the first verse in Genesis, which in English translations
was long rendered, "In the beginning God created the heaven and
the earth. The earth was without form and void." This translation
suggested the idea that the world was created *ex nihilo,* out of absolute
nothingness. Given this translation, the first book of the Bible implied
God's all-powerfulness, because nothing less than absolute omnipotence could have brought our amazing universe into being out of
a complete absence of finite entities.

However, Hebrew scholars have long agreed that this translation
is misleading. More accurately rendered, the passage says: "When

God began to create the heaven and the earth, the world was without form and void." Rather than suggesting that the world was void and without form *after* the deity's initial creative activity, the passage suggests a version of the view articulated in Plato's *Timaeus* and, in fact, most cosmogonies of the Ancient Near East—namely, that our universe was created out of a primeval chaos.

Therefore, the creation of our particular universe was, in the words of Alfred North Whitehead, "not the beginning of [finite] matter of fact, but the incoming of a certain type of order."[17] Insofar as we can say "In the beginning," we should understand this phrase to refer to the beginning of the present "cosmic epoch," meaning *our* world, which evidently began about 14 billion years ago. The beginning of our world in this sense did not require omnipotence in the ordinary sense. Rather, as Whitehead put it, "The Platonic 'persuasion' is required"[18]—a persuasion that, over billions of years, could create a universe such as ours.

Unfortunately, however, Christian theologians near the end of the second century CE replaced the biblical idea of creation out of chaos with the idea of creation out of *nothing* (*creatio ex nihilo*). This replacement left Christianity with an insoluble problem of evil, as discussed in the following chapter. Christianity needs to return to the idea of creation out of chaos, which was affirmed by both Jews and Christians until near the end of the second century CE. The doctrine of creation out of chaos supports the notion that divine power operates by persuasion, which obviously fits the evolutionary creation of our world better than the image of a deity bringing things about by means of a series of *fiats*, which could have created the universe within a week or, actually, in an instant.

God vs. Gawd

The distinction between a deity that created the world out of chaos and one that created the world out of nothing, hence being omnipotent in the traditional sense, can be discussed by means of a distinction between "God" and "Gawd." The term "Gawd" can also be used for the traditional Christian idea of deity as entirely male. In this theology, therefore, the term "Gawd" stands for a deity both omnipotent and male. The term "God" connotes a divine reality understood as not omnipotent and as both male and female, as suggested by Genesis 1:26–27 and Virginia Mollenkott, who wrote that God "transcends and yet contains both male and female, both masculine and feminine.[19]

Mollenkott's books, in fact, constitute one long argument against the view of God as exclusively masculine. Her book *The Divine Feminine* began with a critique of a traditionalist theologian, Vernard Eller, who took issue with the language of Christian feminists. In opposition to their replacement of the term "man" with "humanity" and "humankind," Eller insisted that the only truly personal word for the human race is *man*.[20] Saying that "the male half of the human race comes to be understood [for Eller] as the norm for what humanity is all about," it is no surprise, Mollenkott quipped, "that women are not as good at being *man* as men are." From Eller's point of view, accordingly, it is *man* who was created in God's own image.[21]

"The masculinity of God is as thoroughly rooted in the totality of scripture," Eller said, "as any idea one could name."[22] However, he could make this claim only because he did not really know "the totality of scripture." Mollenkott's book, subtitled *The Biblical Imagery of God as Female*, contained 15 chapters discussing such images.

In any case, the use of the term "Gawd" was inspired by a story about a British philosopher with extremely conservative theological views. During a meeting of a theological discussion group in England, another member of the group made a statement with which this philosopher disagreed. "Are you talking about God," this philosopher asked, "or Gawd?"

By "Gawd" he meant the creator of the universe, characterized by the attributes of traditional theism, especially omnipotence, in which he believed. By "God," he meant a divine reality without some of the attributes of the traditional deity, especially omnipotence—an alleged divine reality that he considered entirely fictitious.

In the present theology book, the same distinction is employed, but in the opposite way, arguing that, although God exists, Gawd does not.[23]

This distinction is crucial for the rise of atheism and the resulting debates between theists and atheists, including the so-called New Atheists,[24] because almost all arguments for the "non-existence of God" are really objections to Gawd. Indeed, there are many good reasons to deny the existence of Gawd, but also many good reasons to affirm the existence of God.[25] One of these reasons is a new version of the teleological argument.

FINE-TUNING FOR LIFE

Down through the ages, theologians who offered arguments for the existence of God have almost always employed some version of the teleological argument, often called the "argument from design." Pointing to evidence that the world, or parts of it, seemed to be designed, they argued that the design could be explained only by a powerful and intelligent creator. A version of this argument, comparing the universe with a watch, became prominent in the eighteenth century. But in the nineteenth and twentieth centuries, this argument lost favor, partly because the argument presupposed the divine designer to be omnipotent and partly because Darwinism seemed to provide explanations for the apparent design.

Because the teleological argument from design had become virtually the only argument for the existence of God that science-based thinkers had taken seriously, atheists for about a century— from the latter part of the nineteenth century to the latter part of the twentieth—complacently assumed that the intellectual case for theism had been permanently destroyed.

In the 1970s, however, a different type of argument for design began to emerge, a type that Darwinian evidence could not touch, because it refers to apparent design of the world long before life emerged. Indeed, the basic argument is that the universe appears to have been "fine-tuned for life." The fine-tuning is exemplified by the constants of physics, such as the four forces of physics—gravity, the strong force, the weak force, and electromagnetism.

Gravity is a long-range attractive force, without which there could be no stars and planets. It is very weak, compared with the other forces. But if it had been still weaker, the stars would have been red dwarfs, which would have burned for a very long time but not hot enough to support planets on which life could develop. However, if gravity had been a bit stronger, all the stars would have been blue giants burning so hot that they could not have lasted the billions of years it takes life to develop.[26]

Another example of how the universe appears to have been fine-tuned for life is provided by the "strong force," which is a very powerful but short-range force. It exerts influence only within an atom's nucleus, where it binds protons and neutrons together. The strong force determines the amount of energy released when simple atoms undergo nuclear fusion. When hydrogen in a star turns into helium, the helium atom is slightly lighter than the two protons and two neutrons that went into making it. So 0.007 of the hydrogen's mass is converted into energy.

However, if this figure were 0.006 instead 0.007, protons and neutrons would not bond together. In that case, helium could not be formed, so there would be an all-hydrogen universe. But if this figure were instead 0.008, then protons would bond together without the aid of neutrons, so that no hydrogen would remain. "[W]hat is remarkable," said Great Britain astronomer royal Martin Rees, "is that no carbon-based biosphere could exist if this number had been 0.006 or 0.008 rather than 0.007."[27]

As this example illustrates, the "fine-tuning" is *extremely* fine. The same is true of the "weak force," which also exerts influence only within the nucleus, where it is responsible for converting neutrons into protons. The weakness of this force has allowed the sun to "burn its hydrogen gently for billions of years," thereby allowing the universe to have time to bring about life.[28] If this force had been much weaker, there would have been no excess protons to make hydrogen, so there would be all-helium stars, which would provide no basis for the emergence of life.[29]

But if this force had been slightly stronger, then "the Big Bang's nuclear burning would have proceeded past helium and all the way to iron," making fusion-powered stars impossible.[30]

Much of the fine-tuning involves ratios. For example, electromagnetism is much stronger than gravity, about 10 to the 36th power stronger—about a trillion, trillion, trillion times stronger.[31] Yet it could not have been much different, or life would have been impossible.

On the one hand, if gravitational attraction were much stronger, stars would be smaller and would burn so hot that their life spans would be too short for life to develop. On the other hand, if the attraction were much weaker, planets would be much smaller, and a miniaturized sun would burn much more quickly. Hence, it might last only 10 thousand years, rather than the 10 billion years needed for the creation of the heavier elements, such as carbon and oxygen, which are needed for the evolution of life.[32]

The ratio of electromagnetism to the strong force also seems to be finely tuned. If the strong force were much stronger, the electromagnetic force would not have been strong enough to prevent protons from sticking together, so there would be no free protons to form hydrogen. But if the strong force had been much weaker, then complex atomic nuclei, upon which life depends, would be unable to form. Stephen Hawking said: "[I]f the electric charge of the electron had been only slightly different, stars either would have been unable to burn hydrogen and helium, or else they would not have exploded."[33]

To give one final example: Neutrons are heavier than protons, but only very slightly: The ratio of their masses is 939.56563 to 938.27231. If the mass of neutrons were increased by one part in seven hundred, hydrogen could not be turned into helium, so stars could not be formed. But if neutrons were slightly lighter, there would be an all-helium universe, hence no possibility for life.[34]

These are only a few of the many fundamental constants that had to be fine-tuned if life were to develop in our universe—26 such constants, by one count.[35]

How Can the Fine-Tuning Be Explained?

The evidence for apparent fine-tuning is so strong that there are virtually no arguments against it. According to physicist Paul Davies,

"There is now broad agreement among physicists and cosmologists that the Universe is in several respects 'fine-tuned' for life."[36] This agreement is shared by traditional theists and deists, which is not surprising, but also by atheists, such as Stephen Hawking,[37] who wrote:

> The laws of science, as we know them at present, contain many fundamental numbers, like the size of the electric charge of the electron and the ratio of the masses of the proton and the electron. . . . The remarkable fact is that the values of these numbers seem to have been very finely adjusted to make possible the development of life.[38]

But is there an acceptable explanation for this remarkable fact?

A Cosmic Fine-Tuner

The simplest explanation is that the fine-tuning was the work of an intelligent cosmic agent. As Paul Davies put it: "It seems as though someone has fine tuned nature's numbers to make the universe. . . . The impression of design is overwhelming."[39]

This impression has converted some erstwhile atheists. For example, philosopher Antony Flew, one of the world's best-known atheists, came to consider a "divine Mind" the "only viable explanation [for] the origin of the laws of nature."[40]

Another convert was astronomer Fred Hoyle, who had been so opposed to theism that he rejected the "big bang" theory in favor of the steady-state view of the universe, because it seemed less suggestive of theism. But after studying the evidence for fine-tuning in relation to carbon, Hoyle was led to his well-known conclusion: "Some supercalculating intellect must have designed the properties of the carbon atom."[41]

The view that the fine-tuning of the universe could only be explained by appeal to a divine creator was also articulated by mathematician and philosopher of science John Lennox, in a book entitled *God's Undertaker,* the subtitle of which asked: *Has Science Buried God?* "[T]he more we get to know about our universe," said Lennox with regard to fine-tuning, "the more the hypothesis that there is a

Creator . . . gains in credibility as the best explanation of why we are here."[42]

However, this is an answer that many philosophers and scientists are not able to accept. Since at least the middle of the nineteenth century, it has been accepted by mainstream science and Western culture generally that "God" cannot be an answer to a scientific question. Presupposing this situation, philosopher Roberto Unger and physicist Lee Smolin said that cosmology's "greatest crisis of its short history" was created by the discovery that the universe appears to be fine-tuned for life. This is regarded as a crisis because there is no explanation for the fine-tuning that is widely considered acceptable by scientists.[43]

Fine-Tuning without a Tuner?

Science-based thinkers have generally been deeply committed to the idea that life came about by accident. The idea that the universe was designed to produce life is considered unscientific, on the grounds that "God" cannot be part of a scientific hypothesis.

Some scientists and philosophers therefore came up with an alternative hypothesis. According to this view, our universe is a tiny portion of a "multiverse," comprised of billions or even trillions of universes, each with different laws. Given so many universes, the argument goes, one of them was bound to just happen to have the laws and variables needed for life to emerge. According to this view, the fact that the universe appears to be extremely fine-tuned does not mean that it was, in fact, produced by a cosmic fine-tuner.[44] From this point of view, the belief that there are billions or trillions of universes removes the need for theism.

The argument: If our universe were the only universe, it would be implausible to hold that it had come about without a purposeful creator. The possibility that our extremely fine-tuned universe came into existence by chance would be so improbable as to be virtually impossible. So an apparently fine-tuned universe would mean that scientists would need to accept theism, even if they hated the idea. This line of thought led scientists who were opposed to the idea of a divine creator to promote the multiverse idea, which allows them to retain their belief that the existence of life was an accident.

Various scientists have explained why many scientists prefer the multiverse hypothesis:

Arno Penzias, who won the Nobel Prize as co-discoverer of the cosmic microwave background, said: "Some people are uncomfortable with the purposefully created world. To come up with things that contradict purpose, they tend to speculate about things they haven't seen."[45]

Cal Tech's Sean Carroll said that most scientists "would prefer a theory that was completely free of appeals to supernatural agents."[46]

"If one does not believe in providential design, but still thinks the fine-tuning needs some explanation," said Martin Rees, the multiverse hypothesis provides an option.[47]

Stephen Hawking said: "The many improbable occurrences that conspired to enable our existence" would seem to be a miracle created by a benevolent God, "if ours were the only solar system in the universe." However, if there are many parallel universes, each with different laws, then the "apparent miracle" that our universe is ideally fit for life disappears: "the multiverse concept can explain the fine-tuning of physical law without the need for a benevolent creator who made the universe for our benefit."[48]

Arguments against the Multiverse Idea

Arguments against a cosmic fine-tuner because it suggests theism are anti-philosophical. As deity-averse philosopher Thomas Nagel said, "it is just as irrational to be influenced in one's beliefs by the hope that God does not exist as by the hope that God does exist."[49] Accordingly, scientists and others should do their best to avoid being unduly influenced by their fears as well as their hopes, looking as dispassionately as possible at which alternative has the best evidence. Also, in explaining why cosmology is in crisis, Unger and Smolin said that, besides the fact that a theistic answer is widely ruled out as a possible answer, the other explanation—the multiverse hypothesis—is an "ontological fantasy."[50]

There are many scientific reasons for rejecting the multiverse theory:

- *Violation of Occam's Razor:* One of the most common objections to the multiverse idea is that it dramatically violates Occam's razor, according to which, all other things being equal, the simplest hypothesis should be chosen. For example, Paul Davies said that "the multiverse represents an inconceivably flagrant violation of Occam's razor— postulating an enormous ensemble of essentially unobservable universes, just to explain our own."[51] To postulate billions— perhaps an infinite number—of universes, rather than a single deity, does seem to violate Occam's principle.

- *Extreme Extrapolation:* There are other reasons for calling the multiverse idea unscientific. According to Australian evolutionist Luke Barnes, the multiverse idea "will surely forever hold the title of the most extreme extrapolation in all of science, if indeed it can be counted as part of science."[52]

- *Not Falsifiable:* It is generally accepted that what makes a hypothesis scientific, rather than merely philosophical, is that it could in principle be refuted by some possible observation. Princeton University's Paul Steinhardt, after having helped create the multiverse idea, turned against it. "It's not even a scientific theory," said Steinhardt, because "it allows every conceivable possibility."[53]

- *Science Stopper:* Another objection to the multiverse theory is that it is unscientific in the sense that it could be used as an excuse to accept a premature answer. Even Brian Greene, who wrote two books advocating the multiverse idea,[54] has admitted that it could be used as a "science stopper," saying:

  > If true, the idea of a multiverse would be. . . a rich and astounding upheaval, but one with potentially hazard-ous consequences. Beyond the inherent difficulty in assessing its validity, when should we allow the

multiverse framework to be invoked in lieu of a more traditional scientific explanation? Had this idea surfaced a hundred years ago, might researchers have chalked up various mysteries to how things just happen to be in our corner of the multiverse and not pressed on to discover all the wondrous science of the last century? . . . When faced with seemingly inexplicable observations, researchers may invoke the framework of the multiverse prematurely—proclaiming some phenomenon or other to merely reflect conditions in our own bubble universe and thereby failing to discover the deeper understanding that awaits us.[55]

- *Does Not Eliminate Fine-Tuning:* Still another problem with the multiverse theory is that, although it was motivated by the desire to eliminate fine-tuning and thereby a divine creator, it does not really do this. According to Paul Davies, "[The] scientific multiple worlds hypothesis merely shifts the problem up a level from universe to multiverse." Explaining why, Davies added:

> The multiverse comes with a lot of baggage, such as an overarching space and time to host all those bangs, a universe-generating mechanism to trigger them, physical fields to populate the universes with material stuff, and a selection of forces to make things happen. Cosmologists embrace these features by envisaging sweeping 'meta-laws' that pervade the multiverse and spawn specific bylaws on a universe-by-universe basis. The meta-laws themselves remain unexplained— eternal, immutable transcendent entities that just happen to exist and must simply be accepted as given. In that respect the meta-laws have a similar status to an unexplained transcendent god.[56]

Which View Is More Scientific?

Some thinkers may reply that, although questions have been raised about the scientific status of the multiverse hypothesis, it is at least more scientific than the idea of a divine fine-tuner. Some years back, *Discover* magazine published an article entitled "Science's Alternative to an Intelligent Creator: The Multiverse Theory."[57] Why did the article refer to the multiverse theory as a scientific theory? Merely because it is not theistic—because it does not attribute the fine-tuning to a being called "God."

But how can that be considered a good reason? What if no one had used the term "God" but a group of scientists had suggested that the best explanation for a cosmic fine-tuning was a cosmic mind? In fact, this is what Fred Hoyle did, speaking of a "supercalculating intellect."

Hoyle was one of the greatest scientists of the twentieth century. Is his view to be considered unscientific because his "supercalculating intellect" could be considered divine—or, more precisely, one aspect of the divine? Let's say that Group A advocated this hypothesis while Group B rejected it. Should Group A's position be considered unscientific by virtue of advocating this hypothesis? Should Group B's position be accepted as scientific by virtue of its rejection of Hoyle's hypothesis?

Surely whether or not a hypothesis is scientific depends on many factors. One of these is that a scientific hypothesis must avoid ad hoc explanations. An ad hoc explanation is one that exists for no reason other than saving a favored hypothesis. That is, it is ad hoc because it does not help explain any other phenomena. The multiverse idea, developed to explain away the apparent fine-tuning of the universe in order to save the hypothesis that the universe has no divine creator, can be considered the ultimate ad hoc hypothesis.

It might seem that the multiverse hypothesis and a cosmic-mind hypothesis would be in the same boat, because both would be ad hoc hypotheses. But this is not true. The existence of a cosmic mind can be used to explain a wide range of phenomena, such as the existence of truth, religious experience, evolution, and the reality and efficacy of moral and mathematical forms.[58] But the multiverse hypothesis does not explain anything except (purportedly) why the universe appears to be fine-tuned although it really is not. Far from being less scientific than the multiverse hypothesis, the theistic explanation for fine-tuning can be considered *more* scientific by virtue of not being ad hoc.

Should Science Avoid Theism at All Costs?

Nagel's above-quoted statement cannot be repeated too often: "[I]t is just as irrational to be influenced in one's beliefs by the hope that God does not exist, as by the hope that God does exist."[59] If philosophers and scientists would follow this dictum, the evidence and arguments discussed above should settle the issue: The fine-tuning of our universe can best be explained by a cosmic mind.

Nevertheless, many philosophers and scientists will stick with the multiverse hypotheses, in spite of all the arguments against it, rather than affirming a cosmic mind. To affirm a "cosmic mind" is to affirm belief in God, and belief in God, it is widely thought, must be avoided in science at all costs, because—many people think—to believe in God is to endorse a terrible view of the universe. Confessing that he shared in the widespread "fear of religion," Nagel wrote: "I hope there is no God! I don't want there to be a God; I don't want the universe to be like that."[60] He is, however, actually thinking of Gawd and the problem of evil.

There are many reasons why some people would want there to be no deity. One of the main reasons, especially important to scientists, is that belief in deity as traditionally understood undermines the scientific enterprise. In explaining why he rejected the idea of a divine creator, Stephen Hawking said: "Religion believes in miracles," which "aren't compatible with science."[61] Harvard biologist Richard Lewontin gave essentially the same argument. While granting the "patent absurdity" of some explanations that been endorsed to avoid theism, he said that scientists must hold fast to atheism anyway, because they "cannot allow a Divine Foot in the door." Why? "To appeal to an omnipotent deity is to allow that at any moment the regularities of nature may be ruptured, that miracles may happen."[62]

However, both Hawking and Lewontin have assumed that to accept theism is to endorse the existence of Gawd. According to the present theology, God's power is unique in being alone capable of creating a universe, but having this power does not necessarily include the power to interrupt the universe's laws—in other words, the power to perform miracles. Once it is clear that theism does not necessarily involve supernaturalism, there is no reason to accept the multiverse theory, which Unger and Smolin rightly called an absurd "ontological fantasy."[63]

The scientific community rightly rejects supernatural theism, with its omnipotent deity, which can interrupt the world's normal cause-effect relations. This type of theism, which affirms the existence of Gawd, *should* be "avoided at all costs." But that notion of deity, which can be seen to be false on other grounds as well, says nothing about the reasonableness of the idea that a cosmic mind provides the best explanation of the recently discovered fine-tuning of the universe. This fine-tuning has provided the strongest empirical evidence ever provided for the existence of a divine creator. In an earlier day, one theologian said: "I believe, because it is absurd." Now one can say: "I believe, because the alternative is absurd."

GOD VS. NEO-DARWINISM

In addition to the issue of the origin of our universe, another major issue in the argumentation about religion and evolution is the acceptability of the biological school of thought known as Neo-Darwinism. Whereas Charles Darwin was a theist, Darwinism was soon replaced with Neo-Darwinism, which is anti-theistic. This anti-theist bias has been the main reason within the scientific community for resistance to the simplest explanation for fine-tuning.

Many traditional Christians have rejected neo-Darwinism because of its naturalism, its rejection of the idea that God has intervened supernaturally in the world, especially in the creation of human beings. Contrary to the view of these questions, naturalism in this sense should be embraced. But some of the implications of neo-Darwinism's atheism should be resisted, partly because these implications result in views that are obviously false.

One of these views is the claim that evolution is *undirected* and hence *not progressive*. When the idea of evolution first spread in the nineteenth century, it was taken by society to mean that progress is built into the world. Darwin himself understood natural selection "as an instrument to manufacture biological progress and moral perfection." In fact, Darwin's belief in progress followed from his idea that evolution was planned by the divine wisdom.[64]

But neo-Darwinists, because of their atheism, have needed to deny progress, saying that, for example, human beings are not higher than amoebae. "[I]f an amoeba is as well adapted to its environment as we are to ours," said Stephen Jay Gould, "who is to say that we are higher creatures?" Darwin's criterion of adaptation, Gould conceded, was "improved fitness," but this meant, Gould insisted, only "better designed for an immediate, local environment," not improvement in any "cosmic sense."[65]

Neo-Darwinism's denial of cosmic progress follows from a closely related feature of its atheism—its view that the evolutionary process is wholly undirected. Neo-Darwinists of course reject the view that a divine being has directly caused every detail of the process. But they also reject the idea that the evolutionary process has manifested any directivity whatsoever, such as an aim toward beauty or greater complexity. They claim that all evolutionary changes can be explained wholly in terms of natural selection based on random variations.

Process theism rejects this view, instead portraying God as luring the world to greater complexity, for the sake of beings with richer experience. "What is inexorable in God," wrote Whitehead, "is valuation as an aim towards 'order'"—a type of order that allows for beings with greater value, for themselves and others. "[T]he purpose of God," Whitehead said, is "the attainment of value."[66]

Besides being the ground of order, God is also the ground of novelty. Like order, novelty is not good in itself; it is good only insofar as it serves the divine aim: "'Order' and 'novelty' are but the instruments of [God's] subjective aim," which is the growth of intrinsically valuable experiences.[67]

Atheists will be inclined to reject this talk of divine influence in the evolutionary process as supernatural interruptionism. However, process theology is based on naturalistic theism. There are no occasional interruptions of the normal cause-effect relations. As stated in this book's Introduction, "divine influence [is] understood as part of the normal cause-effect relations, not an exception to them." Process theism affirms God or Goddess, not Gawd.

Although Thomas Nagel does not affirm theism, process theists are one with him on the two positions he considers unacceptable. He wrote: "I reject both supernaturalism and neo-Darwinism's explanation of the sources of evolutionary change."[68]

Because of process theology's difference from Neo-Darwinism on theism, it also differs with it on morality and meaning. According to historian of evolution William Provine, evolutionary biology implies that "there are no inherent moral or ethical laws." Likewise, said Provine: "The universe cares nothing for us. ... Humans are as nothing even in the evolutionary process on earth. ... There is no ultimate meaning for humans."[69]

By contrast, process theism affirms that our universe was fine-tuned for life. It even affirms a new version of the old view that humans, or at least human-like beings, are the crown of creation (as discussed in Chapter 4). Process theology is definitely good news.

CHAPTER THREE

The Divine Love
and the World's Evil

THE PREVIOUS CHAPTER defended the idea that God is literally the "creator of heaven and earth." Throughout most of its history, Christianity held a supernaturalist worldview, according to which the divine creator of the world is omnipotent. This belief was supported by the creedal confessions of "God Almighty." But this understanding of our creator was undermined in the nineteenth century by the realization that our world has been billions of years in the making. Given evolution operating over billions of years, it no longer seemed obvious that the world needed an omnipotent creator.

The idea that our world was created by an omnipotent deity had been supported by the assumption that the Book of Genesis described the world as created *ex nihilo*. However, this idea was undermined by the realization that the Hebrew Bible actually described the deity as creating our world out of chaos, not out of absolute nothingness.

The traditional idea of how our world came about was also supported by the assumption that beings with consciousness could have been introduced into the world only by an omnipotent creator. Oxford's Richard Swinburne wrote:

[S]cience cannot explain the evolution of a mental life. . . . [T]here is nothing in the nature of certain physical events . . . to give rise to connections [to mental events]. . . . God, being omnipotent, would have the power to produce a soul.[1]

However, microbiologists discovered, as to be discussed in Chapter 4, that all living beings, even bacteria, have experience—a discovery that removed one more reason to assume that the world was created by an all-powerful deity. This position has been reinforced by the growing popularity of panexperientialism, according to which experience is primordial.

Probably the main reason for the decline of the biblical idea of God as the creator of heaven and earth has been the neo-Darwinian idea that the world can be understood perfectly well without postulating a divine creator. However, neo-Darwinism cannot provide a good argument against theism, because it has too many obviously untrue dogmas. For example, it denies various hard-core commonsense ideas, such as freedom, morality, and purpose.[2]

Whereas neo-Darwinism generally limits itself to the evolution of living things, it has been central to cosmology, which had long portrayed an atheistic universe. But in the latter part of the twentieth century, as we saw in the previous chapter, the recovery of the world as God's creation was aided by the discovery that our universe was fine-tuned for life. The conclusion that this was the work of a cosmic mind could be avoided only by means of an unbelievable and unscientific hypothesis of a multiverse. In other words, cosmology now provides extremely strong reasons to regard our world as created by a cosmic mind.

CREATIO EX NIHILO AND EVIL

As stated at the outset of the previous chapter, Christian creeds have attributed omnipotence to God. This would not be problematic if it meant merely that God's power is unique by virtue of being able to create a universe. But the idea of divine omnipotence meant, as the Catechism of the Catholic Church said, that God "can do everything. . . . Nothing is impossible with God."

This power was usually clarified to mean the power to do every-thing except the self-contradictory: God could not make a round square or change the past. Aside from this exception, however, God could do literally anything. One of the main problems with this idea, which especially raises the ire of scientists, is that God can bring about miracles, in the sense of events that are impossible from the point of view of physics and chemistry.

The other major problem caused by this idea of divine power is that it implies that God could prevent any of the events that we normally consider evil—both *moral* evils, due to the sinful acts human beings, and *natural* evils, not caused by the agency of human beings.

Examples of natural evils are earthquakes (if not caused by fracking); hurricanes and tornadoes (at least prior to human-caused climate change); and congenital illnesses. Some children with con-genital illnesses are born with fatal diseases that are destined to kill them before they are 10. The parents must live with the idea that God could cure their children, but does not. The Catechism says: "He does whatever he pleases." It is not surprising that the problem of evil has been the main cause of atheism.

It has even driven some Christian professors of religion to atheism. New Testament scholar Bart Ehrman wrote a book entitled *God's Problem: How the Bible Fails to Answer Our Most Important Question— Why We Suffer*. Ehrman explained that, although he had been raised in a conservative Christian family and had attended fundamentalist schools, he lost his faith in a divine creator:

> I could no longer explain how there can be a good and all-powerful God actively involved with this world, given the state of things. . . . The problem of suffering became for me the problem of faith.[3]

Having in view evils such as the killing fields of Cambodia and the Jewish Holocaust, he asked: "How could God allow this to happen to anyone, let alone his 'chosen people'?"[4]

As Stendhal quipped: "God's only excuse is that he does not exist." Even Christians who are not driven to atheism find the various forms of evil in their lives to be the major challenge to their faith. One of the best pastors I know told me that he preached about the problem of evil at least once a month.

Creation ex Nihilo vs. Creation Out of Chaos

As pointed out in the previous chapter, the Book of Genesis described the world as having been created out of chaos. This idea is crucial for the problem of evil, because to speak of a chaotic realm is to imply the existence of things with some inherent power, some power of their own, which cannot be completely controlled by God. This point is implicit in the title of a book by Harvard's Jon Levenson, *Creation and the Persistence of Evil.*[5] Throughout the Hebrew Bible, said Levenson, chaos was characterized as circumscribed, not annihilated, with the result that evil is a perpetual problem.[6]

Speaking of creation out of chaos was often expressed, with language from Greek philosophy, by saying that God always exists along with "unformed matter." Today, the same point could be better expressed by saying that God has always existed in relation to eternal energy.

Nothing in the New Testament contradicted the idea of creation out of chaos. It is true, to be sure, that some theologians have claimed that *creatio ex nihilo* is implied by various New Testament passages, especially John 1:3, Romans 4:17, Colossians 1:16, and Hebrews 11:3. However, in his book *Creatio Ex Nihilo: The Doctrine of "Creation out of Nothing" in Early Christian Thought*, German Christian theologian Gerhard May said that neither these nor any other New Testament passages provide evidence for *creatio ex nihilo.*[7]

Christian theologians continued to presuppose creation out of chaos through the first two Christian centuries. Early Christian thinkers, including Justin Martyr, Athenagoras, and Clement of Alexandria, held that, said May, the "acceptance of an unformed matter was entirely reconcilable with biblical monotheism." Justin even argued that Plato "took over the doctrine that God made the cosmos out of unoriginate matter from the opening verses of Genesis."[8] (As some scholars have paraphrased this point, Justin said that Plato had plagiarized Genesis!)

A second-century theologian named Hermogenes argued that it was essential to retain the doctrine of creation out of chaos. Saying that theologians needed to "ensure the absolute goodness of the creator God," Hermogenes maintained that only the doctrine of creation out of chaos allowed us to explain why evil occurs. By contrast, he said, the idea of *creatio ex nihilo*, by saying that the creator is the source of literally everything, including evil, would threaten the creator's perfect goodness.[9] Nevertheless, the majority of Christian theologians at the time ignored Hermogenes's argument.

THE REACTION TO MARCION

The stimulus for the shift to *creatio ex nihilo* was provided by a second-century gnostic theologian named Marcion, according to whom the world was created out of evil matter by the Hebrew Bible's creator-deity (in distinction from the perfectly good supreme deity revealed by Jesus). To fence the Church off from this heretical view, Christian thinkers completely rejected the idea of creation out of unformed matter, replacing it with the idea of creation out of nothing.[10]

For continuing to affirm creation out of chaos—which had been the accepted view for over a millenium—Hermogenes was condemned as a heretic. The new doctrine of *creatio ex nihilo* developed very quickly. The phrase was first used by Theophilus of Antioch, who flourished from 170 to 180 CE. Irenaeus, the co-founder "of the church doctrine of *creatio ex nihilo*," was active in the final decades of the second century. And Tertullian and Hippolytus, both of whom lived until about 240 CE, considered it to be "the fixed Christian position that God created the world out of absolutely nothing."[11]

Moreover, the change to this doctrine was evidently made by men who, unlike Hermogenes, were intellectually incapable of dealing with such ideas. "By removing all restrictions on [the deity's] creative activity by declaring the free decision of [the creator's] will [to be] the sole ground of creation," the new doctrine of *creatio ex nihilo*—wrote Gerhard May—was bound to make the biblical concept of the divine creator "a philosophical problem." However, May added, "this is a question far beyond Theophilus."[12]

Irenaeus also rejected the Platonic view, according to which the creator can only will "the best possible." Irenaeus rejected this view in favor of the "the absolute freedom and omnipotence of the biblical God," which "must rule and dominate in everything," so that "everything else must give way to it." However, May said, this position was "only attainable because Irenaeus [was] quite unaware of philosophical problems." Indeed, "cosmological questions scarcely worried Irenaeus."[13]

However, regardless of the hasty and incompetent reflection that led Theophilus and Irenaeus to this radically new doctrine of divine power, this doctrine quickly became a test of orthodoxy. Speaking of "God the Father Almighty," St. Augustine declared in the fifth century:

> [God] is called Almighty for no other reason than he can do whatsoever he willeth and his omnipotent will is not impeded by the will of any creature.[14]

Augustine was, of course, speaking of Gawd. Anyone who denies that "all things are in the hands of the one Almighty," Augustine added, "is a madman," because nothing happens "unless the Omnipotent wills it to happen.... [T]he will of the Omnipotent is always undefeated."[15]

In the sixteenth century, John Calvin formulated essentially the same position. God [Gawd] is called "omnipotent," Calvin said, because "he regulates all things according to his secret plan, which depends solely upon itself."[16] Calvin even affirmed "double predestination," according to which people are predestined to either salvation or damnation:

> Those whom [Gawd] passes over, he condemns; and this he does for no other reason than that he wills to exclude them from the inheritance which he predestines for his own children.[17]

So much for the Christian message as "good news."

Of course, many Christians today reject the idea of predestination to damnation or salvation in an afterlife, considering that whole framework mythical. But to retain the idea of divine omnipotence has essentially the same consequences even apart from that framework: Hundreds of millions of people are consigned to horrible living conditions, through no fault of their own. And yet the doctrine of omnipotence implies that Gawd could have unilaterally changed those living conditions.

This way of understanding God's power is still held by Calvinists today, such as theologian Millard Erickson, who wrote: "[Gawd's] will is never frustrated. What he chooses to do, he accomplishes."[18] According to this view, people today are afflicted by terrorism, starvation, cancer, Alzheimer's disease, climate change, and terrible political leaders because Gawd chose to bring these conditions about.

TWO THEODICIES BASED ON *CREATIO EX NIHILO*

Given this understanding of the creator, how could theologians develop a theodicy? The task of theodicy is to show how the deity could, despite appearances, be perfectly good. Traditional theologies are ones that are based on the idea that Gawd created the world *ex nihilo*. There are two types of traditional theodicies: all-determining theodicies and free-will theodicies.

Traditional All-Determining Theodicies

Traditional theologies hold that Gawd is omnipotent, in the sense of being able unilaterally to determine every detail of all the events in the world. One of the traditional theologies holds that Gawd actually does this. These all-determining theodicies seek to explain how Gawd, in spite of doing this, can be considered perfectly good and loving.

St. Augustine held all-determining theism, as indicated in his previously quoted statement, according to which nothing happens "unless the Omnipotent wills it to happen." But if Augustine held this view, how could he, in light of all the evil in the world, say that Gawd is perfectly good? Augustine's answer was that, actually, there is no evil.

It might seem absurd for anyone to deny the reality of evil. After all, there are painful and fatal diseases, murders, rapes, wars, fatal accidents, and so on. Nobody would deny this. When Augustine and other theologians like him have denied the existence of evil, they have implicitly distinguished between *prima facie* evil, *genuine* evil, and things that are *only apparently* evil.

Many things appear to be evil at first glance, such as having a painful tooth extracted. However, the dentist's extraction will prevent more painful problems later on, so the extraction was only apparently evil. Moreover, assuming that it is good for humans to develop character and virtues, the occurrence of adversity is often a necessary condition for these developments: The existence of poverty provides an opportunity for charity; sins against others provide them the opportunity to forgive; suffering can promote compassion; and so on. Accordingly, what we superficially call evil can, upon closer observation, turn out not to be really evil. It may even be considered good overall, if it was a necessary condition for a greater good that would have been impossible without the *prima facie* evil.

Then, having pointed out that this is sometimes the case, Augustine argued that it is *always* the case. Augustine wrote time and time again that Gawd allowed evil only so that He could bring good out of it. Having an aesthetic theology, Augustine argued that the beauty of the world is achieved by the opposition of contraries. Gawd is able to use the wickedness of humans for good, Augustine said in *The City of God,*

> thus embellishing the course of the ages, as it were an exquisite poem set off with antitheses. ... To the eye that has the skill to discern it, the universe is beautified even by sinners.[19]

In another writing, *Enchiridion,* Augustine left no doubt as to his position:

> [Gawd] judged it better to bring good out of evil than not to permit any evil to exist. ... If it were not good that evil things exist they would certainly not be allowed to exist by the Omnipotent Good.[20]

In response to this type of theodicy, Ivan in Dostoevsky's *The Brothers Karamazov* protested. He said that the world may end with a "higher harmony," and if he were present he might even join a chorus singing with praise, "Thou art just, O Lord, for Thy ways are revealed." But Ivan wanted to state on the record in advance that he hoped he would *not* join that chorus, because he could not accept the idea that any "higher harmony" could justify all the evils that were allegedly necessary for it, such as the suffering of innocent children.[21]

Many theologians support Ivan's position, saying that they cannot but consider obscene the idea that all cases of *prima facie* evil—from the Nazi holocaust to Israel's treatment of the Palestinians to the rapes, starvation, and murders of little children that occur every day—have been necessary to bring about great goods that would not have been possible without them. The suggestion that there has been no genuine evil many people find obscene beyond telling.

Many people also say they simply cannot believe this claim, because it is, in the strictest sense of the term, incredible. Ideas can be called incredible in the strictest sense if they violate any of our *hard-core commonsense beliefs*, which are beliefs that we all presuppose in practice, even if we deny them verbally. To say that we presuppose them in practice is to say that we could not live without presupposing them. To deny them verbally, therefore, involves one in contradiction with one's own presuppositions.

As noted in the introduction, the adjective *hard-core* is used here to distinguish such beliefs, which are truly common to all people, from those beliefs that are often described as "common sense" but are not *common* in the sense of being truly universal. These beliefs, which can be called *soft-core common sense,* can be denied *without* necessarily contradicting any presuppositions of one's practice. Examples of soft-core common sense from earlier times are the beliefs that the Earth is flat and that it is the center of the universe. Today's soft-core common sense includes the belief that bacteria are wholly devoid of sentience and spontaneity.

One example of hard-core common sense is the belief that there is a real world beyond our own experience: One can verbally claim to be a solipsist, but one will reveal, in the very act of stating this claim to an audience, not really to believe it. Another example is the belief that there is causation, in the sense that one thing or event influences other things or events.

The belief that some events are genuinely evil belongs to this class of beliefs: No one can in practice consistently live without presupposing that some events are genuinely evil—that the world would have been better if they had not occurred. Without this presupposition, many of our most basic emotional reactions, such as remorse, guilt feelings, gratitude, and blaming, would not make sense.

When parents learn that their son or daughter has died because of a careless physician's erroneous diagnosis, or when a man learns that his wife and daughters have been raped and murdered, the emotional reactions of even the staunchest Calvinists will show that they do not really believe—in the sense of believing it in practice—that those events happened for the best. Voltaire's *Candide* was devoted, of course, to showing that a young man could not get through life believing that "everything happens for the best in this best of all possible worlds."[22]

Accordingly, all-determining theodicies cannot provide a plausible account of how Gawd could be considered perfectly good, a fact that Mark Twain expressed sardonically:

> It is curious—the way the human mind works. The [traditional] Christian begins with this . . . uncompromising proposition: God is all-knowing, and all-powerful. This being the case, nothing can happen without his knowing beforehand that it is going to happen; nothing happens without his permission; nothing can happen that he chooses to prevent. That is definite enough, isn't it? It makes the Creator distinctly responsible for everything that happens. . . . Then, having thus made the Creator responsible for all [the] pains and diseases and miseries . . . , and which he could have prevented, the gifted Christian blandly calls him Our Father![23]

Traditional Free-Will Theodicies

Some traditional theists, recognizing that all-determining theism cannot provide a satisfactory answer to the problem of evil, have developed a free-will version. It holds that, although Gawd *essentially* has all the power, Gawd has, through a self-limitation, *voluntarily* given a high degree of freedom to some of the creatures, at least human beings—freedom with which they can act in opposition to the will of God.

The basic idea of free-will theism is that, although creaturely free-dom allows genuine evils to occur—namely, sin and the evils resulting therefrom—*the fact that* such evils occur is itself not genuinely evil, because a world with genuinely free creatures, who can freely choose the right and the good and thereby freely develop moral and religious virtues, is a better world than one that, while sin-free, would be devoid of the values made possible by genuine freedom. Accordingly, Gawd is not blameworthy for the world's evils: "It is not logically possible," said Richard Swinburne, "that [Gawd] could give us such free will and yet ensure that we always use it in the right way."[24]

This version of traditional theism, by allowing for both genuine freedom and genuine evil, can provide a more satisfactory answer to the problem of evil than can all-determining theism. But it still has serious problems.

The Problem of "Natural Evil": Given the idea, usually accepted by advocates of traditional free-will theism, that the only earthly creatures with freedom are human beings, free-will theism—with its notion that Gawd essentially has all the power—provides no answer to the question of what is usually called "natural evil," meaning the forms of evil that are not due to human volition.

This type of theism also provides no answer to the fact that the face of our planet is susceptible to earthquakes, tornadoes, and hurricanes; the fact that human beings and other animals are susceptible to cancer and other diseases; and the fact that our planet contains the elements to produce nuclear weapons and other weapons of mass destruction.

The doctrine of *creatio ex nihilo* implies that God could have created a world supportive of human life that would not have had all these dangers. For example, Dale Aukerman—a conservative pacifist theologian—wrote a chapter entitled "Why the Possibility for the Bomb?" in which he said:

> [Gawd] certainly could have created the universe and the earth without uranium and thus without the possibility of these technological breakthroughs that have given human beings the capability of turning the planet into an uninhabitable waste. . . . [Gawd] set us in the midst of a creation which contained that very hidden and most terrible possibility. Why?—when He could so easily have withheld it from us.[25]

Of course, traditional free-will theists can speculate, as did Aukerman, that Gawd did this in order to accentuate the fact that, unless we turn to God, we are doomed. The fact remains, however, that the nuclear peril under which the planet now exists is an evil that was not required by human freedom as such but that Gawd, according to traditional theism's construal of divine power, freely chose to allow.

Gawd Could Prevent Any and Every Evil: According to traditional free-will theism, Gawd could intervene to prevent any specific instance of evil. Gawd could have diverted every bullet headed toward the heart of a young man "too young to die." Gawd could have prevented any of the massacres that have occurred. Gawd could, in fact, prevent any sinful human intention from producing its intended effects. And Gawd could prevent any disease or any natural disaster from producing permanent injury or premature death. This position, therefore, retains the assumption of traditional theism that has led millions to question the existence or at least the goodness of a divine being.

If there were a Superman who could prevent all these kinds of events but refused to do so—perhaps on the grounds that doing so would prevent opportunities for human growth—we would certainly question his moral goodness. A Superman, of course, could not prevent all genuine evils, because, being finite, he could not be everywhere at once. But the God of traditional theism, being ubiquitous, does not have this excuse. (Recall Stendhal's quip: "[Gawd's] only excuse is that He does not exist.")

A Defense Rather than a Theodicy?

Faced with these problems, some traditional free-will theists simply say that, although they cannot explain why Gawd allows so much evil, they need not do so. "If [Gawd] is good and powerful as the theist believes," wrote Alvin Plantinga, "then he will indeed have a good reason for permitting evil; but why suppose the theist must be in a position to figure out what it is?"[26]

Plantinga's answer here is part of his claim that theists need not offer a *theodicy*, which would attempt to provide a *plausible explanation* for the world's evils, but can rest content with a *defense*, which merely shows that there is *no logical contradiction* between holding "evil exists" and "Gawd is omnipotent, omniscient, and wholly good." As long as a proffered explanation shows how these two propositions *might* be consistent, said Plantinga, the fact that it is implausible "is utterly beside the point."[27]

The main problem with this approach is that its contentment with such a minimalist view of theological rationality seems to be based on the assumption that traditional theism is somehow in a privileged position. But theism, especially traditional theism, is no longer in such a position. Accordingly, it must, like any other position, commend itself in terms of plausibility as well as self-consistency.[28] But that is what it is unable to do.[29]

Neither version of traditional theism, in sum, provides a position that shows the world's evils to be compatible with the perfect goodness of Gawd. As Hermogenes warned in the second Christian century, the adoption of *creatio ex nihilo* would give Christians an insoluble problem of evil. It is surely time to try out the kind of theodicy Hermogenes had suggested.

A PROCESS THEODICY

Traditional theism, as defined here, holds that Gawd, the creator of our world, is omnipotent, having the power to determine everything in the world. The term "non-traditional theism," accordingly, simply refers to any type of theism that rejects that doctrine of divine omnipotence. Process theism is a version of nontraditional theism—in fact, now the best-known version. Referring to process theism as "non-traditional theism" does not mean, however, that it differs with traditional theism on all points.

Process theism affirms the existence of a personal creator who is perfect in both power and goodness, including the unique power to bring about a universe such as ours. But it is nontraditional by virtue of affirming a contemporary version of the biblical and Platonic notion of creation out of chaos and thereby a different understanding of divine power.

Creativity and Spontaneity

In the ancient visions of creation out of chaos, the "stuff" out of which our world was created was generally thought of as passive matter. As such, it could be understood to offer resistance to the divine will and thereby to provide a reason for imperfections in the natural world. But it provided little, if any, basis for explaining distinctively human evil.

In process theism, by contrast, the stuff out of which our world was created is not what we normally think of as "stuff" at all, but creative activity. This idea is based in part on recent physics, according to which what we think of as "matter" consists of energy. Generalizing this notion, Whitehead referred to the stuff embodied in all individuals as "creativity." On this basis, the long-standing dualism between "physical nature" and "human experience" is overcome: All genuine individuals, from electrons to living cells to human beings, are embodiments of creativity, or creative activity, which involves a degree of spontaneity.

It must be emphasized that spontaneity is attributed only to genuine individuals, not to "all things" whatsoever. A rock has no capacity for self-determination. Spontaneity belongs only to the genuine individuals making up rocks, such as their electrons, protons, and atoms. The self-determination, and hence spontaneity, of the individuals gets canceled out in aggregates such as sticks and stones by the law of large numbers. But the spontaneity of the tiny individuals is not cancelled out in living individuals, from single-celled organisms (bacteria) to the largest multicellular animals: Over and above the tiny individuals is a higher-level individual, which can coordinate the spontaneities of all the constituent members of the animal body. This higher-level individual, which has a much greater degree of experience and spontaneity, is the animal's mind or psyche.

In human beings, the psyche's spontaneity is freedom. Just as we cannot help presupposing that we have a degree of freedom, we rightly assume that other animals have a degree of spontaneity. Whitehead argued that we must attribute at least an iota of such spontaneity all the way down. Besides the fact that microbiologists increasingly say that living cells have a degree of experience and spontaneity, quantum physicists say that absolute determinism cannot even be attributed to subatomic particles.[30]

Degrees of Spontaneity

Accordingly, rather than an absolute dualism between "humanity," with its freedom, and "nature," assumed to be rigidly determined, process philosophy suggests an evolutionary series of more or less radical differences of degree. In successively bringing forth atoms, molecules, prokaryotic cells, eukaryotic cells, multicelled animals, mammals, and human beings, the evolutionary process has brought forth beings with increasingly greater freedom.

The evolutionary development of our world can be understood to have begun, as suggested in Genesis, with a "formless void" or "chaos," because this development, by hypothesis, arose out of a primordial situation in which the creative activity was completely random, rather than being organized into enduring things, such as quarks, electrons, and protons.

People whose minds have been shaped by *creatio ex nihilo* will be inclined to ask where this chaos came from, contending that it must have been created by Gawd. But what is the self-evident truth behind this *must*? It cannot be simply that "everything that exists must have been created," or else we would have to ask, Who created the divine creator? We do not ask this, because part of what we mean by either "God" or "Gawd" is "a being who exists necessarily."

The correct formulation of the self-evident truth, therefore, is that "everything that exists *contingently*, rather than necessarily, must have been created." Given the obvious truth of the fact that nothing can come from nothing (*ex nihilo nihil fit*), traditional theists were quite right to hold that *something* must exist necessarily. The question is: What is this something?

Rather than being the deity alone, that which exists necessarily, Whitehead suggested, is God-with-a-world, that is, God-with-a-realm-of-finite-existents. In other words, as Charles Hartshorne put it, God is the "soul of the universe."[31] As this term suggests, God is related to the world somewhat in the way our minds or souls are related to our bodies, especially our brains.

In fact, as Gerhard May pointed out, Hermogenes used the biblical designation of God as "Lord" to support this view, arguing that "God was in his unchangeableness always Lord, and so there must have been from eternity something for him to be Lord of."[32]

Hermogenes followed Middle Platonism, according to which the universe consists of three principles—God, the Ideas, and Matter— which are co-eternal.[33] Whitehead's cosmology had the same three ingredients: God, Ideas (which Whitehead called "eternal objects"), and eternal matter (reconceived by Whitehead as "creativity"). However, Whitehead implied that there are *four* eternal principles, because creativity exists eternally as both *divine* creativity (embodied in God), and *creaturely* creativity (embodied in finite existents).

As shown by these summaries of the positions of Whitehead and Hermogenes,[34] they are radically different from the position of *creatio ex nihilo*, according to which all of the universe's power belongs to Gawd alone.

Divine Power as Persuasive, Not Controlling

One implication of the process view is that power is always *shared* power. If God is the supreme but never the only embodiment of creativity, then God has never had a monopoly on power. Also, because the creativity embodied in finite beings is inherent to the realm of finitude, this creativity cannot be withdrawn or overridden. Human freedom is, to be sure, a gift from God, brought about through billions of years of divinely influenced evolutionary development. But because it was evoked out of the capacity for spontaneity inherent in worldly existents as well as God, human freedom—now that it exists—cannot be simply withdrawn.

This view of shared power implies, in turn, that divine power is persuasive, not controlling. Although God, by hypothesis, influences every creature, God cannot wholly determine how any creature will use its own power. Accordingly, as Plato and Hermogenes suggested, our creator could only bring about the best order possible.

Necessary Correlations between Value and Power

If our world arose out of Middle Platonism's "three principles," it makes sense to suppose that there are some necessary principles, inherent in the very nature of things, about the features of finite existents, their relations to each other, and their relations to God. Two of these principles have already been implied: all existents, by virtue of embodying creativity, have both spontaneity and the power to influence other existents; and even the supreme existent can never override the other existents' exercise of their power.

A third principle is that correlations necessarily obtain among the following variables: (1) The capacity to enjoy positive value; (2) the capacity to suffer negative value (evil); (3) the power of self-determination (freedom); (4) the power to influence others, for good or ill. To speak of "necessary correlations" means that, as one variable increases, all the others increase proportionately. For example, for a being to have a great capacity to enjoy positive values is necessarily to have a great capacity to experience evils; to have a high degree of freedom is necessarily to have influence on others, for good or ill.

Because of these necessary correlations, it would not have been possible for the deity to have created beings similar to ourselves, having the same capacity to enjoy positive value, but with less freedom, less capacity to suffer evil, or less power to inflict evil on others. Accordingly, Whitehead has helped us see how the creator of our world could be perfectly good. We cannot reasonably expect God to have done the impossible.

CONCLUSION

It is clear that a successful theodicy cannot be based on the idea that our universe was created out of absolute nothingness. It is also clear that a theodicy based on Hermogenes and Whitehead has a much stronger basis for being considered biblical. It is also clear, moreover, that such a theodicy can succeed with the main task of a theodicy: to portray our creator as perfectly good. But many people, having had their sensibilities shaped by traditional theism, will likely say that the God of process theology is *not really divine,* because the central attribute of a being worthy of worship is omnipotence.

There is a valid point behind this claim: To be God is to be *perfect in power* as well as in goodness. Process theism clearly portrays God as perfect in goodness, but many critics say that it does this by portraying God as imperfect in power—as having less power than a being might have. This criticism is based on the idea that a being perfect in power would have all the power, period. However, argued Charles Hartshorne many decades ago,

> [T]he greatest possible power (which by definition is perfect power) may not be the same as "all the power that exists united into one individual power," for such union of "all" power may be impossible.[35]

Hartshorne argued, in fact, that it *would* be impossible. Here is the argument:

- In discussing the problem of evil, we are discussing an *actual* world (as distinct from an imaginary world in some author's mind).

- An actual world contains actual beings.

- Actual beings have power—the power to influence other things and, in some cases, the power to influence themselves (self-determination).

- An actual world comprised of a multiplicity of actual beings exists necessarily—as necessarily as God.

- Therefore, God could not possibly have all the power.

Making his point in different words, Hartshorne said:

> Instead of saying that God's power is limited, suggesting that it is less than some conceivable power, we should rather say: "[God's] power is absolutely maximal, the greatest possible, but even the greatest possible power is still one power among others, is not the only power.[36]

Moreover, another way of stating that God's power is unique was developed in Chapter 2: God's power is unique in being the only power able to create a universe. It is better, however, not to use the word "omnipotence" for this power, given the connotations it has. Surely, however, there can be no power greater than the power to create a universe.

In response, traditional theists will claim that we can conceive of a being with great power: the power to create an entire universe suddenly, all at once. However, to say that such a being is conceivable it is not sufficient merely to say that we can *verbalize* the notion of such being. Rather, the question is what is *consistently* conceivable. And insofar as we accept the idea that a real world contains *actual* beings, the universe consists of beings with their own power. Accordingly, we cannot truly conceive of a divine being who could have created our universe suddenly, all at once.

Process theism also provides an answer to the charge that God is indictable for having brought forth a universe that is so full of evil. The answer is that in stimulating the universe to bring forth life and then higher forms of life, including human-like beings, God's aim was to evoke the existence of creatures with increasingly higher forms of value. But every increase in the capacity for good necessarily increases the capacity for evil.

Creation is necessarily risky. The stimulation of the evolutionary process, until it brought forth human beings, necessarily brought forth the possibility of the human forms of evil. The only way to indict God for the evils of the world would be to hold that God should not have brought forth life, or at least the higher forms of life. But even this would have been a type of evil: The creation of a universe more trivial, with less capacity for value, than it might have been.[37]

With this revised understanding of the unique power of God, belief in God is not undermined by a contradiction between divine power and worldly evil.

CHAPTER FOUR

Humanity:
Crown of Creation

C HAPTER TWO DEALT with how the universe provided the conditions for the rise of life. An equally major question has been
how human consciousness could have arisen. Chapter Four begins
with this issue. It then turns to the biblical ideas of humans as *imago
dei* and the "crown of creation." Discussion of these ideas leads to
discussions of Soul and Spirit. Finally, the chapter returns to the rise
of human consciousness.

HOW DID HUMAN CONSCIOUSNESS ARISE?

This question has been central to philosophers and scientists since the
seventeenth century, when René Descartes developed his doctrine
of mind-body dualism. Descartes was a supernaturalist, so he did
not worry about how consciousness arose: God had simply created
it, along with matter. But his dualism raised the question of how the
mind could interact with its material body.

According to Descartes, the mind consisted of consciousness,
whereas the body, including the brain, was made of material stuff,
which is entirely insentient. This dualism created a problem, because

it entails that mind and body exert different types of causation. The mind can exercise *final* causation, meaning the attempt to achieve purposes. By contrast, the bits of matter composing the body can only exert *efficient* causation in the sense of billiard-ball causation, in which one thing affects other things by striking them.

But if mind and brain are so different, how can they interact? When I want a glass of water, how does my mind influence my brain, telling it to reach for the water? Likewise, when I burn my finger on the stove, how does my burnt finger make me—my mind—feel pain and withdraw my finger?

Originally it was thought that Descartes' dualism created a problem for him; but it was recently realized that he intended his dualism to be a proof for the existence of an omnipotent deity, because except for Gawd's power, the movements of our minds and our bodies could not be coordinated. This position was expressed more explicitly in later decades by Fr. Nicolas Malebranche, whose position was called "occasionalism": Upon the occasion of my hand being on a hot stove, the divine creator causes me to feel pain; and upon the occasion of my decision to move my hand, that creator causes my hand to move.[1]

One philosopher who holds this position is Oxford University's Richard Swinburne. Stating that there is "no natural connection between brain-events and correlated mental events," Swinburne argued that mind-brain correlation is explained by the fact that "[Gawd] is *omnipotent*: he can do anything."[2]

But what about philosophers who refuse to appeal to an omnipotent deity? Most philosophers who have worked on this issue were either dualists, who continue Descartes' dualism between the mind and the brain, or materialists, who equate the mind with the brain. In recent decades, members of both groups have admitted that they could not solve the mind-body problem.

For example, British philosopher Colin McGinn, a materialist, wrote: "The mind-body problem is a 'mystery' and not merely a 'problem.'"[3] In calling it a "mystery," he meant that it could never be solved. Explaining why, he asked, rhetorically: "How could the aggregation of millions of individually insentient neurons generate subjective awareness?" Indeed, he said: "It would take a supernatural magician to extract consciousness from matter."[4] Of course, being a materialist, McGinn rejected the existence of a deity.

Philosopher Geoffrey Madell of Edinburgh University said that dualism is much better than materialism. Nevertheless, he wrote:

> [I]t is admitted on all sides that the nature of the causal connection between the mental and the physical, as the Cartesian conceives of it, is utterly mysterious.[5]

Madell also extended his analysis to the topic of this section, the rise of consciousness. He wrote:

> [T]he appearance of consciousness in the course of evolution must appear for the dualist to be an utterly inexplicable emergence of something entirely new, an emergence which must appear quite bizarre.[6]

McGinn, as a materialist, expressed the same agnosticism. Speaking of the rise of mollusks and fish, he said:

> [W]e do not know how consciousness might have arisen by natural processes from antecedently existing material things. Somehow or other sentience sprang from pulpy matter, giving matter an inner aspect, but we have no idea how this leap was propelled. . . . One is tempted, however reluctantly, to turn to divine assistance: for only a kind of miracle could produce this from that.[7]

The insoluble problem faced by both dualists and materialists was expressed with great clarity by New York University's Thomas Nagel. Using the French term *pour soi* for that which is something "for itself," because it has experience, and *en soi* for that which, having no experience, is merely "in itself," Nagel famously wrote: "One cannot derive a *pour soi* from an *en soi*," because "the gap is logically unbridgeable." If a deity "wanted to create a conscious being," Nagel continued, "he could not expect to do it by combining together in organic form a lot of particles with none but physical properties."[8]

The problem of how a mind can relate to its body, and how minds arose historically, can be solved neither by dualism nor materialism, because each position presupposes that the human body consists of *en soi*, things devoid of experience. This issue will be taken up again later in this chapter.

HUMANS AS IMAGO DEI AND CROWN OF CREATION

Central to Christian thought have been two biblical terms summarizing the distinctiveness of human beings: *imago dei* (image of God) and "crown of creation." In traditional Christian thought, these terms were thought to apply to men more fully than to women. In recent Christian thinking, however, this sexist way of thinking has been overcome, at least in some types of theology.

The most important biblical basis for humans as *imago dei* is in the first chapter of Genesis (which was written in the sixth century BCE during the Babylonian exile). Genesis 1:26–27 says:

> Let us make humankind in our image, according to our likeness, and let them have dominion [over the earth]. So God created humankind in his image, in the image of God he created them; male and female he created them.

Many theologians today take this passage to point to "an egalitarian anthropology in which male and female are created to reflect the image of God equally."[9]

Traditional Christian thought commonly spoke of humanity— or "man," as our species was long called—as the crown of creation. Although there were many biblical passages used to support this description, the most important one was Psalm 8:3–5:

> When I look at your heavens, the work of your fingers, the moon and the stars that you have established; what are human beings that you are mindful of them, mortals that you care for them? Yet you have made them a little lower than angels, and crowned them with glory and honor.

Although the Bible's high evaluation of human beings was based on its theism, this high evaluation long remained dominant in Western culture, even after it became secular.

However, things started changing in the latter part of the nineteenth century. For reasons discussed in previous chapters, the Bible began losing its authority, and the idea that God created the universe in general seemed refuted by science. As a result, human beings were portrayed not as the crown of creation, but as a cosmic accident. Neo-Darwinists (as distinct from Darwin himself) argued that humanity could not be regarded as something special, which the universe had in some sense intended to produce.

Recently, as discussed in Chapter 2, the discovery of fine-tuning has contradicted this idea of a purely accidental universe. It suggests that the universe had intentionality—the purpose to produce life. This was a startling revelation. But this revelation by itself provides no support for the idea that humanity is in any sense the crown of creation, because some "deep ecologists" have affirmed "biological egalitarianism," according to which all forms of life have equal intrinsic value.[10] From this perspective, the idea that the universe was fine-tuned for life did not necessarily conflict with the neo-Darwinian view that humans are no higher than amoebae. However, our universe was not simply fine-tuned for life. It was also prepared for spirit.

SOUL AND SPIRIT

What is spirit? In discussions of the biblical view of human beings, there has long been a debate between the tripartite view, which says that a human being is composed of body, soul, and spirit, and the bipartite view, according to which soul and spirit are taken to refer to the same entity.

Advocates of the tripartite view point to passages such as I Thessalonians 5:23, which says "may your spirit and soul and body be preserved entire," and Hebrews 4:12, which says that the Word of God, sharper than any two-edged sword, "penetrates even to dividing soul and spirit." But advocates of the bipartite view say that the human being is composed only of the material body and the immaterial soul or spirit. According to this view, "soul" and "spirit" are two terms for the same reality.

The issue of whether one of these views can be called *the* biblical view can be left aside. But if one asks whether one of these views is more helpful in the attempt to understand human beings, there is much to be said for the tripartite view. The statement that a human being is composed of soul and body says nothing distinctive about human beings in relation to other animals: As we have seen, experience goes all the way down to the lowest forms of life. As Whitehead said: "It is not a mere question of having a soul or of not having a soul. The question is, How much, if any?"[11]

When organisms have a lot of soul, spirit can emerge. That is, the term "spirit" can be used to refer to the functions of the soul that are beyond the capacities of other animals, such as the capacities for logic, rationality, mathematics, and science. Non-human animals can demonstrate some degree of capacity for these functions. For example, some animals have a capacity for counting. So there is no absolute dualism—the difference between humans and other animals is a matter of degree. However, the difference is so great that it is in effect a difference of kind.

In addition to logic, rationality, mathematics, and science, there are several other capacities of the human soul that can be labeled "spirit," including morality, religion, human-like freedom, and the various arts, such as music, painting, and sculpture. The universe was ready for creatures with spirit as well as life. In other words, the universe was not merely fine-tuned for life. It was also fine-tuned for living creatures such as us, with the capacities for logic, rationality, mathematics, and the other characteristics of spirit.

However, many modern philosophers and scientists have argued that humans can have no spirit because they have no soul.

THE DENIAL OF SOUL

Biologist Francis Crick, one of the discoverers of the structure of the

DNA molecule, wrote a book entitled *The Astonishing Hypothesis*, in which he said:

> The Astonishing Hypothesis is that "YOU," your joys and your sorrows, your memories and your ambitions, your sense of personal identity and free will, are in fact no more than the behavior of a vast assembly of nerve cells and their associated molecules. As Lewis Carroll's Alice might have phrased it: "You're nothing but a pack of neurons."[12]

This position, which stands in contrast with "the religious concept of a soul," said Crick, puts science "in a head-on contradiction to the religious belief of billions of human beings alive today."[13]

The motivation for such a counter-intuitive claim was the mind-body problem. If there is a mind or soul, how could it influence the body? And how could the body influence the mind or soul in return?

This became a problem because, as Descartes formulated the issue in the seventeenth century, the mind and the body were taken to be *ontologically different in kind*. On the one hand, the body, including the brain, is physical, in the sense of being composed of bits of matter. These bits of matter, such as the brain cells, are completely devoid of feeling or experience of any type. On the other hand, the mind is mental, in the sense that it consists of consciousness, experience, feelings, and intentions.

In this discussion, the term "dualism" always mean this *ontological* dualism, according to which mind and body are different in kind, in the sense of being composed of different stuff: matter and consciousness or experience. As pointed out above, this dualism creates an insoluble problem, because it defines mind and brain such that they could not (apart from divine intervention) interact. The mind, being spiritual rather than physical, could not influence the (physical) brain. And the brain, being completely physical, would have nothing with which to influence the mind.

Ridiculing the idea that something mental could make a physical difference in our brains, philosopher John Searle asked:

Are we supposed to think that thoughts can wrap themselves around the axons or shake the dendrites or sneak inside the cell wall and attack the cell nucleus?[14]

Searle wrote as a materialist, so it is not surprising that he considered Descartes' mind-body dualism unintelligible. But even some dualists agree. As we saw, Madell acknowledged that the mind-body relation, as understood by Cartesians, is "utterly mysterious." The mystery for Madell, moreover, goes beyond the question of how mind and brain can interact. It also extends to the question of how consciousness could have arisen.

Because ontological dualism seems unintelligible, most philosophers came to endorse materialism (also called physicalism). According to this position, the world consists entirely of material (physical) things. But how, then, does consciousness arise? For many decades, materialists tried to argue that conscious states could be reduced to (explained in terms of) bits of matter. But this attempt failed, as no one could successfully refute Nagel's point that something devoid of experience (*en soi*) could produce something *with* experience *(pour soi)*.[15]

Agreeing with Nagel, McGinn made his afore-quoted comment, "It would take take a supernatural magician to extract consciousness from matter."[16] McGinn's comment was, of course, made with tongue in cheek, as McGinn rightly took it for granted that we cannot solve philosophical problems by appealing to a supernatural deity. Referring to the seventeenth century, William James wrote: "For thinkers of that age, ['Gawd'] was the great solvent of all absurdities."[17]

Some philosophers today, such as Richard Swinburne, still use a supernatural deity to explain the interactions between soul and brain. But modern thinkers in general would not appeal to supernaturalism. And so, not knowing of an alternative, they have been led to the conclusion that we cannot intelligibly speak of human beings as having souls: A person is simply "a pack of neurons."

THE DENIAL OF SPIRIT

In the absence of a soul, it is obvious that a person cannot have any of the above-mentioned functions of soul that distinguish humans from other animals. In other words, humans could not have spirit. They could not be said to be the *imago dei* or the "crown of creation." This section looks at the main reasons for denying the reality of three of the types of spirit: freedom, moral experience, and religious experience.

Freedom

Neo-Darwinism, pointed out William Provine, cannot allow for genuine freedom, saying that "free will, as traditionally conceived, the freedom to make uncoerced and unpredictable choices among alternative possible course of action, simply does not exist."[18] Philosophers have explained why materialism in general rules out freedom.

Science, said John Searle, "allows no place for freedom of the will."[19] Assuming that science proves the truth of materialism, Searle said that science tells us that the world "consists entirely of mindless, meaningless, physical particles."[20]

However, while saying that freedom is impossible, Searle also said that we cannot help presupposing it. It is "impossible for us to abandon the belief in the freedom of the will," said Searle, because

> the conviction of freedom ... is built into every normal, conscious intentional action.... [W]e can't act otherwise than on the assumption of freedom, no matter how much we learn about how the world works as a determined physical system.[21]

In saying this, Searle was in effect agreeing with Whitehead. However, Searle did not accept Whitehead's view that "we must bow to those presumptions, which, in despite of criticism, we still employ for the regulation of our lives."[22] Rather, Searle concluded that, even though we necessarily presuppose freedom, it must be an illusion.[23]

Dualists, by contrast, can affirm freedom, in the sense of self-determination, by saying that the mind or soul, understood as an entity distinct from the brain, is able to exert final causation and hence self-determination. However, human behavior can be free, in the sense of self-determining, only if the soul can guide the brain, and dualists are unable to explain causal interaction between the mind and its brain. So they are unable to explain how the soul's self-determination can express itself in bodily practices.

Moral Experience

Another of the dimensions of human spirit is its capacity for moral experience. This capacity allows us to distinguish moral from immoral behavior and, because of our freedom, to chose to act morally. This has widely been considered central to the idea that the human race is "the crown of creation." For example, Charles Darwin saw the evolutionary process as an instrument to manufacture "moral perfection."[24] "[O]f all the differences between man and the lower animals," wrote Darwin, "the moral sense or conscience is by far the most important."[25] But *neo*-Darwinism is completely different on this point, because of its atheism. From this perspective, wrote William Provine, "there are no inherent moral or ethical laws."[26]

Modern thought more generally, insofar as it presupposes atheism, denies the reality of moral values or norms. Oxford University philosopher John Mackie, in a book entitled *Ethics,* said: "There are no objective values"; moral values are not "part of the fabric of the world."[27] For example, said Mackie, we might think that, "if someone is writhing in agony before your eyes," you should "do something about it if you can." But this, said Mackie, is not an objective requirement of the nature of things.[28]

Mackie did grant that objective moral values could be defended if theism could be defended,[29] but he was convinced that it could not be—not surprisingly, because he equated theism with belief in Gawd, who has the crucial attribute: "able to do everything (i.e., omnipotent)."[30]

Religious Experience

Modernity has also been unable to affirm that a person has direct contact with a Holy Reality, traditionally referred to in Western circles as "God."

There have been two main reasons for denying that putative religious experience—the kinds of experiences reported in William

James' *Varieties of Religious Experience* and Maurice Bucke's *Cosmic Consciousness*—are ever genuine. One reason is the denial that there is a Divine or Holy Reality, an experience of which would evoke an "experience of the holy." The other reason is the conviction that human perception is limited to *sensory* perception, so that, just as we could not experience moral norms (even if they existed), we also could not experience a divine reality. For example:

- According to Immanuel Kant, to affirm a "feeling of the immediate presence of the Supreme Being" would be a "fanatical religious illusion," because it would be to affirm "a receptivity for an intuition for which there is no sensory provision in man's nature."[31]

- According to French sociologist Émile Durkheim, the primary problem for the scientific understanding of religion is "explaining the sacred"— that is, explaining why religious people think in terms of the distinction between the "sacred" and the "profane," even though "nothing in sensible [sensory] experience seems able to suggest the idea of so radical a duality to them."[32]

- Religion professor Samuel Preus said that explaining and interpreting religion should be carried out from "an altogether nonreligious point of view."[33]

- Another professor of religion, Robert Segal, said that social scientists should assume that "believers never encounter God."[34]

- When Harvard theologian Gordon Kaufman was asked to what the word "God" refers, Kaufman replied: "Certainly not to anything we directly experience."[35]

These denials of freedom, moral experience, and religious experience follow from the denial of a divine being, understood as Gawd, and the sensationist doctrine of perception, according to which, in Whitehead's words, all perception is by the mediation of our bodily sense-organs, such as eyes, palates, noses, ears, and the diffused bodily organization furnishing touches, aches, and other bodily sensations.[36]

This sensationist theory of perception, combined with atheism, led to the denial of a set of functions of our souls or minds that can be called spirit.

THE RECOVERY OF SOUL AND SPIRIT

An account of the recovery of spirit must begin by providing a more adequate account of the human soul.

How Freedom Is Possible

As discussed above, neither materialists nor dualists can make sense of human freedom, although it is one of our hard-core commonsense ideas, which—as discussed in the Introduction—cannot be denied without self-contradiction. On the assumption that materialism and dualism are the only possible positions, advocates of materialism defend it by pointing to the difficulties in dualism, while advocates of dualism argue that it must be true because materialism has even greater problems.

But there is a third option: panexperientialism (a better term for the position that was traditionally called "panpsychism"). It can account for the freedom we presuppose. This point, which can be called "panexperientialism with organizational duality," can be explained in five steps:

1. Rather than being composed of two types of entities— physical and mental—all fully actual entities are of one type. The ultimate elements of the universe are momentary experiences. Each momentary experience—called an "occasion of experience"—begins by receiving influences from previous experiences. Each experience then exercises self-determination. In very low-grade experiences, this self-determination is trivial.

But a trivial capacity for self-determination is qualitatively different from a complete absence of it. The fact that every experience has at least an iota of self-determination provides the basis for more self-determination at higher levels of the evolutionary process—in, for example, bacteria, DNA molecules, bees, squirrels, chimpanzees, and humans.

2. These momentary experiences get organized into enduring individuals of various types, called *societies*. "The real actual things that endure," said Whitehead, "are all societies."[37] The simplest type of societies are serially ordered societies, such as atoms, DNA molecules, and animal souls, in which there is only one member at a time. The human mind or soul is a serially ordered (or personally-ordered) society, in which there is only one member at a time. The fact that the mind is a personally ordered *society* of actual occasions, rather than simply a single entity, allows freedom to enter into the mind, because each actual occasion is more or less self-determining. When the actual occasions are living, the personally ordered society is called a "living person."

3. Very low-grade enduring individuals, such as electrons and protons, can organize themselves in one of two basic ways. On the one hand, the low-grade societies can form "compound individuals," such as atoms, molecules, macromolecules, organelles, prokaryotic cells, eukaryotic cells, and animals, including humans.[38] These beings are individuals by virtue of having an inclusive experience, which allows the individual to act as a whole. For example, the ordinary molecules composing a macromolecule, such as DNA, have their own experiences, but the DNA molecule as a whole has its own experience, which gives it the capacity to exercise self-determination and then to act as a whole on other things. On the other hand, the low-grade enduring individuals can be organized into aggregational societies, such as rocks, bicycles, and toasters. Not being compound individuals, these entities have no capacity for self-determination.

4. The modern idea that "everything is determined," so that there is no freedom in the world, is based on the failure to distinguish compound individuals from aggregational societies. For example, philosopher William Lycan treated human beings as if they were structurally no different from electric toasters. A "physical macro-event," such as the explosion of a toaster, he said, is fully determined by forces beyond the toaster: It exerted no self-determination. Likewise, Lycan said, when a human being does something (such as buying dinner for a homeless person), that is also a "physical macro-event." Therefore, Lycan concluded, this event was as fully determined as was the explosion of the toaster.[39]

5. However, a toaster is not analogous to a human being. A toaster is composed of billions of atoms, all at the same level. Any self-determination exerted by the individual atoms is canceled out by the actions of the billions of other atoms. As Whitehead put it, the individuals composing a toaster have spontaneous functionings, but "for lifeless matter these functionings thwart each other, and average out so as to produce a negligible total effect."[40] So the behavior of the toaster is completely determined by the forces acting on it; the toaster cannot exert even an iota of self-determination.

But a human is hierarchically organized. Its atoms are organized into ordinary molecules, which are organized into macromolecules, which in turn are subordinated to the compound individuals known as prokaryotic cells, some of which are compounded into eukaryotic cells. The human brain consists of approximately 100 billion of the eukaryotic cells known as neurons. Insofar as it has a living brain, a human being is a compound individual, with the soul being the dominant member. The soul can influence various parts of the brain, by means of which the soul can guide its body. Given the complete difference between a human being and a toaster, it is incredible that materialist philosophers insist that they must behave in the same way. As Whitehead said, "diverse modes of organization" can produce "diverse modes of functioning."[41]

How the Soul and Brain Can Interact

Presupposed in the above discussion is the idea that the soul and the brain can interact: The soul influences the brain cells, which in turn influence the soul.

The idea that the soul can influence the brain is generally called "mental causation." This idea has been problematic for both materialists and dualists. Indeed, there is a philosophical position known as *epiphenomenalism,* according to which the mind is a non-efficacious product of the brain. In other words, the (physical) brain somehow produces (mental) experiences, but then these experiences make no difference to bodily states and actions.

However, the reality of mental causation is a hard-core common-sense idea. As philosopher Ted Honderich said, the main reason for affirming mental causation is "the futility of contemplating its denial." "Off the page," said Honderich about epiphenomenalism, "no one believes it."[42]

The reason mental causation has been an insoluble problem for dualists was discussed earlier: There is no way to understand how an entirely non-physical mind could influence entirely physical brain cells. Materialism is not much different. Charles Hartshorne, in fact, called materialism "covert dualism," because it says that the world consists of individuals with experience and individuals without experience.[43]

Philosopher Jaegwon Kim spent much of his career trying to show that physicalism (equated with materialism) does not entail epiphenomenalism. Indeed, he dismissed epiphenomenalism with a *reductio ad absurdum*: If our reasons and desires have no causal efficacy at all in influencing our bodily actions, then perhaps no one has ever performed a single intentional action! However, after working on this problem for many years, he at the end confessed "to be up against a dead end"—the problem of the mind appeared "intractable."[44]

However, given panexperientialism, the idea of mental causation is not a problem. As Charles Hartshorne put it:

[C]ells can influence our human experiences because they have feelings that we can feel. To deal with the influences of human experiences upon cells, one turns this around. *We have feelings that cells can feel.*[45]

The Possibility of Moral and Religious Experience

As discussed earlier, modern philosophers have said that genuine religious and moral experience is impossible, because a divine reality and moral norms cannot be perceived by means of our senses. Whitehead showed, however, that sensory perception is a secondary mode of perception, being derivative from a more fundamental, nonsensory type of perception, or *prehension*, through which moral norms and divinity might be experienced.

Given the idea that sensory perception is the only way of knowing anything about the world beyond ourselves, claims about telepathy—a kind of nonsensory perception normally called "extra-sensory"—have been ridiculed, because telepathic experiences would be the only exception to the idea that all perception occurs by means of our senses.

However, that is far from the truth. Whitehead pointed out that we constantly presuppose the occurrence of various types of nonsensory perception. Here are three examples:

An External World: "The belief in an external world independent of the perceiving subject," declared Einstein, "is the basis of all natural science."[46] However, sense perception does not assure us of the existence of a world beyond our present moment of experience. "[T]he mind [cannot] go beyond what is immediately present to the senses," said philosopher David Hume, "to discover the real existence . . . of objects."[47] Hume's point was that sensory perception as such gives us only sense-data, such as shapes and colors, not the fact that these shapes and colors betoken real objects.

On the basis of sensory perception alone, therefore, we would be left with solipsism—the idea that we do not know whether or not there is anything real beyond ourselves. That, of course, would be absurd: We *know* that we are in a world of real objects and people.

Philosophers, to be sure, have debated this point. But as Hume himself said, no one doubts this in practice—that is, in the course of living. And this is the test of what we *really* believe. To repeat Whitehead's statement about hard-core common sense: "we must bow to those presumptions, which, in despite of criticism, we still employ for the regulation of our lives."[48]

One's Own Body: Behind our knowledge of the external world is our nonsensory prehension of our own bodies. Hume claimed that "the mind [cannot] go beyond what is immediately present to the senses." But in that statement, Hume showed that he was aware of something actual beyond his mind: his body. In asking where we get the idea of substances—that is, of actual things as distinct from mere sense impressions—Hume asked which of our body's sensory organs could have provided this idea:

> If it be perceived by the eyes, it must be a color; if by the ears, a sound; if by the palate, a taste; and so of the other senses.[49]

In asserting the lack of any perception of anything beyond our own minds, Hume had implicitly presupposed the existence of something beyond our mind. Whitehead asked: "What is the meaning of '*by*' in '*by* the eyes [and] '*by* the ears'?" The answer is that the sense-data "are given *by* the causal efficacy of actual bodily organs."[50]

Our awareness of our body's causal efficacy for our experience is due to our *nonsensory perception of this efficacy*. In fact, Whitehead referred to our most fundamental mode of perception, more basic than sensory perception, as "perception in the mode of causal efficacy," otherwise called "prehension."

This perception of our bodily organs is obviously not itself a form of sensory perception: I do not see my eyes providing sensory data for me or hear my ears providing sounds. My capacity to enjoy sights and sounds through my eyes and ears depends upon my nonsensory perception of my body, through which I receive the information that its sensory organs have brought in from the world beyond my body.

My most *direct* perception of my body, furthermore, is not my perception of these organs but my pre-sensory prehension of my brain.

In Whitehead's words:

> Common sense, physical theory, and physiological theory, combine to point out a historic route of inheritance . . . first physically in the external environment, then physiologically— through the eyes in the case of visual data—up the nerves, into the brain.[51]

In other words, I receive sense-date from my eyes, which I perceive indirectly by directly perceiving (prehending) my brain.

The Past: Philosopher George Santayana, who taught at Harvard prior to Whitehead's arrival there, took Hume's insight about solipsism a step further. Besides not telling us that we live in a real world, sense-perception also, observed Santayana, does not tell us of the existence of the past. Therefore, if sense-perception were our only source of information, we would be afflicted with "solipsism of the present moment."[52]

As to why we know that we have a past, it is because we *remember* it. That may seem too obvious to mention. But the point is that memory is *a form of nonsensory perception.* We don't see the past, or hear it, or smell it, or taste or touch it, and yet we know about it. In Whitehead's view, "the most compelling example of non-sensuous perception is our knowledge of our own immediate past."[53]

To summarize the argument thus far: Modern philosophers have argued that putative moral and religious experience cannot be genuine, because such experience would require nonsensory perception. This would make it different from every other type of experience, hence too odd to be plausible. Whitehead showed, however, that nonsensory perception, far from being a great exception, is more fundamental than sensory perception, being presupposed by it. Indeed, Whitehead said that "science conceived as resting on mere sense perception, with no other source of observation, is bankrupt."[54]

Whitehead argued, in addition, that we directly experience moral norms. He wrote:

> There are experiences of ideals—of ideals entertained, of

ideals aimed at, of ideals achieved, of ideals defaced. This is the experience of the deity of the universe.[55]

Of course, the fact that the experience of ideals is an experience of the deity does not necessarily make the experience a religious experience. As will be discussed below, our experience of both logic and mathematics are also experiences of the deity of the universe. These are secular effects of the deity.

But our experience of the deity of the universe is a religious experience if we experience it *as holy*. In at least most religious traditions, the divine reality is described as the "holy" or the "sacred." Rudolf Otto wrote a famous book about religious experience entitled *The Idea of the Holy;* Mircea Eliade wrote an equally famous book named *The Sacred and the Profane*.[56] "[A]t the foundation of all religion," said Whitehead, is "the intuition of holiness, the intuition of the sacred."[57]

As indicated above, modern philosophers and social scientists believe that there is no such intuition. They make this judgment based not on interviews and surveys, but on the dogma that there could be no experience of holiness, because our sensory system could not detect holiness. This judgment led to Durkheim's question of how the distinction between sacred and the secular ever arose, because nothing in sensory experience suggests this contrast. More recently, Samuel Preus asked: "if 'God is not given,' how is one to explain religions— that is, their universality, variety, and persistence until now?"[58]

However, neither Preus nor anyone else has been able to answer this question.[59] It appears that the universality, variety, and persistence of religion can only be explained on the assumption that the universe is holy, or contains holiness, which can be experienced by people of every culture.

William James, who influenced Whitehead on this issue, rejected the sensationist view of perception, which had been pioneered by Hume. Against Hume's sensationist empiricism, James advocated a "thicker and more radical empiricism." On that basis, James affirmed that we have a "religious sense," through which we can experience a "larger power which is friendly to [us] and to [our] ideals."[60]

MORE MANIFESTATIONS OF SPIRIT

Spiritual activities differentiate humans from other animals, with their less developed souls. The previous section discussed three types of spiritual activity: freedom, moral experience, and religious experience. This section discusses three more.

Mathematics

Given our culture's heavy association of mathematics with science and technology, probably not many people would place it alongside of moral and religious experience as a mark of spirit. However, there is no doubt that it is one of the major ways in which human souls greatly exceed those of other animals. Also, mathematical experience is equally dependent upon the deity of the universe.

Mathematical Objects: The objects of mathematics, such as the number 2, and mathematical truths, such as that 2 and 2 are 4, appear to exist objectively. But many philosophers of mathematics argue that this cannot be because numbers are abstract, and, as such, they cannot be perceived. "How does this [alleged] immaterial realm," asked philosopher of mathematics Reuben Hersh, "make contact with flesh and blood mathematicians?"[61] Hilary Putnam said: "We cannot envisage *any* kind of neural process that could even correspond to the 'perception of a mathematical object.'"[62] In other words, even if numbers exist, there would be no way we could know about them.

Some philosophers have decided to avoid the problem by simply denying the reality of mathematical objects, as illustrated by book titles such as *Science without Numbers* and *Mathematics without Numbers*. According to this approach, mathematics is just a game, with no reference to real objects.[63]

Most commentators agree, however, that this "nonrealist" or "formalist" solution is inadequate to the presuppositions of mathematicians themselves. As Y. N. Moschovakis said, it violates "the instinctive certainty of most everybody who has ever tried to solve a [mathematical] problem that he is thinking about 'real objects.'"[64] Similar observations have been made by other philosophers.[65]

Famous mathematical physicist Roger Penrose has provided an illustration of the certainty that mathematical objects are really objective. Speaking of the mathematical structure called the Mandelbrot Set—which was described in 1980 by Benoit Mandelbrot—Penrose said: "The Mandelbrot Set is not an invention of the human mind: it was a discovery. Like Mount Everest, the Mandelbrot Set is just *there!*"[66]

Kurt Gödel, one of our most brilliant mathematicians and logicians, argued that it is false to say that mathematics is not based on perception, for we "have something like a perception" of mathematical ideas.

> I don't see any reason why we should have less confidence in this kind of perception, i.e., in mathematical intuition, than in sense perception.[67]

Gödel's proposal was laughed out of court by lesser minds, but wrongly so, given the fact that, as Whitehead showed, there are many kinds of nonsensory perception.

Hersh had another objection: "Ideal entities independent of human consciousness violate the empiricism of modern science."[68] The valid point behind this objection goes back to Aristotle—that abstract, non-actual (ideal) things can exist only in actual things. In response to Aristotle, Middle Platonism held that Plato's eternal forms exist in the divine logos, the mind of God.[69] The question of how numbers and other ideal entities can exist was not a problem as long as philosophers were theists.

In the eighteenth century, as Hersh pointed out, Leibniz and Berkeley still held that abstractions like numbers are thoughts in the mind of God. But then this theistic solution went out of fashion: "Heaven and the Mind of God," said Hersh, "are no longer heard of in academic discourse."[70]

However, Whitehead decided that the arguments against a cosmic mind were invalid (unless the mind were conceived as omnipotent). Developing a new version of the Middle Platonic view, Whitehead renamed Aristotle's insight the *ontological principle*, according to which: "[A]part from things that are actual, there is nothing—nothing either in fact or in efficacy."[71]

It was this realization that led Whitehead to affirm the existence of a reality worthy to be called "God." He wrote:

Everything must be somewhere; and here "somewhere" means "some actual entity." Accordingly the general potentiality of the universe must be somewhere.... The notion of "subsistence" is merely the notion of how eternal objects can be components of the primordial nature of God.[72]

Whitehead's argument, in other words, was that mathematical objects can exist because they exist in God—that is, in the mind of the universe, which makes the universe an experiencing whole. This is the position known as *panentheism.*

Deciphering the Universe: Besides the fact that the universe contains mathematical objects, the universe is itself mathematical, a fact that is usually considered a mystery. Roger Penrose said that for him and many other physicists, the fact that "somehow the structure of the physical world is rooted in mathematics" is "a very great mystery."[73] "Why nature is mathematical is a mystery," agreed Richard Feynman."[74]

Equally remarkable, however, is the fact that the human mind has proved capable of understanding the universe's mathematical principles. In a book asking *Is God a Mathematician?* Mario Livio discussed Isaac Newton's discovery of the law of gravity:

Newton took the laws of falling bodies discovered by Galileo, combined them with the laws of planetary motion determined by Kepler, and used this unified scheme to put forth a universal, mathematical law of gravitation.... The accuracy to which Newton himself could verify his law of gravity... was no better than about 4 percent. Yet the law proved to be accurate beyond all reasonable expectations. By the 1950s, the experimental accuracy was better than one ten-thousandth of a percent.[75]

One of the remarkable facts about the universe, physicist and science writer James Trefil has argued, is the fact that, in spite of its enormous size, "the laws of nature we discover here and now in our laboratories are true everywhere in the universe." Referring to this fact as the "principle of universality," he asked how it could be explained. Suggesting that it cannot, he referred to it as a mystery.[76]

But Whitehead said that the question had already been answered by Plato: He held (in Whitehead's words) that "the agency whereby ideas obtain efficiency in the creative advance" was "*a basic Psyche whose active grasp of ideas conditions impartially the whole process of the Universe.*"[77]

The scientific discovery that the universe was fine-tuned for life is arguably science's most important discovery for understanding the place of humans in the universe. But the idea that the universe was fine-tuned for life is too modest. For this idea says only that the universe was prepared for life as such—as prepared for humans as for bacteria.

The world of Platonic forms contains an enormous wealth of possibilities that have no relevance for bacteria and amoebae. Neo-Darwinists argue that evolution has been shaped by interaction with the physical world. But how could such interaction lead to higher mathematics, which for our ancestors 10,000 years ago would have no survival value at all?

It seems that the universe is fit not simply for life, but for beings such as us—beings with spirit. This does not mean that God created the realm of Platonic forms. "[God] does not create eternal objects, for his nature requires them in the same degree that they require him."[78] But it does mean that human beings have been born into a universe that was ready for them—a universe that provides the conditions for mathematical as well as moral and religious truths.

LOGIC AND RATIONALITY

Although logic and rationality are not the same, they are closely related, in that logic is basic to rationality and rationality would be impossible without logic. Indeed, Whitehead called logic "the general analysis of self-consistency."[79]

The capacity of human beings for logic and rationality is another manifestation of spirit. Although some other animals, such as chimpanzees and crows, are clearly able to act logically, there is no reason to think that they are able to think about logic and rationality.

Logic: There are various ways to define, or characterize, logic. Thomas Nagel, for example, said that logic is "the system of concepts that makes thought possible."[80] This statement suggests that logic has some authority over us. But how can this be?

Hilary Putnam observed that "the nature of mathematical truth" and "the nature of logical truth" have one and the same problem.[81] This means that logic faces this twofold problem: Where do logical truths exist, and how can they be effective in the world?[82]

For materialists, these problems are insoluble. A logical truth is a *meaning*, called by Whitehead a "proposition." If the world consists entirely of bits of matter, there is by definition no place where meanings, such as logical truths, could exist. And there is no way these truths could make a difference. The logical rule known as *modus ponens* says: "If p then q; p holds; therefore q is true." For example:

- If it is raining outside, my balcony is wet.

- It is raining outside.

- Therefore, my balcony is wet.

There is no question about the soundness of this rule.

What is questionable is how this logical truth can affect us. Colin McGinn, writing from a materialistic perspective, asked "how a physical organism can be subject to the norms of rationality. How, for example, does *modus ponens* get its grip on the causal transitions between mental states?"[83]

Thus phrased, the answer would be: In no way. But rephrased in terms of panexperientialism, there is no problem, because it is not you as a "physical organism" that must deal with *modus ponens*, but you as a mind—as the dominant member of your psychophysical organism. And just as you can (non-sensorily) perceive mathematical truths, you can perceive (prehend) propositions, such as logical truths.

In fact, Whitehead discusses various types of prehensions, one of which is *propositional prehensions.*

Also, just as mathematical principles can affect us because their presence in God makes them efficacious, the same is true of logical principles. Logical principles can influence us because their existence in God makes them efficacious.

Rationality*:* Whereas logic makes rationality possible, actually thinking rationally about some topic, be it physics, engineering, or theology, is to operate in terms of rules of rationality. The necessity of rules of rationality can be illustrated by what is usually considered the first rule of rationality, the law of non-contradiction. As philosopher Charles Larmore wrote, to argue that there are no objective rules of rationality "would mean that the idea that we *ought* to avoid self-contradiction is merely a preference, with no inherent authority."

> Imagine thinking that even so basic a rule of reasoning as the avoidance of contradiction has no more authority than what we choose to give it. Imagine thinking that we could just as well have willed the opposite, seeking out contradictions and believing each and every one. Has anyone the slightest idea of what it would be like really to believe this?[84]

The fact that we presuppose rules of rationality shows that materialism provides a completely inadequate basis for understanding human nature. Materialism insists that all causation is *efficient* causation—the influence of one thing or event on another.[85] But the rational activity of a philosopher of science is action in terms of some norm, such as the norm of self-consistency.

Hilary Putnam complained that most science-based schools of thought have produced "philosophies which leave no room for the rational activity of philosophy," with the result that "these views are self-refuting."[86] By contrast, said philosopher Jaegwon Kim, our self-image involves thinking of ourselves "as reflective agents capable of deliberation and evaluation—that is, . . . as agents capable of acting in accordance with a norm."[87] Beings within a materialistic world would not be capable of acting in terms of norms.

But would this be possible within any naturalistic world? Thomas Nagel called this difficult, because reasoning involves infinite thoughts. Although the infinity of thought is easiest to see with regard to arithmetical reasoning (once we are able to count, we realize that "every number has a successor, larger by one," so the number of arithmetical truths is infinite). But it is equally true with logical truths.[88]

And this produces a puzzle: "How is it possible for finite beings like us to think infinite thoughts?" After rejecting what he called "the religious answer," Nagel observed that it would be difficult to avoid a position with no religious ring to it whatsoever. Noting that "the existence of mind is certainly a *datum* for the construction of a world picture," he wrote:

> I admit that this idea—that the capacity of the universe to generate organisms with minds capable of understanding the universe is itself somehow a fundamental feature of the universe—has a quasi-religious "ring" to it.[89]

It certainly does. It does *not* require a supernatural explanation. But the fact that the universe has produced creatures such as us—with logical and rational capacities that allow us to understand the universe that produced us—implies that the universe is "spiritual" in a deeply significant meaning of the term.

In describing our nature as human beings, accordingly, we need to say not only that we have spirit as well as soul but also that we are children of a universe that has the capacity to produce creatures such as us. The phrase "creatures such as us" means creatures with not only life but also with capacities for logic, rationality, morality, religion, human-like freedom, higher mathematics, and the various arts. All of these capacities can be explained by the same agency that explains the universality of the laws of nature, namely, "a basic Psyche whose active grasp of ideas conditions impartially the whole process of the Universe."[90] In other words, God is understood as the soul of the universe, and the universe is understood as existing in God (panentheism).

Accordingly, we can reaffirm the traditional doctrines that humans are the *imago dei* and the crown of creation.

HOW DID ANIMAL CONSCIOUSNESS EMERGE?

This section continues the discussion in the first section, which concluded with the statement that both dualism and materialism fail to explain the relation of consciousness to the body because they presupposed that the body, including the brain, consists of things devoid of experience. But new developments in microbiology have helped overcome this problem (just as new developments in physical cosmology have helped, as discussed in Chapter 2, to weaken the scientific community's commitment to atheism).

Neurons

As early as 1974, an article in *Science* was entitled "Decision-Making in Bacteria."[91] Since then, the idea has become commonplace, with books and dozens of scientific journals on the topic.[92]

Famous and once-controversial biologist Lynn Margulis[93] is best known for her theory of "symbiogenesis," which began with her discovery that the eukaryotic cell is a composite resulting from a symbiotic union of primitive prokaryotic cells. In other words, eukaryotes resulted when large prokaryotes absorbed smaller ones.

Her theory of symbiogenesis was based on the idea that all living organisms are sentient. Saying that her worldview "recognizes the perceptive capacity of all live beings,"[94] she held that "consciousness is a property of all living cells," even the most elementary ones: "Bacteria are conscious. These bacterial beings have been around since the origin of life."[95]

Given the meaning usually given to the term "consciousness," it is not the best term to describe the experience of bacteria. The term "feeling" is much better. In fact, Whitehead used this term for experience at every level, with "consciousness" saved for the higher forms of feeling. The crucial point, nevertheless, is that an ultimate dualism is rejected.

The importance of this discovery cannot be overemphasized. Since the time of Descartes, as stated above, the mind-body problem, for both dualists and materialists, has presupposed that the brain is composed of insentient matter. As we saw in Section I, Colin McGinn, in explaining why the mind-body problem is insoluble, asked: "How could the aggregation of millions of individually insentient neurons generate subjective awareness?"[96]

Pointing out the relevance of the new view of bacteria to this problem, Margulis said:

> Thought and behavior in people are rendered far less mysterious when we realize that choice and sensitivity are already exquisitely developed in the microbial cells that became our ancestors.[97]

Neurons (brain cells) are much more sophisticated than bacteria, which are prokaryotic cells. If cells in general are, in the words of University of Chicago microbiologist James Shapiro, "capable of sophisticated information processing,"[98] then brain cells are capable of even more sophisticated processing.

Panexperientialism

Given the fact that experience goes down to the most primitive form of life, there is no need for a supernatural explanation of the existence of consciousness, because brains are not composed of insentient neurons. Rather, neurons, which are eukaryotic cells, consist of bacteria (prokaryotic cells), which have low-level experiences, best called feelings.

But this raises the question of the source of the experiences of these prokaryotic cells. The answer to this is suggested by articles speaking of decision-making at a *subcellular* level.[99] The first subcellular level would be organelles. (It was long said that bacteria had no organelles, but this view is changing.)[100] But where does this reference to lower levels come to an end?

The answer being increasingly given is that it does not—that experience goes all the way down. The name for this position is *panexperientialism* (a better term for the view previously known as "panpsychism"). This view was endorsed by some leading philosophers of previous generations, such as William James, Alfred North

Whitehead, Charles Hartshorne, and Charles Peirce.[101] More recently, it has been endorsed by Thomas Nagel and Galen Strawson.[102] Still more recently, many more philosophers have endorsed this view.[103]

Just as the fine-tuning of the universe does not require an omnipotent deity, the same is true of the existence of consciousness.

DISTINCTIVELY HUMAN CONSCIOUSNESS

However, what about distinctively human consciousness? It was long thought that the transition from pre-human animals to human beings required a supernatural intervention. This was even true of Darwin's older friend Charles Lyell, a geologist who was famous—and, in conservative religious circles, notorious—for advocating "uniformitarianism," according to which explanations of things in the past should not employ causes not operating today, such as miracles.

Lyell, however, made an exception with regard to the human mind. Believing that its origin could not be explained in terms of natural causes alone, Lyell argued that divine intervention added "the moral and intellectual faculties of the human race, to a system of nature which had gone on for millions of years without the intervention of any analogous cause." This suggestion meant, Lyell added, that we must "assume a primeval creative power which does not act with uniformity."[104]

Darwin rejected this idea of divine additions to explain the distinctive capacities of the human mind, saying: "I would give nothing for the theory of natural selection, if it requires miraculous additions at any one stage of descent."[105]

Agreeing with Darwin that there is no need to posit supernatural intervention to account for human existence, process theologian John Cobb described how the transition from the pre-human primates' structure of existence to the structure of human existence could have occurred. The distinctiveness of human beings, he suggested, involves "surplus psychic energy," meaning energy beyond that needed for the well-being of the body. The threshold dividing humans from other primates occurred, he suggested, when the surplus psychic energy became sufficient in quantity to enable the psychic life to become its own end rather than primarily a means to the survival and health of the body. This surplus psychic energy was the precondition for religion and all those other activities (such as music and mathematics) in which the mind treats itself as an end in itself, not simply as the director of its bodily activities.[106]

With regard to what is distinctive about human existence, Cobb agreed with standard evolutionary accounts, according to which symbolism is central. But he did not agree with those who focus only on the practical advantages for survival provided by symbolic language. Rather, suggested Cobb—who was influenced by the Jungian historian of consciousness Erich Neumann—the evolutionary development constituting human distinctiveness consisted of "the greatly increased unconscious psychic activity organizing the whole of experience for its own sake." Although the much greater supply of surplus psychic energy existed primarily in what we call the unconscious portion of the mind, the unconscious psychic activity of symbolization resulted in "a new and incomparably richer mode of consciousness."[107]

Referring to the first stage of human existence as *primitive existence*, Cobb then dealt with the emergence of *archaic existence* and then, about 500 years BCE, *axial existence*. Moreover, he portrayed axial existence as taking various forms, which he discussed as Buddhist, Homeric, Socratic, Prophetic, and Christian existence.

Various scholars would describe the developments from primitive to axial existence differently. But Cobb's portrayal describes how the type of human existence we exemplify today could have gradually emerged from the earliest humans. Standard histories say that the first humans [genus *Homo*], which emerged about 8 million years ago, led to *anatomically* modern humans (*Homo sapiens)* about 300,000 years ago, and then *behaviorally* modern humans (having traits such as abstract thinking, deep planning, and symbolism), which emerged about 50,000 years ago.[108]

Cobb's account, which deals with behaviorally modern humans, assumes that the entire history leading to them developed naturalistically. No supernatural infusion was necessary.

CONCLUSION

A theology of human beings, to be adequate, must fulfill two conditions: It must do justice to human experience, including the
experiences of spirit, and it must do this without resorting to supernaturalism. This has proved to be difficult. This was impossible even
for Charles Lyell, who was famous for insisting on the doctrine there
are no events that violate the uniformity of nature. This chapter has
shown how Whitehead's philosophy explains how the "moral and
intellectual faculties of the human race" could have evolved within a
fully naturalistic worldview (albeit a naturalism that includes divine
influences). At the root of this position is panexperientialism, which
explains how mind and body can interact without supernaturalism.

The Prophets, Jesus,
and Other Religions

CHAPTER FIVE

The Hebrew Prophets

MANY SYSTEMATIC THEOLOGIES have no discussion of the prophets; they go directly from Scripture, God, and Humanity to Jesus.[1] But to understand Jesus, it is essential to know something about the prophets.

PROPHETIC EXISTENCE

In Cobb's *The Structure of Christian Existence,* he placed "prophetic existence" in the context of the evolutionary development of human consciousness—from primitive existence to archaic existence and then to axial existence.[2] "Axial existence" refers to the new mode of consciousness that emerged almost simultaneously in China, Greece, India, Israel, and Persia, in what Karl Jaspers named the *axial period,* which occurred roughly from 800 to 200 BCE.[3]

Cobb went beyond Jaspers by portraying axial existence as taking various forms, five versions of which he discussed as Buddhist, Homeric, Socratic, Prophetic, and Christian existence. (Cobb also went beyond Jaspers by including Jesus in the axial period.[4]) In contrast with the axial developments in India and Greece, the Hebrews took a third path:

107

As their power of rational reflection grew, they accepted the tribal myth of a divine lawgiver, much as the Indians accepted the myth of transmigration and the Greeks that of their ancestral gods. Their critical and reflective activity was directed toward rationalizing the understanding of their relationship to their deity.[5]

Focusing not on scattered and partial foreshadowings of the axial revolution in Israel, but on its decisive and distinctive embodiment, Cobb pointed to the prophetic movement of the eighth and seventh centuries BCE. "I see in the great prophets—especially in Jeremiah— the decisive breakthrough into a new structure of existence."[6]

Although Biblical scholar Marcus Borg used very different language, he also described the prophets as exceptional:

The classical prophets of ancient Israel are among the most remarkable people who have ever lived. Such is the indelible impression made by their words. Their language is memorable, poetic, and powerful. Their passion and courage are exceptional. Their message combines radical criticism of the way things are with urgent advocacy of another way of being.[7]

As Borg's statement indicated, he was referring to the "classical" prophets, meaning the ones from the eighth to the sixth century BCE, whose messages are contained in books bearing their names.[8]

THE CLASSICAL PROPHETS

Four of the classical prophets—Amos, Micah, Isaiah, and Jeremiah— are discussed here. The earliest of these prophets was Amos (the Hebrew Bible does not present the prophets in chronological order).

To understand these prophets, it is necessary to understand the agrarian societies in which they lived. By the time of the prophets, these societies had social systems, comprising economic, political, religious, and social structures, which "were controlled and shaped by elites of power and wealth to serve their own interests."[9] The development of this type of society in Israel was described by Marcus Borg thus:

> This type of society began to develop within Israel with the emergence of the monarchy around 1000 BCE. By the time of Solomon, Israel's third king, the major features of the ancient domination system were in place: a politics of oppression centered in monarchical authority; an economics of exploitation centered in the monarchy and aristocracy; and a religion of legitimation centered in the temple built by Solomon in Jerusalem.

> Thus, by the time the classical prophets began to speak in the eighth century, Israel and Judah had become miniature versions of the ancient domination system that had enslaved their ancestors in Egypt. The victims (the majority of the population) were Israelites, of course, but now the elites at the top were also Israelites! Egypt had been established in Israel.[10]

Accordingly, when the prophets indict Israel or Judah, the indictments are not directed against the people in general, but "against the elites who were responsible for creating and maintaining the structures of domination and exploitation."[11]

> [These elites] had deformed Israel, changing her from the exodus vision of an alternative community living under the lordship of God to just another kingdom living under the lordship of a native pharaoh.[12]

The economy of exploitation to which Borg referred was an *economy of extraction*, in which Judah and Israel were, in Walter Brueggemann's words, "committed to economic extraction from the common population to produce surplus wealth for the governing elite, who had arranged the economy for their own benefit."

> The prophetic corpus [said Brueggemann] offers a sustained critique of an economy of extraction that thrived in the kingdoms of Samaria and Jerusalem and in the larger imperial powers that displaced those kingdoms.[13]

Exhibiting "an acute practice of social analysis," these prophets "rather consistently followed the money," in light of their conviction that "the ultimate intent of the creator God—expressed in the traditions of covenant—was for a neighborly economy."[14]

The relation of the prophets to the Mosaic covenant was especially developed by Richard Horsley in his *Covenant Economics*. In condemning the rulers of Judah and Israel, "The criteria that the prophets applied," said Horsley, "were covenantal."[15]

> The crimes for which the rulers were indicted and sentenced were violations of the commandments and principles of the Mosaic covenant. In broad general terms, the prophets charged the rulers and officers with brutal oppression of the poor, in violation of the covenantal principles given to protect them.[16]

As this quotation shows, the target of the prophetic indictments, as Borg pointed out, was not the people in general but a much more specific target. But instead of speaking simply about the "elite," Horsley referred to the "rulers and officers of the monarchy," with the officers including "chiefs, elders and princes." Horsley explained:

> These were precisely the kings and their officers who took the tithes of the people's produce from which they lived in luxury. . . . The officers of the monarchy were the ones who presided over the collection and storage of the goods. Their positions of political power also gave them expanding economic power over the producers. They used their control over the resources gathered from the people to then enhance their own position at the expense of the people.[17]

These policies created an enormous economic gap between the haves and have nots—a gap that evoked protest from the classical prophets. According to Brueggemann,

> A predominant theme of the prophetic corpus is the conviction that a predatory economy that permits powerful moneyed interests to prey upon the vulnerable peasant population is

unsustainable..., because a viable social order cannot endure such exploitative conflict and differential.[18]

The protests by the classical prophets against the predatory economy began with Amos.

Amos

Amos lived in the southern kingdom, Judah. (When king Solomon died at the end of the ninth century, the United Kingdom split into two kingdoms, Israel and Judah.) Nevertheless, Amos felt called to travel to the Northern Kingdom (also called the Samarian Kingdom, for its capital city, Samaria). In approximately 750 BCE, Amos began speaking there, warning Israel's leaders that unless they gave up idolatry and began treating its people fairly, their kingdom would be destroyed. This prophecy was based partly on the fact that the powerful Assyrian Empire was using its military power to expand.

Amos began his message by denouncing Israel's enemies, such as Damascus and Tyre, indicting them for their barbaric cruelty in warfare. Announcing God's judgment on them, Amos stated that they would be conquered and sent into exile. But after thereby winning over the audience, Amos indicted Israel's elite class for its social injustice. Beginning with "Thus says the Lord," Amos explained why Israel's elite deserved punishment:

> [B]ecause they sell the righteous for silver, and the needy for
> a pair of sandals—
> they who trample the head of the poor into the dust of the
> earth,
> and push the afflicted out of the way. (Amos 2:6-7)[19]

In so acting, the king and his officers violated the egalitarian ideal embodied in the covenant with God. Referring to the elite class's indifference to the poor people's need, Amos condemned its greed:

> Hear this, you that trample on the needy,
> and bring to ruin the poor of the land,
> saying, "When will the new moon be over

so that we may sell grain;
and the sabbath,
so that we may offer wheat for sale?
We will make the ephah small and the shekel great,
and practice deceit with false balances,
buying the poor for silver,
and the needy for a pair of sandals,
and selling the sweeping [gleaning] of the wheat.
(Amos 8:4-6)

Amos also condemned the leaders for living in luxury while being unconcerned with the misery of the poor:

Alas for those who lie on beds of ivory,
    and lounge on their couches,
and eat lambs from the flock
and calves from the stall. . . .
who drink wine from bowls,
and anoint themselves with the finest oils,
but are not grieved over the ruin of Joseph
    [the people of Israel]. (Amos 6:4-6)

Finally, given the fact that the elite, including the priests, have ignored justice and righteousness, Amos had God say:

I hate, I despise your festivals,
and I take no delight in your solemn assemblies.
Even though you offer me your burnt offerings and the grain
    offerings,
I will not accept them;
and the offerings of well-being of your fatten animals,
I will not look upon. (Amos 5: 21-22)

Micah

The covetousness and greed of the elite were also condemned by Micah, who spoke a few decades after Amos and, unlike Amos, issued his message in the Southern Kingdom, where he lived. Expressing the concerns of the rural farmers and villagers, Micah castigated the monarchy, its officers, and the wealthy for violating the Mosaic covenant. Micah complained:

> They covet fields, and seize them;
> houses and take them away;
> they oppress householder and house,
> people and their inheritance. (Micah 2:1-2)

Besides robbing the poor, they also cheated them with dishonest commerce. Micah had God ask:

> Can I tolerate wicked scales
>   and a bag of dishonest weights?
> Your wealthy are full of violence;
> your inhabitants speak lies,
> with tongues of deceit in their mouths. (Micah 6:11-12)

In addition, Micah had God say to the rulers:

> Should you not know justice?—
>   you who hate the good and love the evil,
> who tear the skin off my people,
> and the flesh off their bones;
> who eat the flesh of my people,
> flay the skin off them,
> break their bones in pieces;
> and chop them up like meat in a kettle,
> like flesh in a caldron. (Micah 3:1-3)

In one of the most famous passages in the Hebrew Bible, Micah told the people and their leaders how they should behave:

> Do justice, … love kindness, and … walk humbly with your God. (Micah 6:8).

Isaiah

The behavior of the elite in the Southern Kingdom being no better, their behavior was denounced by Isaiah of Jerusalem—also known to scholars as First Isaiah.

To explain the name "First Isaiah": The Book of Isaiah is the longest of the prophetic books, partly because it contains the messages of three different men: First Isaiah, or Isaiah of Jerusalem (Chapters 1–39), reflects the period of 740–697 BCE; Second Isaiah, or Isaiah of the Exile (40–55) reflects the period of 539–535; and Third Isaiah, or Isaiah after the Exile (55–66) reflects the 515–500 period.[20]

Although Isaiah of Jerusalem (First Isaiah) "seem[ed] to be of high social status and to have free access to the king,"[21] his message was not entirely different from that of Amos and Micah. Isaiah condemned the elite for their thievery and their failure to take care of their people, especially widows and orphans.

> Your princes are rebels
> and the companions of thieves.
> Everyone loves a bribe
> and runs after gifts.
> They do not defend the orphan,
> and the widow's cause does not come before them.
> (Isaiah 1:23)

Isaiah of Jerusalem also complained that the officers of the monarchy, in order to make them themselves richer, took from the poor what little agricultural land and housing they had:

> Ah, you who join house to house,
>   who add field to field,
> until there is room for no one but you,
> and you are left to live alone in the midst of the land. (Isaiah 5:8)

In light of the execrable policies of the elite, this prophet gave God a chance to raise a question.

> Yahweh comes in judgment
> against the elders of his people and their officials.
> "It is you who devour the vineyard,

the spoil of the poor are in your houses!
What do you mean by crushing my people,
by grinding the face of the poor?" (Isaiah 3:15)

The basic crime of the elite was that they had renounced the covenant, with its moral laws:

The earth lies polluted
    under its inhabitants;
for they have transgressed laws,
violated the statutes,
broken the everlasting covenant.
Therefore a curse devours the earth,
    and its inhabitants suffer for their guilt. (Isaiah 24:5–6)

In a summary indictment, First Isaiah said:

Ah, you who make iniquitous decrees,
    who write oppressive statutes,
to turn aside the needy from justice
and to rob the poor of my people of their right,
that widows may be your spoil,
and that you may make the orphans your prey!
(Isaiah 10:1–4)

In one of the best-known passages—which begins by comparing the ruling class with the leaders of the most notorious cities in Hebrew scripture: Sodom and Gomorrah—First Isaiah criticized formal worship that is not based on morality.

Hear the word of the Lord,
you rulers of Sodom!
Listen to the teaching of our God,
you people of Gomorrah!
What to me is the multitude of your sacrifices?
says the Lord;
I have had enough of burnt offerings of rams

and the fat of fed beasts;
I do not delight in the blood of bulls,
or of lambs, or of goats.
When you come to appear before me,
who asked this from your hand?
Trample my courts no more;
bringing offerings is futile;
incense is an abomination to me.
New moon and sabbath and calling of convocation—
I cannot endure solemn assemblies with iniquity.
Your new moons and your appointed festivals my soul hates;
they have become a burden to me, I am weary of bearing them.
When you stretch out your hands,
I will hide my eyes from you;
even though you make many prayers,
I will not listen;
your hands are full of blood.
Wash yourselves; make yourselves clean;
remove the evil of your doings
from before my eyes;
cease to do evil,
learn to do good;
seek justice,
rescue the oppressed,
defend the orphan,
plead for the widow.
(Isaiah 1:10–17)

Third Isaiah (Isaiah after the Exile) stated more fully why the worship of God had been worthless:

[D]ay after day they seek me
and delight to know my ways,
as if they were a nation that practiced righteousness
and did not forsake the ordinance of their God;
they ask of me righteous judgments, they delight to draw near
    to God.

"Why do we fast, but you do not see? Why humble ourselves,
    but you do not notice?"
Look, you serve your own interest on your fast day,
and oppress all your workers.
Look, you fast only to quarrel and to fight
and to strike with a wicked fist.
Such fasting as you do today
will not make your voice heard on high.
Is such the fast that I choose,
a day to humble oneself?
Is it to bow down the head like a bulrush,
and to lie in sackcloth and ashes?
Will you call this a fast,
a day acceptable to the Lord? (Isaiah 58:1-5)

Third Isaiah then stated the kind of worship God would like:

Is not this the fast that I choose:
to loose the bonds of injustice,
to undo the thongs of the yoke,
to let the oppressed go free,
and to break every yoke?
Is it not to share your bread with the hungry,
and bring the homeless poor into your house;
when you see the naked, to cover them, and not to hide yourself
    from your own kin?
Then your light shall break forth like the dawn,
and your healing shall spring up quickly;
your vindicator shall go before you,
the glory of the Lord shall be your rear guard.
Then you shall call, and the Lord will answer;
you shall cry for help, and he will say, Here I am.
If you remove the yoke from among you,
the pointing of the finger, the speaking of evil,
if you offer your food to the hungry
and satisfy the needs of the afflicted,

then your light shall rise in the darkness
and your gloom be like the noonday. (Isaiah 58:2-10)

Jeremiah

The prophet Jeremiah lived in challenging times, both for Judah and for him.

The content of the book of Jeremiah spans the tumultuous period from about 622 until shortly after 587. Jeremiah's emergence as a major prophetic figure and his message coincide with the years following Josiah's reforms[22] (ca. 622–609), the rather chaotic period immediately following his death in 609, and the subjugation of Judah first by Egypt (609–605, 601–598), and then Babylon (604–601, 597–538). The book thus covers the wildly shifting fortunes of the nation, from its brief nationalistic exuberance under Josiah to a desperate search for security and leadership amid Egypt's and Babylon's international contest for control of Syria-Palestine.[23]

Of all the prophets, Jeremiah easily had the most dramatic life. "Jeremiah was beaten, put in stocks, threatened with death, forced into hiding, imprisoned, and lowered into a muddy cistern to starve and die."[24] In the present chapter, however, the focus is on some features of Jeremiah's message. Although his prophecy contained novel elements, it also reiterated many of the complaints of his predecessors, saying:

Woe to him who builds his house by unrighteousness,
and his upper rooms by injustice;
who makes his neighbor serve him for nothing,
and does not give him wages;
who says I will build myself a great house
with spacious upper rooms. . . .
Do you think you are a king?
because you compete in cedar?
Did not your father eat and drink
and do justice and righteousness?
Then it was well with him.
He judged the cause of the poor and the needy;
then it was well. Is not this to know *me?*

says the Lord.
But you have eyes and heart
only for your dishonest gain,
for shedding innocent blood,
and for practicing oppression and violence. (Jeremiah 22:13-18)

Like previous prophets, Jeremiah warned that worshiping in the Temple is worthless, unless it is backed up by obedience to the stipulations of the covenant. Jeremiah reported that he was told to proclaim this:

Hear the word of the Lord, all you people of Judah, you that enter these gates to worship the Lord. Thus says the Lord of hosts, the God of Israel: Amend your ways and your doings, and let me dwell with you in this place. Do not trust in these deceptive words: "This is the temple of the Lord, the temple of the Lord, the temple of the Lord." For if you truly amend your ways and your doings, if you truly act justly one with another, if you do not oppress the alien, the orphan, and the widow, or shed innocent blood in this place, and if you do not go after other gods to your own hurt, then I will dwell with you in this place, in the land that I gave of old to your ancestors forever and ever. (Jeremiah 7:1–7)

In many of the indictments by the prophets, wrote Horsley, they focus on the violation of one commandment or another. But the indictment in 7:9–11 "lists most of the commandments together, suggesting that the Temple, along with the practices of the monarchy, are in violation of the whole covenant."

Will you steal, murder, commit adultery, swear falsely, make offerings to Baal, and go after other gods that you have not known, and then come and stand before me in this house, which is called by my name, and say, "We are safe!"—only to go on doing all of these abominations? Has this house, which is called by my name, become a den of robbers in your sight? (Jeremiah 7:9–11)

Jeremiah then said, in God's name, that the temple would be destroyed:

> Go now to my place that was in Shiloh, where I made my name dwell at first, and see what I did to it for the wickedness of my people Israel. And now, because you have done all these things,…and when I spoke to you persistently, you did not listen, and when I called you, you did not answer, therefore I will do to the house that is called by my name, in which you trust, and to the place that I gave to you and to your ancestors, just what I did to Shiloh. (Jeremiah 7:12-14)

Jeremiah's warnings were especially notable because of his practice of using symbolic acts to dramatize them, acts he understood to have been ordered by God. One of his best known of such acts involved a broken jug.

> Thus said the Lord: Go and buy a potter's earthenware jug. Take with you some of the elders of the people and some of the senior priests, and go out to the valley of the son of Hinnom at the entry of the Potsherd Gate, and proclaim there the words that I tell you. You shall say: Hear the word of the Lord, O kings of Judah and inhabitants of Jerusalem. Thus says the Lord of hosts, the God of Israel: I am going to bring such disaster upon this place that the ears of everyone who hears of it will tingle. Because the people have forsaken me, and have profaned this place by making offerings in it to other gods whom neither they nor their ancestors nor the kings of Judah have known, and because they have filled this place with the blood of the innocent, and gone on building the high places of Baal to burn their children in the fire as burnt offerings to Baal. . . . Then you shall break the jug in the sight of those who go with you, and shall say to them: Thus says the Lord of hosts: So will I break this people and this city, as one breaks a potter's vessel. (Jeremiah 19:1–11)

This was the symbolic act that led Jeremiah to be placed in public stocks, to humiliate him (Jeremiah 20:2). In any case, Jeremiah's warnings proved to be justified when in 586 the Babylonian army brought a permanent end to the kingdom of Judah.[25]

However, Jeremiah's pronouncements were not all doom and gloom. While they were in exile, Jeremiah gave the people hope, saying in God's name:

> The days are surely coming, says the Lord, when I will make a new covenant with the house of Israel and the house of Judah. It will not be like the covenant that I made with their ancestors when I took them by the hand to bring them out of the land of Egypt—a covenant that they broke, though I was their husband, says the Lord. But this is the covenant that I will make with the house of Israel after those days, says the Lord: I will put my law within them, and I will write it on their hearts; and I will be their God, and they shall be my people. No longer shall they teach one another, or say to each other, "Know the Lord," for they shall all know me, from the least of them to the greatest, says the Lord; for I will forgive their iniquity, and remember their sin no more. (Jeremiah 31:31–34)

PATHOS

How can we understand the emergence of the classical prophets, especially the first one, Amos? Biblical scholar James Sanders persuasively argued that Amos was deeply influenced by "the Wisdom circle of thinkers for which his village, Tekoa, had been known" (see next section).[26] Abraham Joshua Heschel, the great Jewish theologian, argued that the convictions of the Hebrew prophets, such as Amos, came also from their direct experience of God.

Heschel's View

Whereas Greek philosophers typically described God as impassible, incapable of feeling emotion, Heschel described the God of the prophets as the opposite. Being "open to the presence and emotion of the transcendent Subject," said Heschel, the prophets spoke out of a "state of suffering in sympathy with the divine pathos."[27] The "divine pathos" refers to God's suffering with the suffering of the people. It was the prophets' experience of this divine *pathos*, Heschel suggested, that led them to their cry for justice. Speaking of the prophets' "breathless impatience with injustice," Heschel believed that this impatience was based on their "fellowship with the feelings of God, a sympathy with the divine pathos."[28]

Whether or not Heschel was influenced by Alfred North Whitehead, his idea that God has feelings, and that we can feel those feelings sympathetically, was similar to Whitehead's view.

Whitehead's View

According to Whitehead's panexperientialism (see Chapter 2), all genuine individuals feel (prehend) other individuals. When one individual feels another individual (as distinct from an abstraction), it is called a "physical feeling. A physical feeling has both a datum—which is *what* is felt—and a subjective form—which is *how* that datum is felt. The term "feeling," explained Whitehead, brings out "this double significance of subjective form and of the apprehension of an object."[29]

A physical feeling is also called a "conformal feeling," because its subjective form conforms to the subjective form of the prior feeling. This point is so important that Whitehead gave it a name, "the Doctrine of Conformation of Feeling."[30] He also used the language of "sympathy," saying:

> The primitive form of physical experience is emotional—blind emotion—received as felt elsewhere in another occasion and conformally appropriated as a subjective passion. In the language appropriate to the higher stages of experience, the primitive element is *sympathy,* that is, feeling the feeling *in another* and feeling conformally *with* another.[31]

In Whitehead's view, we feel God directly, and this feeling is analogous to our feelings of other individuals (even though God is unique in including the entire universe). So in feeling God, we tend to sympathize with, and hence conform to, the subjective form of

God's feelings. Of course, most of us most of the time feel God only subconsciously. Some people, such as the prophets, have felt the divine feelings more consciously than do most of us.

Accordingly, Whitehead's philosophy supports the possibility of Heschel's view—that the proclamations of the prophets were based on "fellowship with the feelings of God, a sympathy with the divine pathos."

The views of Heschel and Whitehead were also similar on this issue to the view of Japanese theologian Kazoh Kitamori.

Kazoh Kitamori's View

In 1946, Kitamori published a book entitled *Theology of the Pain of God*. "[T]he theology of the pain of God," said Kitamori, "is literally concerned with his pain."[32] The title of his book was derived from Jeremiah 31:20, which in Kitamori's Bible was translated "My heart is pained."[33] Kitamori indicated that his position here was based on experience, saying: "The heart of the gospel was revealed to me as the 'pain of God.' This revelation led me to the path which the prophet Jeremiah had trod (Jer. 31:20)."[34]

Back to Heschel

In any case, all the prophets, held Heschel, were called to speak because of their feelings of God's feelings. But Jeremiah was evidently the one who felt the divine impulse to prophesy most deeply, being called to do so against his will. Speaking to God, Jeremiah said that his feeling of the divine call overpowered him, making him seem like a fool:

> O Lord, you have enticed me,
> and I was enticed;
> you have overpowered me,
> and you have prevailed.
> I have become a laughingstock all day long;
> everyone mocks me.
> For whenever I speak, I must cry out,
> I must shout, "Violence and destruction!"
> For the word of the Lord has become for me

a reproach and derision all day long.
If I say, "I will not mention him,
or speak any more in his name,"
then within me there is something like a burning fire shut up
    in my bones;
I am weary with holding it in, and I cannot. (Jeremiah 20:7–10)

WISDOM AND MONOTHEIZING

One more important fact about the classical prophets is that they were crucial to the process of monotheizing—a term coined by James Sanders. The meaning of the term was explained in Sanders's 2014 book, *The Monotheizing Process: Its Origin and Development*. Most people would agree with his definition of monotheism: "belief in there being one God of All."[35]

However, because of the way the Hebrew Bible was constructed, people have tended to believe that the Hebrew Bible as a whole witnessed to monotheism. After all, the first verses of the Bible suggest that the world and all its peoples were created by the God of the Hebrews. Accordingly, it seemed, the Hebrew scriptures were monotheistic from the beginning.

However, Sanders pointed out, biblical passages that reflect the earliest traditions express polytheism (belief in several gods) or at best henotheism (wherein people in one tradition worship one deity while accepting that people in other traditions worship different deities).

To flesh out the statement about "the way the Hebrew Bible was constructed": As reviewed in the first chapter above, the Hebrew Bible was written by many different authors at very different times. Moreover, some of the latest-written chapters come early in the Bible as ultimately constructed. This is the case with the first chapter of Genesis, which speaks of God as creating "the heaven and the earth." This chapter was written in the fifth or sixth century BCE, many years later than the passages reflecting polytheism or henotheism. Realizing this fact makes it possible to understand the title of Sanders's book, as explained in this statement by him:

Reading carefully, moving from the older passages through to the later, the careful reader is able to trace a process that is best called *monotheizing*.[36]

In other words, the Hebrew Bible is not fully monotheistic, but it moved *toward* full monotheism.

Although monotheism was defined above as "belief in there being one God of All," it is also important, Sanders added, not simply to believe it but "to act like it, to view not only God as One but all humanity as creatures of the One God." In other words, to be fully monotheistic is to treat all people as creatures of the same God.[37]

The classical prophets were crucial to this issue, especially Amos. When he began his ministry, the Kingdom of Israel was doing well and gaining land, because Egypt's power had been waning. "Israel's leaders," wrote Sanders, "felt that Yahweh must surely be proud of them for expanding to borders almost as extensive in the north as they had been in Solomon's day."[38]

In this situation, with Israel basking in pride in its exceptionalism as God's chosen people, which God had brought from Egypt, Amos said:

Are you not like the Ethiopians to me,
O people of Israel? says the Lord.
Did I not bring Israel up from the land of Egypt, and the
Philistines from Caphtor and the Arameans [Syrians] from
Kir?[39]

Israel regarded all of these peoples as enemies. It was as if conservative people in the United States, proud of American exceptionalism, were asked to believe that God loved Russians and Chinese as much. "Amos's message was such a shock to exceptionalist thinking," wrote Sanders, "that he was thrown out of town and kingdom for preaching such negative things."[40]

The idea that the God worshiped by the Hebrews was also the God of other peoples, including hated enemies, was repeated by later prophets. After the Northern Kingdom was destroyed by Assyria,

Isaiah of Jerusalem (First Isaiah) came to accept the idea that the God of the Hebrews was also the God of the Assyrians. Jeremiah came to accept the same about Babylon's Nebuchadnezzar, who was to destroy Jerusalem.[41]

As a result of this process, the Hebrews' God became understood as the creator. Although many early traditions in the Bible suggested that Yahweh was merely "Israel's tribal, protective deity," Amos portrayed God as "not just Yahweh, but the One God of All," including the natural world.[42]

Asking how Amos, in the little village of Tekoa, could have advanced the monotheizing process so effectively, Sanders pointed to the Wisdom circle of thinkers for which Tekoa had been known.

[The Wisdom thinkers] did not cite national epic recitals or traditions to support the[ir] message. On the contrary, Wisdom thinkers garnered their advice from observing common human actions and practices unlimited by national boundaries, and from observing phenomena of nature that also know no national boundaries (I Kings 4:33). . . . In Wisdom literature, in other words, God was perceived as unlimited by Israel's national boundaries or traditions.[43]

The Wisdom thinkers, therefore, engaged in what would later be called "natural theology."

Accordingly, what came to be accepted as the biblical view of God was decisively shaped by Amos and his successors. "Jeremiah," said Sanders, "made it clear that Yahweh was creator of the whole world as well as judge and redeemer." Likewise, Isaiah of the exile (Second Isaiah) "offered anthems praising God as creator of all the world and all peoples (Isa 45:12–31) and yet also as judge and redeemer of Israel."[44]

CONCLUSION

The Hebrew prophets of the eighth to the sixth centuries BCE were remarkable and important people. They introduced a new form of human existence. They strongly expressed the belief that the creator of the universe cared about human morality, and that our creator felt suffering for the sufferings of the world. The prophets therefore strongly protested against the leaders of Israel and Judah insofar as they violated the moral and economic principles of the Mosaic covenant, which they ostensibly followed. Instead, the leaders of Israel and Judah adopted the same policies as the Egyptian pharaohs, from which God and Moses had rescued their ancestors. Finally, the prophets led the Hebrew world toward the full embrace of monotheism, according to which all people are loved by the creator of the entire universe.

The Hebrew prophets are of irreplaceable importance for Christians, because without the prophets we cannot understand Jesus, and without them, in fact, Jesus surely could not have emerged.

CHAPTER SIX

Jesus and the Roman Empire

CHRISTIANS IN AMERICA today have two reasons to learn something about the Roman Empire. In the first place, we cannot understand why other peoples hate our country and what we might do about it unless we, as Chalmers Johnson has said, "grasp what the United States really is."[1] And if America now *"is* Rome," as Andrew Bacevich has said,[2] having some understanding of what Rome *was* can help us grasp what America *now is.*

A second reason for examining the nature of the Roman Empire is that Christianity arose during its heyday, and many scholars of the historical Jesus have said that we cannot understand the message of Jesus without understanding the nature of the Roman Empire. "Trying to understand Jesus," said Richard Horsley,

> without knowing how Roman imperialism determined the conditions of life in Galilee and Jerusalem would be like trying to understand Martin Luther King without knowing how slavery, reconstruction, and segregation determined the lives of African Americans in the United States.[3]

This chapter, accordingly, looks at the Roman Empire as a basis for understanding both the nature of America's empire and the person our religious tradition has called the Christ—our central revelation of God, to whom we have pledged our ultimate loyalty.

THE ROMAN EMPIRE

After achieving dominance over the rest of Italy, Rome became the dominant power in the western Mediterranean world by the end of the third century BCE. By the close of the second century, it had become the dominant power in the east as well, replacing the Macedonian empire established by Alexander. By the end of the first century BCE, it had subjected most of the known earth to its rule, and the goal of Augustus Caesar was "to conquer what remained of the world."[4]

Students of imperialism have identified at least five features of the Roman Empire that are also exemplified by the American Empire: (1) the sense that the empire is divinely authorized; (2) the development and employment of overwhelming military power to spread and maintain the empire; (3) the use of terror, or simply the *threat* of terror, to intimidate; (4) rule through puppets backed up by the empire's pervasive military presence; and (5) the collection of taxes in order to enrich the empire's center and to finance its imperial rule. This section discusses these five features in general, after which the next section explores how they were exemplified in Palestine.[5]

Sense of Divine Authorization

After the decade of civil war that followed upon the assassination of Julius Caesar, his adopted son Octavian defeated Marc Anthony in 31 BCE. Octavian took the name "Augustus," meaning "Revered," and was widely called the "savior of the whole human race" because he had brought "peace" to the whole world.[6] Soon, however, the adjectives applied to Augustus became even stronger, elevating him to the status of deity. He was called "the Divine Augustus" and "the most divine Caesar." Horace, making him parallel to Pluto (who reigns in heaven), referred to him as "god on earth."[7] Statues of him were erected next to those of traditional gods, and ritual sacrifices, shrines, and temples were established for him.[8]

The official view of Augustus is illustrated by an inscription from 9 BCE, which reads:

> The most divine Caesar . . . we should consider equal to the Beginning of all things. . . , [t]he beginning of life and vitality. . . . Whereas Providence, which has regulated our whole existence . . . , has brought our life to the climax of perfection in giving us [the emperor] Augustus, whom it filled with strength for the welfare of men, and who being sent to us and our descendants as Savior, has . . . become [god] manifest, Caesar has fulfilled all the hopes of earlier times . . . , and whereas, finally, the birthday of the god has been for the whole world the beginning of good news (*euangelion*) . . . [therefore let a new era begin from his birth].[9]

The Greek word *euangelion* is, of course, the term in the New Testament translated as "good news" or "gospel."

In any case, implicit in this description of Augustus as god and savior for bringing peace—the peace that came to be known as the *Pax Romana*—was the idea that the spread of the Roman Empire was the work of Divine Providence working through him. For example, Virgil, having referred to Augustus Caesar as "son of a god," said that he "shall spread his empire . . . to a land that lies beyond the stars."[10]

The Development and Use of Overwhelming Military Power

The primary basis for the spread of the Roman Empire was the military power exercised by the Roman legions, which was so far superior to that of most other peoples as to make their defeat a foregone conclusion. In conquering peoples, Rome portrayed itself as pacifying them, bringing peace to them, by incorporating them within the *Pax Romana*. Indeed, one of the titles taken by the emperors was "Pacifier of the World."[11] But this was pacification through military might, which the Romans used ruthlessly. As a Caledonian chieftain at the time put it, the Romans "rob, butcher, plunder, and call it 'empire'; and where they make desolation, they call it 'peace.'"[12]

The Use of Terror to Intimidate

The Romans used their overwhelming power not merely to conquer but also to terrorize and thereby intimidate their conquered subjects to keep them in line. Whenever there was disobedience, Rome would not only retaliate but would do so disproportionately, often slaughtering vast numbers of people. They would do this even in regions with little strategic or economic value, in order to maintain what they called "honor" (which is similar to what US leaders have called "credibility"). In her study of Rome's imperial strategy, Susan Mattern wrote:

> What mattered most [to the Roman elite] was how the empire [was] perceived by foreigners and subjects. . . . Terror and vengeance were instruments for maintaining the empire's image.[13]

This view, incidentally, is not simply an inference by modern scholars. The contemporary historian Polybius, after viewing the corpses filling a city destroyed by the Romans, said: "It seems to be that they do this for the sake of terror."[14]

The security and endurance of Rome, its elite class believed, depended "on the image of the force it could wield and on its apparent willingness to use that force at whatever cost."[15] When the Roman legions were sent on expeditions, accordingly, their main mission was usually not defensive but "to punish, to avenge, and to terrify—that is, to reassert a certain state of mind in the enemy"—a state of "awe and terror."[16] This state of mind was supposed to bring what they called *fides*, that is, fidelity, loyalty.[17]

One of the chief means of terrorist intimidation was crucifixion, which was called the worst form of death by both Cicero and Josephus. The idea was that people would be intimidated by learning about the terribleness of crucifixion, which Josephus called "the most wretched of deaths."[18]

Also, the victims of this tactic of state terrorism were displayed in prominent places for all to see.[19] As one Roman put it:

Whenever we crucify the condemned, the most crowded roads are chosen, where the most people can see and be moved by this terror. For penalties relate not so much to retribution as to their exemplary effect.[20]

The use of crucifixion was not unique to the Romans. It had been used by Alexander the Great and many prior hegemonial powers. By the time of the Jesus movement, however, it had become a distinctively Roman symbol of intimidation.[21]

The Use of Puppet Rulers

Upon conquering regions, the Romans generally did not exercise direct rule on the basis of military occupation.[22] Rather, they typically employed local strongmen as puppet rulers. The Romans maintained military garrisons somewhere in the general area, however, to make sure that these local leaders remained puppets and to put down any attempts to overthrow them.

Tribute and Taxation

One motive that some of the Roman rulers had for spreading and maintaining the empire was the enjoyment of power. Caesar, said Plutarch, had "an insatiable love of power and a mad desire to be first and greatest."[23]

But the more general motive was to enrich Rome itself by laying the conquered regions under systems of tribute (a tax on the land) and other forms of taxation. The price exacted by the Romans was severe enough not only to support the expense of maintaining the empire in its various regions but also to make the elite class of Roman society "obscenely wealthy."[24]

Rome's taxation was severe enough to lead to widespread poverty in the territories. The Romans themselves believed that "it was the empire's most onerous and deeply resented burden on provincials" and the one that most often led to rebellion.[25]

PALESTINE UNDER ROMAN DOMINATION

"The politics of first-century Palestine," said K. C. Hanson and

Douglas Oakman in their *Palestine in the Time of Jesus*, "must be interpreted in light of its domination by Roman interests." Having been under the control of successive empires for 600 years—with the exception of one interlude lasting less than a century—Palestine had been under Roman domination for almost a century by the time of Jesus.[26]

There was a difference between the way in which Galilee and Judea were ruled. Until 4 BCE., they had both been under rule from Jerusalem, first the rule of the Hasmonean high priesthood and then that of Herod the Great (sometimes called "Herod the Monstrous"[27]). Herod was a local military strongman who was appointed "king" of Palestine by Julius Caesar to be his client ruler—his puppet. But upon Herod's death, Galilee was put under his son Herod Antipas, designated "tetrarch," while Judea was (after problems with the original client ruler) put under a Roman governor, Pontius Pilate.

Both Galilee and Judea were, nonetheless, under Roman rule, and this rule was devastating militarily, culturally, and economically.

Militarily, the Romans were brutal, employing systematic slaughter, the destruction of villages, and mass enslavement.[28] In Galilee, the Roman legions had, by the time of Jesus, killed tens of thousands of people and enslaved many more. One of the most traumatic attacks occurred in Magdala, evidently the home of Mary Magdalene, about 50 years before her birth. Another traumatic event was the burning of Sepphoris, only a few miles from Nazareth, at about the time of Jesus's birth.[29] To try to deter future challengers to Roman rule in Palestine, the Romans, of course, used crucifixions. For example, at about the time of Jesus's birth, some 2,000 rebels were crucified.[30]

The Galileans were subjected as well to the violence of the Herods. After being appointed king, Herod the Great inflicted much death and destruction in the three years it took him, with help from Rome, to subdue his subjects. He then "established massive military fortresses and ruled with an iron fist"—indeed, a reign of terror employing ruthless secret police.[31] This system was continued by Herod Antipas.

Violations of Religious Sensibilities

Culturally, Roman imperialism meant flagrant violations of the people's traditions and sensibilities. Because the emperor was declared to be divine, any acknowledgment of him was considered idolatrous by the Jewish people. And yet King Herod, to curry favor, built temples and even whole cities named for Augustus Caesar. He also built numerous other pagan buildings and monuments and engaged in what was considered "the shameless worship of foreign gods." Herod even, after deciding to rebuild the Jerusalem Temple, had it built in grand Hellenistic style.[32]

Herod's son Antipas continued this invasion of pagan architecture, building two Roman-style cities in Galilee within two decades. One of these cities, called Autocratoris (meaning "belonging to the Emperor"), was built near Nazareth on the ruins of Sepphoris. The other city, called Tiberias—named for Tiberius, the successor of Augustus—was built at the opposite end of the Sea of Galilee from Capernaum (where Jesus evidently spent much of his time[33]).

The High Priests

Even stronger cultural resentment was directed at the client rulers in Judea, the high priests of the Jerusalem Temple, who since the Roman subjugation of the region had been selected by representatives of Rome—first by King Herod, then by the Roman governor of Judea. The criterion for appointment was not piety and reverence for tradition but subservience to Roman rule. Herod, in fact, appointed Jews from the Hellenistic world, who had no prior relation to the Palestinian people. Their aloofness from the people was shown by the fact that, amassing great fortunes from the revenues they extracted from the people, they lived in great luxury in elegant villas overlooking Jerusalem.

Besides being regarded as illegitimate for these reasons, the high priests violated the Temple by offering sacrifices in honor of the Roman emperor. Moreover, "the high priest and temple authorities," Marcus Borg said, had become "the mediators of imperial rule." Indeed, "Jerusalem and the temple, the sacred center of the Jewish world, had become the center of native collaboration with an imperial domination system."[34]

Given all of these facts about the temple, it is not surprising that Jesus was an "anti-temple prophet," as had been John the Baptist.[35] Jesus had, of course, begun his public activity as a disciple of John, and said that "among those born of women no one has arisen greater than John the Baptist" (Matthew 11:11; cf. Luke 7:28). The relationship between Jesus and John lasted until the Baptizer was executed by Herod Antipas, whom Jesus called "that fox" ("a very negative term," said Borg, "better translated in English as 'that skunk'").[36]

Taxation and the Tribute

In any case, the legitimacy of the high priests was further undermined by the fact that it was their task to collect the tribute to Rome, which they did brutally, using hired thugs to do the collecting.[37] Given the emperor's claim to be divine, moreover, the tribute was regarded as "a direct violation of the Mosaic laws against idolatry."[38]

The volatile nature of this issue is shown by the fact that the issue of payments to the Roman Empire was involved in a revolt at about the time of Jesus's birth, another revolt when Jesus was about 10 years old, and the big Jewish revolt about 36 years after his death, which led to the destruction of Jerusalem and its temple.[39]

Economically, the effects of incorporation into the Roman Empire were devastating to Galilee, as the region was "drawn into an increasingly centralized economy where some people prospered mightily and others sank into helplessness and debt."[40] The people not only had to pay tithes to the Temple but also taxes to Herod the Great, which he made very high in order to pay for his massive building projects and lavish life style.[41] The idea that the taxes were oppressive should not, incidentally, be considered an exaggeration of certain scholars: Josephus, writing at the time, said that Herod had "reduced the entire country to helpless poverty."[42]

After Herod Antipas became tetrarch, furthermore, the tax-collection process become even more rigorous. From Autocratoris and Tiberias—which were built to be efficient administrative centers— Antipas dispatched a veritable army of auditors, tax collectors, and soldiers to the groves, vineyards, and threshing floors of every village at harvest time to ensure that his share of the harvest ... was duly handed over.[43]

Although most of the peasants were earning only a subsistence living, the overall tax burden took 40 per cent or more of their total income.[44] To pay these taxes while retaining enough crops and animals to feed their families, many peasants were forced to borrow money, using their land as collateral. Their debts often became greater each year, until they were forced into foreclosure, so that more and more land passed into the hands of aristocratic families.[45]

This loss of land was a catastrophe, because like people in most agrarian cultures, the peasants of Galilee "cherish[ed] one goal above all others: family survival on the land of their ancestors." By the time of Jesus, there was "a crisis of debt and dispossession that touched and transformed the lives of nearly every peasant family in Galilee."[46]

As this summary of indicates, Jesus and his fellow Jews were facing conditions very similar to those against which the classical prophets—such as Amos, Micah, Isaiah of Jerusalem, and Jeremiah—had protested.

THE ANTI-IMPERIAL GOSPEL OF JESUS

By viewing the message of Jesus within this context, with its military, political, cultural, and economic oppression, it makes sense that, as Richard Horsley put it, Jesus preached an "anti-imperial gospel."[47]

"The message of Jesus" here means the words and deeds of the historical Jesus as based on conclusions of modern Jesus scholars. These scholars have devised several criteria for distinguishing the authentic sayings of Jesus himself from statements that, while attributed to Jesus in one or more of the gospels, reflect the theological and apologetic concerns of Christian communities at later times—40 or more years after the life of Jesus. Those concerns were especially shaped by beliefs engendered by the resurrection of Jesus. Jesus scholars have worked hard to distinguish reports based on those beliefs from reports based on the events that occurred in Jesus's life prior to his resurrection.[48]

The idea that Jesus had an anti-imperial gospel goes against the idea, accepted by many American Christians, that Jesus's message was not political. This widespread notion has been based most strongly on the Gospel of John, which has Jesus saying, "My kingdom is not of this world" (John 18:36). But as pointed out in Chapter 1 above, information about the historical Jesus is found almost entirely in the Synoptics (Matthew, Mark, and Luke); one should not use the Gospel of John to find out what Jesus was like.

The Kingdom of God

New Testament scholars have long known that Jesus's message was oriented around the idea of the reign—or kingdom—of God. The prayer that we call "the Lord's Prayer" is a modification of the Kaddish, a prayer for the establishment of God's kingdom that was recited regularly in Jewish synagogues at the time of Jesus. This fact shows that Jesus's prayer, rather than being about a variety of topics, was focused around the petition "thy kingdom come"—which was an abbreviation of the Kaddish's petition: "May God establish his kingdom in your lifetime."[49]

But what kind of kingdom did Jesus have in mind? A good clue for answering this question is provided by the next lines: "thy will be done, on earth as it is in heaven."

Many scholars, on the basis of a too-literal reading of apocalyptic literature in general and apocalyptic passages in the gospels in particular, have assumed that Jesus was talking about a dramatic end of this world brought about by God's overwhelming power. But the God of Jesus would have evidently been satisfied with a more modest development: a world in which God's will is done.[50]

Marcus Borg offered two arguments against the view that Jesus was predicting that God would soon bring the world to an end. First, some of the material that clearly implies a literal end of the world is best understood as originating after the resurrection of Jesus, which was interpreted by some Christians as the beginning ("first fruits") of the end. Also, some of this material is best understood as originating only after the destruction of Jerusalem in 70 CE, which—given association in some traditions of the destruction of Jerusalem with the beginning of the endtime—led some Christians to believe that the (literal) end of the world was near.[51]

Borg's second argument was that, although there are a few "apocalyptic" sayings that are best understood as originating with Jesus himself and that do seem, if taken literally, to be predicting the near end of the world, taking them literally involves a failure to appreciate the metaphorical nature of apocalyptic imagery. For example, now that most of the "imminent expectation" passages have been dated after the death of Jesus, much of the weight for the claim that Jesus expected an imminent end of the world, in a cosmic cataclysm effected by a supernatural act of God, is borne by Mark 13:24–27, which reads:

> But in those days, after that tribulation, the sun will be darkened, and the moon will not give its light, and the stars will be falling from heaven.... And then they will see the Son of man coming in clouds with great power and glory.

However, there was precedent for using this language—the darkening of the sun and the moon and the falling of stars—to refer metaphorically to the "day of Yahweh" as a judgment upon a particular nation. This language was used, for example, with reference to Egypt in Ezekiel 32:7, to Babylon in Isaiah 13:10, to Gentile nations in Joel 3:15 and IV Ezra 5:4–6, and to Israel in Amos 8:9 and Joel 2:10 and 2:30–31.

Indeed, this latter prophecy in Joel, which refers to the sun's darkening and the moon's turning to blood, is cited in Acts 2:19–20 as having been fulfilled on the day of Pentecost.[52] The author of Luke-Acts certainly did not believe the world had literally come to an end some 60 years before he was writing his books.

Finally, while it is Mark 13 in general, sometimes called the Little Apocalypse, that is the primary basis for thinking that Jesus expected a cataclysmic end of the world, Jesus in verses 14–16 tells people that when these events come, they should flee to the mountains—a recommendation that implies that the mountains were *not* about to collapse. Jesus's advice, Borg suggested, was more consistent with the view, supported by other evidence, that he was predicting the destruction of Jerusalem.[53]

In any case, a further clue to the nature of the kingdom Jesus had in mind was provided by the prayer's central petition: "Give us this day our daily bread, And forgive us our debts, As we also have forgiven our debtors." This petition reflected the fact that, in Borg's words,

> The two central issues of peasant life were food and debt. Because many no longer produced their own food, they had to buy it with their meager earnings. Debt was a perennial fear.[54]

The fact that forgiving our debts, as well as food, was mentioned in this very brief prayer shows how central these issues were.[55]

The word used in these lines referred to debts and debtors, not "sins" or "trespasses." To understand what Jesus was about, we need to keep in mind that he was not providing a prayer to be recited by Christians in future centuries. He was focused on the problems faced by his own people—the people of Israel—at that moment of their history, in which they were victims of Roman imperialism. Horsley wrote:

> It is important to keep in mind that "the kingdom of God" is a political metaphor and symbol. In Jesus' preaching and action the kingdom clearly includes the social-economic-political substance of human relations as willed by God. . . . Before it was spiritualized and etherealized in Christian discourse, "salvation" *(soteria)* meant the peace . . . and prosperity provided by the divine . . . emperor for his subjects. . . . For Jesus and many of his Palestinian Jewish contemporaries. . . . , however, the blessings of individual and social-political life would be provided by God as king, in contrast to the emperor. . . . Thus God's activity was political and Jesus' preaching of that

activity was political—with obvious implications for the "imperial situation" then prevailing in Palestine.[56]

In proclaiming the coming kingdom of God, in other words, Jesus was proclaiming an end to the present subservience of the people of Israel to the Roman Empire and its local collaborators. This would not be a minor change. It would involve not only overcoming the religious problem of idolatry. It would also involve a complete change in social, political, and economic relations, which would henceforth reflect divine principles, rather than the demonic principles embodied in the present order.

Demonic Rule

Jesus clearly believed, in line with widespread beliefs of the time, that the world was presently under demonic rule. This belief was reflected in the final petition of his prayer: "Save us from the Evil One."

But Jesus also believed that this demonic rule was coming to an end, as illustrated by his exorcisms. "If it is by the finger of God that I cast out demons," he said, "then the kingdom of God has come upon you" (Luke 11:20). The allusion to Exodus 8:19 in this statement, said Horsley, suggested that a new liberation from political-economic bondage was underway.[57]

The fact that people were possessed by demons was not unrelated to Roman rule. In the story in Mark 5:1–20, the exorcised demoniac identifies itself as "Legion," which the original hearers would have immediately recognized as a reference to the Roman troops. The drowning of the troop of swine, after Legion entered into them, would have reminded them of the drowning of the troops of Pharaoh, the head of an earlier empire.[58]

This view, incidentally, was not unique to Jesus and his followers: The Dead Sea Scrolls show that the Qumran community saw history as presently ruled over by two superhuman spirits, Light and Darkness, with the Romans being under the sway of the power of Darkness.[59] "Jesus's overall perspective," said Horsley, "was that God was bringing an end to the demonic and political powers dominating his society so that a renewal of individual and social life would be possible."[60]

The New Social-Political-Economic Order

At the center of this new social life would be a just economic order, with sufficient food for everyone—as indicated by the fact that the second petition of Jesus's prayer was for "our daily bread." This petition involved an allusion to Proverbs 30:8, which says:

> Give me neither poverty nor riches, but give me only my daily bread, otherwise I may have too much and disown you and say, "Who is the Lord?" Or I may become poor and steal, and so dishonor the name of my God.

The insight behind this proverb is that it is dangerous for people to have either too much money or too little, as either situation tempts them to reject God's rule in their lives. Implicit in Jesus's simple petition for daily bread, therefore, was a critique of an economic system that leads to a division between the very rich and the very poor.[61] Closely related is the petition about forgiving debts: Under the reign of God, the poor will not become even poorer by losing their property to the rich, who will thereby become even richer.[62]

If one thinks that this concern with a new political order, which would bring about a just economic order, would be too prosaic to be what Jesus could have meant by the coming reign of God, one should look at Third Isaiah 65, in which the prophet has God speaking about creating "a new heaven and a new earth"[63] (a phrase that would be repeated in Revelation 21:1). In this new situation, Third Isaiah's God says: "No more shall there be in it an infant that lives but a few days" (Isaiah 65:20). Furthermore, the people

> will build houses and inhabit them, plant vineyards and eat their fruit. They will not build for others to live in, or plant so that others can eat. They will not toil in vain or beget children to their own ruin.[64]

In the time of Jesus, the situation criticized in this passage, in which the common people of Israel were forced into servitude to rich landlords, was even worse. This situation formed the background to the parable of the wicked tenants.[65]

Taxes and the Temple

Besides the fact that Jesus regarded the present situation, with its economic injustice and political servitude to foreign rulers, as controlled by demonic power, there are still other signs that his was an anti-imperial gospel. One of these signs is the evidence, embodied in the traditions (Mark 12:13–17; Luke 23:2), that Jesus had challenged the payment of the tribute to Rome[66]—which, as stated earlier, was the most volatile of all issues.

Furthermore, given the widely held conviction that the Temple had become illegitimate and idolatrous through its subservience to Rome, a challenge to the Temple would also have anti-imperialist implications. The evidence firmly supports, moreover, the view that Jesus's final action—the one that led to his death—involved a challenge to the Temple and its high priests. Just as the parable of the vineyard suggests that he had indicted this ruling group,[67] the evidence also suggests that he had challenged the payment of the half-shekel tax to the Temple.[68]

Finally, and probably most important for understanding why Jesus was put to death, he evidently, besides prophesying that the Temple would be destroyed,[69] created a disturbance in the Temple in protest against the system set up there to collect money from the people. Whatever the exact nature of this disturbance, it was probably a symbolic action, with the primary antecedent being the prophet Jeremiah's acts symbolizing the imminent destruction of Jerusalem and its temple.[70]

The Trial and Crucifixion of Jesus

With regard to the crucifixion of Jesus, scholars point out that, for numerous reasons, the gospel accounts of the "trial of Jesus," especially their attempt to portray "the Jews" as responsible for the death of Jesus, are surely fictional. For example, the actual Pontius Pilate—in extreme contrast with the indecisive, vacillating figure portrayed in the Gospels—was "not one to waste time on legal niceties." His administration was known, in the words of Josephus, for "frequent murders of untried prisoners."[71] But these scholars also agree that the high priests, who were made nervous by any threat to their system of privilege, were probably involved.

The responsibility for the crucifixion of Jesus, however, finally had to rest with the Roman authorities. The death penalty could be authorized only by them, and crucifixion was then and there an exclusively Roman manner of execution. It was also a manner used primarily for those regarded as challengers to Roman authority. "That Jesus was *crucified* by the Roman governor," summarized Horsley, "stands as a vivid symbol of his historical relationship with the Roman imperial order."[72] Saying that "the Bible is *essentially* critical," William Stringfellow called the Gospels' accounts of the crucifixion of Jesus "the most political part of the New Testament."[73]

But why did the Romans crucify Jesus? It has long been thought that it was because Jesus claimed to be the long-expected Messiah (Anointed One). However, said Horsley, "there appears to have been no standard expectation of 'the Messiah' in first-century Judea and Galilee."[74] Unsurprisingly, therefore, neither Mark nor Q, the two main sources for information about Jesus (see the discussion of Q above in Chapter 1), portrayed Jesus as understood by himself or others as a popular king or Messiah.

As for Q: "[T]he Q speeches behind the speech material in Matthew and Luke," wrote Horsley, "give not a hint that Jesus was understood or crucified as a popular king, much less as acclaimed (or 'anointed') by his followers." Instead, the Q speeches "understood Jesus primarily as a prophet."[75] More particularly,

> the Q speeches depict Jesus as the latest and most important in a long line of Israelite prophets, and at points the speeches present him as killed by the rulers as many of the prophets had been (Luke/Q 7:18–35; 11:47–51; 13:34).[76]

As for Mark: "while some disciples may have pictured Jesus in the role of a popular king, Jesus pointedly rejected such a role." Moreover, "the only time that the term *messiah* (*christos*, in Greek) is mentioned, in Peter's confession, Jesus sharply rebukes Peter, clearly rejecting the role of a popular king leading an insurrection for independence

(8:31–33)." Instead, said Horsley, "Jesus's arrest and execution are the rulers' responses not to his or his followers claims of messiahship, but to his actions and pronouncements as a prophet."[77]

> Mark indicates explicitly and repeatedly that what provokes the high priestly rulers to arrest Jesus and hand him over to Pilate for crucifixion are his bold public actions and pronouncements as a prophet.... Once he enters Jerusalem and the Temple, the very center of high priestly control, the official plotting to kill him escalates in response to his repeated prophetic condemnations of Temple, high priesthood, and the Roman tribute.[78]

The high priests and scribes were evidently moved to make plans to kill Jesus after he said: "Is it not written, 'My house shall be called a house of prayer for all the nations'? But you have made it a den of robbers" (Mark 11:17–18; quoting Jeremiah 7:1). Horsley concluded:

> This portrayal of the reason why the Judean client rulers and their representatives want to have Jesus killed fits squarely into the main plot of the overall narrative presented in Mark: as *a prophet like Moses and Elijah.*[79]

Marcus Borg gave a similar explanation to the question of why Jesus was killed, saying that Jesus "was crucified as a political threat to Roman order." In different words, Jesus was killed because "of his role as a social prophet who challenged the domination system in the name of God.... The domination system killed Jesus as the prophet of the kingdom of God. This is the political meaning of Good Friday."[80]

Borg also pointed out that the mode of crucifixion shows that Jesus was not killed by the temple authorities: If these authorities had had the power to impose capital punishment (which is uncertain), "the mode of execution would have been stoning," not crucifixion.[81]

CHRISTIANITY AND EMPIRE

If Jesus's message of the kingdom of God was a direct challenge to the continued rule of the Roman Empire over his people, it would seem to follow that Christians down through history would have been radically anti-imperialistic. But this, especially since the age of Constantine in the fourth century of the Christian era, has seldom been the case. There are several reasons for this fact.

Changing the Enemy

For one thing, the complete opposition of Jesus and his early followers to the imperialism of their day has been largely hidden to readers of the gospels. The main reason for this hiddenness is that the authors of the gospels, seeking to present the message of Jesus so as to serve the needs of the Christian movement 40 or more years after the death of Jesus, sought to make it appear that Jesus's message was directed against, and evoked opposition from, "the Jews," rather than the Roman Empire and those who collaborated with it.

This strategy was carried out most fully and effectively by the author of Luke-Acts, which was written to show Roman authorities that Christianity was utterly harmless to the Roman Empire, because Christians, unlike Jews, were faithful subjects, and to convince Christians that the continued existence of the empire would facilitate, not hinder, the coming of the kingdom of God.

For example, although Paul, in reality, according to tradition, suffered the same fate at the hands of the Romans as did Jesus, the Book of Acts ends with Paul peacefully "proclaiming the kingdom of God...with complete freedom and without hindrance from anyone."[82] Given this picture, the Book of Revelation, which portrays the Roman Empire as the very embodiment of Satan, seems like a foreign body in the New Testament.

It is now well known that, whatever its merits at that time, this strategy of portraying Jesus's enemies as "the Jews" later contributed to the despicable history of Christian anti-Judaism, the deadly effects of which led to the Nazi-caused Jewish Holocaust.[83] Also vitally important, however, is the fact that this strategy has led most later

Christians to fail to understand the original thrust of their religion. Horsley and Silberman said that, for the early Christians,

> Rome was the Beast, the Harlot, the Dragon, Babylon, the Great Satan. They knew that Rome's empire was made possible not by divine order but by the acquisition of vast territories through the deadly violence of the Roman legions and the self-serving acquiescence of their own local aristocracies.[84]

This failure of later Christians to understand the beginnings of their religion has contributed to what is arguably the most fateful reversal in history: Christianity, in origin probably the most explicitly anti-imperial religious movement ever, has since the fourth century provided the religious foundation for the growth of empires even more extensive than Rome's.

The Idea of Unilateral Divine Action

A second reason for the fact that Christian faith has not been oriented against empire is the assumption, already evident at the time of Paul, that God would bring in the kingdom of God unilaterally. We do not know exactly what Jesus's view of this matter was—that is, whether he saw himself as merely proclaiming and dramatizing the inbreaking of the kingdom that God would bring about unilaterally, or whether Jesus believed that the activities of his movement would be the *means* by which God would bring the kingdom fully into existence.

Nevertheless, whatever the view of Jesus himself may have been, his later followers clearly assumed that the replacement of demonic by divine rule would be effected unilaterally by God. As Horsley and Silberman said, Paul, expecting an "imminent divine intervention" that would result in "the utter destruction of 'this evil age,'" encouraged his followers to "separate themselves from the ways of the wicked and await the impending climax of a divine drama that had been unfolding for thousands of years." Given this stance of passive waiting for God to act, "The weekly meetings of the *ekklesiai* . . . and the ritualized reenactment of Christ's resurrection through baptism and the Lord's Supper became sacred ends in themselves," so the Christian movement "increasingly lost touch with its goal of forming a practical worldwide alliance against the forces of empire."[85]

Changing the Focus

Closely related to this development was the one-sided emphasis of some New Testament authors, especially Paul, on the cross and resurrection of Jesus, to the neglect of his life and message, and on Jesus himself as the savior. As a well-known slogan among New Testament scholars put it, "The proclaimer became the proclaimed." This meant a shift of emphasis from what God is now doing to what God has already done.

This shift was implicit in the confession of Jesus as "the Christ," a term that was originally simply a translation of "the Messiah." For Jews, this term was to be applied to the person through whom the kingdom of God on earth would actually be brought about. From that perspective, it was self-contradictory to say that the Messiah had already come, given the fact that the world had not fundamentally changed.

Christians avoided this self-contradiction by understanding the "salvation" achieved by Jesus in a different way, according to which people, as individual sinners, have been saved from hell through the death and resurrection of Jesus. This way of understanding salvation implied that the idea of a reign of divine values on earth was at best a secondary dimension of Christian salvation.

This dimension of complete salvation did not, of course, completely drop out of Christian thought and imagination. For one thing, its presence in the Lord's Prayer made it too prominent to ignore. But the main focus shifted to the idea that the cross of Christ has saved people from hell and for heaven. When Karl Marx called religion the "opiate of the masses," he had in mind primarily this otherworldly form of Christian faith, in which salvation does not require overcoming the evils of this world.

Giving Caesar His Due

A fourth factor contributing to the misunderstanding of Jesus's message by later Christians is the traditional understanding of Jesus's statement in Mark 12:17: "Give back to Caesar the things that are Caesar's, and to God the things that are God's." According to this traditional interpretation, Jesus meant that, since the coin had Caesar's likeness on it, one should go ahead and pay the tribute.

This text has therefore been seen as providing the basis for a dualism, especially emphasized by Luther, between "two kingdoms"— the divine and the secular, the eternal and the temporal—and for the later doctrine of the "separation between church and state." Such a dualism, according to which there is no expectation that this world is to be ruled by divine principles, is often portrayed as the central difference between Christianity and Islam.

However, if Jesus's message was focused on the expectation of a divine rule on earth, that difference should not exist. Horsley argued, in any case, that the traditional interpretation of the passage in question was wrong. For Jesus and other Jews at that time, it was self-evident that *everything* belonged to God, so that *nothing* belonged to Caesar. With his ambiguous remark, therefore, Jesus was able to avoid being trapped into explicitly advocating nonpayment while still implicitly doing so.[86]

Given this interpretation, which fits with the rest of Horsley's portrayal of Jesus as preaching the reign of God as an alternative to the reign of empire, this passage provides no basis for turning the present world over to be ruled by those with the most power, regardless of the principles being used to direct this power.

The Idea of Plenary Inspiration

Still another fact aiding the transmutation of Jesus's anti-imperial gospel into an empire-supporting religion was the doctrine of inerrant, plenary inspiration, according to which all parts of the Bible are equally inspired. Not all traditional Christian theologians have held this doctrine. Luther, for example, regarded the Bible as "the cradle of Christ," meaning that other parts are to be evaluated in terms of how well they conform to the gospel of Jesus Christ. On this basis, Luther felt quite free to criticize various parts of the Bible.

Calvinism, however, taught that all parts of the Bible are equally inspired. This doctrine, in conjunction with the Protestant view that all parts of the Bible are to be given a literal interpretation, implied

that the most bellicose passages in the Bible, including those ordering
the Israelites to exterminate the Canaanites, actually reflected the
divine will.

Accordingly, these passages were used by European Americans,
seeing this land as "the New Israel,"[87] to justify the extermination of
Native Americans, as a step needed for the creation of an American
Empire.

The Traditional Doctrine of Divine Omnipotence

Underlying at least some of these factors, which contributed to the
emergence of an empire-supporting Christianity, was the traditional
doctrine of divine omnipotence, based on the idea of *creatio ex nihilo*,
which emerged near the end of the second Christian century (as discussed above in Chapter 3). Besides creating an insoluble problem
of evil, as discussed in Chapter 3, this idea of divine power implied
that God could inspire scriptures inerrantly and bring about a reign
of God on earth unilaterally. This conception of divine power also
influenced Christians not to regard opposition to empire as part and
parcel of Christian faith. It also led to the trivialization of the idea
of demonic power (discussed in Chapter 3).

CONCLUSION

The traditional picture of Jesus, which was based heavily on the
Gospel of John, is very different from the picture of Jesus as recon-
structed by Jesus scholars from the Synoptic Gospels. Rather than
understanding his task as that of dying for the forgiveness of sins,
Jesus saw his task as that of proclaiming, by word and deed, the
coming Reign of Divine Values.

Rome's rule of Palestine exemplified its standard way of ruling its
empire. Also, Rome's rule anticipated the policies America has used
to control its empire. Accordingly, understanding the Roman Empire
is necessary to understand both Jesus and the American Empire.
He was crucified by the Romans—*not* by "the Jews—because he
was perceived as a threat by Roman authorities. Given the nature of

Jesus's life and his death, American Christians today should be anti-imperialistic, rather than basking in the pleasures of Empire, as did the Roman populace two thousand years ago—ignoring the terror and poverty brought to other provinces by Roman rule.

CHAPTER SEVEN

Christology, Trinity, and the Resurrection

BEGINNING IN THE SECOND CENTURY CE, theologians developed doctrines about "the person and work of Jesus Christ." The doctrine about the *person*, known as "Christology proper," sought to explain how Jesus was related to God. The doctrine of "the work" of Jesus Christ, known as "soteriology," sought to explain how Jesus, being thus related to God, brought about salvation. This latter issue is reserved for Chapter 15.

The discussions of Christology proper in the centuries after the creation of the New Testament were carried out in terms of supernatural ideas. In developing a theology for Americans in the twenty-first century, it is necessary to free Christology from supernatural doctrines. But this does not require losing connection with traditional Christological themes: God as incarnate in Jesus, God as trinitarian, and Jesus as resurrected can be understood in non-supernatural ways.

The issue of how Christological doctrines can be reconceived in nonsupernatural terms will be discussed after a review of some of the problems in the traditional doctrines.

TRADITIONAL DOCTRINES: THE INCARNATION

The early church, said John Cobb in his book *Christ in a Pluralistic Age*, "made incarnation the central Christian dogma."[1] Still today, although many traditional Christians consider the resurrection of Jesus the ultimate miracle, others award this praise to the incarnation. Referring to it as "the Grand Miracle," C. S. Lewis said: "The central miracle asserted by Christians is the Incarnation," and Karen Armstrong, in her *A History of God,* wrote: "The greatest miracle of all is that wonderful, incomprehensible act by which God became a human, and was born to a young Jewish girl named Mary."[2]

The first major controversy about the incarnation involved the relation of God to Jesus, understood as the Son of God. The language of Father and Son suggested that the Son was subordinate to God the Father. This idea was promulgated by an Alexandrian presbyter named Arius (256–336 CE), who held that the Son of God did not exist eternally but was begotten by God the Father at a point in time.

Opposing Arianism was the *homoousion* doctrine, according to which the Son is equal to the Father, being "of the same substance or essence" (*homoousious*) with the Father. In 325 CE, the Nicene Creed rejected Arianism. After confessing belief in "one God, the Father Almighty," the creed professed belief in

> Lord Jesus Christ, the Son of God, begotten of the Father before all worlds, Light of Light, very God of very God, begotten, not made, being of one substance with the Father; . . . and was incarnate and was made man.

Although this view became the orthodox doctrine of the church, its meaning always remained mysterious. For one thing, how could the Son have been begotten by the Father and yet be equal—even if the Son was said to be begotten eternally, rather than in time. Equally serious: How could the Nicene doctrine, according to which the Father and the Son are distinct, be compatible with monotheism, according to which there is only one God? As Chapter 5 pointed out, central to the history of the Hebrew Bible was the movement toward monotheism. Was the affirmation of Jesus as "very God of very God" not a regression to polytheism?

TRADITIONAL DOCTRINES: THE TRINITY

In any case, once this doctrine was (somewhat) settled, debate shifted to the Holy Spirit, about which the Nicene Creed simply said, "We believe in the Holy Spirit." This statement was ambiguous and hence unclear: Was the Spirit simply another name for God, or was the Spirit a third divine being?

After more than a half-century of debate, the Council of Constantinople in 381 declared the Spirit to be distinct and equally divine. Enlarging the Nicene Creed of 325, the Nicene-Constantinopolitan Creed—which today is what is usually meant when the Nicene Creed is mentioned—contains this statement:

> We believe in the Holy Spirit, the Lord, the giver of life, who proceeds from the Father and the Son. With the Father and the Son he is worshiped and glorified. He has spoken through the Prophets . . . .

With this creed, the church described God as a trinity, according to which God, while consisting of three divine persons, was said to be a unified being. But this description did not clear things up.

"For many Western Christians," said Karen Armstrong, "the Trinity is simply baffling." This is not surprising, she said, because the doctrine made no logical or intellectual sense; rather, "the Trinity only made sense as a mystical or spiritual experience."[3]

The Athanasian Creed

The judgment that the "three-in-one" doctrine makes no logical sense is suggested by an examination of the Athanasian Creed, which was widely considered the best formulation of trinitarianism. (Although this creed was historically attributed to a fourth-century deacon named Athanasius, it was actually written about 500 CE.) Leaving no doubt that it advocated a *social trinity,* according to which there are three divine "persons," the Athanasian Creed said:

> [W]e worship one God in Trinity, and Trinity in Unity;
> Neither confounding the Persons; nor dividing the Essence.

For there is one Person of the Father; another of the Son; and another of the Holy Ghost.

Besides being unintelligible, the idea that God is a trinity of three persons was used to support the doctrine of creation out of absolute nothingness. One problem produced by that doctrine of creation had been that it seemed to contradict the New Testament assertion that "God is love"—that it belongs to the very nature of God to be loving. Love is a relationship between two or more beings. If there were only one being, it could not be loving. But the doctrine of *creatio ex nihilo* seemed to imply just this—that prior to the creation of the world, God existed all alone.

Some theologians who accepted the idea of a social trinity suggested that it explains how God could always have been loving: The biblical statement that God is love, these theologians argued, refers primarily to the love that the members of the trinity have for each other. This position is still held by many supernaturalists. For example, Austin Farrer, a prominent twentieth-century Anglican theologian, argued that God does not need a world, being "what he is above and apart from the world." God did not need a world to be loving, Farrer said, because there is "life of God in God, above and before all worlds," this being the "fellowship of Blessed Trinity."[4] The doctrine of the trinity has thereby served as a tertiary doctrine to support the secondary doctrine of *creatio ex nihilo*.

Moreover, in attempts to give an intuitive idea of the doctrine, the trinity was sometimes painted as three men.[5] We can, of course, understand the idea of three persons; but we cannot understand how three persons can be one. The more the Athanasian Creed said about the Trinity, the more unintelligible it seemed to become. It said, for example:

[T]he Godhead of the Father, of the Son, and of the Holy Ghost, is all one. . . . The Father eternal; the Son eternal; and the Holy Ghost eternal. And yet they are not three eternals; but one eternal. . . . So likewise the Father is Almighty; the Son Almighty; and the Holy Ghost Almighty. And yet they are not three Almighties; but one Almighty. So the Father is God; the Son is God; and the Holy Ghost is God. And yet they are not three Gods; but one God.

The idea of divine impassibility, according to which God is not affected by the occurrences in the world, was one basis for the idea that God must be a Trinity, consisting of three divine persons. Theologians who rejected this view were sometimes called *Modalists*, which held that God the Father, God the Son, and God the Holy Spirit were simply three modes in which the divine essence existed. Trinitarians accused Modalists of affirming *Patripassianism*, according to which, when Jesus was crucified, God the Father suffered. On the basis of the assumption that God is impassible, the idea that God suffered with Jesus's suffering on the cross was denounced as heretical. The doctrine of the social trinity was originally advocated in part to defend the dogma that God cannot suffer (a dogma that also required an absurd distinction between the human and divine natures of Jesus [see below]).

Some Christians have been taught that the idea of the divine trinity—the idea that God consists of three persons—is of the essence of Christian faith. However, trinitarianism in this sense is a secondary doctrine and, as Unitarians have always insisted, a false one.

In any case, besides being unintelligible,[6] the social trinity created an irreconcilable conflict with Judaism. Jews have traditionally repeated twice daily the Shema, which begins: "Hear, O Israel: The Lord our God is one Lord." Jews (and other unitarians, including Muslims) have always regarded the social trinity as polytheism, not unjustly.

The All-Male Trinity

The pictorial presentation of the trinity as three men was also problematic for another reason. Even if a social trinity of three divine persons were intelligible, there was no reason why all the persons had to be described as male (or two of them male and the Holy Spirit as neutral). Indeed, pointed out scholar Valerie Abrahamsen, "an all-male trinity is fairly unusual historically."[7] Some trinities were all-female (such as the Virgin Hebe, the Mother Hera, and the Crone Hecate in Greek mythology). There were also trinities of two females and one male; of two males and one female; and of father, mother, and child.

Within Christianity, Julian of Norwich (1342–1420) portrayed the trinity as Father, Mother, and Lord. And some thinkers have described the Holy Spirit as female, perhaps by equating the Spirit with Sophia as discussed in Proverbs 8:1–5).[8] But these attempts to bring femininity within the Godhead still portray the deity as overwhelmingly masculine, with the implication that men more than women are created in the divine image.[9]

The all-male trinity is expressed in the brief, off-repeated song of praise that came to be known as simply "the Doxology":

> Praise God, from whom all blessings flow;
> Praise him, all creatures here below;
> Praise him above, ye heav'nly host;
> Praise Father, Son, and Holy Ghost.

Jesus: Truly God and Truly Man

In any case, if the traditional doctrine of the trinity is unintelligible, the same is true of the answer given to the next issue raised by the creeds. As stated above, Nicaea said that Jesus Christ was "very God of very God, . . . of one substance with the Father" and yet "was made man." How could Jesus be both divine and human?

The answer to this question that became orthodox was provided by the Chalcedonian Creed (451 CE), which explained that Jesus was "truly God and truly Man" while being "One Person." In emphasizing that Jesus was truly human, the Creed said (with reference to Hebrews 4:15) that he was "like us in all things, sin apart." This account raised some difficult questions, such as:

> How could Jesus be "one person" if the divine nature of Jesus is omniscient and omnipotent, while the human nature is not omniscient and omnipotent?
>
> How could Jesus be "truly Man"—"like us in all things, sin apart"—if he was omniscient and omnipotent while we are not?

As can be seen even from this brief discussion, the traditional doctrines of God as trinitarian and Jesus as the God-man are not intelligible.

Why Traditional Doctrines of Incarnation and Trinity Are Unintelligible

The basic reason why the traditional doctrine of the incarnation of God in Jesus could not be made intelligible was the assumption that *God as an experiencing subject* was incarnate in Jesus. This assumption entailed that Jesus contained two subjectivities: the (omniscient) divine subjectivity and the (non-omniscient) human subjectivity. The attempt to portray Jesus as a unified, fully human person was hopeless from the outset.

The assumption that the aspect of the Trinity that was incarnate in Jesus—that is, the divine Logos (or Word)—is an experiencing subject also guaranteed that the attempt to describe the divine three-foldness would end in failure. This assumption about the divine Logos meant that the divine threefoldness had to involve three persons, each with its own subjectivity.

In Greek philosophy, the divine Logos was "the divine reason implicit in the cosmos, ordering it and giving it form and meaning." [10] As such, the Logos was not a personal being. This idea of the Logos was central to the Jewish philosopher Philo. According to Philo,

> God is revealed to His creation through the Logos, though not in a personal way. The Logos is the wisdom of the divine and the organizing principle of matter. . . . The Logos is the "first-born" of God, but inferior to God. God expresses Himself and His acts through the Logos. [11]

By contrast with both Philo and Greek philosophers, the prologue of the Gospel of John described the Logos—translated "the Word"— as a personal being. A personal being, moreover, who is co-eternal with God and is, in fact, God: "In the beginning was the Word, and the Word was with God, and the Word *was* God. This one was in the beginning with God." [12]

This twofold way of describing the relation of the Word (Logos) to God was repeated in the creeds of Nicaea and Chalcedon: The Son is distinct from God and yet *is* God. Insofar as the Logos (Word) was God, the Logos had to be treated as a personal being and hence could be called the "Son of God." So by virtue of taking John's prologue literally, the theologians condemned Christology and trinitarianism to unintelligibility.

TRADITIONAL DOCTRINES: THE RESURRECTION OF JESUS

In Christianity, the resurrection of Jesus has always been fundamental. St. Paul wrote:

> If Christ has not been raised, then our proclamation has been in vain and your faith has been in vain. We are even found to be misrepresenting God, because we testified of God that he raised Christ. (1 Corinthians 15:14–15a)

"This is a strong claim," observed Dutch theologian Marcel Sarot, "and Paul makes it about the Resurrection only, not about any of the other miracles."[13]

Indeed, although C.S. Lewis and others have called the incarnation the greatest miracle, many Christian thinkers, like Sarot, have assigned this status to the resurrection. "The resurrection of Jesus," said well-respected Catholic New Testament theologian Raymond Brown, "was the supreme intervention of God in human existence, the supreme miracle."[14]

However, traditional Christianity's account of the resurrection of Jesus, speaking of the "resurrection of the body," implies supernaturalism. There is no way in which the resurrection of the body could be understood within the framework of naturalistic theism.

The traditional ideas of Christology proper, God as trinitarian, and the resurrection of Jesus cannot be reaffirmed by people who see supernaturalism as impossible. But these doctrines can be reconceived within a postmodern framework based on naturalistic theism.

CHRISTIAN DOCTRINES RECONCEIVED:
JESUS AS INCARNATION OF GOD

To solve the problems in the traditional ideas of Jesus as incarnating God, we need not, as many modern theologians have suggested, quit speaking of God as literally incarnate in Jesus. Rather, the problem can be solved by simply saying that God was present in Jesus not as experiencing, but *as experienced.*

In other words, God was incarnate in Jesus as an ongoing object of Jesus's experience, not as presently experiencing. By analogy, when you remember an experience that you had yesterday, that previous experience is in your present experience as an object of this experience, but not as presently experiencing.

Once this adjustment is made, there is no problem in principle of speaking of God as incarnate in Jesus. Thus understood, the divine presence in Jesus does not render the full humanity of Jesus problematic, because God is present in all human beings—in fact, in all sentient (experiencing) beings whatsoever. In Whitehead's words: "Every event on its finer side introduces God into the world. . . . The world lives by its incarnation of God in itself."[15] Whitehead also said: In affirming "the direct immanence of God in the one person of Christ" and "some sort of direct immanence of God in the World generally," the early Christian theologians in Alexandria and Antioch "have the distinction of being the only thinkers who in a fundamental metaphysical doctrine have improved upon Plato."[16]

Jesus as Revelatory Incarnation of God

However, although the doctrine that God was incarnate in Jesus is of utmost importance, Christian faith does not only say this. It also says that, in Borg's words, "Jesus is for Christians the decisive revelation of God."[17] That confession is an example of soteriology, the work of Jesus, for it says that one of the ways Jesus provides salvation for us is by giving us our decisive revelation of God. However, the doctrine that Jesus was a *revelatory incarnation* of God combines soteriology with Christology proper: The description of Jesus as an incarnation of God is to describe (our view of) Jesus himself; adding "revelatory" makes the statement also soteriological.

How could Jesus have revealed God? This seemed easy in traditional theology: Being divine and hence omniscient, Jesus could simply reveal truths about the nature of God, about how God created the world, and so on. However, this view was made problematic by the synoptic gospels, because they do not suggest that Jesus was omniscient. Indeed, Mark 13:32, speaking of the end of the world, said that "of that day or that hour no one knows, not even the angels in heaven, nor the Son, but only the Father" (Matthew 23:36 says the same).

So now the question is: How can we understand how Jesus, not being divine, could have been a revelatory incarnation of God?

Moreover, it belongs to faith to regard Jesus this way not merely as a matter of fact, but to hold that Jesus's relation to God was such that it has been *appropriate* for Christians to regard Jesus this way. For that to be the case, the life and death of Jesus had to be a *special* act of God. The challenge is how to say this without reverting to supernaturalism.

Special Act of God. In 1961, Langdon Gilkey, long-time professor of theology at the University of Chicago, wrote:

> What we desperately need is a theological ontology that will put intelligible and credible meanings into our analogical categories of divine deeds and of divine self-manifestation through events. Only an ontology specifying what God's relation to ordinary events is like, and thus what his relation to special events might be, could now fill the now empty analogy of mighty acts, void since the denial of the miraculous.[18]

Gilkey saw that unless we have a way of thinking of God's action as analogous to our own, we have no way to speak of *special* divine acts.

As Gilkey said, special divine acts are acts of self-manifestation, in which the nature and purpose of God are especially revealed. In traditional theology, special divine acts were ones in which God acted differently from the way God acts in relation to most events. In other words, special acts were miracles. It was through Jesus's miracles, and especially his resurrection, that God's nature and purpose were manifested, with the central attribute of God's nature being omnipotence. That view presupposed, of course, supernaturalism. The question for today is: What can be meant by special divine acts in a worldview in which supernaturalism is rejected?

In process theology, the human mind or soul is a "living person," meaning a serially ordered society of living occasions of experience. The person's acts in the primary sense are acts of self-constitution, in which the soul constitutes what it is to be in the next moment, with its aims for its body. What people usually mean by "human acts" are bodily acts, including the acts in which the person speaks. These are the person's acts in a secondary sense. In this secondary sense, a person acts in many different ways: speaking, dancing, singing, running, driving, playing tennis, preparing food, and so on. But in the primary sense, human action is always the same: The mind provides aims for various parts of its body.

Special acts by a person are bodily acts through which the person's fundamental character and purpose are manifested. Obviously, some external, bodily acts are more capable than most acts of manifesting the person's character and purpose. For example, if John Jones is a kindly person, his act of tying his shoelaces will generally not do much to express this fact. Much more suited to being special acts are ones in which he flashes a forgiving smile or gives an encouraging pat on the back.

A second requirement for a special act would be that an act really expresses ("presses out") the person's character and purpose. For example, say John Jones in a parking lot suddenly stops his automobile, thereby allowing an old lady to have the last parking place. But this would not be a special act, manifesting his kindness, if he stopped only because he saw a pile of tacks in front of his car.

A third factor in a special act is that the person's behavior must conform to a high degree to the person's intentions for his or her body. For example, if Jones accidentally hit his car's accelerator instead of its brakes, so that his car ploughed into the old lady's car, this would do nothing to reveal his kindly nature.

Accordingly, to be a special act of a person, (1) it must be the type of act that in principle could express the person's basic character and purpose; (2) it must be based on an intention that especially reflects this character and purpose; and (3) the person's body must actualize that intention to a high degree.

Moreover, when one's bodily members actualize the soul's intentions, this is not an external relation. Rather, the mind enters into the members of the body. In other words, the soul is incarnate in the person's bodily members.

This discussion can be applied analogically to divine action. God, like a human soul, is a "living person," consisting of divine occasions of experience. God's acts in the primary sense are those occasions of experience in which God formulates divine aims for various parts of the world. God's primary activity is, accordingly, always the same: God presents aims to various parts of the world.

God's acts in the secondary sense are worldly events (including the acts of Jesus). Every event in the world is influenced by God, so every event in the world is an act of God to some extent. But worldly events differ enormously in the degree to which particular events respond to the divine aims and reflect the divine purpose. Therefore, some worldly events are special, divinely provided initial acts, much more than are most events in the world.

Accordingly, to speak of God's special acts does not involve saying that God has acted structurally in a different way, thereby interrupting the world's normal causal relationships. Also, God's action is never coercive, but always persuasive,[19] calling worldly individuals to actualize the best possibilities for them, given their location in time and space. The events in the world are partially self-creative subjects, which can decide for or against the highest possibilities offered to them by God.

The conceptualization of special acts of God can be based on the three-fold analysis outlined above. First, for an event to be a special act of God, it will need to be the kind of event that is especially suited for expressing God's eternal character and purpose. Especially suited are the words and deeds of human beings through which they express a vision of reality.

Second, the event will need to be based on aims from God that especially reflect God's general aim. Again, God's aim for a finite individual is always the best possibility for it, given its actual situation. Accordingly, although God acts formally in the same way for every worldly event—by providing it aims—the *content* of God's aim for different individuals and events will differ radically.

For example, the best possibilities for ants differ greatly from the best possibilities for monkeys. God's aims for young children will generally be less complex than the highest possibilities for adults. The human race could not produce poetry until it had formed language. And the best possibilities for people in one religious tradition will be quite different from the best possibilities for people in other religious traditions. Accordingly, the divine aims for human beings will differ radically, and some of them will more directly reflect the divine character and purpose than others.

Third, the bodily action of a person, to be a special act of God, must actualize the aims provided by God to him or her to a high degree. Human beings are very complex creatures, and the divine aim given to a person contains a hierarchy of possibilities. Therefore, normal human beings have a very high degree of freedom. Persons can reject the highest aims toward which God was luring them in favor of lower aims. Persons can even act radically contrary to the divine will for them at a particular time and place. In such a situation, a person's act cannot be considered a divine act to a significant extent. Contrary to Augustine and Calvin, sinful acts are not acts of God to the same degree as acts that conform to divine aims. The crucifixion of a proclaimer of God's will is not a divine act to the degree that the proclamation was.

In summary: A special act of God is a human act (1) that expresses a vision of reality, (2) for which God's aim was a direct reflection of the divine character and purpose, and in which (3) the divine aim was actualized to a high degree.

Appropriately Received as Special Act of God: This suggestion shows that it is possible to describe how Jesus could have been a special act of God in such a way that he has been appropriately received as the decisive revelation of God. It is crucial that Jesus was born into a tradition that understood the world as the product of a personal creator, one that wants human beings to treat each other fairly and with love. Central to Jesus's vision of reality was, of course, the kingdom of God, in which all people are to have their daily bread and be treated with dignity and love.

Given that context, in which Jesus had, among other things, accepted and radicalized the vision of the Hebrew prophets, it was possible for God to give aims to Jesus that, if actualized, would reflect God's eternal character and purpose.

Given this account, it is necessary only to suggest that Jesus did indeed live in terms of the highest aims presented to him. As to how this could have happened, Marcus Borg, building on Abraham Heschel, has emphasized the centrality of divine compassion in the message of Jesus. Accepting Borg's view that Jesus was one of—indeed the greatest of—the Hebrew prophets, we can assume that Jesus's words and acts were based on his experience of the divine *pathos*. As Borg suggested, the idea that Jesus directly experienced God's compassion for the world could account for the centrality of compassion in Jesus's preaching and acting. And in experiencing God's compassion and internalizing God's aims for him, the soul of Jesus incarnated God. Accordingly, God was incarnate in Jesus in a special way. We can thereby understand how Christians can appropriately regard Jesus as the decisive revelation of God for them.

Jesus as the Christ

Although it is of utmost importance to say, as did Borg, that Jesus is the decisive revelation of God for Christians, there is more to say about Jesus. Christians have always, as the term "Christian" indicates, said that Jesus was the Christ. There have been many ways to understand this term, most of which have been supernaturalist. But John Cobb advocated a non-supernaturalist understanding, building on his idea of structures of existence, which was discussed above in Chapter 5 on the Hebrew prophets.

In a book entitled *Christ in a Pluralistic Age,* Cobb defined "Christ" as the Logos as incarnate in the world:

Christ is the incarnate Logos. As such Christ is present in all things. The degree and the kind of Christ's presence varies. The fullest form of that presence is that in which he coconstitutes with the personal past the very selfhood of a person. That would be the paradigm of incarnation. In that case Christ would not simply be present in a person but would *be* that person. The distinctive structure of Jesus's existence was characterized by personal identity with the immanent Logos. . . . In all things Christ is present. Jesus *was* the Christ.[20]

In Whiteheadian terms, Christ or the immanent Logos is the initial aim.

The Logos is immanent in all things as the initial phase of their subjective aim. . . . The initial aim is the immanence of the Logos. It is God's gift and presence to the occasion, God's grace. . . . Christ means predominantly the immanence of the Logos in the living sphere, and it is especially among human beings that he is to be found.[21]

Although it is correct to say that Jesus was a prophet, his status as the Christ made him somewhat different from the classical prophets.

The structure of the prophet's existence, at least in those experiences which inspired the prophecies, differed from the ordinary Jewish existence chiefly in the relation to God. Jews knew themselves as agents of decision and action, responsible before God to obey the divine law. Thus their existence centered in the will . . . . The law was known by instruction and study. The prophet, however, was grasped by a direct awareness of divine purposes and requirements . . . . The point at which the prophets were distinctive, i.e., their relation to God, is also the point at which Jesus appears distinctive. . . . The prophets spoke of a Word of God received by them, whereas Jesus presented his message on his own authority.[22]

This difference reflected the fact that in Jesus there was "a distinctive incarnation because his very selfhood was constituted by the Logos."[23]

CHRISTIAN DOCTRINES RECONCEIVED: THE DIVINE TRINITY

If the doctrine of Jesus as the incarnation of God can be understood in a nonsupernatural way, what about God as threefold? The idea of three divine persons, each with its own subjectivity, certainly cannot and should not be saved. But there are other, and more helpful, ways to understand God as threefold.

A Temporal Trinity

One way to speak of God as trinitarian is to think in terms of a "temporal trinity," which refers to God's activity at the *beginning*, the *middle*, and the *end* of the world, such as God as Creator, Revealer, and Consummator.

According to Whitehead, "The essence of Christianity is the appeal to the life of Christ as a revelation of the nature of God *and of his agency in the world*."[24] Could this conception of Christianity be applied to the temporal trinity? Traditional, supernaturalist theologians would say No.

While saying that Jesus was the decisive revelation of God, they did not take this to mean that Jesus revealed the divine *modus operandi*. Although they recognized that Jesus said we should not respond to evil by resorting to violence, and they added that Jesus himself lived by this dictum, these theologians did not think of Jesus as having revealed God's way of acting in general. In particular, they would have said that the revelation in Jesus did not give us a clue as to how God created the world and how God would eventually overcome evil.

Traditional theologians granted that God's method of acting in Jesus was primarily persuasive, and that the same is true of God's activity in human history. Aside from occasional miracles and the unique incarnation in Jesus, God was said generally to abstain from using coercive power in relation to humans. God called, and we either accepted or rejected the call. Jesus's call to people to follow him could be regarded as revelatory of God's way of relating to human beings in general. However, traditional theology said that God's activity at the beginning and the end of the world—at the creation of the world and the consummation of history—could not be understood as divine persuasion.

As for the destruction of evil at the end of the world: Although traditional theologians granted that God's method of acting in Jesus was primarily persuasive, they considered this only a temporary strategy. The method of suffering love, they said, is not God's only or even primary method for overcoming evil: Although Jesus died softly on the cross, he held a big stick in reserve.

For example, in a critique of pacifist theology, one author said: Christ may have acted nonviolently during his life, but "Jesus will at the end bring all criminals (sinners) to judgment by violent means (overcoming the armies of the Antichrist by force and casting sinners into hell)."[25] As a book entitled *Armageddon* put it:

> In his first coming to earth, Jesus Christ was born in a stable.... The second coming of Jesus Christ to earth will be no quiet manger scene. It will be the most dramatic and shattering event in the entire history of the universe.... Cities will literally collapse, islands sink and mountains disappear. Huge hailstones, each weighing a hundred pounds, will fall from heaven.... The rulers and their armies who resist Christ's return will be killed in a mass carnage.[26]

No more Mister Nice Guy!

According to this theology, in other words, God's past mode of activity in Jesus would not suffice to bring about the eventual victory of divine over demonic power. God would have to resort to a degree of violence that would outdo the violence of the forces of evil. The revelation of God's love in Jesus was not, accordingly, a revelation of the divine *modus operandi*: The true nature of divine power, which is supernatural, has been, for the most part, held in reserve, and will be fully manifested only at the end.

Many conservative Christians, of course, do not endorse the Armageddon theology. And yet the dualism between the *modus operandi* of Jesus and that of God has been so ingrained in the Christian mind, especially in the West, that most Christians have assumed that persuasive love would never be sufficient for overcoming evil. Rather, it is widely thought that evil can be overcome only by the threat of, and the occasional use of, violence.

For example, Anglican Bishop William Temple, in support of just-war theology in the 1940s, claimed that God had two modes of dealing with the world. The "love method" supplements, rather than replaces, the use of coercive methods to establish justice and law. Persons who will not acknowledge love must be treated by means of the other method.[27]

Charles Raven's Theology

By contrast, another twentieth-century Anglican theologian, Charles Raven, said that the resolution of the Arianism controversy provides a basis for overcoming the idea that there is dual mode of divine operation. If we rightly understand the implications of the doctrine of the trinity, with its *homoousion* doctrine, said Raven, we see that Temple's kind of theology is heretical. Truly rejecting the Arian heresy—according to which the pre-existent one who became incarnate in Jesus was a subordinate deity—means recognizing

> Christ's way of redemption as universally characteristic and effective. If we agree that God uses other means ... in respect of the Last Judgment ... we are Arians, however much we may recite the Nicene Creed.[28]

God, in other words, will not resort to coercive power to bring about the ultimate victory of good over evil. Indeed, if we say that the power of love cannot overcome the power of evil, we are in effect denying that love is the ultimate power of the universe.

To be sure, the possibility of understanding how love can finally overcome our subjugation to evil is connected with another primary doctrine of Christian faith: the idea that, although the divine purpose as revealed in Jesus is to bring about as much salvation (wholeness) as possible in this life, it is also (as stated above in the Introduction) "to bring about an even more complete salvation in a life beyond bodily death." This issue is to be discussed in Chapter 15. In the meantime, Raven's understanding of the trinitarian structure of God should be explored more fully.

Besides implying that God's activity of overcoming evil at the end of history is the same as God's activity in Jesus, the *homoousion* doctrine also implies that God's activity in creating the world is the same kind of activity, that is, persuasion. As pointed out in Chapter 2, if our stupendous universe had been created in six days, the creator would have required overwhelming coercive omnipotence. But given the new idea that it took some 15 billion years for our universe to be created, the idea that the creation involved persuasive power makes sense.

By thinking of these three roles—Creator, Revealer, Consummator—in conjunction with the idea that Jesus revealed the divine *modus operandi*, we have a repudiation of Marcion's dualism, according to which our world was created by an evil deity, different from the redeeming God revealed in Jesus. By including the book of Genesis in the Christian canon, the early church repudiated this dualism, declaring creation and redemption to be two actions of one and the same divine reality.

Unfortunately, Raven said, traditional theology missed the full significance of this identification, taking it to mean that the one God operates in two different ways, using coercive power to create the world, next using persuasive love to save human beings, and finally using coercive power to punish those who rejected the divine offer of salvation. However, argued Raven, the true significance of the rejection of Marcionism is that we should understand God's creative activity in the light of the nature of God's revealing activity in Jesus.[29] As stated in Chapter 2, God's activities of creating, revealing, and saving should be understood as persuasive.

Christians, therefore, should reject the idea of a dual mode of divine operation, instead regarding, in Raven's words, "love not force as the ultimate power."[30] A reconceived doctrine of the Trinity can help us see this doctrine as an expression of naturalistic theism.

CHRISTIAN DOCTRINES RECONCEIVED: THE RESURRECTION OF JESUS

Insofar as Christians no longer find appeals to supernatural miracles credible, what can be said about the resurrection of Jesus? Many Christian theologians have believed that talk of the resurrection of Jesus had to be rejected (with the denial often hidden beneath ambiguous language). But there is a much better approach: Recognizing that the resurrection could be real without being miraculous.

To explain: It has widely been thought that the reported "miracles of Jesus," including the resurrection, had to be classified either as supernatural miracles or else as myths or fabrications. For thinkers who thus classify them, the assumption is that events of the types traditionally classified as miracles simply do not happen. The assumption that they never happen is supported by the late modern worldview, with its sensationist epistemology, its mechanistic ontology, and its equation of the mind or soul with the brain.

The Hermetic Tradition

However, there was an alternative worldview, known as Hermeticism, which thrived between the fifteenth and seventeenth centuries. Dealing with philosophy, theology, mathematics, and science (including medicine, astrology, and alchemy), it allowed for "action at a distance" as a natural phenomenon. From this Hermetic perspective, the "miracles" of Jesus—such as mind-reading and physical healings—could be regarded as fully natural, if extraordinary, events. They could, therefore, be regarded as not different in kind from similar events that have reportedly occurred in other traditions, such as Hinduism and Buddhism.[31]

This Hermetic tradition was deeply threatening to the seventeenth-century church, which held that the Christian miracles showed Christianity to be the One True Religion. Without this interpretation of these events, the church's claim to possess the "keys to the kingdom" would have seemed groundless. If the miracles could be given a naturalistic interpretation, it was thought, the church's authority would be in peril.

Hermeticism was involved in a three-cornered battle, in competition with Aristotelianism and mechanism, to become the new worldview.[32] Marin Mersenne, who paved the way for the mechanistic philosophies of Descartes, Boyle, and Newton, regarded the Hermetic tradition as "public enemy number one," because it denied the supernatural character of the miracles upon which the Christian Church was built. By regarding all wonders as natural, the Hermetic philosophy in effect denied laws of nature, and without laws of nature to be broken, complained Mersenne, there could be no miracles in the true sense of the term.[33]

By virtue of developing a mechanistic worldview, Mersenne and his fellow mechanists defended miracles and hence Christianity as the One True Religion. Mersenne did acknowledge that events similar to the miracles of Jesus were reported in other religious traditions. However, engaging in special pleading, he said that those extraordinary events were produced by the devil. (Although Mersenne held that God alone possessed truly supernatural power, he said that the devil had *preternatural* power, through which miracles could be simulated.)[34]

Psychical Research

Although Hermeticism (along with Aristotelianism) was trounced by the mechanical philosophy, it in some respects reemerged in the latter part of the nineteenth century. The Society for Psychical Research stated its purpose thus:

> [T]o investigate that large body of debatable phenomena designated by such terms as mesmeric, psychical and spiritualistic . . . in the same spirit of exact and unimpassioned enquiry which has enabled Science to solve so many problems.[35]

The founders of this society hoped to provide scientific grounding for a positive creed to undermine the materialistic worldview, which was increasingly (but falsely) thought to be scientifically validated.[36] Because the materialistic worldview had gained enormous prestige due to its supposed association with the physical sciences, the alternative worldview, which the Society for Psychical Research hoped to provide, was largely ignored. It was, nevertheless, endorsed by several first-rate thinkers, including:

Psychologists Pierre Janet, Carl Jung, and William McDougall, and Sigmund Freud (after having long scorned it).

Physicists Sir William Barrett, David Bohm, Sir William Crookes, Thomas Edison, and Nobel Prize-winners Brian Josephson and Lord Rayleigh.

Astronomers Camille Flammarion and Sir Arthur Eddington.

Biologists Hans Driesch and Nobel-prizewinner Charles Richet.

Philosophers Henri Bergson, C. D. Broad, and William James.

William James, in particular, advocated a "thicker and more radical empiricism," which includes an examination of "the phenomena of psychic research so-called."[37] We need a scientific worldview, he argued, that would allow these phenomena to be regarded as fully natural, albeit exceptional, occurrences. He said:

Science, so far as science denies such exceptional occurrences, lies prostrate in the dust for me; and the most urgent intellectual need which I feel at present is that science be built up again in a form in which such things may have a positive place.[38]

James also thought his radical empiricism to be equally important for religion. He wrote:

Let empiricism once become associated with religion, as hitherto, through some strange misunderstanding, it has been associated with irreligion, and I believe that a new era of religion as well as of philosophy will be ready to begin.[39]

Thus far, religious leaders have for the most part spurned James' proffered assistance. The present theology is intended to be a step toward the acceptance of James' proffer.

The three major types of psychical research—or *parapsychology,* as it is now often called—are extrasensory perception (telepathy and remote viewing), psychokinesis (the mind causing changes in the physical world without using its body), and evidence for life after death—upon which the present chapter focuses.[40]

There are many types of evidence suggestive of life after death, such as communications through mediums, experiences suggestive of reincarnation, experiences suggestive of possession, out-of-body experiences, and apparitions. Most relevant to the present discussion are apparitions, because phenomena reported in relation to apparitions are analogous to, even often identical with, phenomena reported in relation to the post-crucifixion appearances of Jesus. (Although this book does not have a chapter on life after death as such, it does have treatments of the resurrection of Jesus [here] and out-of-body experiences [Chapter 15].)

Orthodox theologians tend to reject any suggestion that the appearances of Jesus can be understood in terms of the kinds of apparitions studied in psychical research. Anglican theologian Alan Richardson said:

> Against all modern attempts to explain the resurrection as something natural and comprehensible, it is necessary to insist that the resurrection of Jesus is a *miracle.*[41]

By that, of course, Richardson meant that the resurrection was produced supernaturally. Likewise, fellow Anglican theologian Austin Farrer said:

> Christ's Resurrection, as faith conceives it, is unique in its kind; Christians will always resist the reduction of it to a level with any class of facts whatsoever.[42]

However, some prominent New Testament scholars, while accepting the historicity of the resurrection, have disagreed with the view that it was absolutely unique. This disagreement involves a difference in how the event called "the resurrection of Jesus" is understood. Those who speak of the uniqueness of this event usually think in terms of the "bodily resurrection of Jesus." But those who think in terms of analogies with modern-day apparitions speak of "the *appearances* of Jesus after his death"—as did St. Paul, who wrote nothing about an empty tomb, but instead spoke of life after physical death in a "spiritual body."[43]

Types of Apparitions

A judgment as to the appropriateness of speaking of analogies requires an understanding of the types of apparitions and their standard features. A summary of some of these standard features, as provided by psychical research, shows that they support the possibility that the postmortem appearances of Jesus might have reflected the continuing existence of the personality of Jesus.

Veridical Apparitions: Some apparitions are veridical, meaning that the persons who saw the apparitions acquired from them true information that would not have been knowable by normal means. The existence of veridical apparitions counts against the common assumption that all apparitions can be dismissed as pathological hallucinations.[44] For example, there are well-documented cases in which family members of a deceased person have learned from an apparition the location of some money or an important document. There are also some cases in which one learns that and how the person seen in the apparition had been killed.[45]

Multiple Apparitions: Although most apparitions are seen by only one person, some of them are multiple, meaning that *two or more persons at different locations* see the apparition within roughly the same time period.[46] Multiple cases strengthen the claim that some appartions are objective.

Collective Apparitions: In these phenomena, two or more persons simultaneously see the apparition at the same place. Sometimes, moreover, the apparition is seen by at least one person who had never seen the person while he or she was alive. Collective apparitions count heavily against the assumption that all apparitions are subjective hallucinations.

Auditory and Tactual Apparitions: Although apparitions are primarily visual, they are sometimes auditory and occasionally tactual as well.[47]

Reports of the Appearances of Jesus

Some of the apparitions reported by psychical researchers have had features similar to the reported postmortem appearances of Jesus. According to the New Testament reports, the resurrection appearances of Jesus included these features:

- There are multiple apparitions (e.g., Luke 24:34; Luke 24:36–38).

- There are collective apparitions (e.g., Matthew 28:9–10; 1 Corinthians 15:6; Acts 1:3).

- There are apparitions in which Jesus spoke (e.g., Matthew 28:9; Matthew 23:16–18; Mark 16:14–16; Luke 24:13–30; Luke 24:36–38; John 20:16; John 20:24–29; John 21; Acts 1:3).

- There are apparitions in which Jesus was touched (Matthew 28:29; Luke 24:39; John 20:26–28).

- Whereas some apparitions seemed to be entirely physical (e.g., Luke 24:36–43; Matthew 28:9; John 20:20), some of them seemed physical in some respects and nonphysical in others, such as when Jesus entered into houses with locked doors (John 20:26; Mark 16:12; Luke 24:30–36; Luke 24:5–53; Acts 1:1–11).

To cite these reports is not to say that all or even some of them happened precisely as reported; we have no way of knowing. The purpose, instead, is to show that the features of apparitions as reported by psychical researchers in our time are similar to stories about apparitions in New Testament times.

New Testament Scholars

Some New Testament scholars, having become aware of such similarities, have treated the postmortem appearances of Jesus as instances of apparitions. For example:

- In 1907, Kirsopp Lake, who taught at the universities of Leiden and Harvard, published a book entitled *The Historical Evidence for the Resurrection of Jesus Christ*, in which he said: "[T]he phenomenon which we call the Resurrection cannot be isolated, but must be considered in connection with others which belong to the same class."[48]

- B. H. Streeter, professor of Biblical Exegesis at Oxford University and a member of the Archbishop's Commission on Doctrine in the Church of England, published a book in 1912 entitled *Foundations: A Statement of Christian Belief in Terms of Modern Thought.* Streeter said that the resurrection appearances to the disciples were visions "directly caused by the Lord himself, veritably alive and personally in communication with them."[49] A few years later, Streeter published a book entitled *Immortality: An Essay in Discovery Coordinating Scientific, Psychical, and Biblical Research.*[50]

- In 1941, C. J. Cadoux, professor of church history at Oxford University, published a book entitled *The Historic Mission of Jesus.* Cadoux said that the appearances were "real manifestations given to his followers by Jesus himself, not by means of his physical body resuscitated from the empty tomb, but by way of those strange processes sufficiently attested to us by psychical research, but as yet very imperfectly understood."[51]

- In a 2007 book about Jesus (co-authored with N. T. Wright), Marcus Borg pointed out that St. Paul, who gave the first accounts in the New Testament about the resurrection, reported four times in First Corinthians that Jesus *appeared* to various people. In the Bible, Borg pointed out, the word "appeared" is often "used in connection with 'apparitions' [and] an apparition is a paranormal kind of experience, not visible to everybody who happens to be there." That Paul thought of the resurrection appearances as apparitions, Borg continued, "is further suggested by his inclusion of himself in the list of people to whom the risen Christ appeared," which implied that Paul "regards his own experience of the risen Christ [his vision on the Damascus Road] as similar to the others." Borg also said that "apparitions do not involve a physical body, even though what is seen often includes seeing a person in bodily form." Borg added that "visions and apparitions can be true," so we need "not put them in the category of hallucinations."[52] In other words, Borg was saying, the resurrection appearances could be categorized as *veridical apparitions.*

Pichas Lapide

The fact that the resurrection of Jesus need not be categorized as a supernatural miracle is illustrated by the position of orthodox Jewish theologian Pichas Lapide (who died in 1997). Lapide believed in the resurrection of Jesus, but he did not believe that Jesus was in any way absolutely unique. Although "the resurrection belongs to the category of the truly real and effective occurrences," Lapide said, it was not a "miracle" in the supernaturalist sense.[53]

CONCLUSION

Traditional theologians tend to believe that, if theologians reject supernaturalism, they will inevitably produce very thin Christologies. This chapter, however, shows that a naturalistic Christology can do the following:

Describe God as having been incarnate in Jesus in a special way.

Conceptualize how Jesus could have appropriately been taken by Christians as the decisive revelation of God.

Conceptualize God as trinitarian.

Endorse the belief that the post-crucifixion appearances originated with the still-experiencing Jesus of Nazareth.

The discussion of life after death is continued in Chapter 15.

CHAPTER EIGHT

The Christian Way
and Other Ways

PERHAPS THE MOST COMMON name for earliest Christianity was "the Way" (Acts 19:9, 19:23, Acts 14), with Christians known as "followers of the Way" (Acts 22:4, 24:14). This chapter deals with the question of how people of the Christian Way should think about other Ways, such as the Buddhist Way, the Jewish Way, the Muslim Way, and so on.[1] This chapter advocates the approach known as *religious pluralism*.

RELIGIOUS PLURALISM

For members of a particular religious tradition to accept religious pluralism is to accept two points—one negative, one positive. The negative point is the rejection of religious absolutism, which means rejecting the *a priori* assumption that one's own way is the only way that provides saving truths and values to its adherents—that it has been divinely established as the only legitimate religion, intended to replace all others.

The positive point, which goes beyond the negative one, is the acceptance of the idea that there are indeed religions other than one's own that provide saving truths and values to their adherents.

This twofold affirmation provides a summary account of what can be called "religious pluralism in the generic sense." To accept generic religious pluralism is not necessarily to deny that one's own religious tradition has distinctive truths and values of universal importance, the acceptance and implications of which members of that tradition could seek to spread. But it means that, if the adherents of that tradition do believe that it has such truths and values, they assume that other religions do as well.

Religious pluralism stands in opposition to the two types of Christian absolutism: exclusivism and inclusivism. According to exclusivism, only Christians can be saved. Inclusivists, by contrast, hold that people in other religious traditions can be saved—perhaps if they have followed the light available to them in those traditions— but only by virtue of the salvation effected by Jesus Christ.[2]

The present chapter is based on two major convictions. The first is that the promotion of religious pluralism in our world today is vitally important: If civilization is to have much hope of surviving even the present century, we must find solutions to our global problems, especially the problems of war, imperialism, nuclear weapons, and global warming plus ocean acidification.

The world's religions, with their ability to motivate people, could provide a powerful force for the kind of civilizational transformation we need, if they cooperate toward that end in the name of their common values. But thus far the religions have been sources of discord as much as sources of solidarity. The growth of religious pluralism in the various traditions could encourage a mutual respect and appreciation that would facilitate cooperation.

A second conviction is that this growth of religious pluralism is now especially important among Christians. This is because the tendency to religious absolutism has been very strong among Christians and also because Christians have in recent centuries had far more power—militarily, economically, and culturally—than adherents of other religions, making the Christian tendency to accept religious absolutism the most destructive.

This tendency is, furthermore, far from being a thing of the past.

Indeed, the possibility of "civilizational wars," with the "Christian West against the rest," is more of a threat now than at any time in recent centuries. This chapter focuses, accordingly, on Christian religious pluralism, beginning with the ideas of four of the leading Christian pluralists of recent decades.

John Hick

In an essay entitled "The Non-Absoluteness of Christianity," Presbyterian John Hick (1922–2012) rejected the "absolutist position," which affirms "a Christian monopoly of salvific truth and life" and thereby the conviction that the Christian religion should seek "to dispossess the non-Christian religions."[3] The pluralistic position, he said, holds instead that "Christianity is not the one and only way of salvation, but one among several."[4]

In a chapter named "The Pluralistic Hypothesis," Hick wrote that pluralism rejects the view that "there can be at most one true religion, in the sense of a religion teaching saving truth." The traditional belief that "God must intend [Christianity] to supersede all other religions and to embrace the entire human race," Hick added, is "incompatible with a pluralist understanding of Christianity as one salvific response among others."

In a chapter headed "A Christianity That Sees Itself as One True Religion Among Others," Hick attributed an "implicitly pluralistic theology" to Christians who assume that their "Jewish or Muslim or Hindu or Sikh or Buddhist friends and acquaintances are as fully entitled in the sight of God to live by their own religious traditions as we are to live by ours," because they have "their own authentic form of faith."[5]

Paul Knitter

This generic pluralism was also clearly affirmed by Roman Catholic Paul Knitter (b. 1939), who spoke of "the simple but profound insight that *there is no one and only way*" and of the "possibility that other religions may be ways of salvation just as much as is Christianity."[6] Describing the "paradigm shift" from either exclusivism or inclusivism to pluralism as the move from an insistence on the absoluteness of Christianity "toward a recognition of the independent validity of other ways,"[7] Knitter held with other pluralists that there are "many equally valid religions" and that "no one religion can claim to be absolutely ... superior over all others."[8]

Whereas absolutists insist that Christianity has a total or virtual monopoly on religious truth, Knitter affirmed "the plurality of religious truth."[9] Endorsing "historical consciousness," which realizes that "insofar as every existing reality is historical, it is limited," Knitter explicitly drew the conclusion that Christianity, like every other religion, is limited. This conclusion leads to the "dialogical imperative," Knitter said, because it is through dialogue with members of other religious traditions that "we can expand or correct the truth that we have," thereby overcoming the "limitations of our own viewpoint."[10]

Wilfred Cantwell Smith

The endorsement of generic pluralism by Wilfred Cantwell Smith (1916–2000)—who began life as a Presbyterian and ended as a member of the United Church of Canada—was illustrated by his dismissal of the "fallacy" held by traditional Christians that "they alone were in God's grace, were saved."[11]

Smith instead affirmed "pluralism," according to which "the figure of Christ" is only "one form among others [through] which God has entered history," so that we can hold that "God has played in human history a role in and through the Qur'an, in the Muslim case, comparable to the role in the Christian case in and through Christ." Given the notion that the meaning of *idolatry* is "to treat, mistakenly, something mundane as if it were divine," Smith considered idolatrous the tendency of Christians "to hold that their own forms [doctrines and practices] are given by God, others' forms are not."[12]

Marjorie Suchocki

Marjorie Suchocki (b. 1933), a member of the United Methodist Church, developed the implications of the Whiteheadian view of the God-world relation in her highly readable book, *Divinity and*

Diversity, which is subtitled *A Christian Affirmation of Religious Pluralism*. Because all creatures have their own creativity, hence their own freedom of response—as the creation narrative in Genesis itself suggests—God's activity in the world, she argued, must take the form of "call and response."

Because the various creatures will often use their freedom to respond in different ways, diversity arises. God's call at any time will be relevant to the responses previously made by a particular species, or a particular religious tradition. Accordingly, Suchocki concluded:

> If God works through call and response, and if human freedom introduces variety into the response, then shouldn't we expect to find different stories, rituals, orders of social structure, and senses of the sacred, but all tending toward creating the good within human forms of community?[13]

In developing the implications of this view for the Christian understanding of the "reign of God," Suchocki said that we are today called to this task:

> [T]o live a reign of God that reaches not toward an imperialism of one religion—our own!—sweeping the planet, but that reaches toward a new form of community: a community made up of diverse religious communities, existing together in friendship.[14]

John Cobb

Generic pluralism has also been clearly affirmed by United Methodist John Cobb (b. 1925). In *Christ in a Pluralistic Age*, Cobb indicated that the pluralism he accepted involves the rejection of the traditional view "that Christianity is the one right or true way."[15] In his first book on interreligious dialogue (*Beyond Dialogue*), Cobb said that he "join[ed] with Paul Knitter, John Hick, and Wilfred Cantwell Smith in their rejection of the deep-seated tendency of Christians to absolutize their tradition in some way."[16]

Cobb's endorsement of generic pluralism was also illustrated by his acceptance of this normative judgment:

> [I]n a plurality of religious movements each deserves respect
> in its own terms and Christians should not make claims for
> their doctrines of a sort that they do not accept as equally
> legitimate for others to make about theirs.[17]

This judgment, added Cobb, implies that the various movements are "on the same level." Besides recognizing the *descriptive* fact that we live in a pluralistic age, meaning one in which "almost everyone is forced to come to terms with religious differences," Cobb also endorsed the *normative* interpretation that "the diversity is acceptable and that people should learn to live with it in mutual appreciation."[18]

As well as supporting the need for Christians to engage in dialogue with members of other religious traditions, Cobb endorsed the implication of this engagement—that the Christian thereby "sets aside all claims of an exclusiveness that entails a monopoly of wisdom" and respects the other traditions "as comparable in worth."[19] While regarding the Christian experience of salvation as distinctive, Cobb accepted "the Hindu account of *moksha* or the Zen Buddhist account of *satori* [as] just as authentic."[20]

WHY RELIGIOUS PLURALISM HAS EMERGED

Religious pluralism, which has become an increasingly important factor in the Christian world since it began to emerge in the seventeenth and eighteenth centuries, has developed for at least five motives: theological, ethical, sociological, scientific, and dialogical.

Theological Motive

The major theological motive has been the doctrine of divine love. John Hick said that he became a pluralist because he could not reconcile the idea that God is "infinite love" with the idea that "only by responding in faith to God in Christ can we be saved," because this would mean that "infinite love has ordained that human beings can be saved only in a way that in fact excludes the large majority of them."[21]

Paul Knitter, having felt a tension "between two fundamental beliefs: God's universal love and desire to save, and the necessity of the church for salvation," decided that he had to affirm the former—that the doctrine of God's universal salvific will implies that the revelation given to others must be a potentially saving revelation. In other words, "Christians not only can but must look on other religions as possible *ways of salvation.*"[22]

Ethical Motive

The ethical motivation behind religious pluralism begins, Mark Heim (b. 1950) observed, "with revulsion at the crimes of religious pride."[23] Illustrating this point, Hick devoted several pages to the "destructive effects of the assumption of Christian superiority," pointing out that, for example,

> there is a clear connection between fifteen or so centuries of the "absoluteness" of Christianity, with its corollary of the radical inferiority and perverseness of the Judaism it "superseded," and the consequent endemic anti-Semitism of Christian civilization.[24]

This anti-Semitism, of course, led to the holocaust.[25]

If each religion could overcome its absoluteness "by the realization that one's own religion is one among several valid human responses to the Divine," Hick argued, "religion could become a healing instead of a divisive force in the world."[26]

Sociological Motive

These theological and ethical motivations for pluralism have been supported by a sociological fact about the modern world—that many people, through increased familiarity, are overcoming old stereotypes about other religions. Besides learning about these religions from books and mass media, people in historically Christian countries increasingly have neighbors belonging to other religious traditions. When they compare the lives of these people with that of fellow Christians, it becomes increasingly difficult to maintain the old view that the spiritual and moral fruits produced by Christianity prove it to be in a class by itself.[27]

Scientific Motive

Another external push toward pluralism has come from the encounter with modern science. More important than any particular discovery or teaching of modern science is what can be called its *presumption of naturalism*. Although sometimes the term "naturalism" is used to mean a materialistic, atheistic worldview, the basic meaning of naturalism—and the only type of naturalism that science necessarily presupposes—is the denial of supernatural interruptions of the world's normal causal processes.

Much modern theology—that broad movement often called "liberal theology"—has accepted naturalism in this sense. Hick, for example, said that the form of Christianity that "believed in miracles which arbitrarily disrupt the order of nature" is "incompatible with the scientific project."[28]

The rejection of supernaturalism does not require a rejection of theism. As discussed in this book's Introduction, many liberal theologians have developed doctrines that can be called "theistic naturalism," or "naturalistic theism." The denial of supernatural interventions does not even entail the rejection of ongoing divine activity in the world, as process theologians have especially shown.

But the presumption of naturalism does mean that pluralist theologians no longer assume that the founding events of Christian history involved a divine incursion into the world, different in kind from the way God works always and everywhere. For example, the German theologian Ernst Troeltsch (1865–1923), the first major pluralist of the twentieth century, rejected (in Knitter's words) "concepts of revelation that had God swooping down from heaven and intervening into history at particular spots."[29] Wilfred Cantwell Smith rejected the idea "that God has constructed Christianity" in favor of the idea that God "inspired us to construct it, as He/She/It has inspired Muslims to construct what the world knows as Islam."[30]

The doctrinal revisions undertaken by pluralistic theologians have especially focused on traditional Christian theology's supernaturalistic Christology. According to that Christology, pointed out Hick, Jesus "was God—more precisely, God the Son, the second person of the Holy Trinity—incarnate." That doctrine implied "that Christianity, alone among the religions, was founded by God in person," so it was "God's own religion in a sense in which no other can be."[31]

In the first book in which John Cobb stated his pluralistic position—*Christ in a Pluralistic Age*—he rejected the traditional "supernaturalist and exclusivist" interpretation of the incarnation of the divine Logos in Jesus, according to which Jesus was "a supernatural being," namely, "the transcendent, omnipotent, omniscient ruler of the world . . . walking about on earth in human form."[32]

The rejection of supernaturalism applied also to the traditional idea of salvation, according to which it involves a divine decision, based on arbitrary standards, that saves some people from eternal damnation. Recognizing that Christian exclusivism and inclusivism both depend on some such definition of salvation—for example, "being forgiven and accepted by God because of the atoning death of Jesus"—Hick suggested that "we define salvation . . . as an actual change in human beings," which involves "a long process," not a sudden, supernaturally effected transformation.[33] Cobb, likewise, spoke of "salvation as something we participate in here and now rather than, or in addition to, life beyond."[34]

Dialogical Motive

A fifth motivation behind the development of pluralistic forms of Christian theology has been what Paul Knitter and David Lochhead have called the "dialogical imperative."[35] An *ethical* motivation for dialogue is the recognition that many of our planet's problems are so great that they can be overcome, if at all, only through the cooperation of the world's various religions. For example, Knitter argued that all the religions today are facing the human demand for "some form of this-worldly, earthly (as opposed to purely spiritual) *liberation*," so that "*liberation*—what it is and how to achieve it—constitutes a new arena for the encounter of religions."[36]

A theological impetus for dialogue is that, once we see that our own religion is not the one and only true religion, we realize that other traditions may have truths and values that are not provided, at least as clearly, in our own religion. The conclusion that Christianity, like every other religion, is limited, said Knitter, leads to the dialogical imperative, because it is through dialogue with members of other religious traditions that—to repeat Knitter's statement quoted above—"we can expand or correct the truth that we have," thereby overcoming the "limitations of our own viewpoint."[37] This motive, as discussed below, is also central to Cobb's pluralistic theology.

CRITICISMS OF HICK'S IDENTIST RELIGIOUS PLURALISM

Although for many theologians, the need for Christianity to embrace pluralism is now beyond question, not all theologians agree. From the perspective of some theologians, "Christian pluralism" is a self-contradiction. One cannot hold Christian faith in an authentic form, they believe, and be a pluralist. Much of this rejection of Christian pluralism arises from an absolutist, supernaturalist notion of Christian faith, which simply presupposes that the only authentic form of Christian faith is one that assumes, *a priori*, that it is the only religion supported by God.

This kind of criticism can be largely ignored by pluralists, because the controversy is not about pluralism as much as it is about the proper Christian response to modern thought—whether the liberal rejection of the supernaturalist framework for Christian theology is a necessary adjustment by Christian faith or a betrayal of that faith.

There is another criticism, however, that must be taken more seriously. According to this criticism, pluralism inevitably leads to a kind of relativism that is antithetical to Christian faith. The centrality of this issue was pointed out in Alan Race's landmark book (see endnote 2, this chapter), in which he said:

> The pertinent question mark which hovers over all theories of pluralism is how far they succeed in overcoming the sense of "debilitating relativism" which is their apparent danger.[38]

By "debilitating relativism," Race meant the view that all religions are equally true in a way that makes them all equally false.[39]

At least one pluralist theologian, Langdon Gilkey (1919–2004), believed that this danger could not be avoided. Seeing "no consistent theological way to relativize and yet to assert our own symbols," Gilkey concluded that giving up our absolute starting point leads to an "unavoidable relativism."[40]

The reason this concern looms so large is not only the fact that the way to affirm pluralism without relativism is not immediately obvious, but also the fact that some of the most prominent pluralists have been led to relativism. For example, besides that fact that Ernst Troeltsch (1865–1923) has been called first great Christian pluralist, he has also been called (by Cobb) "the first great Christian relativist."[41]

Also, the position of John Hick has been widely criticized as leading to a complete relativism. This fact is of great significance because Hick's version of pluralism, besides being the version that has been discussed far more than any other,[42] has been widely taken as stating *the* pluralist position.

For example, Kevin Meeker and Philip Quinn, in an edited book, *The Philosophical Challenge of Religious Diversity*, said that they reserved the term *religious pluralism* "to refer to the position John Hick adopts in response to the fact of religious diversity."[43] Similarly, Mark Heim (b. 1950), seeing Hick as having made "the philosophical case for a pluralistic outlook," treats Hick's position as the paradigmatic pluralistic theology.[44]

Any weaknesses in Hick's position, therefore, have widely been taken to be weaknesses of pluralism as such. It is, therefore, important to see that the weaknesses in Hick's position, which have led to such widespread criticism, follow from his particular version of pluralism, rather than from pluralism as such (generic pluralism).

Although Hick's move to pluralism began, as we saw, with his conviction about what divine love would not do, the particular way Hick worked out his pluralistic position led him, ironically, to the conclusion that personalistic words, such as "love," could not be applied to the Divine Reality in itself.

What led Hick to this conclusion was a fact combined with an assumption. The fact is that the reports of profound religious (mystical) experience can be divided into at least two major types: (i) those that describe communion with a good, loving, personal deity, distinct from the experiencer, and (ii) those that describe a realization of identity with ultimate reality experienced as formless, impersonal, ineffable, and "beyond good and evil."

The existence of these two types of religious experience creates a problem partly because they are both reported—as Caroline Franks Davis pointed out in her book *The Evidential Force of Religious Experience*—as apprehensions of "the nature of ultimate reality."[45]

But this fact would not have created a problem except for Hick's assumption that, as Cobb put it, "what is approached as 'ultimate reality' must be one and the same."[46] Hick himself said that "there cannot be a plurality of ultimates."[47] Given that assumption, Hick faced a serious question, which had been articulated by Davis:

> How can "ultimate reality" be both a personal being and an impersonal principle, identical to our inmost self and forever "other," loving and utterly indifferent, good and amoral, knowable and unknowable, a plenitude and "emptiness"?[48]

Hick, in seeking to answer this question, decided that, as a pluralist, he could not play favorites by saying that one kind of religious experience was more authentic—more revelatory of ultimate reality—than the other. He decided, accordingly, that ultimate reality in itself—which he often called simply the "Real in itself"—must be considered completely unknowable (like Immanuel Kant's *noumenal reality*), and must, therefore, be distinguished from all human ideas about ultimate reality.

Hick then divided these human ideas into two types: (i) divine *personae*, such as the biblical God and Advaita Vedanta's *saguna Brahman* (Brahman with qualities), and (ii) *impersonae*, such as Advaita Vedanta's *nirguna Brahman* (Brahman without qualities) and Buddhism's *Sunyata* (usually translated "emptiness"). But none of these human ideas correspond to the Real in itself, said Hick, because it "cannot be said to be one or many, person or thing, substance or process, good or evil, purposive or non-purposive."[49]

We therefore cannot, Hick asserted, apply to ultimate reality in itself any substantive predicates, such as "being good," "being powerful," and "having knowledge."[50]

Hick's position thereby did lead to the "debilitating relativism" of which Alan Race spoke. In his eagerness to show all religions to be equally true, Hick in effect declared them all to be equally false, thereby undercutting their support for moral and spiritual attitudes. Hick did, to be sure, claim that "the major world religions constitute varying human responses to the transcendent Reality, and are thus at least to some extent *in alignment with that Reality*," so that they can provide criteria for valuing various human attitudes.[51]

For example, pointing out that saints in all religious traditions manifest "compassion/love towards other human beings or towards all life,"[52] Hick implied that this attitude is in alignment with "transcendent Reality." However, given Hick's assertion that this "transcendent Reality" is entirely devoid of purpose, goodness, compassion, and love, he could not intelligibly say that the saint's "compassion/love" is any more in alignment with transcendent Reality than Hitler's loathing/hatred. Because its complete relativism undermines Christian faith and ethics, Hick's version of religious pluralism has been widely rejected.[53]

Another charge that has been leveled is that Hick's religious pluralism is not really pluralistic. Mark Heim, referring primarily to Hick's version of pluralistic theologies, said: "Despite their appropriation of the title, these theologies are not religiously pluralistic at all."[54] That criticism is, however, not true: As we have seen, Hick affirms all the points that characterize *generic* religious pluralism.

Heim's criticism was much better stated when he said that Hick's "pluralism is real but superficial."[55] It is superficial, Heim pointed out, because Hick in effect treated all religions as essentially the same. Hick did this, Heim said, because of two dubious assumptions: "a metaphysical dogma that there can be but one religious object, and a soteriological dogma that there can be but one religious end."[56] Because of these dogmas—which Cobb had previously criticized— Hick regarded all religions as oriented around an identical religious ultimate and as seeking a salvation that is essentially identical. Hick's position can, therefore, be called "identist pluralism."

One problem created by identist pluralism, Heim pointed out, is that by implying that "the specific and special aspects of another faith tell us [nothing] that is of significant importance," this position provides no motivation for dialogue.[57]

But Heim's equation of Hick's position with pluralism as such led him to an inconsistent conclusion. On the one hand, Heim said, "Despite their appropriation of the title, ['pluralistic'] theologies are not religiously pluralistic at all," so we need a "truly pluralistic hypothesis."[58] On the other hand, repeatedly referring negatively to "pluralism" and "pluralistic theology,"[59] Heim called for a "post-pluralistic" theology.[60] How could Heim call for a theology that is "truly pluralistic" and also "post-pluralistic"?

In any case, Heim's second conclusion—that we need a post-pluralistic theology—came through as the dominant message of his book. This fact is illustrated by a review of Heim's book by Paul J. Griffiths entitled "Beyond Pluralism."[61] This message reinforced the view that, given the deep problems inherent in Hick's version of pluralistic theology, pluralistic theology as such should be left behind.[62]

PROCESS THEOLOGY'S COMPLEMENTARY RELIGIOUS PLURALISM

Whitehead's process philosophy provides the basis for a different version of religious pluralism, free from the problems inherent in Hick's position. Two features of Whitehead's philosophy are especially relevant.

One of these was Whitehead's concern, in dealing with different systems of thought, to show how assertions that at first sight appear to be contradictory may actually express complementary truths. He suggested this approach with regard to science and religion, saying that a clash between their teachings is "a sign that there are wider truths . . . within which a reconciliation of a deeper religion and a more subtle science will be found."[63]

Whitehead also suggested this approach with regard to Buddhism and Christianity, saying that, instead of sheltering themselves from each other, they should look "to each other for deeper meanings."[64] In this case, as in the previous one, the task is to overcome formulations that, while expressing a measure of truth, have done so in "over-assertive" ways, "thereby implying an exclusion of complementary truths."[65]

The other feature of Whitehead's philosophy that is especially germane to religious pluralism is his view of the relation between God and creativity.

Two Ultimates: God and Creativity

Whitehead's "creativity" involves a generalization of the physicist's "energy." Creativity is the power embodied in all actual things—both God and finite actualities.

As explained in Chapter 4, actual entities are momentary "actual occasions," which come into existence out of the causal influence of the past, exercise a degree of self-determination in the present, when they come to completion, after which they exert causal influence on future actual occasions.

Your experience during a few seconds, for example, is composed of a number of actual occasions, also called "occasions of experience." Whitehead's term *creativity* points to the twofold power of each occasion of experience to exert a degree of self-determination in forming itself and then to exert causal influence on the future. Whitehead's term *creativity* thus provides a new understanding of what previous philosophers have called "being" or "being itself," and that theologian Paul Tillich also called "the power of being." However, whereas Tillich equated the power of being with God, Whitehead distinguished them.

The distinctive feature of Whitehead's position is that creativity (being itself) and God are equally primordial. Although traditional theologians regarded the power to create as eternal, they held that this power belonged to God alone: The fact that a world with its own power exists was due to a voluntary divine decision. This idea was enshrined in the doctrine of *creatio ex nihilo*, according to which—as discussed in Chapter 3—our world was created out of a complete absence of finite actualities.

Whitehead rejected this doctrine, suggesting instead that our world was created, as the Bible itself suggests, out of a primeval chaos (see Chapter 3). Although our particular world is a contingent divine creation, there has always been *a* world, in the sense of a multiplicity of finite actualities embodying creativity. To say that God has always co-existed with creativity, therefore, means that creativity has always been embodied in a world as well as in God—that there has always been worldly creativity as well as divine creativity.

This doctrine is doubly important for the issue of religious pluralism. In the first place, this doctrine explains the impossibility of supernatural interruptions. Traditional theism's supernaturalism was undergirded by its doctrine of *creatio ex nihilo*. By saying that the very fact that there is a finite world at all is due to God's free decision, traditional theists implied that all the principles embodied in our world—not only what we call the "laws of nature" but also the universe's most fundamental causal principles—were freely created. And what was freely created could be freely interrupted. This doctrine, besides giving traditional theists an insoluble problem of evil, also lay behind their absolutist view of Christianity as the only divinely approved religion.

Equally important for religious pluralism is the fact that Whitehead's distinction between God and creativity provides a basis for speaking of *two ultimate realities*. This idea was most fully worked out by John Cobb, whose position, in contrast with Hick's identist pluralism, can be called "complementary pluralism." Different religions, Cobb said, have seen different truths and have offered different paths to salvation.

In developing the idea that there are two ultimates, Cobb suggested that one of these, corresponding with Whitehead's *creativity*, has been called "Emptiness" (*Sunyata*) or "Dharmakaya" by Buddhists, "nirguna Brahman" by Advaita Vedanta (nontheistic) Hindus, "the Godhead" by Meister Eckhart, and "Being Itself" by

Martin Heidegger and Paul Tillich. This is the *formless* ultimate.

The other ultimate, corresponding with what Whitehead called "God," is not Being Itself but the *Supreme* Being. Far from being formless, it is the world's source of all forms, such as truth, beauty, and justice. It has been called "Amida Buddha" or "Sambhogakaya" by Buddhists, "saguna Brahman" or "Ishvara" by theistic Hindus, "Yahweh" by Jews, "God" by Christians, and "Allah" by Muslims.[66] In contrasting the two ultimates, Cobb suggested that, while creativity is the ultimate *reality*, God is the ultimate *actuality*.

Cobb gave several reasons for preferring this hypothesis to Hick's. One reason was that he simply found it not illuminating to say that God, who is *worshipped*, and Emptiness, which is *realized*, are "two names for the same noumenal reality."[67]

Cobb's hypothesis also allows Christian theologians to avoid the "relativization and even negation of basic Christian commitments" implicit in Hick's hypothesis."[68] According to Hick's hypothesis, "those who assume that all traditions must be focusing on the same aspects of reality," Cobb said, are led to believe that what Zen Buddhists call Emptiness "must be the same as God," which can in turn lead the Christian thinker to

> employ the negative theology on the Christian heritage so radically as to dissolve God into Emptying. In that process everything distinctive of the biblical heritage is lost.[69]

The acceptance of two ultimates overcomes a problem that has made it difficult for some of our best Christian theologians to understand how they can continue to a affirm the morality-supporting attributes of God while taking Buddhist Emptiness seriously.

David Tracy's Rejection of Two Ultimates

For example, David Tracy of the University of Chicago agreed with Cobb that God must be understood by Christians as an ultimate that can be trusted and worshipped. But whereas Cobb distinguished between creativity as the *ultimate reality* and God as the *ultimate actuality*, Tracy rejected the idea of two ultimates.[70] In retaining the traditional equation of God and ultimate reality, Tracy thereby affirmed that Buddhist Emptiness is identical with what Jews, Muslims, and Christians call "God."[71]

Thanks to his involvement in interreligious dialogue with Buddhists, however, Tracy realized that this equation could be very threatening. Trying to think of ultimate reality as emptiness, he said, is "a deeply disorienting matter, for any Christian who holds her/his profound trust in and loyalty to the one God." It was in the Buddhist-Christian dialogue, he added, that he experienced "the full terror of otherness."[72]

The Buddhist idea of ultimate reality as emptiness led him, he said, to explore the apophatic neo-Platonic theologies of Meister Eckhart and other Christian mystics.[73] Tracy "nevertheless remain[ed] puzzled," he admitted, "whether the Christian understanding of God can receive as radically an apophatic character as Eckhart sometimes insists upon."[74]

Given his commitment to liberation theology and his faith in God as the one by whom "hope is granted" for "acts of resistance to the status quo," Tracy had to pull back from a *completely* negative theology.[75]

However, although Tracy saw the need not to go as far as Hick in negating all the positive and thereby morality-supporting attributes of God, the fact that he felt impelled to go even part way was due to the fact that he, like Hick, could not relinquish the metaphysical assumption that there must be only one ultimate reality.

John Cobb: Pluralism without Relativism

Whiteheadian pluralists, by contrast, can affirm the existence of a Divine Actuality with many characteristics in common with the biblical God, including those that support the concern for a just social order, without disagreeing with the description, provided by nontheistic Hindus and Buddhists, of ultimate reality as formless. Finally, Cobb said,

> When we understand global religious experience and thought in this way, it is easier to view the contributions of diverse traditions as complementary.[76]

This last point is crucial, given Cobb's view that the challenge of interreligious dialogue is "to transform contradictory statements into different but not contradictory ones," thereby moving "toward a more comprehensive vision in which the deepest insights of both sides are reconciled."[77]

One basis for such reconciliation is to recognize that sometimes claims that may at first glance seem contradictory are really answers to different questions.

> [T]here is no contradiction in the claim of one that problem A is solved by X and the claim of the other that problem B is solved by Y.... The claims are complementary rather than contradictory.[78]

For example:

> Consider the Buddhist claim that Gautama is the Buddha. That is a very different statement from the assertion that God was incarnate in Jesus. The Buddha is the one who is enlightened. To be enlightened is to realize the fundamental nature of reality, its insubstantiality, its relativity, its emptiness. ... That Jesus was the incarnation of God does not deny that Gautama was the Enlightened One.[79]

Another example involves the tension between the Christian assertion "that Jesus is the Christ" and the Jewish insistence "that the Messiah has not come." Jews and Christians, Cobb suggested, should "work together repeatedly to clarify the difference between what Jews mean by 'Messiah' and what Christians legitimately mean by 'Christ.'"[80]

In his landmark book on religious pluralism, Alan Race, after warning of the danger of "debilitating relativism," pointed to Cobb's version as an exception. "The virtue of Cobb's contribution," said Race, "is that he combines fidelity to Christ with unqualified openness to other faiths."[81] Cobb illustrated this assessment by saying that, to enter into interreligious dialogue,

> we do not need to relativize our beliefs.... We can affirm our insights as universally valid! What we cannot do, without

lapsing back into unjustified arrogance, is to deny that the insights of other traditions are also universally valid.[82]

THREE ULTIMATES

Although thus far Cobb's complementary pluralism has been discussed in terms of Whitehead's distinction between God and creativity, Cobb actually affirmed *three* ultimates, with the third being the cosmos or the universe, in the sense of the totality of [finite] things. These three ultimates, pointed out Cobb, can be related to the three types of religion—theistic, acosmic, and cosmic—described by former Claremont religion professor Jack Hutchison.[83]

The distinction between God and creativity helps us compare the theistic and acosmic types of religion. But there is also a type of religion, illustrated by forms of Taoism and many primal religions, including Native American religions, that regards the cosmos as sacred. By recognizing the cosmos as a third ultimate, we are able to see that these cosmic religions are also oriented toward something truly ultimate in the nature of things.[84]

Although traditional Christian theology, with its doctrine of *creatio ex nihilo*, could not regard the cosmos as in any sense ultimate, Whitehead's philosophy does. Although our particular cosmos (our "cosmic epoch") is contingent, being rooted in a divine volition, the fact that there is *a* world—some world or other consisting of a multiplicity of finite actual entities—is not contingent. What exists necessarily is not simply God, as in traditional Christian theism, and not simply the world understood as the totality of finite things, as in atheistic naturalism, but God-and-a-world, with both God and worldly actualities being embodiments of creativity.

Although these three ultimates within the totality are distinct, they are, Cobb emphasized, "not in fact separable from one another," adding:

> I would propose that without a cosmic reality there can be no acosmic one, and that without God there can be neither. Similarly, without both the cosmic and acosmic features of reality there can be no God.[85]

Cobb's position here reflected a statement by Whitehead:

> There is no meaning to "creativity" apart from its "creatures," and no meaning to "God" apart from the "creativity" and the "temporal creatures," and no meaning to the "temporal creatures" apart from "creativity" and "God."[86]

Those who have been conditioned, especially through the doctrine of *creatio ex nihilo*, to believe that there can be only one ultimate tend to hear any talk of multiple ultimates as polytheism. But this characterization would not, Cobb pointed out, be appropriate for his Whiteheadian worldview, because the three ultimates do not exist on the same level. They differ as the one Supreme Being, the many finite beings, and Being Itself, which is embodied by both God and finite beings. Creativity, as Being Itself, is in no way a second god alongside the Supreme Being, because it is not a being and has no reality apart from its embodiments in the divine and finite actualities.

It makes no sense to say, as some have, that Whitehead's God is subordinate to creativity, because, as Cobb argued,

> between reality as such and actual things there can be no ranking of superior and inferior. Such ranking makes sense only among actualities. Among actualities [God] is ultimate.[87]

This statement also made clear that Whitehead's position did not make the world of finite beings equal with God. Although Tillich said that a Supreme Being would be merely "one being alongside other beings," this pejorative description would not fit the Whiteheadian idea of God. As the "worldsoul," understood as "a unity of experience that contains all the multiplicity of events," God is "the being that includes all beings."[88]

This pluralistic ontology allows us to understand the possibility that a wide variety of religious experiences could be authentic. Although these three ultimates are inseparable, individuals and religious traditions can concentrate on one or two features alone. Insofar as there is concentration solely on God, or on the universe in distinction from

God, or on creativity, there would be the pure case of theistic, cosmic, or acosmic religious experience. In fact, Sri Aurobindo reported having had all three types of experience.[89]

However, Cobb added, "much religious language blurs the distinctions and relates to more than one of the three ultimates." For example, "The universe reverenced as ultimate is the embodiment of Being Itself or [nirguna] Brahman and is pervaded by God." This fact is "often attested unintentionally in the rhetoric of those who find meaning in appreciating their part in this whole."[90]

Likewise, "Language about God often draws on what is strictly true only of Being Itself." This mixing occurs especially in Western theism, Cobb points out, because "it has incorporated acosmic elements from its Neo-Platonic sources" with the result that

> the religious experience of Western mystics seems to be at once of theistic and acosmic reality—one might say that it is of the theistic as embodying the acosmic reality, or of the acosmic as qualified by the theistic reality.[91]

As a final example, the truth that "Being Itself does not exist at all except in God and the creatures" is reflected in a twofold fact. On the one hand, "Being Itself, being the being of all things, is also closely associated with the thought of the whole." On the other hand, "Very little is said of Being Itself or [nirguna] Brahman that does not hint at characteristics that actually belong to God."[92] Cobb illustrated this latter idea by pointing out that, although many Buddhists would say that Emptiness or *Dharmakaya* can be realized "as such apart from all forms," it is always expected that those who fully realize ultimate reality, thus understood, will be characterized by wisdom and compassion.[93]

Cobb's view that the totality of reality contains three ultimates—along with the recognition that a particular tradition could concentrate on one, two, or even all three of them—gives us a basis for understanding a wide variety of religious experiences as genuine responses to something that is really there to be experienced. "When we understand global religious experience and thought in this way,"

Cobb emphasized, "it is easier to view the contributions of diverse traditions as complementary."[94]

(Marjorie Suchocki had earlier made a similar suggestion. Whereas Whitehead had included three notions—"creativity," "many," "one"—within the Category of the Ultimate,[95] Suchocki suggested that we could think of these as "three different ultimates," each of which can be seen as the central focus of different religions.[96])

Mark Heim, who subtitled his book "Truth and Difference in Religion," said that the overarching task of a more adequate approach to religious diversity is "to find a fruitful way of combining recognition of truth or validity *and* difference across the religions." Contrasting (identist) pluralists, who "are committed to limiting their attribution of truth to what is convergent," with inclusivists, who "are almost equally inclined to stress the truth of what is similar ... and to deny validity to what is different," Heim said: What is needed is a perspective that "can recognize the effective truth of what is truly other."[97]

Heim thereby said what Cobb had been saying for many years. (The subtitle of Heim's book, in fact, could have been employed by Cobb.) "I continue to push [my proposal] forward against great resistance," stated Cobb, "because I believe it helps those who accept it to acknowledge the deep differences among religious traditions without denying that each has its truth."[98]

CONCLUSION

The rejection of supernaturalism entails the denial of Christian absolutism and hence of both exclusivism and inclusivism, as those terms have come to be understood. The rejection of supernaturalism, therefore, leads to the acceptance of religious pluralism. The present chapter shows that pluralism does not necessarily lead to a debilitating relativism. Rather, people can strongly affirm the primary doctrines of the Christian gospel without denying the truth and saving value of the primary doctrines of other religious traditions.

The Whitehead-Cobb distinction between God and creativity is of immense importance for Christian resistance to imperialism. If theologians affirm religious pluralism while holding that there is only one religious ultimate, as John Hick and David Tracy illustrate, it is difficult for them to have a view of deity that condemns imperialism.

Sin and the
Demonic

CHAPTER NINE

The Divine
and the Demonic

AFTER POINTING OUT that the American Empire is now often compared with that of Rome, Chapter 6 looked at the Roman Empire as a basis for understanding not only the American Empire but also the message of Jesus. Although Rome saw itself as divinely authorized to impose its *Pax Romana* on the world, the nature of this "peace" was far from divine. It was not even benign. Jesus and the final book of the New Testament regarded it as the very opposite of divine—as demonic.

This fact raises the question of whether Christians today should regard the American Empire as demonic. That question is to be discussed in Chapters 11–14. The present chapter deals with a prior question: Is the notion of demonic power necessarily a mythological idea, which can no longer be taken seriously by modern (and postmodern) minds, or is it possible to develop a nonmythological notion of demonic power? This chapter argues that the latter is the case. It also argues that the concepts of "divine" and "demonic" are of crucial importance in developing a form of Christian faith that is able to deal realistically with the nature of America today.

This chapter begins with a discussion of the divine and the demonic in traditional Christian thought, then uses that discussion as background for developing a new understanding of demonic power.

THE DIVINE AND THE DEMONIC IN
TRADITIONAL CHRISTIAN THOUGHT

The contrast between the divine and the demonic is implicit every time Christians repeat the first petition of the Lord's prayer, "Thy kingdom come." The contrast is explicitly brought out by the final petition, "rescue us from the evil one" (Matthew 6:13). The contrast between divine and demonic power, including the fervent desire that the former will defeat the latter, is at the very heart of Christian faith.

The New Testament's Mythological but Realistic View of the Demonic

This contrast is certainly central to the New Testament. Although the authors of the various New Testament writings surely believed our world to be essentially good, because created by God, they shared Jesus's view that it at present was under demonic control. The Gospel of Luke, for example, has the devil say that the kingdoms of the world are under his control (4:5–6). The Gospel of John speaks of the devil as "the ruler of this world" (14:30, 16:11). The First Letter of John says that "the whole world is in the power of the evil one" (5:19). Paul speaks of "the present evil age" and of Satan as "the god of this age" (Galatians 1:4; 2 Corinthians 4:4). And the New Testament view of this matter—that the world is the scene of a deadly battle between the divine and the demonic—is the theme of the New Testament's final book in its entirety.

The New Testament, we can say, has a view of the demonic that is mythological but realistic. It is *mythological*, because it understands demonic power in terms of an individual creature with power, knowledge, and cosmic scope rivaling deity itself. Given the qualitative difference that must exist between the creator of the universe and any of its creatures, this view of the demonic must be regarded as mythological: No creature could approximate the omniscience, omnipresence, and unique power—power to create a universe—that belong to God alone.

And yet this picture is *realistic*, because it regards the demonic as a real power, with genuine autonomy, which is driving the world in a direction diametrically opposed to divine purposes.

Can we look at the past century of our world without thinking that the human race must be under the influence of such a power? The twentieth century was by far the bloodiest century in history, with unprecedented slaughter and genocide, and yet we have taken no steps to overcome the war-system of settling disputes. Americans created nuclear weapons and then, when we learned how deadly they are, built thousands more, until we had the world wired to be destroyed many times over. After we learned that a relatively modest exchange of nuclear weapons could initiate a "nuclear winter," leading to the death of human civilization and other higher forms of life, we still did not abolish them.

Furthermore, we learned over three decades ago that, even if nuclear war were avoided, the continuation of our present trajectory, with its increasing population and pollution—especially excessive carbon dioxide in the atmosphere and the ocean—would soon lead to extinction. But we have made no real efforts to change this trajectory. This has remained the case even after climate change turned out to be occurring much faster than predicted.

Although the scientific consensus is that we must turn from a carbon-based to a solar-based energy system, with the rich countries reducing their carbon emissions by 90%, and although the needed technologies are already available, the focus—especially in the United States, long the global leader in emitting carbon dioxide and other greenhouse gases[1]—has relied far too long on coal, oil, and natural gas.

We are, furthermore, highly educated, smart creatures. It does seem that we are possessed by some demonic power that is leading us, trance-like, into self-destruction. But is there any nonmythological way in which we can understand how this could be?

We could approach this question by looking more closely at the biblical idea of the relation between the divine and the demonic.

In the centuries prior to the New Testament period, the Hebrew tradition moved toward becoming thoroughly monotheistic (see Chapter 6): There is only one God, the creator of our world, who has acted in the history of Israel and that of other peoples and spoken through the prophets.

Monotheism is the doctrine that there is only one truly divine power—only one power worthy of worship. Monotheism does not, however, imply *monism*, the doctrine that there is only one power, period. Monotheism is compatible with the belief in one or more centers of power that have some power of their own, and hence some autonomy, *vis-à-vis* divine power. Because a partially autonomous power could go bad—using its power to oppose the divine purposes—monotheism could be compatible with belief in a demonic power.

In fact, Jeffrey Russell, in his well-received volumes on the history of the idea of the devil, has argued that the New Testament view is best called "semidualistic monotheism."[2] In contrast with full-fledged dualism, a semidualistic position does *not* hold, as would a fully dualistic position, that the demonic is fully autonomous and equal to God in cosmic scope and power. But it does allow some real autonomy to the demonic.

We can express this semidualism by saying that *the demonic is a creature and yet more than a creature*. To say that the demonic is a creature is to say that it, unlike the divine, does not exist necessarily and eternally but came about through the creative power of the divine. Once it has been created, however, it is not *merely* a creature, in the sense of being totally under the control of divine power. Rather, it can really oppose divine power and threaten its purposes. The demonic has potentially deadly consequences.

Something like this does seem to have been the view assumed in the New Testament. Such a view would, of course, presuppose that the creation has a degree of autonomy in relation to the creator. This was, as pointed out in Chapter 3, the view of the Hebrew scriptures, a view that was presupposed by New Testament writers. But in following centuries, after the adoption of the doctrine of *creatio ex nihilo*, the creatures, including Satan, had no independence vis-à-vis God.

A decisive figure in this development was St. Augustine, who at the beginning of the fifth century rigorously worked out the implications of the doctrine of creation out of nothing. His resulting doctrine of divine omnipotence required that all power belongs to God alone, so that nothing contrary to the divine will could happen. As quoted in Chapter 3, Augustine said that God "is called Almighty for no other reason than that he can do whatsoever he willeth and because the efficacy of his omnipotent will is not impeded by the will of any creature."[3] Moreover, Augustine said, "[God] does in the hearts of even wicked men whatsoever He wills."[4]

Popular Christianity at that time thought of the devil as in some sense independent of God and as hostile to God's purposes, carrying on a life-and-death battle of cosmic proportions. But within Augustine's theology, the devil could no more oppose God's will than could any other creature.

> By the power given to the devil [Augustine said with regard to Peter's denials], "he was tempted so that he might not think too highly of himself. . . . God himself. . .did all things justly by the power he gave to the devil.[5]

In this monistic theology, according to which all power belongs to God, the devil plays no essential role, being merely one more instrument through which the Sole Power unilaterally works its will.

This theology retains the mythological aspect of the New Testament's view of the demonic while giving up its realism. This view is mythological, to repeat, because it thinks of the demonic in terms of an individual creature who rivals God in cosmic scope, knowledge, and power. This view thereby attributes capacities to a creature that no creature could possibly have.

But this view loses the New Testament's realism by depriving the demonic power of any shred of autonomy, regarding Satan instead as wholly under the divine thumb. Because all power is said to be ultimately God's, the battle between God and the demonic is a mock battle, not a real one. The demonic is safely domesticated, brought within the household of God's instruments. Christians could be complacent.

A NEW VIEW OF DEMONIC POWER: REALISM WITHOUT MYTHOLOGY

Implicit in the foregoing historical overview of traditional thinking about the divine and the demonic is a constructive suggestion: If we return to the biblical idea of creation out of chaos, we can have a view of demonic power that overcomes the mythological character of the New Testament's view while retaining its realism. First, however, the very idea of the demonic needs discussion.

The Reintroduction of the Demonic

Thanks in large part to Paul Tillich, the symbol of *the demonic* became widely used in theology in the twentieth century. In 1963, Tillich said: "The symbol of the demonic does not need justification, as it did thirty years ago, when it was reintroduced into theological language."[6]

It was necessary for this symbol to be reintroduced because the Enlightenment had called for all mythological notions to be abolished, and the traditional notion of the demonic was certainly mythological. This symbol needed to be reintroduced because the entire rejection of the category of the demonic made religious thought in the eighteenth and nineteenth centuries overly optimistic: Because we are not really in the clutches of some demonic power, it was thought, we will be able to use reason to analyze the human mind and society, thereby bringing human civilization under control—just as natural science and technology had brought the natural world under control. But since the outbreak of World War I, this optimism has been in retreat. Perhaps the complete rejection of the idea of the demonic was premature.

As stated above, it seems that our political leaders are possessed by some demonic power that is leading them lemming-like into self-destruction. But can the way this occurred be understood without appeal to superhuman agency?

God, Creativity, and the World

One of Alfred North Whitehead's greatest gifts to theology, as discussed in the previous chapter, is his doctrine that the basic stuff of which the world (including human life) is made is creative energy, which he called simply "creativity." Besides being implied by Whitehead's view that our world was created out of chaos, this doctrine of creativity also turns out to provide a basis for a contemporary version of the semidualistic monotheism presupposed in the New Testament. It thereby provides the basis for a doctrine of demonic power as truly demonic—as really threatening to divine purposes.

Creativity, like Plato's unformed matter, never exists by itself. It exists only as embodied in actual beings. God is the primordial embodiment of creativity. Being primordial, God has always existed. Creative power, therefore, has always existed as embodied by God. Thus far, process theology is in agreement with traditional theology.

Process theology rejects, however, the traditional view that creative power is primordially embodied *only* in God. That view implied that God could completely control the creatures. The biblical tradition gave no clear answer to this question. On the one hand, there are passages suggesting that the creatures have no power *vis-à-vis* God, such as those passages saying that God molds human beings like a potter molds clay.[7]

On the other hand, the idea that the world was created out of primordial stuff left open the possibility, emphasized by Hermogenes and Jon Levenson (see Chapter 3), that the creatures, by virtue of embodying this primordial stuff, might have some power of their own with which they can resist the divine molding. The biblical tradition was, accordingly, ambiguous on this issue.

But this ambiguity was eliminated with the adoption of the doctrine of *creatio ex nihilo*. Monotheism became *monism*, according to which all creative power essentially belongs to God alone. If the creatures have any creative power, this is only because God has freely given them some. And, having been freely given, it could be withdrawn at any time. This is why traditional theists could be complacent about creaturely power, including demonic power.

In process theism, by contrast, creative power is primordially embodied in a world of finite beings as well as in God. This does *not* mean that our particular world has always existed. Whitehead's view, like Plato's, was that our particular world started coming into existence out of a primordial chaos, at a particular time in the past.

This view is now supported by scientific evidence, whether or not one accepts the currently dominant view, according to which, as mentioned in Chapter 2, our cosmos originated about 14 billion years ago.[8] The present idea of most cosmologists is that our world originated out of a vacuum, perhaps with a Big Bang. This view might seem to imply *creatio ex nihilo*. But the idea of a vacuum is really the idea of a condition in which, although there is no matter, there is tremendous energy.[9]

This view is similar to Whitehead's. Primordial chaos, in Whitehead's view, was a situation with creative energy but no matter. It was chaotic because the embodiments of creativity, or energy, were simply momentary events, each one lasting perhaps on the order of a billionth of a second. There were, as Carl Sagan would have said, billions of billions of billions of these events. But none of them were channeled into enduring structures. Besides no electrons or neutrinos, there were not even any enduring individuals as simple as quarks. There were, by hypothesis, simply very brief energy events happening at random. That is what Whitehead meant by "chaos."

Creation of Our Cosmos out of Relative Nothing

Given this idea, there is a sense in which creation out of nothing can be affirmed. When we speak of "things," we normally have in mind *enduring* things, which retain their identity over time, such as rocks, molecules, electrons, and protons. In this sense of the term, there were no *things* in the chaotic situation out of which God created our world. God, accordingly, created our world "out of no-thing."

Simply putting it that way, however, could cause confusion. This confusion can be avoided by using the phrase provided by Russian Orthodox theologian Nicholas Berdyaev. The Greek language, Berdyaev pointed out, has two terms for nothing: *ouk on*, which refers to *absolute* nonbeing, and *me on*, which refers to *relative* nonbeing. On this basis, Berdyaev, who had a view of creation somewhat like Whitehead's, affirmed creation out of *relative* nothing.[10] This doctrine affirms that everything of value in our world is due to God. Christian faith in God as creator—of the heavens and the earth, of life, and of human life—requires no stronger affirmation than this.

The rejection of the doctrine of creation out of *absolute* nothingness means that the creation of our world did not involve the beginning of finite existence as such. It involved, instead, God's bringing order out of chaos. Our world started coming into existence when, out of this chaos, God evoked the most primitive forms of order at the base of our particular world. Rather than all events happening at random, some of them came to be ordered into enduring strings of events, in which each event in the string repeated the form of its predecessors.

A more complex order emerged when these simplest enduring individuals, such as quarks and gluons, combined to form compound individuals, such as protons and neutrons. Then these in turn merged in various combinations to form more complex enduring individuals, such as atoms and molecules, then macromolecules, then living cells— first prokaryotic cells and then eukaryotic cells. Eukaryotic cells then led to multicellular organisms. And so on.

Self-Determination All the Way Down

This process of creation took a very long time, because God was not working with passive stuff, which could simply be manipulated. Rather, each enduring individual consists of a series of events, each of which has its own creativity, its own power. This creative power has two dimensions. It is, in the first place, the power of each event to respond to prior events with at least some iota of self-determination. We know of this responsive power from our own experience: In each moment, we are affected by all the events in our environment. But we decide just how to respond to them. For example, if a waiter accidentally spills scalding water on me, I will feel the pain; this is forced upon me. But I have the power to respond with either anger or understanding.

On the basis of this act of self-determination, I then exercise the second kind of creative power, which is usually simply called "causation." I cause my body to act in particular ways, so the waiter may hear me say "You stupid idiot!" Or, if I use my freedom differently, he may hear: "That's OK. I realize you didn't mean to do it."

Whitehead's doctrine that all individuals embody creativity means that at least some iota of responsive, self-determining creativity, as well as some degree of outgoing, causal creativity, is exercised by all events, even those in the primordial chaos. In other words, freedom, like the lady's turtles, goes all the way down.

Such a view would have been ridiculed in the nineteenth century, when science was heavily committed to a strict determinism. But since the discovery of quantum indeterminacy, this idea is not ruled out.[11] This idea is also supported by the microbiologists who discovered, as discussed in Chapter 2, that bacteria make decisions. Likewise, Nobel prize-winning chemist Robert S. Mullikan, who was known as "Mr. Molecule" because of his intimacy with this form of existence, once said that if molecules were as big as dogs, we would unhesitatingly attribute the power of decision-making to them.[12]

The idea that freedom goes all the way down might seem to be obviously false. There is surely no freedom in a rock or a pile of sand. But this apparent problem is avoided by the recognition, emphasized by Whitehead and Hartshorne, that low-grade individuals can be organized in two basic ways. On the one hand, they can form aggregational entities, such as rocks and mountains, in which there is no dominant center of activity to exercise self-determination.

On the other hand, low-grade individuals can form "compound individuals," such as living cells, which do have a dominant center of activity, through which the individual as a whole can act. The idea that some degree of freedom goes all the way down applies only to individuals (both simple and compound). This doctrine is not falsified, therefore, by the fact that things such as rocks and styrofoam cups have no freedom.[13]

Divine Power as Persuasive

The idea that our world was created out of actualities with some power of self-determination has theological implications. If God is the supreme, but never the only, embodiment of creative power, then power is always shared power. God never has a monopoly on power and hence can never unilaterally determine what will occur. Because the creativity embodied in finite beings is inherent, rather than freely bestowed, it cannot be withdrawn or overridden.

This view of shared power implies that divine power is persuasive, not coercive. God influences every finite event, but God cannot wholly determine how any event will use its own creativity and thereby its twofold power to exert self-determination and causal influence on others. Because living cells, viruses, bacteria, and DNA molecules have the twofold power to act with spontaneity and then to influence other things, for good or ill, we should not suppose that there is some level of the world that fully reflects the divine will—as if God for some mysterious reason wanted there to be cancer, AIDS, and genetically deformed babies.

Rather, as Plato suggested, our creator at each level brought about the best order that was possible. In emphasizing the importance of this point, Whitehead said that Plato's view—"that the divine element in the world is to be conceived as a persuasive agency and not as a coercive agency"—should be considered "one of the greatest intellectual discoveries in the history of religion."[14]

Creation as Risk

Another theological implication of this view of the God-world relation is that the creation of a cosmos with very complex compound individuals is necessarily a risky business. This is so because the higher the form of existence, the greater its power of self-determination, with which it can resist the divine preferences, and also the greater its power to influence others, for good or ill.[15] Although electrons, atoms, and molecules have some power of self-determination, this power is surely vanishingly small. During most of the history of our universe, therefore, the freedom in the creation would not have been great.[16]

The rise of living organisms, such as bacteria, would have been the first truly significant increase in the power of self-determination. But even the freedom of these prokaryotic cells was trivial in comparison with that of eukaryotic cells, which evidently emerged only a little over a billion years ago. Then about 550 million years ago, most of the basic life forms of today were created. This period, known as "biology's big bang," increased the freedom within the creation many times over.[17] The next major increase would have been the rise of the higher forms of mammals within the last 100 million years, especially the simians. Surely the greatest single increase in freedom, however, occurred when one line within the simians gave rise to human beings (homo sapiens).

This very recent event in the history of our planet was God's greatest gamble, because creativity as embodied in human beings had the potential to become qualitatively more destructive than any of the other species. Because of our unprecedented power of self-determination, we can make decisions that run strongly counter to the divine influences upon us, which are always calling us to truth, beauty, and goodness. Because of our unique ability to understand these divine norms, furthermore, our ability to deviate from the divine will is our power to sin.

Also, thanks to our distinctive minds, by means of which we can grasp and manipulate symbols, combined with our opposable thumbs, by means of which we can grasp and manipulate external things, we have far more ability to exert coercive power than any other creatures. Our power to sin is, accordingly, matched by an equally unprecedented power to dominate.

Our unprecedented power to influence other things is, moreover, not limited to coercion: Our linguistic power has given us an unprecedented form of persuasive power, a form of power that was greatly augmented with the invention of writing and, more recently, the technologies of mass communication. Because of the distinctive capacities of human beings, our emergence meant the rise of creatures who could, over time, come to exercise forms of power that could threaten the very purposes for which God created the world.

Divine Creativity and Creaturely Creativity

Whitehead's notion of creativity provides a basis for reconceiving demonic power. Creativity is embodied both in God and the world. Developing an idea of demonic power, however, requires that we distinguish clearly between these two embodiments.[18] We can make this distinction terminologically by calling creativity as embodied in God "divine creativity," and creativity as embodied in the world "creaturely creativity."

Although this distinction is implicit in Whitehead's thought, he did not emphasize it. He spoke simply of creativity, being intent on distinguishing it from God, because it was that distinction that explained creaturely freedom and thereby avoided the traditional problem of evil. Most of Whitehead's discussion of creativity, therefore, focused on creativity as embodied in creatures. He did make clear, nevertheless, that creativity is embodied in God as well, referring to God as the "aboriginal instance" and "primordial exemplification" of creativity.

Making this distinction is important because these embodiments are qualitatively different. In one sense, to be sure, creativity as embodied in God is the same as that embodied in creatures: It involves the twofold power to exert both self-determination and then causal influence on others. In other respects, however, divine and creaturely creativity are radically different from each other. For one thing, every creaturely embodiment of creativity is a local embodiment, which is significantly influenced by only a small portion of the universe and has significant influence back upon only a small portion. Creativity as embodied in God, by contrast, is universal, because the divine experience encompasses the whole universe. Likewise, creaturely creativity is always directed by limited knowledge, even in the most informed human beings, whereas divine creativity is always directed by omniscience, the knowledge of everything knowable at the time.[19]

Because of these metaphysical differences, divine creativity is *morally* different from creaturely creativity.

Divine Compassion

It is morally different in both of its dimensions. On the one hand, the responsive, self-determining creativity of God is always characterized by compassion for all sentient beings. The word "compassion," like its synonym "sympathy," literally means *feeling with*—feeling the others' feeling as one's own.

Jewish theologian Abraham Joshua Heschel, as pointed out in Chapter 5, argued that the God of the Bible, unlike the deity of some Greek philosophers, suffers with the sufferings of the people.[20] Building on Heschel, Marcus Borg emphasized the centrality of divine compassion in the message of Jesus.[21]

Process theology provides philosophical support for this view, saying that it belongs to the very nature of God to feel the feelings of the creatures as God's own feelings, so that God suffers with our sufferings and rejoices with our joys. The divine knowledge of the world, therefore, is not neutral. It is *sympathetic* knowledge. We can call this the *responsive love of God*.

To understand why God responds with sympathy or compassion for *all* sentient beings, even though humans do not, we can begin by reflecting on the fellow creatures to whom we most naturally *do* respond with sympathy. These are primarily the cells composing our own bodies. We have a natural sympathy for our bodily cells, feeling their pains and enjoyments as our own. This sympathy, moreover, extends equally to all parts of the body. A person would not, for example, take good care of one foot while deliberately causing pain to the other one. Nor do people have compassion for their feet while being indifferent to their hands. Given the fact that love in the most basic sense is being sympathetic with the feelings of others, feeling their feelings as one's own, we can say that a person has a natural and equal love for all parts of his or her body.

However, one's natural compassion for one's own bodily parts does not extend to the beings making up most of the rest of the world, at least not very strongly. One can remain pretty indifferent to most of them. One may have a deep sympathy, which is partly natural and partly developed through intimate association, for a few other creatures, such as one's family members, close friends, and pets. But for the most part, most people do not have strong natural sympathy or compassion for most of the life of the planet.

Some degree of compassion can, to be sure, be cultivated, perhaps by regarding all other creatures as, like oneself, sentient creatures loved by God, or perhaps through prayer or meditation. But this cultivated compassion will not lead people to feel the feelings of most other creatures with anything like the depth with which they feel the feelings of their own bodily members. As one honest man put it, he was more preoccupied with the discomfort caused by a hangnail than he was with the starvation of millions of people. Because we are very local beings, having a relation of direct sympathetic awareness of only, for the most, our own bodily members, we can be pretty indifferent to, or even take sadistic delight in, the sufferings of others.

God, however, is not a localized being, but the Omnipresent One. And as Charles Hartshorne emphasized, we should think of God as the soul of the world, related to the world as a whole in somewhat the same way we are related to our own bodies.[22] It is natural for God, therefore, to feel the feelings of all sentient beings with the kind of sympathetic, compassionate awareness with which we feel our own bodily cells.

For Christians, this idea should come naturally, given our acceptance of Jesus's sufferings on the cross as God's own sufferings. And insofar as we take Jesus as the supreme revelation of God, the cross becomes revelatory of how God responds to the sufferings of creatures in general. As Matthew 25 suggests, insofar as we bring either joy or suffering to "one of the least of these," we bring either joy or suffering to God.

In any case, we can say that God's responsive creativity is always informed by compassion for the experiences of all the creatures. Unlike us, God cannot love some while hating or being indifferent to others. God naturally—by nature—responds to all creatures with responsive love.

On the basis of that statement, one might ask whether God loves the demonic, which is a creature. The answer is No, because the statement that God loves all creatures refers to *individual* creatures, meaning those with experience and hence intrinsic value. Only they have feelings that can be felt with sympathy or compassion. But the demonic (by hypothesis) is not an individual, but a complex abstraction or structure (as discussed in the following chapter). It is a set of symbols, habits, dispositions, beliefs, values, and so on that inform the creativity of a society and thereby the individuals that make it up. God (by hypothesis) wants to overcome the demonic, because it is destructive of the experience of individual beings, whom God loves.

The importance of the idea that God loves all creatures can become clearer by looking at the argument of some philosophers who have suggested that God might not be perfectly loving. Henry David Aiken, arguing that "there is no logical connection between the metaphysical attributes [of God] and the moral attributes," added: "Logically, there is no reason why an . . . omniscient being might not be a perfect stinker." Likewise, P. H. Nowell-Smith said: "There is nothing in the idea of an . . . omniscient creator which, by itself, entails his goodness."[23]

Both of these philosophers contended, therefore, that from the idea of God's omniscience, which means having perfect knowledge of past and present beings, it does not follow that God would be perfect in goodness, having love for all sentient beings.

But for philosophers to say this is for them to ignore the kind of knowledge we have of our own bodies. Many people, perhaps especially philosophers, are inclined to think of our most basic kind of knowledge as that which we obtain through sense perception, as when we see a deer. It is true that knowledge of that type does not necessarily involve sympathy. The deer hunter can, therefore, pull the trigger on his rifle, wounding or killing the deer, without any remorse. By analogy from this kind of knowledge, Aiken and Nowell-Smith could infer that, although God knows everything happening in the world, God might not be compassionate.

But the knowledge we get through our eyes is a very indirect kind of knowledge, mediated first by trillions of photons, which carry information from the deer to the hunter's eye, then by billions of neurons, which mediate that information from his eyes to his brain, from which the hunter's conscious experience derives it. We cannot imagine that God's knowledge of the world is this indirect, highly mediated form of knowledge. Rather, if God is omnipresent, then God's knowledge must be more like the knowledge that hunters have of their own bodily cells, to which their experiences are directly connected. And this knowledge is, of course, highly sympathetic—as when a hunter accidentally shoots himself in the foot.

Given this more adequate understanding of knowledge, we can see that, contrary to Aiken and Nowell-Smith, the divine omniscience *does* imply the divine goodness. Or, to use the language of philosopher J. Brenton Stearns, we can say that (contrary to Stearns) God's "metaphysical eminence" *does* imply God's "moral eminence." Stearns argued that a "metaphysically supreme being" might be evil. But once we see that direct, immediate knowledge is always *sympathetic* knowledge, we can see that an omnipresent, omniscient being would necessarily have compassion for all sentient creatures.[24]

This difference between God and the creatures with regard to responsive creativity leads to a parallel moral difference in *outgoing* creativity. Because we can feel indifference or even hatred toward others, we can use our outgoing creativity—our creative influence on others—in ways that are not intended to promote their welfare. Indeed, we can use our power in order to inflict pain upon, or even destroy, them. But because of God's compassion for all creatures, God's influence on the world always aims to promote the good of all creatures. We can call this the *creative love of God.*

The doctrine that it belongs to the very nature of God to have creative and responsive love for all creatures—because the relation of God to the world as a whole is analogous to our relation to our own bodies—is process theology's way of explaining the New Testament's insight that God *is* love.

The resulting understanding provides another way (beyond what was discussed in Chapter 7) to understand God as trinitarian, with the three dimensions here being (a) the divine creativity, (b) the responsive love of God, and (c) the creative love of God. It does not make sense, however, to try to correlate these three dimensions of God with the language of Father, Son, and Holy Spirit (even apart from sexism in these terms). If language using personal terms is to be retained, it should be understood as a symbolic or metaphorical way to point to the fact that the divine use of power is necessarily and hence always characterized by universal compassion and active good will.

The Demonic

There is no one right way to understand the demonic. But in the present book, it is understood as having two characteristics. First, the demonic involves creaturely power that is exercised in a way that is diametrically opposed to divine purposes. Therefore, demonic power would involve *creaturely creativity that is exercised on the basis of greed, hate, or indifference, and therefore without the intent to promote the welfare of those affected by it.*

However, if this were the only characteristic of "the demonic," it would be equatable with "evil," or perhaps "terribly evil." But in this book, being diametrically opposed to divine creativity is only one of the two characteristics of "the "demonic." The other one is that creaturely creativity is *powerful enough to threaten divine purposes.* As discussed earlier, the rise of human beings introduced the potential for creaturely creativity to become this powerful.

CONCLUSION

This account provides a possible theoretical explanation of how demonic power is possible in a monotheistic universe. This position, to repeat, can be called semidualistic monotheism. It is not *fully* dualistic, because demonic power is not eternal. The demonic is a creature, which arose in time as a result of God's creative activity: If God had not stimulated the evolutionary process to bring forth human-like beings, demonic power would not exist. But God is not indictable for the fact that our world contains demonic power, because the possibility of the existence of demonic power could have been ruled out only by having no human-like beings whatsoever.

The demonic, as the Bible and Christian tradition have held, is a creature. Although the power out of which the demonic arose—creaturely creativity—is eternal, it is not inherently evil. It is neutral, capable of becoming either good or evil.

Process theology, therefore, agrees with Marcion that, contrary to Augustine, God's purposes can be truly threatened by a transhuman power. But process theology rejects Marcion's view that our world was created by an evil deity out of evil stuff, and also his view that demonic power is eternal. Many billions of years of evolution occurred in our universe and on our planet before demonic power arose. As Matthew Fox has emphasized, what has been called "original sin" is a latecomer in the universe.[25]

But this position, in contrast with monistic monotheism, is semi-dualistic, because it says that, once the demonic has emerged, it has its own power, so that it cannot be unilaterally controlled or eliminated by God. The battle between the divine and the demonic is, therefore, a *real* battle, with the outcome on our planet still undecided. One problem with the traditional doctrine of divine omnipotence is that it trivializes the notion of the demonic, by implying that there can be no such battle.

CHAPTER TEN

The Emergence
of the Demonic

THE IDEAS DEVELOPED in the previous chapter explain only how demonic power is *possible*. They do not explain why it actually arose. The potential for demonic power may have existed for an indefinitely long period without becoming realized. The precondition for it to emerge was the appearance of creatures having the human level of creativity, but it is unclear where that should be placed.

Modern humans (Homo sapiens) emerged about 500,000 years ago.[1]

Homo sapiens sapiens, which are fully human *anatomically,* emerged between 200,000 and 300,000 years ago.[2]

Homo sapiens sapiens that are also human *behaviorally*, with features such as language and music, emerged about 50,000 years ago.[3]

So whenever one dates the beginning of "the human level of creativity," it existed a long time before the rise of the demonic, which came into being very recently. Why did this finally happen? The answer lies, in great part, in the dynamic that has been called "the parable of the tribes."

THE PARABLE OF THE TRIBES

The phrase "parable of the tribes" is taken from the title of a book by Andrew Bard Schmookler.[4] The basic idea is that once the war-system arose, the various human societies—the various tribes—inevitably became locked in a competitive spiral that led not only to increasingly lethal technology but also to many correlative developments. The emergence of demonic power was part and parcel of this process.

The War-System

Schmookler's argument took off from the fact that the war-system began within the past 10,000 years, because it was closely related to the rise of civilization, with its cities and agriculture.[5] During the prior existence of human beings, when they supported themselves by hunting and gathering, human life was, to be sure, filled with human-caused evils of various sorts. Desires for revenge and other motives would have led tribes to carry out savage raids on each other from time to time. But the hunting-and-gathering mode of existence would have provided no motive to develop a war-system as such.

For example, captives, who could not be given enough freedom to share in the hunt, would have simply provided more mouths to feed. But the rise of civilization gradually changed all this. Slaves could be assigned the drudge work involved in agriculture and the building of walls and water canals. Women captives could, besides working in the homes and the fields, bear more children, in order to build up the city's defensive and offensive capacity. The cities, with their cultivated lands and their domesticated herds, provided additional targets for attack. The rise of civilization provided a precondition for the institutionalization of war.

Once the war-system began, everyone was forced to participate. Even if most societies wanted to be peaceful, any one society could force the rest to prepare for war, or else risk being subjugated or annihilated. As Schmookler wrote, "Nice guys are finished first."[6] Schmookler's perspective in many respects follows the classic analysis provided in the seventeenth century by Thomas Hobbes, which became the basis for the presently dominant approach to international relations called "political realism."

The State of Anarchy

According to the Hobbesian-Realist analysis, the interstate realm is a state of anarchy. The term *anarchy* is not used here in its popular sense, to mean a totally lawless, chaotic situation, but in its technical sense, to mean simply the absence of a superior power to regulate the behavior of the states to each other by enforcing rules based on moral norms. In an edited book entitled *The Perils of Anarchy,* Christopher Layne wrote:

> International politics is an anarchic, self-help realm. "Anarchy," rather than denoting chaos or rampant disorder, refers in international politics to the fact that there is no central authority capable of making and enforcing rules of behavior on the international system's units (states).[7]

In other words, in this anarchical situation, it is simply power—not power qualified by moral principles—that determines the relations between the tribes. The classic formulation was provided by Thucydides, who has the Athenian general give other peoples only this choice: Do you want to be taken over peacefully or violently? The general added that, if the other peoples had the superior power, they would do the same to the Athenians.

Anarchy, according to this Hobbesian-Realist analysis,[8] means "the war of all against all." The point is not that you actually fight against everyone else, but that every other society is at least potentially your enemy, and that there is no overarching power to protect you. It is a "self-help" world.[9]

War is brought on not only by the desire of one society's leaders for additional power, riches, and glory. It can be brought on simply by one society's fear that another society is amassing enough military power to attack it. Thucydides again provides the classic statement, having his general say with regard to taking Sicily: "If we cease to rule others, we are in danger of being ruled ourselves."[10]

It is important to understand that the doctrine of political realism, strictly speaking, is limited to this analysis, with its twofold point: (1) that the present world order is anarchical; (2) this fact makes power the determining factor in international relations. For example, the editors of *The Perils of Anarchy* gave this summary statement of the position of political realists:

> [R]ealists regard anarchy—the absence of any common sovereign—as the distinguishing feature of international life. Without a central authority to enforce agreements or to guarantee security, states must rely on their own means to protect their interests.[11]

Most realists, however, go beyond this descriptive analysis to include a prediction: that this is not only the way the international situation has always been but also the way it always will be. These realists, in other words, believe that it is an aspect of realism to hold that it would be impossible to overcome anarchy through the creation of a global government.

They do recognize, to be sure, that a *de facto* global government might be created by a sufficiently strong imperial power, which could simply impose its own rule on the rest of the world. But they reject as unrealistic the idea that anarchy could be overcome by the free decision of the states or peoples of the world to create a global democratic government. Those who hold otherwise are dismissed as "utopians."

However, even though the political realists who add this prediction about the future have been in the majority, this prediction does not belong to political realism as such. That this is so can be seen from the fact that there have been political scientists and political philosophers who completely accept the realist analysis while calling for the creation of a global government.

The Selection for Power

The next crucial point of Schmookler's analysis is that, in the present anarchical state of civilization, coercive power inevitably grows. Two examples will be given in Chapter 16. A new offensive weapon created by one tribe forces the other tribes to create new defenses against it. These defensive advances then lead to new offensive weapons, and so on.

Likewise, each technological advance by one tribe will soon spread to the other tribes within striking distance. Once this occurs, the advance no longer gives the first tribe an advantage, so it is impelled to develop still more deadly weapons. For example, after the United States created atomic bombs in 1945, the Soviet Union created its own by 1949; then in 1952, the United States created a hydrogen (thermonuclear) bomb, and the Soviets had their own thermonuclear bomb by 1953 (see Chapter 13).

Furthermore, a move that may be intended defensively will often look offensive to others, evoking further efforts by them to increase *their* power. And there is no stopping point. Although the development of nuclear weapons might have occurred considerably later than it actually did, the fact that it did eventually occur was made virtually inevitable by the dynamics of the system, given the facts about physics and geology. Even the creation of this seemingly ultimate weapon did not slow down the drive to invent more weapons to get an edge over potential enemies, as illustrated by the drive to weaponize space and create a "nuclear shield."

The development of ever greater coercive power does not, however, involve only the creation of new forms of weapons and defenses. The most obvious additional element is military strategy and tactics, to which a major portion of any history of warfare is devoted. But a society's ability to wage war is also to a great extent a function of its political and economic systems. Any development that gives a society a temporary military edge will tend to spread to the neighboring societies. For example, the success of an early form of capitalism in the Italian city-states in the fourteenth century gave them an edge over their rivals, because they had more money to buy weapons and pay their troops. Accordingly, this early form of capitalism soon spread to other countries.

The main point of this analysis is that the evolution of civilization in the state of anarchy is necessarily shaped in large part by a principle similar to that of natural selection in Darwinian evolution, according to which only the fit survive. Schmookler called this principle the "selection for power." This analysis is not reductionistic, as if the drive for power were at the root of all cultural developments. The point is, instead, that of those developments that do occur, those that increase a society's power *vis-à-vis* other societies will tend not only to survive but also to spread.

In the long run, the direction of civilization has been shaped decisively by this selection for power. And, as civilization evolves, the need for power increasingly shapes every aspect of a society. In recent decades, for example, something like half of America's science has been devoted to military-related research. Anarchical civilization, with its war-system, results in a reign of power.

Implicit in this analysis is the idea that the reign of power in the realm *between* the states leads to the reign of power *within* each state. This is not to say that the rise of hierarchical, domination societies, historically associated with the rise of patriarchy, was motivated entirely or even primarily by the demands of the war-system. That interstate system did, however, provide the context in which hierarchical societies were virtually inevitable. As Gerda Lerner pointed out in her study *The Creation of Patriarchy*, nonhierarchical societies for the most part simply did not survive.[12]

It is hard, furthermore, to argue with the claim that survival must take priority over all other considerations. But the argument from "necessity" in relation to external dangers has provided, probably from the outset of the war-system, an excuse for the worst kinds of internal inequities. The war-system has also provided an ever-increasing basis for the human domination of nature.

Increasing Domination by the Demonic

It is through this process, only briefly sketched here, that demonic power, which the rise of human existence made possible, actually came to dominance on our planet. In recent millenia, human civilization has increasingly been oriented around the drive to increase human power, in the sense of the power to control, the power to destroy, the power to intimidate. Human beings in this context have wanted more power over nature, in order to increase their power over other human groups, in order to give them more power over nature, and on and on. Civilization has been significantly shaped by the drive to produce coercive power, which could be used with greed and hate, or at least indifference. Since the rise of civilization, it has increasingly been in the grip of this drive for domination.

Although the evolution of this dominance involved a step-by-step process, rather big steps occurred now and then, when significantly new inventions, ideologies, and institutions emerged. One of the first great increases in coercive power occurred in the Bronze Age, some 6,000 years ago. The next big jump evidently occurred near the outset of the Iron Age, about 3,000 years ago, with the rise not only of empires but also of patriarchy and androcentric belief systems. It is, indeed, only here, when ideology became a central dimension of the parable of the tribes, that civilization irreversibly headed toward domination by demonic power.

In that respect, two fateful developments were the marriage of Christian theology with Graeco-Roman forms of thought, which occurred in the early centuries of Christianity's existence, and the Constantinian exploitation of the resulting theology for imperialistic purposes in the fourth century. Subsequent crucial preconditions for the rise to global dominance of the demonic were the market economy, European colonization of the globe, ideologies of nationalism and capitalism, Social Darwinism, and the Industrial Revolution, which was based on the unprecedented exploitation of fossil fuels.

The grip of demonic power on our planet was further increased in the twentieth century by a number of developments, including Marxism-Leninism, Fascism, *Realpolitik,* the two world wars, the creation of nuclear weapons, and American and Soviet imperialism.

Due to these and other developments and the consequences thereof, the demonic's domination of the planet, both in extent and intensity, now dwarfs that of its incarnation in the Roman Empire, the effects of which New Testament writers had observed. Divine values, which as incarnated would lead to a peaceable, sustainable form of existence, are increasingly overridden by demonic values, which lead to greater warfare against each other and the rest of the earth.

If this warfare continues, the creator's hopes for this planet, which in principle could support the harmonious and joyous flourishing of human beings and other forms of life far into the future, God's experiment with human beings could come to a grossly premature end. This would be, we can only suppose, one of the supreme tragedies of the universe.

We do not, of course, have to imagine this future tragedy in order to speak of divine purposes being threatened and even thwarted by demonic power. In looking back at human history from the time of the Bronze Age forward, the violations of our creator's will—that we have life and have it abundantly—have been massive. Hegel was not wrong to call this history a *slaughter bench*.[13]

Hegel's view was that, as tragic as this history was, it was inevitable. We need not accept Hegel's rather monistic, pantheistic view of the relation between the divine and the human spirit to see an element of truth in his opinion. Given creaturely freedom, the trajectory of human civilization could have been enormously different. But the parable of the tribes suggests that, in broadest terms, our present crisis would have come about, sooner or later, in one way or another, as long as human beings do not understand what has been going on.

What is not inevitable, however, is that we continue to acquiesce in the trajectory that has brought us to this point. Now that we have the ability to understand what has happened, we could make the decision to break free from the parable-of-the-tribes trajectory.

DEMONIC POWER

Given the above sketch of an explanation of how demonic power is possible in a monotheistic universe, plus an account of how it arose historically, the notion of the demonic can be fleshed out more fully. This fleshing-out can begin with the idea that the demonic involves an objective symbolic structure, which presupposes the idea, discussed previously, that creativity as embodied in humans is capable of becoming demonic because of our linguistic power.

The Demonic as Objective Symbolic Structure

This dimension of the demonic can be approached through a suggestion made by theologian Arthur McGill. Much discussion of human evil has suggested a voluntaristic and individualistic understanding of sin, according to which it is perversity of will originating from within the individual human being. McGill, by contrast, pointed out that sin is understood in the New Testament as a state of subjugation to destructive, enslaving powers that seem to come "from beyond all human agency."[14] The most complete statement of the demonic as referring to transhuman powers occurs in Ephesians 6:11-12 (NKJV):

> Put on the whole armor of God, that you may be able to stand against the wiles of the devil. For we do not wrestle against flesh and blood, but against principalities, against the rulers of the darkness of this age, against the spiritual hosts of wickedness in the heavenly places.

This passage reflects the conviction that the world, though created by God, is presently under virtual enslavement to demonic power. This picture also seems true of our contemporary world, apparently rushing towards mass suicide in a hypnotic trance. Our battle seems to be against "blood and flesh" less than against some demonic power to which human civilization is in bondage. The demonic, therefore, is not simply the destructive use by humans of their tremendous powers out of greed, hate, or indifference, but some objective, transhuman power that leads us to embody these attitudes and act in these ways.

Helpful in understanding the nature of this transhuman power was cultural theorist Ernest Becker, who offered this naturalistic account of the demonic's emergence:

> The Demonic has a naturalistic basis. It comes into being on the basis of a real evolutionary development: man is the animal in nature who, par excellence, can create vast

structures of power by means of his symbolic manipulation of the world of energy.[15]

Although Becker was correct to focus on the "symbolic manipulation of the world of energy," equally important are the vast structures of power based on the symbolic control of the world of human experience itself. We all live largely in terms of the symbolic world provided by the culture in which we are raised. Our psychic energy is largely channeled by this inherited symbolic world. Accordingly, the demonic can largely be understood as *symbolic structures that channel human creativity toward destructive activities based on greed, hate, and/or indifference.*

Our understanding of the effects of this symbol system can be aided by McGill's description of two ways in which the demonic has been understood to work:

> Sometimes it crushes and violates with overwhelming force. . . . In this mode the demonic is represented as a giant or a dragon, full of brutally destructive violence. At other times the demonic is experienced as securing its mastery over human beings, not by brute force, but by subtle insinuation. . . seducing people to give themselves over into its power. In this mode the demonic is presented as a wily serpent taking on the appearance of a lovely woman or handsome man, manipulating and enslaving the human ego by means of enticing forms.[16]

If this second form is literalized, the demonic involves the sexual. However, if we interpret the demonic out of our contemporary situation and the New Testament, we will see this side of the demonic as the seduction to resort to destruction in the name of achieving good. Rather than having two forms, the demonic has two moments. Human destructiveness has become demonic, but an essential component of this demonic destructiveness is the whole symbolic framework of myths, images, beliefs, ideologies, traditions, and habits that seduce us to employ our power destructively.

The myths, images, and beliefs in the demonic cluster of symbolic structures contain a wide variety of ingredients, such as ideas of what it means to be a "man"; stories and myths of deliverance and regeneration through violence; ideas of superior and inferior peoples; notions of tribal pride; images of fulfillment through power, glory, and riches; stories and statues, even in churches, glorifying military heroes; national flags and anthems; religious scriptures or interpretations of them that provide divine sanction for military conquest and the domination of nature; interpretations of the universe implying that ultimate success and security come through coercive power; economic theories mandating the destruction of nature and traditional cultures for the sake of prosperity; and on and on. This cluster of symbolic structures can become an objective power by being incarnated in institutions, in public and private documents, in public and private habits, and now in the mass media.

The Demonic as the Quasi-Soul of a Culture

Although the previous elements descriptive of the demonic are essential, they do not explain why demonic power is so massive, why it appears to radiate from some all-pervasive demonic spirit, infiltrating every aspect of our lives and penetrating every dimension of our psyches. If the mythological idea of such a spirit is rejected and demonic power is instead understood entirely in terms of human agency, how are we to explain its seeming to radiate from a ubiquitous, transhuman source? The explanation could be found in the idea that a nation or culture can have a demonic soul.

It is important to be clear what is *not* implied by this idea. Human beings and other animals are genuine individuals, because out of the organization of cells emerges a series of dominant experiences, which we call the mind or soul. The idea that a nation or a culture has a soul might be taken to mean that, out of a cohesive organization of human beings, a higher-level series of experience emerges, constituting the literal soul of that nation or culture, thereby turning that nation or culture into a true individual. But there is no soul of a nation or a culture in this literal sense.

The idea of a national or cultural soul need not, however, be entirely metaphorical. We can say, instead, that a nation or culture has a *quasi*-soul. The meaning of this idea can be approached by reflecting upon the kind of unity possessed by a living plant. Unlike an animal, a plant has no *anima*, no dominating soul to make it a genuine individual. And yet every cell in the plant is what it is partly because it is part of that plant. Each cell is partly constituted by its relations to the other members of that plant. The identity of each cell is, therefore, significantly constituted by patterns pervasive of the whole plant. Although the plant does not have a literal soul, it has a quasi-soul—a pattern of interactions that acts to some extent as if it were a soul that informs all its members.[17]

By analogy, and in a more complex sense, we can speak of the quasi-soul of a nation. Because we are all internally related to each other, we enter into and help constitute each others' souls. Insofar as a nation has a set of shared symbols, memories, myths, ideologies, and habits that are often and widely rehearsed, these shared elements are reinforced through this repetition. These shared elements, constituting a quasi-soul, are closely related to Carl Jung's *archetypes*, of which he said:

> There are as many archetypes as there are typical situations in life. Endless repetition has engraved these experiences into our psychic constitution, not in the forms of images filled with content, but at first only as *forms without content*, representing merely the possibility of a certain type of perception and action.[18]

The quasi-soul of a nation is constituted only by those elements that are shared by most of its members, at least most of its dominant members, not the elements that are idiosyncratic to individuals or restricted communities. Of course, elements that were originally idiosyncratic to some individual or group can enter into the national quasi-soul, thereby changing it, but only by no longer being idiosyncratic. This process can now occur quite rapidly, thanks to the rise of the mass media.

Because this national quasi-soul is not a genuine soul, there is no unified national experience, in a literal sense, and no capacity for the nation to act as a unity. The quasi-soul of a nation is, nevertheless, objective to each of its members, confronting each of them with a pervasive set of beliefs, values, habits, mannerisms, and symbols. Most individuals make only a tiny contribution to the national quasi-soul, but this quasi-soul typically makes a massive contribution to each individual.

Only the individual soul has concrete existence and thereby intrinsic value; the notion of a national quasi-soul provides no justification for subordinating the individual to the nation. But the causal power of the national quasi-soul dwarfs that of the individual soul, because this quasi-soul is constituted by the causal power of millions or billions of individuals, including those of past generations whose present effects are mediated not only through their objective symbolic products but also through members of the present generation.

This point provides a basis for a reconciliation of McGill's description, according to which the demonic is experienced as coming from transhuman agency, with the explanation of the demonic in terms of human agency. Insofar as the national quasi-soul is constituted by constantly repeated beliefs, images, symbols, and values that encourage us to use our awesome powers with greed, hate, and/or indifference, the national quasi-soul can contribute to the demonic.

The individuals whose souls are formed in that society will tend to be ready servants of demonic evil. Insofar as they remain subject to this pattern, their contribution back to the national quasi-soul will reinforce its demonic character, so that it will exert its influence undiminished, even strengthened, on the next generation of its members.

Although this discussion has thus far been carried out in terms of a quasi-soul of a nation, in the sense of a *country*, it is more true that it is a *culture* that is constituted by shared memories, stories, ideologies, beliefs, images, symbols, values, and habits, and a culture may or may not be coterminous with a country. On the one hand, a country may embody two or more cultures. On the other hand, a culture may be largely common to two or more countries. For example, although their political structures and histories differ, England, the United States, and other Anglo-Saxon countries have to a considerable extent a shared culture, so that one could speak of an Anglo-Saxon quasi-soul.

Likewise, although the various nations of Europe are very different in many ways, with (for example) the quasi-soul of Germany being very different from that of France, Italy, and Great Britain, we can also speak of a European quasi-soul, although it exists at a more abstract level and has a far more tenuous hold on its members than do the quasi-souls of their more immediate cultures. The power of a quasi-soul at any level depends upon the intensity of memories, beliefs, myths, symbols, attitudes, emotions, and habits that constitute it. The degree to which a cultural quasi-soul is demonic depends upon the content of those beliefs, myths, and so on. Children in some cultures inherit more bellicose souls than do children in other cultures.

Ideological Selection

Because the power of a society is determined partly by its ideology, the selection for power operates with regard to it as well as the other determinants of its power.[19] Accordingly, we should expect that, as long as the parable of the tribes continues, the history of civilization's ideologies will involve the gradual ascendancy of those that are most effective in producing a warrior-mentality and thereby a warrior-society.

An effective ideology of power may, for example, lead people to believe that by being warriors they are obeying the will of, and even imitating the behavior of—the deity of the universe; it may lead them to believe that by dying in the service of this deity, they will be especially rewarded; it may lead them to hate, or at least be indifferent to, the welfare of people in other societies; it may convince them that they are a chosen people, so that by subjugating others they are actually bringing about divine rule on earth; and so on.

Within the framework of the parable of the tribes, an effective ideology of power will tend to promote political and economic systems that increase a society's military capacity; it will also tend to produce philosophies, sciences, and technologies through which nature can be effectively dominated. The growth of such ideologies of power has been an intricate part—in many ways the most important part—of the growth of demonic power over the past few thousand years.

Walter Rauschenbusch, in his great book *A Theology for the Social Gospel*, emphasized this psychical or spiritual dimension of what he called "the kingdom of evil." Pointing to the structures and habits of modern society that promote sin, Rauschenbusch showed how people are seduced into sin, through the power of authority and imitation, from very young ages.[20]

By providing this nonmythical way to understand the traditional view that people are led into sin by "supra-personal forces of evil," Rauschenbusch made a valuable contribution to the rediscovery of the reality of demonic power.

By discussing the "supra-personal forces of evil" and the "kingdom of evil," Rauschenbusch provided a way to understand the idea of "original sin." As many theologians have said, it should really be called "originating sin," because it is a disposition to feel and act in ways to which the term "sin" is usually applied.

But even the term "originating sin" is problematic, insofar as people tend to think of sin as something for which the individual is primarily responsible. But insofar as children are born into cultures that have more or less demonic quasi-souls, their own souls will be shaped by these beliefs, images, attitudes, and feelings long before they have reached the age of accountability.

There is, to be sure, always at least a slight degree of freedom, even at the youngest age. But at this age the freedom is too slight to be made the focus of attention, as the term "sin" does. By speaking instead of "the demonic," we can better convey the idea of a power to which people are subjugated and from which they need help if they are to break free.

This demonic power is now, even more completely than in New Testament times, in effective control of the trajectory of civilization. This control is now so complete that, although we are on the verge of destroying human civilization and much of the rest of the planet's advanced forms of life, our leaders are, rather than changing course, actively fanning the flames of conflict.

The trajectory through which demonic control of civilization has grown has run primarily through the history of empire. Two thousand years ago, that trajectory was most strongly embodied in the Roman Empire. Although Rome saw itself as divinely authorized, the authors of the New Testament saw it as the ultimate embodiment of the demonic. For example, the Book or Revelation, pointed out Marcus Borg, used the ten-horned beast from the sea, which rules the world and demands worship, to symbolize Rome. The book also described Rome as "the great whore," and Babylon the Great. Finally, the number of the beast is "666," and "[u]sing the rules of *gematria*, the number 666 decodes into 'Caesar Nero.'"[21]

Today, the trajectory of empire is primarily embodied in the United States, which, as pointed out earlier, has an empire that dwarfs Rome's in both power and reach. Whereas it presents itself as divinely led—even if in secular dress—an increasing numbers of the world's people see it as more demonic than divine.[22]

A Way Out?

The condition that gave rise to the war-system and hence imperialism, and that also allowed them to continue, Schmookler emphasized, is the anarchical state of civilization. Like many other thinkers, he argued that the spiral of violence will be overcome only when civilizational anarchy has been overcome by a global government.

There are two paths through which such a government could be created. One path would be for the peoples of the world to form a global democracy. The other path would be for one country to become the de facto government of the world. The United States, which since its inception has been increasing the scope of its empire, has since the end of the Cold War, and especially since 9/11, been seeking to use its military superiority to move closer to that goal. The ideology of the neoconservatives says that a truly global American Empire, a *Pax Americana*, would be a good thing for the world, not only by bringing universal peace by bringing the reign of anarchy to an end, but also by bringing about regimes around the world that are committed to freedom, democracy, and human rights.

In its most extreme form, this ideology has promised that American rule will bring "an end to evil."[23] That apocalyptic notion suggests, of course, that a global empire run by America would be an approximation of the reign of God on earth desired by Christians, Jews, and Muslims.

CONCLUSION

The next two chapters discuss the fact that the American Empire, with its movement toward becoming all-inclusive, *is not moving toward* an approximation of a reign of God on earth. It has instead been a demonic empire.

CHAPTER ELEVEN

The American Empire: Divine or Demonic?

WHEREAS Chapters 9 and 10 discussed the demonic abstractly, the present chapter begins a discussion of demonic power as illustrated by the American Empire.

As discussed in Chapter 6, the Roman Empire claimed that it was divinely authorized and even that its emperor was divine. But the methods it used to create and maintain its empire were far from godly: It deployed overwhelming military power to spread and maintain its empire. It used terror, or simply the threat of terror, to intimidate its subjects and enemies. It ruled other peoples through puppets backed up by its pervasive military presence. And it collected exorbitant taxes to enrich its center and finance its imperial rule, thereby impoverishing its subjects.

Maintaining the primacy of the empire was the supreme value. The empire's subjects, such as the peasants of Galilee, had value only insofar as they served this primacy. From the perspective of the empire, the values taught by the prophets of Israel as divine values—justice, mercy, compassion for the poor—were nonvalues. The empire, being the embodiment of divinity, was the true measure of value. From the biblical point of view, however, the empire was the chief embodiment of demonic values: Besides flagrantly and massively violating the truly divine values, it was idolatrous, claiming that its emperor, with his perverted system of values, was divine and hence deserved the people's ultimate loyalty.

The present chapter asks whether this evaluation of the Roman Empire by Jesus and early Christians applies today to the American Empire. Or is America the exception to the general rule, having created a benign and even benevolent empire, which can be regarded as furthering the divine purposes for the world?

THE DRIVE FOR A UNIVERSAL EMPIRE

There have been various ways in which Americans in earlier centuries expressed the view that their empire-in-the-making was divinely authorized. One of these ways was to refer to America as the "new Israel."[1] But the phrase that really caught on was "manifest destiny," which John O'Sullivan coined in 1845 to signify the mission of the United States "to overspread the continent allotted by Providence for the free development of our yearly multiplying millions."[2] In 1850, the idea that this destiny was to create a universal empire was expressed by an editor in New Orleans named James Debow in the following words:

> We have a destiny to perform, a 'manifest destiny' over all Mexico, over South America, over the West Indies and Canada. The Sandwich [Hawaiian] Islands are as necessary to our eastern, as the isles of the gulf to our western commerce. The gates of the Chinese empire must be thrown down ... and the haughty Japanese tramplers upon the cross be enlightened in the doctrines of republicanism.... The eagle of the republic shall poise itself over the field of Waterloo, after tracing its flight among the gorges of the Himalaya or the Ural mountains, and a successor of Washington ascend the chair of universal empire![3]

Such ideas were, in fact, expressed from almost the founding of the United States. David Humphreys, a protégé of George Washington's, wrote in a poem:

Our constitutions form'd on freedom's base,
Which all the blessings of all lands embrace;
Embrace humanity's extended cause,
A world of our empire, for a world of our laws.[4]

But this kind of talk, common in the eighteenth and nineteenth centuries, was heard much less in the twentieth century. Early in that century, "imperialism" took on negative connotations, so it became taboo in respectable circles to speak of "American imperialism" and the "American empire." These terms were, for the most part, said American military historian Andrew Bacevich, used only by left-wing critics of American foreign policy.[5] There were, however, a few exceptions.

PRAISE OF THE AMERICAN EMPIRE

One of these exceptions was Ronald Steel, who in 1967 published a book entitled *Pax Americana*. Writing as the criticism of the Vietnam War was heating up, Steel acknowledged that "by any conventional standards for judging such things," America is "an imperial power," having an empire "the scope of which the world has never seen."[6]

However, Steel argued, "America has been engaged in a kind of welfare imperialism, empire building for noble ends rather than for such base motives as profit and influence"—the chief noble end being "permitting other nations to enjoy the benefits of freedom, democracy, and self-determination."[7] When America intervenes, Steel said, it does so with "the most noble motives and with the most generous impulses."

Steel later recanted this view.[8] But his previous position became one of the central points in the promotion by neoconservatives of a truly global American empire.

Journalist Charles Krauthammer of the *Washington Post* was one of the earliest ones to start trumpeting this theme. In a 1991 essay, he said that although "historically, the world recoils at the thought of a single dominant power for fear of what it will do with its power...America is the exception to this rule," because "the world generally sees it as benign"—as a power that "acts not just out of self-interest but a sense of right."[9] In that same year, fellow neocon Ben Wattenberg, in a book entitled *The First Universal Nation*, wrote:

> The American empire is not like earlier European imperialisms. We have sought neither wealth nor territory. Ours is an imperium of values.[10]

In 1996, arch-neocons William Kristol and Robert Kagan, arguing that America needed a foreign policy that did not bore Americans, proposed a policy of "benevolent global hegemony." This proposal was not unrealistic, they assured their readers, because America's moral ideals and its vital interests are "almost always in harmony."[11]

In 1998, Kagan developed this notion further in an essay entitled "The Benevolent Empire." Saying that "the benevolent hegemony exercised by the United States is good for a vast portion of the world's population," Kagan argued that this is no surprise:

> Ever since the United States emerged as a great power, the identification of the interests of others with its own has been the most striking quality of American foreign and defense policy.[12]

In 2002, Krauthammer took up the theme again, saying that America's claim to being a benign power is not mere "self-congratulation" but is verified by its "track record."[13] Dinesh D'Souza, in that same year, described America as "the most magnanimous imperial power ever."[14]

Max Boot, in an essay published in May 2003 after America's apparently easy victory in Iraq, argued that America's primary foreign policy goal should now be to preserve and extend what Krauthammer had called "the unipolar moment." Saying that "[t]hat moment has now stretched into a decade and shows no sign of waning," Boot asked why the general rule that "any hegemon will call into being an opposing coalition . . . hasn't happened to America." The answer is obvious, he said:

> America isn't like the empires of old. It does not seek to enslave other peoples and steal their lands. It spreads freedom and opportunity.[15]

The war in Iraq, Boot added, should be seen as simply one important step "in a larger campaign to make the world safe for democracy."[16]

This idea—that the purpose of the American empire is to bring about democracy globally—was a central theme of most neocons. In 1991, Joshua Muravchik published a book entitled *Exporting Democracy: Fulfilling America's Mission*. Ben Wattenberg wrote: "Americans have a missionary streak, and democracy is our mission."[17] For most neocons, theological ethicist Gary Dorrien pointed out critically, "the crusade for world democracy and the struggle to preserve America's unipolar dominance were the same thing."[18]

The idea that America is in the business of spreading freedom and democracy, and thereby serving a universal cause, was often articulated by President George W. Bush. His address to the nation on September 7, 2003, closed with these words: "We are serving in freedom's cause—and that is the cause of all mankind."[19] In his State of the Union address earlier that year, Bush explicitly declared this cause also to be God's cause, saying: "The liberty we prize is not America's gift to the world; it is God's gift to humanity."[20] In the inaugural address at the outset of his second term, Bush said that "it is the policy of the United States to seek and support the growth of democratic movements and institutions in every nation and culture."[21] The next day, Krauthammer wrote: "The great project of the Bush administration [is] the strengthening and spread of democracy."[22]

American Exceptionalism

The favored way for secular Americans to brag about their country has long been the description of it as the *exceptional* nation. For awhile, the disastrous Vietnam War seemed to destroy the America-is-the-greatest-nation-in-the-world version of American Exceptionalism. In 1975 sociologist Daniel Bell wrote:

> Today, the belief in American exceptionalism has vanished with the end of empire.... The American Century foundered on the shoals of Vietnam.... There is no longer a Manifest Destiny of mission. We have not been immune to the

corruption of power. We have not been the exception.... We are a nation like all other nations.[23]

However, said *Newsweek*, "the belief in exceptionalism came roaring back with Ronald Reagan's 'shining city on a hill' in the 1980s."[24] The twentieth century closed with American Exceptionalism being alive and well.

But then the Iraq War did to this myth the same thing the Vietnam War had done earlier. Besides leading to a great increase in anti-Americanism around the world,[25] the Iraq War led many Americans to reject the idea that America is exceptional in a positive sense. However, there are Americans for whom American Exceptionalism in the self-congratulatory sense is still endorsed as strongly as before. One of those was former Vice President Dick Cheney (who was primarily responsible for the Iraq War[26]).

In 2015, Cheney and his daughter Liz Cheney co-authored a book entitled *Exceptional,* which began by asserting, "Yes, We Are Exceptional." Spelling out their self-praising beliefs, the Cheneys wrote:

> We have guaranteed freedom, security, and peace for a larger share of humanity than has any other nation in all of history. There is no other like us. ... We are, as a matter of empirical fact and undeniable history, the greatest force for good the world has even known.[27]

Our children need to know, they continued, "that they are citizens of the most powerful, good, and honorable nation in the history of mankind, *the* exceptional nation."[28] In particular, the Cheneys bragged:

> [W]e have been the last, best hope of earth because we are freedom's defender, not just for ourselves, but also for millions around the world. We do it because it is right. ... No nation has ever worked so successfully to extend freedom to others.[29]

In sum, the neocons and President Bush, reinvigorating rhetoric from an earlier time, argued that, because of America's wonderfulness, the emergence of an all-inclusive empire under American leadership would be the best possible result for the world. This claim was implicit in the subtitle of the book by the Cheneys, *Why the World Needs a Powerful America.*

Insofar as religious language is used, the American empire can be described, according to this view, as not only benign but also divine, in the sense that it is being used by God to bring divine values, especially freedom, to the whole world. Unlike other empires, from this perspective, America can be trusted with sufficient power to bring these values to other peoples by force, if necessary, because there is no conflict between American interests and its ideals: Its primary interest is to spread these ideals.

Contrary Views by Erstwhile Believers

During the Cold War, Andrew Bacevich confessed, he had assumed that American foreign policy was actually guided by its stated objectives, which were "quite limited—to protect our homeland, to preserve our values, to defend our closest allies." However, after the Cold War ended, Bacevich saw that America did not greatly decrease its military spending, weapons systems, and overseas bases. This fact led him to examine the historical evidence again. On the basis of this examination, he decided that some left-wing critics of American foreign policy, such as Charles Beard and William Appleman Williams, had been basically right all along.[30]

Bacevich then began criticizing the neocon claims. Krauthammer, as we saw, said that America's claim to be a benign empire is supported by its "track record." But Bacevich, having re-examined this track record, rejected the claim "that the promotion of peace, democracy, and human rights and the punishment of evil-doers—not the pursuit of self-interest—[has] defined the essence of American diplomacy." Instead, Bacevich said, "unflagging self-interest and large ambitions underlay all US policy."[31]

Pointing out that the aim of the US military has been "to achieve something approaching omnipotence," Bacevich mocked the idea that such power in America's hands "is by definition benign" because the leader of the free world "does not exploit or dominate but acts on behalf of purposes that look beyond mere self-interest."[32] Against those who justify American interventions in other countries on the grounds that America's foreign policy is to promote democracy, Bacevich pointed out that in previous countries in which America intervened, "democracy [did not] flower as a result." America intervenes not for altruistic purposes, he added, but "to sustain American primacy."[33]

Many other intellectuals have expressed similar views. Chalmers Johnson, who like Bacevich was once a conservative who believed that American foreign policy aimed at promoting freedom and democracy, later came to describe the United States as "a military juggernaut intent on world domination."[34] A book written some years ago by Noam Chomsky was entitled *Deterring Democracy*. A more recent book by Chomsky was subtitled *America's Quest for Global Dominance*.[35] Richard Falk wrote of the Bush administration's "global domination project," which, far from promising to usher in global democracy, poses the threat of "global fascism."[36]

Adjudicating between the Two Views

To have a basis for deciding whether the positive or the negative view of the American Empire is closer to the truth, making a judgment about this issue requires some agreement about moral principles. That issue will be saved until Chapter 16. Also, whether increasing the American Empire would be good for the world, we must look at some facts about how the world has fared under American leadership thus far. The next section discusses America's planning to become a global empire. The three sections that follow provide evidence relevant to the question of whether US foreign policy has actually been devoted to the promotion of freedom, democracy, human rights, and has, in fact, served the global good. The chapter concludes by dealing with the question of whether America, after charging the Soviet Empire with being an "evil empire," has been one itself.

PLANNING FOR A GLOBAL EMPIRE

Americans have been taught that our country's plans and policies during World War II were entirely virtuous, intended to promote the general good. Americans have also been taught that our behavior during the Cold War was equally virtuous, seeking only to defeat an evil empire. The truth, however, is very different.

During the Cold War, the United States, working through the CIA and NATO (and hence the Pentagon), supported various kinds of clandestine operations, including false flag terrorist attacks (see Chapter 12), to prevent the rise of any Communist or even socialist governments in Europe. These operations were part of a much broader strategy aimed at extending the American empire.

Planning for this strategy began within weeks after World War II started in Europe in 1939, at which time the Council on Foreign Relations—in collaboration with the US Department of State— formed a committee to devise strategy for the war and the ensuing peace. Laurence Shoup and William Minter, who referred to this committee as the "imperial brain trust," said that it "worked out an imperialistic conception of the national interest and war aims of the United States," a conception that "involved a conscious attempt to *organize and control a global empire*."[37]

The basic idea was that the United States, which was struggling to come out of the depression, was not self-sufficient, even though, thanks to its interpretation and enforcement of the Monroe Doctrine, it already had the entire Western Hemisphere as a source of markets and raw materials. In addition, these strategists decided, America needed a "Grand Area" that included China, Japan, the Dutch East Indies (now Indonesia), and the British Empire and Commonwealth. Control of this Grand Area was, moreover, only a temporary measure. "The preferred ideal," in the words of Shoup and Minter, "was even more grandiose—one world economy dominated by the United States," with "international political and economic institutions" that would "integrate all of the earth's nations under the leadership of the United States."[38]

Besides setting these goals, the brain trust also pointed out that US policy makers, while privately formulating these actual war aims, recognized that they needed to announce different war aims for public consumption. "[F]ormulation of a statement of war aims for propaganda purposes," the brain trust pointed out, "is very different from formulation of one defining the true national interest."[39] In particular, the authors said:

> If war aims are stated which seem to be concerned solely with Anglo-American imperialism, they will offer little to people in the rest of the world, and will be vulnerable to Nazi counter-promises. . . . The interests of other peoples should be stressed, not only those of Europe, but also of Asia, Africa, and Latin America. This would have a better propaganda effect.[40]

In practice, this policy of the Grand Area meant not only preventing as many countries as possible from aligning themselves with the Soviet Union (and later China), but also preventing countries from developing socialist economies or any form of *nationalist* economy, in which a country's raw materials would be used for its own people rather than being offered up to the global capitalist economy led by the United States. If countries resisted the US policies, they were likely to be overthrown.

OVERTHROWING GOVERNMENTS DURING THE COLD WAR

During the Cold War, the United States overthrew dozens of governments (many of which had been democratically elected) and tried but failed in several more countries. This overthrowing of governments during the Cold War was the continuation of US policies in previous decades, beginning in 1898, when America took over Hawaii, Cuba, Puerto Rico, and the Philippines. But the discussion here is limited to the Cold War. The US overthrow of Iran's democratically elected government in 1953 is here used for illustrative purposes.

Iran

During the 1940s, the Anglo-Iranian Oil Company, which was owned by Great Britain, was exploiting Iran, giving it only 20 percent of the profits when the going rate was 50 percent. After failing to budge

Britain during negotiations, Iran in 1951 nationalized the company. This move was led in the parliament by Mohammad Mossadegh, who after that was elected prime minister. Although the British government was given a generous settlement—25 percent of the profits, as compensation—it organized, with American support, an economic blockade, which plunged the already impoverished country into destitution. The British then, in late 1952, approached the CIA about organizing a coup, believing that the incoming Eisenhower administration would be amenable. They were right.

The Eisenhower administration had many reasons to desire regime change. Iran's nationalization of a foreign oil company, if allowed to stand, might inspire similar seizures elsewhere.[41] Also, if there were a friendlier government in Tehran, Iran could be used for surveillance of the Soviet Union and for otherwise protecting US interests in the Gulf region.[42] Furthermore, Eisenhower's secretary of state, John Foster Dulles, and his brother Allen Dulles—the new director of the CIA—had both previously worked for the law firm representing Standard Oil of New Jersey.[43] Finally, although Mossadegh was not a Communist, the claim had been made that he was, and the Eisenhower administration had swept into office by charging the Democrats with having lost both China and Korea to the Communists.[44]

The CIA planned a coup with the young shah of Iran, along with a former Nazi collaborator, General Zahedi. Having been supplied by the US army, Zahedi's forces were easily victorious.[45] The shah then became America's puppet ruler of Iran.

Although the US-backed ouster of Mossadegh was bitterly denounced by the people of Iran, the young shah gave thanks to Allah and the CIA[46]—as presumably did Standard Oil, which started receiving 40 percent of Iran's oil profits. The *New York Times*—in spite of having earlier pointed out that Mossadegh had "acquired a reputation as an honest patriot"[47]—declared that his ouster would be a good learning experience:

> Underdeveloped countries with rich resources now have an object lesson in the heavy cost that must be paid by one of their number which goes berserk with fanatical nationalism.[48]

"Fanatical nationalism" was, of course, the idea that a country's resources should benefit its own people, rather than the corporations of America and its allies. This object lesson provides an example of the way in which the US government has, like Rome and other empires, used terror to intimidate.

The aftereffects of this object lesson were even more deadly. Although Allen Dulles declared that Iran had been saved from a "Communist-dominated regime,"[49] democratic freedom was not to be the result. The shah's regime instituted, in the words of Amnesty International, "a history of torture which is beyond belief."[50] This torture was the work of the shah's secret police, SAVAK, which was trained by Norman Schwartzkopf, the father of the Norman Schwartzkopf who was to lead US forces in the first Bush administration's attack on Iraq.[51]

For saddling the Iranian people with this regime and stealing their one source of wealth, America earned their long-term hatred, which was manifested when the shah was replaced in 1979 by a rabidly anti-American government.[52]

Since then, the United States has repeatedly threatened to overthrow the Iranian government, accusing it of destabilizing the Middle East. The Bush-Cheney administration wanted to attack Iran. As it was preparing in 2003 to attack Iraq, there was a quip going around in neocon circles, "everyone wants to go to Baghdad; real men want to go to Tehran."[53] And in 2017, President Donald Trump made no secret of his desire to topple the Iranian government.[54] Then, in 2018, Trump made John Bolton, a neocon who had long advocated bombing Iran, his new national security advisor.[55] Much mutual hatred has followed from the regime change brought about by America in 1953.[56]

Other Cold War Overthrows

Although the overthrow of the Iranian government was the earliest of America's successful attempts to bring about regime change during the Cold War, it was far from the only one. Indeed, the United States during this period overthrew—counting Iran—a total of 30 governments.[57] Here are a few of those:

- Iran 1953
- Guatemala 1954[58]
- Vietnam 1954–73[59]
- Laos 1958, 1959, 1960, 1964[60]
- Ecuador 1960, 1962, 1963[61]
- The Congo 1960[62]
- Brazil 1962–64[63]
- Dominican Republic 1963[64]
- Indonesia 1965[65]
- Chile 1973[66]
- Greece 1967[67]

OVERTHROWING GOVERNMENTS AFTER THE COLD WAR

It was widely thought that the United States was so aggressive in trying to overthrow governments during the Cold War because it was battling against "the Soviet menace." But after the collapse of the Soviet Union, the United States, if anything, became more aggressive in overthrowing governments, with many of the attempts being successful.[68] The regime change in Panama can serve as an illustration.

Panama

Just six weeks after the fall of the Berlin Wall, which symbolized the collapse of the Soviet Empire (on December 20, 1989), the administration of George H. W. Bush invaded Panama in what was called, with or without a straight face, "Operation Just Cause." In the previous months, the White House, with the aid of the US media, had orchestrated a campaign to demonize Panama's ruler, General Manuel Noriega.[69] The claimed reason for the invasion was that Noriega had stolen the 1989 election and that he was involved in the drug racket.[70] But these were far from the real reasons, because the

US government had long known about Noriega's involvement with drugs and had supported him when he stole the election in 1984.[71]

One of the real reasons was based on a coup in 1968, which had been led by Noriega's predecessor, General Omar Torrijos. This coup had displaced the rule of the white elite, who constitute about 8 percent of the population. Although Torrijos and Noriega were dictators, they were *populist* dictators, and their two decades of rule brought major changes. In Noam Chomsky's words:

> Black, Mestizo, and Indigenous Panamanians gained their first share of power, and economic and land reforms were undertaken. . . . [I]nfant mortality declined from 40 percent to less than 20 percent and life expectancy increased by nine years. . . . Indigenous communities were granted autonomy and protection for their traditional lands, to an extent unmatched in the hemisphere.[72]

On January 1, 1990, America was going to lose even further control, because the Panama Canal was scheduled to pass back into Panamanian hands. Bush's 1989 invasion put the government back into the hands of the white-skinned pro-American elite.[73]

The attack on Panama, which was massive, was also intended to serve the elite in another way. Especially singled out for attack was El Chorillo neighborhood. At 1:00 a.m., while its residents were sleeping, it was attacked by tanks, helicopters, rockets, and flame-throwers. People burned to death in the incinerated buildings or leaped from their windows. People running through the streets in panic were cut down in crossfire.[74] Eyewitnesses reported that US helicopters fired at strictly civilian buildings, that US troops shot at ambulances and bayoneted wounded people to death, and that US tanks ran over dead bodies and even a bus, killing all its passengers.[75]

Washington originally claimed that only 200 Panamanian civilians were killed, then raised the figure to around 500.[76] But the Central American Human Rights Commission said, as did Catholic and Episcopal Churches, that an estimate of 3,000 would be conservative. The title of the commission's report was "Panama: More than an

Invasion, ... a Massacre." Why did the US government focus on the Chorillo neighborhood? The owners of this neighborhood had wanted "to transform this prime piece of real estate into a posher district," but Noriega had stood in the way, allowing the poor to live there rent-free. US forces removed this obstacle "by bombing the neighborhood into rubble and then leveling the charred ruins with bulldozers."[77]

Still another motive was suggested by a human rights commission report that "the U.S. Army used highly sophisticated weapons—some for the first time in combat—against unarmed civilian populations."[78] Among these weapons were F-117A stealth fighters, which were used to bomb facilities that had no fighter planes or even any radar. An aviation journal, explaining the likely rationale, said:

> By demonstrating the F-117A's capability to operate in low-intensity conflicts, ... the operation can be used by the Air Force to justify the huge investment made in stealth technology [to] an increasingly skeptical Congress.[79]

The same conclusion was reached by a retired military officer. Saying "100 Special Forces guys" would have sufficed to capture Noriega, he suggested that "this big operation was a Pentagon attempt to impress Congress just when they're starting to cut back on the military."[80]

Although the official reason for the attack had been to capture Noriega, the Panamanian Defense Forces had had Noriega in custody and offered to turn him over to the United States, but the Bush Administration declined the offer.[81] When President Bush was asked by a reporter, "Was it really worth it to send people to their death for this? To get Noriega?" Bush replied that "every human life is precious, and yet I have to answer yes, it has been worth it."[82]

The reversion to the pre-1968 state of things was confirmed by a 1990 story in the *Miami Herald*, which said:

> Six months after the U.S. invasion, Panama is showing signs of growing prosperity—at least for the largely white-skinned business class that has regained its influence.... The upper class and the middle classes are doing great.... But the poor

are in bad shape. . . . The Catholic Church has begun to denounce what it sees as a lack of government concern for the poor.[83]

A final reason for the invasion was for the US to announce its new status since the demise of the Soviet Union. The day after the invasion, General Colin Powell, the new Chairman of the Joint Chiefs of Staff, said: "We have to put a shingle outside our door saying, 'Superpower lives here.'"[84]

But the people of Latin America did not need this shingle. An article in *El Tiempo*, calling Operation Just Cause an "imperialist invasion of Panama," said: "We live in a climate of aggression and disrespect... [in] absolute submission... to the service of an implacable superpower." An editorial, denouncing "international totalitarianism in the guise of democracy," said that Bush "declared plainly to Latin America that for the North American government, there is no law— only its will—when imposing its designs on the hemisphere."[85]

Other Post-Cold War Overthrows

- Yugoslavia 1999–2000[86]
- Afghanistan 2001[87]
- Iraq 2003[88]
- Haiti 2004[89]
- Libya 2011[90]
- Syria 2012 to 2018 (attempted)[91]
- Ukraine 2014[92]

The Fall

Writing in 1973, theological lawyer William Stringfellow, describing the Fall as "the era in which persons and nations exist in profound and perpetual strife," said:

> The Fall is where the [American] nation is. . . . The people have been existing under a state of such interminable warfare

that it seems normative. There is little resistance to the official Orwellian designation of war as peace.[93]

GLOBAL APARTHEID

The previous section provided examples of US violations of the rights of individual people and countries. The present and the following sections look at some effects of US imperialism—or "leadership," as its advocates like to call it—on the world as a whole. The advocates of the American Empire might pose the issue thus:

> We could grant that US imperialism has required the violation of the rights of some people, even millions of people, and also violated the sovereignty of many countries. After all, as the saying has it, "you can't make an omelet without breaking some eggs." Is it not true, nevertheless, that US leadership, especially as exercised since World War II, has contributed to the general good of the world so that, overall, that leadership can be considered benign, even benevolent?

In many ways, the most important event of the twentieth century occurred during and after World War II, when the United States replaced Great Britain as the leader of the global capitalist economy (as intended by the imperial brain trust). From that point onward, the United States has borne increasing responsibility—and hence credit or blame—for the overall welfare of our world. The best way to predict whether an even more inclusive American empire would be good or bad for the planet as a whole is to look at some dimensions of planetary trends from 1945 to the present. These trends must be regarded as crucial, especially from the perspective of Christian faith. The present section examines the growth in "global apartheid." The following section looks briefly at some other dimensions of American imperialism that bear on the question of its effects on the general good of the world.

The Reality of Global Apartheid

The term "global apartheid" was introduced into the discussion of global inequality primarily through a booklet of that title published in 1978 by Gernot Köhler.[94] Writing long before apartheid in South Africa was dismantled, Köhler defined global apartheid thus:

> [A] structure of world society [in which] a minority of whites occupies the pole of affluence, while a majority composed of other races occupies the pole of poverty, [and in which] the affluent white minority possesses a disproportionately large share of world society's political, economic, and military power. . . . [G]lobal apartheid is thus a structure of extreme inequality in cultural, racial, social, political, economic, military and legal terms, as is South African apartheid.[95]

Köhler did, however, point to one major difference—that "global apartheid is even more severe than South African apartheid."[96] In particular:

> Income inequality is even worse: In South Africa, the poorest 40% of the population receive only 6.2% of the national product, while the poorest 40% of the world receive . . . [only] 5.2% of the world product. . . . [T]he richest 20% of South Africa's population take 58.0% of the income, while the richest 20% of the world take . . . 71.3% of world income.[97]

Köhler's moral conclusion: "Just as the world community opposes apartheid in South Africa, it should also oppose the global apartheid."[98]

In 1992, the concept was discussed by Thomas Schelling, a Harvard economist who had contributed to US strategy during the Vietnam War. Asking which country the world as a whole most closely resembled, he said: "I find my own answer stunning and embarrassing: South Africa." Spelling out the implications, Schelling, while not mentioning Köhler's discussion, gave a similar analysis:

> We live in a world that is one-fifth rich and four-fifths poor; the rich are segregated into the rich countries and the poor into poor countries; the rich are predominantly

lighter skinned and the poor darker skinned. . . . There is no systematic redistribution of income.[99]

In 1993, Richard Falk, referring to the discussions by both Köhler and Schelling, pointed out that Schelling, a well-known military strategist, should have extended his analysis to include the fact that "the rich, light-skinned countries enjoy a decisive military superiority and engage in frequent interventionary operations against the poor, dark-skinned countries."[100] Falk's point was that, as we saw above, the countries with military superiority, especially the United States, often use that superiority to prevent the poor countries from improving their economic situations.

Another controversial feature of Schelling's discussion was his failure to draw the same moral conclusion as had Köhler, namely, that global apartheid should be condemned and dismantled. Schelling instead told fellow Americans that we must *safeguard* what we possess, including "our material standard of living."[101]

The year 1992, which brought Schelling's study, also brought the first book-length discussion: *Unravelling Global Apartheid*, by Titus Alexander. In explaining the parallel between global and South African apartheid, Alexander said:

> Three-quarters of the land [in apartheid South Africa] and all its natural resources could only be owned by whites, a sixth of the population. The West also has a sixth of the world's population and commands over three-quarters of global resources. . . . [In South Africa,] democracy for a few meant oppression for the many. So it is for most people in the global economy. . . . Free trade and consumer choice for a few means low incomes, long hours and a struggle for subsistence among the many.[102]

After citing these and several other parallels, Alexander concluded:

> The profound parallels between apartheid and the global system mean that people in the West are as much part of institutional injustice towards the world's majority as white South Africans were towards their non-white neighbours.[103]

Given the fact that apartheid as practiced in South Africa "was declared illegal and a 'crime against humanity' by the UN General Assembly in 1973," Alexander added, "Inequality between the West and the world's majority . . . is just as immoral and illegitimate. It deserves the same condemnation."[104]

All of the sources cited thus far in this section were published in the previous century, when global apartheid was first discussed. But the fact that it is now less discussed does not mean that there has been a reduction in the reality of the phenomenon. Indeed, a 2016 article about global apartheid said:

> The gap between the most wealthy and those living in the deepest poverty continues to grow, and the reality of the rich and the reality of the poor can feel like two different worlds altogether.[105]

Any doubt about the continued growth of inequality was eliminated in 2017 by an Oxfam report, which said:

> [T]he richest 1% now have more wealth than the rest of the world's population combined. Global inequality is worse than at any time since the 19th century.[106]

Given the prominence of the gap between the rich and poor criticized by both the prophets and Jesus, Christians cannot say that America's role as the leader of the global economy has manifested biblical virtues. Insofar as America claims to be a Christian nation, it must be given a failing grade with regard to the Son of Man's statement in Matthew 25:

> Truly, I say to you, as you did it to one of the least of these my brethren, you did it to me. . .; as you did it not to one of the least of these, you did it not to me.[107]

Historical Origins of Global Apartheid

People in the affluent world have tended to assume that the great disparities between their societies and those in poor countries are "natural," perhaps because they have always existed, maybe due to differences in character. Recent studies have shown, however, that the disparities arose rather recently as a result of a well-known historical development: colonialism.

In the 1750s, according to economist Paul Bairoch, "living standards in what we today call the North were not notably higher than those in the South." Writing in 1980, Bairoch said: "Over the next 230 years the average citizen in the capitalist world grew to be eight times richer than one in the noncapitalist world." Why? Primarily because of "the drainage of wealth from the underdeveloped Periphery to the developed Center."[108]

This drainage of wealth occurred during the period of European expansion, during which it colonized most of what is now sometimes called the "third world." As Colin Parkins explained,

> the European powers' expansion profoundly affected the local economic and social structures in these areas and tied them into global economic relationships that shaped their subsequent development.
>
> [The impact of this colonial relationship took several forms]: the disruption of indigenous processes of development, the imposition of market relations, the consolidation of authoritarian political structures, and above all the formation of an international division of labour in which the colonized areas acted as primary commodity producers and labour reserves for the industrialized world.[109]

What this "division of labour" meant is that the economies of the colonized countries were structured not to meet their own peoples' needs but to serve the desires of the colonizers. One result "was an unprecedented accumulation of wealth and capital in the metropolitan countries." So, rather than being natural and eternal, "The patterns of global apartheid are a product of this history."[110]

Developments since World War II

When the United States took over leadership of the global economy after World War II, the patterns of global apartheid did not significantly change. America was, in other words, no less exploitative than had been Great Britain and the other European colonial powers. Indeed, the United States was determined to maintain the great disparity that obtained at that time. In 1947, George Kennan, who was Director of the Policy Planning Staff in the US State Department, said in a "top secret" memo that has since been quoted countless times:

> We have about 50% of the world's wealth, but only 6.3% of its population. . . . In this situation, we cannot fail to be the object of envy and resentment. Our real task in the coming period is to devise a pattern of relationships which will permit us to maintain this position of disparity without positive detriment to our national security.[111]

Kennan thereby expressed the same attitude that had been manifested by the "imperial brain trust."

The chief instruments for carrying out this policy, aside from the CIA and the US military, were the so-called Bretton Woods Institutions: the International Monetary Fund (IMF), the World Bank (technically known as the International Bank for Reconstruction and Development), and the General Agreement on Tariffs and Trade (GATT), which later became the World Trade Organization (WTO). As John Cobb observed in his "theological critique of the World Bank," although the establishment of the United Nations captured much more of the world's attention in 1944, "the actions taken at Bretton Woods would prove, in the long run, more fateful."[112]

There was again, as David Korten explained, a difference between public and private aims:

> The public purpose of what became known as the Bretton Woods system was to unite the world in a web of economic prosperity and interdependence that would preclude nations' taking up arms. Another purpose in the eyes of its architects was to create an open economy unified under U.S. leadership that would ensure unchallenged U.S. access to the world's markets and raw materials.[113]

The best indicator of which of these two purposes was most important, as Korten pointed out, was provided by the results.

> If measured by contributions to improving the lives of people or strengthening the institutions of democratic governance, the World Bank and the IMF have been disastrous failures— imposing an enormous burden on the world's poor and seriously impeding their development. In terms of fulfilling the mandates set for them by their original architects— advancing economic globalization under the domination of the economically powerful—they both have been a resounding success.[114]

Commenting further on what the World Bank and the IMF have done to the poor around the world, Korten wrote: "They have arguably done more harm to more people than any other pair of non-military institutions in human history."[115] This harm has been especially great since the 1980s, when loans to borrowing countries resulted in enormous debts, which were followed by "structural adjustment programs," which forced the countries to spend less and less money on programs for their own people and more and more money simply to pay the interest on the loans.

The way this worked has been described in many works, such as Walden Bellow's *Dark Victory: The United States, Structural Adjustment, and Global Poverty,* and various writings by John Cobb, including one entitled "Imperialism in American Economic Policy."[116] In *Confessions of an Economic Hit Man*, moreover, John Perkins explained how he, while working on behalf of US interests, claimed that he was working to alleviate poverty in other countries, using deceptive development loans and other means to further impoverish them while further enriching US interests.[117]

As a result of these and related processes, the disparity between the rich and the poor of the world has continued to increase. In 1960, people in the richest fifth of the world population were 30 times wealthier than the poorest fifth. By 2000, they had become 134 times wealthier.[118] The *Human Development Report* of 2005 said that the richest 10 percent of the world's population was receiving 54 percent of the world's total income, while 40 percent of the world's population—meaning 2.5 billion people—was receiving only 5 percent.[119] As quoted above, Oxfam reported in 2016 that the richest 1% had more wealth than the rest of the world combined.[120]

One consequence of the resulting absolute poverty is lack of sufficient food, clean water, and even the simplest medical care by about a billion people. Primarily as a result of these deficiencies, some 18 million people die from poverty-related causes every year, 11 million of whom are children under the age of 5. This would mean, at the present rate, 180 million people, including 110 million children, dying from poverty-related causes every decade.[121]

Accordingly, whereas the United States has portrayed itself as the great champion of the right to life, it has been presiding over, and using its power to enforce, an economic system that denies the right to life to people on a massive scale, by denying them the means even to a subsistence living. This global economic system does not merely allow billions of human beings to sink below what Henry Shue calls "the line beneath which no one [should] be allowed to sink." It *pushes* them under.

The fact that the United States was fully conscious of what it has been doing, and intended to keep doing so, was expressed in a document entitled "Vision for 2020." Having said that the mission of the US Space Command is to "dominat[e] the space dimension of military operations to protect US interests and investment," this 1997 document added: "The globalization of the world economy ... will continue with a widening between 'haves' and 'have-nots.'"[122]

George Kennan's 1947 memo said that, because of the disproportionate share of the world's resources that we in the United States use, "we cannot fail to be the object of envy and resentment." This new document, written 50 years later, recognized that the increasing disparity between the rich and the poor, caused by the US-led global economy, will make the "have-nots" of the world increasingly resentful. Accordingly, the US military will need ever more sophisticated weapons to keep them in line.[123] One could hardly imagine a less Christian foreign policy.

In light of the facts discussed in this section, we can only wonder how Robert Kagan was able to write with a straight face about "the benevolent hegemony exercised by the United States," saying that this hegemony "is good for a vast portion of the world's population."[124]

EVIL EMPIRE

During the Cold War, American leaders characterized the Soviet Union as an "evil empire." This characterization was based on several factors, especially the Soviet Union's murder of some 9 million during the Stalinist period,[125] its brutal interventions in Eastern European countries, and its (alleged) desire to create an all-inclusive global empire. "Throughout the Cold War," Gary Dorrien wrote, "American political leaders maintained that Soviet Communism was evil because it was ideologically driven to rule the world."[126]

The other regime that Americans have regularly called evil is the Nazi regime, partly because it brutally attacked other countries, partly because its genocidal holocaust murdered some 6 million Jews as well as 5 million non-Jews,[127] and partly because World War II, which it initiated in Europe, resulted in the deaths of some 70 million people, more than any other war.[128] We rightly consider both the Stalinist and Nazi regimes extremely evil.

But if we apply the same criteria to the American empire, how can we withhold the judgment that it, too, is an evil empire? For one thing, America has invaded far more countries than Germany and the Soviet Union combined.

Also, the United States has been far more "ideologically driven to rule the world" than the Soviet Union. During the Cold War, Dorrien pointed out, US political leaders claimed that "America built a global military system and fought proxy battles with the Soviet Union not because it aspired to dominate the world, but to keep the Soviet Union from doing so."[129] But the fact that American leaders did not dismantle this global military system after the Soviet Union crumbled, and even continued to expand its global military system, showed that this claim was false. (This was the fact that drove Bacevich to rethink the true goals behind US foreign policy.)

Now, moreover, neocon thinkers and US military documents have openly proclaimed that a global *Pax Americana* is the goal. If it would have been evil for the Soviets to want to dominate the world, is it not evil for America to seek this kind of domination?

According to neocon ideology, of course, this does not follow, because the Soviet Union was inherently evil, whereas America is inherently good. So whereas a Soviet-imposed global empire would have been evil, an American-imposed global empire would be good. As neocon Ben Wattenberg put it: "A unipolar world is a good thing, if America is the uni."[130] We have, however, seen that this part of neocon ideology is patently and massively false.

Finally, although Soviet and Nazi leaders were each responsible for many millions of deaths, American leaders, through their interventions in dozens of countries and their apartheid-causing leadership of the global economy, have been responsible for far more deaths than the Nazi and Soviet regimes combined.

In the first couple decades after World War II, to be sure, one could not pin much of the responsibility for poverty-caused deaths on the United States, except for those that occurred in countries in Latin America, whose economies the United States had largely controlled for many decades. The millions of people who died from poverty-related causes in other parts of the world were primarily the responsibility of imperial powers in Europe, especially the British empire. Processes that had been set in motion by those powers could not have been changed overnight, or even in a few years. As the years wore on, however, the responsibility of the United States increased, insofar as it, besides not creating structures to decrease global poverty, actually took measures to sustain and even increase it.

For the most part, to be sure, US leaders did not consciously want other people to get poorer. But the preservation and even increase of global poverty was a consequence—a *predictable* consequence—of their policies. US leaders, in other words, did not hate the people whose economic hopes they dashed. They were simply indifferent to their welfare, while seeking to maximize their own power and riches.

American policies and actions were, accordingly, evil, because US leaders used their enormous power with indifference to the welfare of those upon whom it was exercised.

In 2002, South African President Thabo Mbeki, in speaking of the "social behaviour [that] has produced and entrenches a global system of apartheid," described it as "social behaviour that has pity neither for beautiful nature nor for living human beings."[131] A social-economic system that was in harmony with the will of God, who has compassion for all people and all other living creatures, would be one that did have pity for the poor and other forms of life. It would be aimed at overcoming the poverty of the poor and the needless destruction of nature.

CONCLUSION

We Americans must face the fact that we have been living in an extraordinarily evil empire. Moreover, given the definition of the demonic articulated in Chapter 9—power that is diametrically opposed to divine purposes and powerful enough to threaten those purposes—we can even call the American Empire demonic.

CHAPTER TWELVE

False Flag Attacks

T HIS CHAPTER continues the attempt, begun in the previous chapter, to discuss ways in which American foreign policy has been demonic. One of the demonic features of US policy has been the use of "false flag attacks." Originally, a false flag attack was one in which the attackers, perhaps in ships, literally showed the flag of an enemy country, so that it would be blamed. But the expression has come to be used for any attack made to appear to be the work of some country, party, or group other than one responsible for the attacks. From at least the time of the Roman Empire, imperialist and would-be imperialist powers have staged false flag attacks to justify various types of action, such as "retaliatory" attacks on countries they wanted to conquer.

FALSE FLAG ATTACKS BY OTHER COUNTRIES

As Stephen Kinzer pointed out in 2018, "False flag operations are a well-established tactic."[1] Summarized in this section are three famous false flag attacks by other countries: One by Japan and two by Nazi Germany.

The Mukden Incident

In the early decades of the twentieth century, Japan, hoping to establish economic self-sufficiency, was exploiting resource-rich Manchuria. The chief instrument of this exploitation was the South Manchuria Railway. In 1930, Chiang Kai-shek's increasingly successful effort to unify China was causing Japanese leaders to fear that their position in Manchuria was threatened.

On September 18, 1931, Japanese army officers secretly blew up a portion of the railway's tracks near the Chinese military base in Mukden, Manchuria. Then, blaming the sabotage on Chinese solders, the Japanese army used this incident as a pretext for taking control of all of Manchuria. This military operation is considered by many historians to be the beginning of World War II. Accordingly, the Mukden incident—which the Chinese call 9/18—was one of the most important false flag incidents of the twentieth century.[2]

The Reichstag Fire

An equally fateful false flag operation was the burning of the Berlin Reichstag, the home of Germany's parliament, on the night of February 27, 1933. The fire—which occurred less than a month after the Nazis took power—is now known to be have been orchestrated by Hermann Göring, the president of the Reichstag, and Joseph Göbbels, Hitler's propaganda minister, who had the fire started by members of the SA (Storm Troops).

The Nazis then blamed the arson on the German Communist Party, claiming that the fire was intended to be the signal for a Communist uprising. The only evidence the Nazis presented for this claim was the presence on the site of Marinus van der Lubbe, a feeble-minded left-wing radical from Holland, who had evidently been brought to the site by the SA troops.[3]

The Reichstag fire then became "the excuse for a hitherto unparalleled persecution of Communist and Social Democratic workers, intellectuals and party leaders."[4] Thousands of people allied with the workers movement were arrested; all left-wing newspapers were shut down; and two so-called fire decrees annulled civil rights that had been provided by the constitution of the Weimar Republic. These decrees "formed the pseudo-legal basis for the entire Nazi dictatorship."[5]

Operation Himmler

On the morning of September 1, 1939, Nazi Germany attacked Poland. In Hitler's speech to the Reichstag later that day, he referred to 21 "border incidents" of the previous night, in which Polish troops had allegedly initiated hostilities. The attack on Poland was hence presented as a defensive necessity. But this attack had been planned as a pretext, so that the war would not be strongly opposed by the German people and, hopefully, other nations. The pretext, dubbed "Operation Himmler," was named for Heinrich Himmler, the head of the notorious paramilitary organization Schutzstaffel (usually called simply the SS).

The plan was to have members of the Gestapo and the Security Service, dressed as Poles, stage various raids near the Polish-German border on the night of August 31. The plan in some cases was to dress some German convicts as Poles, give them fatal injections and take them to the sites, then shoot them and leave them there as proof that they had been killed while attacking German troops. The invasion of Poland on September 1 was the beginning of the European part of World War II, as France and the United Kingdom declared war on Germany two days later.[6]

There also have been false flag attacks by other countries, including the Soviet Union[7] and Israel.[8]

AMERICAN WARS BASED ON FALSE FLAG ATTACKS

These three false flag operations—the Mukden Incident, the Reichstag Fire, and Operation Himmler—were all crucial events on the road to World War II. The fact that this war caused some 70 million deaths,[9] as well as enormous suffering, illustrates how fateful false flag operations can be. Americans have generally assumed that US leaders would never engage in such deadly deceit. In reality, however, American leaders have several times used false flags to start wars.

Here are two examples, one from the nineteenth century, the other from the twentieth.

The US War in the Philippines

In 1898, the United States decided to take islands from Spain. It went to war against Spain in Cuba by falsely claiming that Spain had sunk the battleship *U.S.S. Maine,* which President William McKinley had sent to Havana Harbor.[10] America's taking of Cuba led to a long history of antagonism with that country. But the most important reason to go to war against Spain, from the point of view of US imperialists such as Theodore Roosevelt, was to take control of the Philippine Isles, partly for their own sake, partly as a stepping-stone to the fabled China market.[11]

The United States quickly overpowered the Spanish forces and then, at the peace talks, demanded and obtained the entire Philippine archipelago for the tiny sum of $20 million. However, the Filipinos, who were not party to this agreement, claimed independence. This meant that to control this island nation, the United States would have to go to war against the Filipinos, who had just recently been allied with America against Spain.

In January of 1899, General Arthur MacArthur—father of Douglas MacArthur—ordered all Filipino soldiers out of a village they had occupied for several months. Another US general set up a sentry at a position in this disputed area known as the "pipeline," ordering the men to fire on any intruders. On the evening of February 4, the sentries, approached by four Filipino soldiers—who were probably drunk and unarmed—opened fire on them. US troops, having been prepared for this "pipeline incident," then fired on Filipino positions for the next six hours. Few shots were fired in return by the Filipinos, but the war was on. The US secretary of war, giving the official version of what happened, said:

> On the night of February 4th...,an army of Tagalogs...attacked, in vastly superior numbers, our little army . . . and after a desperate and bloody fight was repulsed in every direction.[12]

This statement was part of a more general "propaganda offensive to prove that the Filipino army started the war." Years later, MacArthur and three US officers who had been on the scene confessed that the whole battle was prearranged and that American troops had fired first.[13]

By then, however, it did not matter much. The Philippines lost 250,000 people in this war—which was so dreadful that the usually ironic William James was provoked to say: "God damn the U.S. for its vile conduct in the Philippine Isles."[14]

The Vietnam War

In June of 1964, advisors of President Lyndon Johnson discussed the idea of escalating the war in Vietnam by bombing North Vietnam. Pointing out that this escalation would require a congressional resolution, they counseled that without some "drastic change in the situation to point to," such as an "armed attack" by the North Vietnamese, it would be hard to get this resolution. Shortly thereafter, a clandestine operation known as OPLAN 34A was formulated.[15]

In mid-July, the US destroyer *Maddox* was sent to the Gulf of Tonkin to carry out electronic espionage. On July 30, South Vietnamese gunboats, with American advisers, made commando raids against North Vietnamese islands in the Gulf.[16] Then on August 2, the *Maddox* cruised near North Vietnamese islands that were under attack by the South Vietnamese gunboats. Three patrol boats of the North Vietnamese, who rightly believed that the *Maddox* and the gunboats were part of one operation, charged repeatedly at the *Maddox*, veering off at the last moment. The *Maddox* then opened fire on them. The gunboats fired torpedoes in return, but missed. On August 3, Secretary Dean Rusk sent a cable saying: "We believe that present Op Plan 34 A activities are beginning to rattle Hanoi."[17]

On the night of August 4, the *Maddox* and another destroyer fired their huge guns for several hours, having evidently been told by their sonarmen that torpedoes were headed at them. But no torpedoes hit them. A naval commander flying directly over the destroyers saw "nothing but black sea and American firepower." Commodore Herrick of the *Maddox*, realizing he might have been firing at nothing, sent a radio message saying: "Review of action makes many reported contacts and torpedoes fired appear very doubtful." The next morning, nevertheless, US troops were given orders to "retaliate" against North Vietnamese targets. At the same time, President Johnson was telling congressional leaders that the North Vietnamese had made "unprovoked attacks" against American ships in international waters.[18]

Secretary of Defense Robert McNamara, when asked by Congress if we had done anything to provoke the attacks, declared that the attacks were "deliberate and unprovoked" against a ship on "routine patrol in international waters." When he was asked whether there was a connection between the *Maddox* and the South Vietnamese commando raids, he said: "Our Navy was not associated with, was not aware of, any South Vietnamese actions."[19]

Congress, accepting these lies, passed the Tonkin Gulf Resolution, which authorized the president "to take all necessary measures to repel any armed attack against the forces of the United States" and to help South Vietnam defend its freedom.[20] With that blank check in hand, the Johnson administration soon initiated a full-scale war, using the resolution in precisely the way he had assured his "good friend" Senator William Fulbright—the chairman of the Senate Foreign Relations Committee—that he would not. Years later, Fulbright said: "I don't normally assume a President lies to you."[21]

The war would go on for another eight years and result in the deaths of over 58,000 Americans and as many as 4 million Vietnamese.[22]

US-NATO FALSE FLAG ATTACKS IN EUROPE

Some Americans, being confronted with the preceding evidence of the willingness of US leaders to provoke and lie about incidents to justify going to war, might reply: "I grant that American leaders have done such things to enemies, but they would not deliberately kill citizens of friendly countries for political reasons." That assumption, however, would be false.

In a 2005 book entitled *NATO's Secret Armies: Operation Gladio and Terrorism in Western Europe*, Swiss historian Daniele Ganser extensively documented the fact that during the Cold War, the United States sponsored false flag terrorist incidents in many countries of Western Europe in order to discredit Communists and socialists. (Ten years later, the story was also told by Paul Williams in book entitled *Operation Gladio,* which told essentially the same account while adding the roles of the Vatican and the Mafia.[23] But this brief account is based on Ganser's book alone.)

In 1947, the Truman administration passed the National Security Act, which created the Central Intelligence Agency (CIA) and its boss, the National Security Council (NSC). Existing primarily to prevent the victory of Communist parties in European elections, the NSC and its CIA first targeted Italy. Directive NSC 4-A ordered the CIA to undertake covert activities to prevent a victory by the Communists in the 1948 elections. After these operations succeeded, directive NSC 10/2 created the Office of Policy Coordination, which was authorized to carry out covert operations in *all* countries in the world. Such operations were to include "propaganda; economic warfare; preventive direct action, including sabotage [and] demolition [and] assistance to underground resistance movements."[24]

With the creation in 1949 of the North Atlantic Treaty Organization (NATO), these operations came to be coordinated by a secret unit within NATO called the Clandestine Planning Committee (CPC), which was guided primarily by the CIA and the Pentagon. US control of NATO was guaranteed by the fact that its Supreme Commander would always be an American general. When NATO was expelled from France in 1966 by French President Charles de Gaulle, it moved to Brussels, Belgium. But the real headquarters—of NATO in general and the CPC in particular—remained in the Pentagon.[25]

These operations involved the creation of secret armies, comprised of members of the extreme right. In Germany, for example, they included former members of Hitler's SS.[26] These armies engaged in false flag operations in several countries, including Italy and Belgium.

Italy

The Italian secret army, which came to be called Gladio, and other right-wing extremists with which Gladio linked up, had together been waging a secret war since the end of World War II. But from 1969 to 1974, during the presidency of Richard Nixon, Operation Gladio became even more violent.

For example, in 1969, bombs exploded in Milan's Piazza Fontana, killing 16 people and injuring another 80. This attack, known as the Piazza Fontana massacre, was blamed on the left by the military secret service, which destroyed evidence and then planted bomb parts in a leftist editor's villa.[27] The deadliest attack in Italy occurred in 1980, when a massive explosion at the Bologna railway station killed 85 people and wounded another 200.[28] Evidence was planted to implicate a Communist organization, the Red Brigades.

For over a decade, the Italian public believed that Communists had committed these atrocities.[29] But in 1984, Italian authorities discovered that these crimes were actually orchestrated by right-wing forces. Judge Felice Casson, who spearheaded the investigation, said the attacks were carried out "to create tension within the country to promote conservative, reactionary social and political tendencies."[30] This interpretation was later confirmed by a member of the extreme right-wing organization Ordine Nuovo, who said:

> You had to attack civilians, the people, women, children, innocent people. ... The reason was ... to force these people, the Italian public, to turn to the State to ask for greater security. This is the political logic that lies behind all the massacres and the bombings.[31]

In 1990, Judge Casson discovered documents revealing the existence of Gladio and its connection to NATO and the United States.[32] That the massacres were organized by US Intelligence was confirmed in 2001 by General Giandelio Maletti, former head of Italian counter-intelligence, who said of the Piazza Fontana massacre:

> The CIA, following the directives of its government, wanted to create an Italian nationalism capable of halting what it saw as a slide to the left.

It seemed to him, he added, that to achieve this goal, "the Americans would do anything."[33]

Belgium

In the 1980s, Belgium suffered a terrifying series of terrorist attacks known as the Brabant massacres. (Brabant is the geographic area around Brussels, where NATO has been headquartered since 1966.) The attacks usually occurred at shopping areas, especially supermarkets. In November of 1985, for example, three hooded men got out of their car and started firing at shoppers with a pump-action shotgun. Eight people were killed. "A husband and wife and their 14-year-old daughter were finished off in cold blood . . . . Another father and his nine-year-old daughter were killed in their car trying to flee." Between 1982 and 1985, there were 16 such attacks, which "reduced Belgium to a state of panic."[34]

Although the responsibility for the Brabant Massacres remained a mystery for many years, evidence later surfaced that they were carried out by a neo-Nazi organization known as Westland New Post (WNP). Michel Libert, a former WNP member, confirmed in 1992 that from 1982 to 1985, it was his job to scout out supermarkets, seeing if they had any protection that could interfere with WNP's operations. Libert's orders came from WNP commander Paul Latinus, who was paid by the Pentagon's Defense Intelligence Agency. A Belgian journalist reports that when he asked Latinus who had asked him to set up the WNP, he said: "American military secret services."[35]

With regard to the motivation behind the massacres, a member of WNP later said that the plan was to "make the population believe that these terrorist attempts were done by the Left."[36] A report issued by the Belgian parliament in 1990 said that the Brabant killings were "part of a conspiracy to destabilize Belgium's democratic regime, possibly to prepare the ground for a right-wing coup."[37]

Transition to Attacking Fellow Americans

Following the exposure of Operation Gladio in Italy in 1990, the discovery that other NATO countries had similar clandestine units became a major scandal in Europe—although it was scarcely mentioned in the US media. NATO officially denied the whole story, but in 1990 Secretary General Manfred Wörner reportedly confirmed to the NATO ambassadors that "the military command of the allied forces—Supreme Headquarters Allied Powers Europe (SHAPE)— coordinated the activities of the 'Gladio Network.'"[38]

As these revelations show, the assumption that US military leaders would not order the killing of innocent civilians in allied countries for political purposes is false. Some Americans, however, might grant this and still assume that our military leaders would not run deceitful operations that would involve sacrificing fellow Americans. The idea that US leaders would sacrifice American lives in deceitful operations to start wars is the idea that is most difficult for most Americans to accept. But if evidence suggests that this has indeed been done, we must be willing to examine the evidence. (Loyalty to God means that we must put truth above patriotism.) And there is indeed such evidence, three examples of which will be discussed next: the evidence about (i) the Pearl Harbor attack, (ii) a planned scam called Operation Northwoods, and (iii) the 9/11 attacks.

SACRIFICING AMERICANS I: PEARL HARBOR

Americans have been taught that the United States entered World War II in response to Japan's unprovoked surprise attack on Pearl Harbor (which killed over 2,000 servicemen, sank or heavily damaged 18 navel vessels, and destroyed 188 planes). "According to this [false] view," said historian Stephen Sniegoski, "the cause of the war stemmed from the malign effort by Japan, run by aggressive militarists, to conquer the Far East and the Western Pacific."[39]

The day after the attack, President Franklin Delano Roosevelt (FDR) began his address to Congress by calling December 7, 1941, "a date which will live in infamy." The date should be so regarded, he said, because the attack on Pearl Harbor was "a surprise offensive" that had been "unprovoked."[40] However, there has long been a revisionist view.

Was the Attack on Pearl Harbor Unprovoked?

World War II had begun in Europe in 1939. Most Americans, at least 80 percent of them,[41] did not want our country to get involved in another European war. As a result, Roosevelt in his 1940 reelection campaign pledged to keep America out of the war. But he had usually qualified his pledge by saying, "unless we are attacked."[42]

FDR did want to get into the war, and he had promised England's leader, Winston Churchill, that he would do so. So he decided he would be able to get into the war only by going in the "back door"— inducing Japan to attack America. Secretary of War Henry Stimson wrote in his diary: "We face the delicate question of the diplomatic fencing to be done so as to be sure Japan is put into the wrong and makes the first bad move—overt move."[43]

Lieutenant Commander Arthur McCollum, the head of the Far East desk of the Office of Naval Intelligence, regularly provided FDR with reports about Japan. In his 2001 book, *Day of Deceit: The Truth About FDR and Pearl Harbor*,[44] Robert B. Stinnett reported that in October of 1940, McCollum provided FDR with a plan for inducing Japan to make the first move. McCollum gave FDR an eight-action memorandum making the following argument:

- It is essential for the USA to get into the war—mainly because if the Axis Powers were to defeat Great Britain, thereby taking control of the British naval fleet, they could virtually rule the world.

- American public opinion would not presently allow the US government to declare war against Japan "without more ado."

- The recent signing of the Tripartite Pact, in which Germany, Italy, and Japan agreed to treat an attack by a new belligerent on any of them as an attack on all, provided an opportunity for more ado, because if Japan could be provoked into a war on the USA, then Germany would join in, providing the USA with a "back door" into the war in Europe.

Of the eight actions proposed, one was to keep most of the US Fleet in Hawaii as bait (rather than, at the conclusion of the spring training exercises, returning much of it to its normal location in San Diego).

Another important action in McCollum's list was to give more aid to the Chinese government of Chiang Kai-shek in support of its war with Japan. The US aid to China stiffened its resistance, making it see no reason to agree to a peaceful settlement with Japan. "It was Japan's inability to terminate the war with China successfully," said Sniegoski, "that motivated its military expansion elsewhere."[45]

The third major part of McCollum's memo was to pinch Japan economically. The United States closed the Panama Canal to Japanese shipping, thereby reducing Japanese imports drastically, causing a spiral downward in the economy and thereby food shortages. Most damaging, FDR froze all Japanese assets in the US and—in cooperation with the Dutch and the British—placed a total embargo on all trade with Japan, including oil. This would mean that Japan would not be able to continue its war with China, "because neither Japan nor Japanese-controlled territory in China produced oil." The *New York Times* referred to this action as "the most drastic blow short of war."[46]

By such actions, McCollum said, Japan might "be led to commit an overt act of war."[47] In fact, said Stinnett, all the suggested actions were carried out before Japan's final decision to attack Pearl Harbor.[48] These actions left Japan little choice. According to Robert Smith Thompson, "Japan had to strike—and strike first. . . . Japan's only salvation lay in taking out the U.S. Pacific fleet."[49]

The day after Roosevelt received McCollum's memo, he explained his plan to Admiral James Richardson, the fleet's commander. When Richardson refused to accept the idea of retaining the fleet in Hawaii, Admiral Husband Kimmel, who was *not* told of the plan, was put in charge of the Pacific Fleet. General Walter Short, who was responsible for the defense of Hawaii, was also not told.[50]

Was the Pearl Harbor Attack a Surprise?

The Japanese attack was not a surprise to the nation's leaders in Washington. There were several means by which the Japanese plan was known.

Code "Purple": One of the ways involved Japan's secret diplomatic code, known as Purple.

> The code was so complex that it was enciphered and deciphered by machine. A talented group of American cryptoanalysts broke the code in 1940 and devised a facsimile of the Japanese machine.... The deciphered texts were nicknamed Magic.[51]

Although the texts did not reveal that Pearl Harbor was the target, they did let Washington know what Japanese leaders were thinking.

Copies of Magic were promptly delivered to FDR and to secretaries of State, War, and Navy, the Army Chief of Staff (General George Marshall) and the Chief of Navel Operations (Admiral Harold Stark). Although Kimmel and Short asked for a code-breaking machine, this request was refused.[52]

"Winds" Signals: The Japanese had set up a "Winds System," by means of which consulates not having the code or a code-breaking machine could learn from weather reports about Tokyo's intentions. If diplomatic relations were broken, so that war was near, the message was to be repeated three times during a weather report. The message was "East wind, rain," with "East wind" indicating the United States and "rain" signifying the cut off of diplomatic relations. This message was broadcast, and picked up by Washington intelligence, on December 4.[53]

The Naval Code: As important as Stinnett's discovery of the McCollum memorandum was his discovery that US intelligence did *not*, as almost universally believed, lose track of the Japanese strike force while it was making its approach to Hawaii. That account—which has been part of the official story, according to which Washington could not have warned Hawaii of the impending attack because it had no precise advance knowledge of it—had been widely accepted. For example, famous historian Stephen E. Ambrose, repeating the story that "intelligence 'lost' the Japanese aircraft carrier fleet," charged in 1995 that US intelligence was "terrible."[54]

One of the two crucial elements in this story was that, although US cryptographers had deciphered the diplomatic code (Purple), the cryptographers were unable to read any of the intercepts of military (naval) messages until *after* Pearl Harbor. For example, in his 1997 book, *The Clash,* the great historian Walter LaFeber said that "the intercepts—codenamed MAGIC—allowed US officials to listen in on the many secret Japanese diplomatic and, [only] after the Pearl Harbor attack, the military messages."[55]

However, Stinnett discovered, the naval code had been partly deciphered by the fall of 1940, and all four of the codes employed for the expedition to Hawaii had been solved by the fall of 1941.[56]

Radio Contact: The other crucial element in the official account was that the Japanese maintained radio silence during the strike force's approach to Hawaii. For example, Lafeber said that "U.S. intelligence had no idea where the fleet was located" because it sailed "without radio contact."[57]

However, far from being silent, wrote Stinnett, the Japanese were "blasting away on the lower marine frequencies," averaging over 6 messages a day.[58] Thanks to the intercepts of these messages, US intelligence was able to track the movement of the strike force to the Kurile Islands, then eastward, and then southward to Hawaii.[59] Beginning on November 20, several intercepts, which FDR himself received,[60] indicated that "Hawaii" or "Pearl Harbor" was the target, with intercepts on December 2 and 3 revealing that the "Hawaii attack" would occur on December 7.[61]

Spy Messages: All this information was reinforced, furthermore, by intercepted messages from Japan's spy in Honolulu, who in response to requests from Tokyo sent grid coordinates for Pearl Harbor, from which Tokyo could prepare bombing maps.[62] On December 6, his intercepted message informed Tokyo that "a considerable opportunity is left for a surprise attack."[63]

The "Pilot" Message: Early in the morning of December 6, US intelligence intercepted the so-called "pilot" message, which contained Japan's response to America's demands. This message came in 14 parts, the first 13 of which were received and decoded on that day. FDR said that the message "means war." Then the 14th part was received and decoded on the morning of December 7. It indicated that the Japanese ambassador to the United States was to deliver the message breaking diplomatic relations to Secretary of State Cordell Hull at 1:00 p.m. (Eastern time), which meant that this was about when the attack was to begin.[64]

Accordingly, the Pearl Harbor attack was not a surprise for Washington, which knew where and when the attack would come, almost down to the minute.[65] But it was a surprise for Hawaii.

Kimmel and Short Kept in the Dark: FDR and General Marshall had taken pains to ensure that Admiral Kimmel and General Short did not know the attack was coming. Besides the fact that none of the intercept information summarized above was given to them, they were also explicitly lied to by their intelligence officers, being told the day before the attack, for example, that the "[aircraft] carriers are lost."[66]

They were also not told after Kimmel, who had sent part of his fleet to the sea north of Hawaii for surveillance purposes, was ordered to bring the ships back to Oahu. This order reflected a more general "Vacant Sea" policy, which was evidently implemented to ensure that the Japanese strike force would not encounter any US ships.[67]

On November 27, Kimmel and Short did receive a war warning, but it was explained so as to prevent them from making preparations: They were told that the attack would probably be "against either the Philippines or KRA Peninsula or possibly Borneo."[68] Finally, after Washington on December 7 received the information about the exact time of the attack several hours in advance, General Marshall sent this information to Hawaii in such a way that it would arrive only after the attack had begun.[69]

Was the Attempted Cover-Up Successful?

The authorities went to great lengths to prevent the public from knowing the truth about the Pearl Harbor attack. This cover-up, which to a great extent still continues, was achieved by various means.

The first investigation, which occurred in 1942, concluded that the lack of preparedness for the attack was the fault of Kimmel and Short. This should have been no surprise, because the investigation was headed by Supreme Court Justice Owen Roberts, who had been handpicked by FDR, and the Roberts Commission was comprised of, with only one exception, "personal cronies of Roosevelt and Marshall."[70]

The one member of the Commission who was not a crony was Admiral William Standley, and he said that Roberts's handling of the investigation was "as crooked as a snake." Admiral Richardson called the report "the most unfair, unjust, and deceptively dishonest document ever printed by the Government Printing Office."[71] Kimmel and Short were called traitors, and there were cries for courts-martial. Kimmel and Short actually wanted them, as the only way in which they could save their reputations. But the administration delayed them until 1944.[72]

In preparation for the Naval Court of Inquiry, a defense attorney obtained 43 of the Magic intercepts. He wrote:

> The admirals on the Court listened to them being read with looks of horror and disbelief. . . . The verdict of the Roberts Commission was overturned. Admiral Kimmel was exonerated on all charges.[73]

The intercepts were also leaked to the Army Pearl Harbor Board, which said that the guilt was not that of General Short but that of General Marshall. (The proceedings of the inquiry were not allowed to criticize the President.)[74]

It was announced, however, that the courts-martial verdicts would not be released until the war was over, and this gave the Roosevelt administration time to reverse the verdicts, which it succeeded in doing. For example, a naval officer who had testified at the Naval Court of Inquiry "was thrown into a psychiatric ward at Bethesda Naval Hospital" and told that "his testimony had better change or he'd be in the ward for the rest of his life."[75]

Having gotten all the testimonies reversed, the administration publicized the revamped versions of the courts-martial findings, and the public never knew what the actual findings of the courts-martial had been.[76] In the mind of the general public, accordingly, the standard story is still the truth about the Pearl Harbor attack. For those who know the facts, however, it is obvious that the official story was a lie. The Pearl Harbor attack was not a false flag operation: The Japanese army did attack Pearl Harbor. But it was similar to a false flag operation in being a deadly operation that was based on a lie—the claim that the attack was unprovoked and unexpected and hence could not have been prevented.

Of course, people who agree on the facts can differ on the question of whether FDR was justified in sacrificing the lives of sailors, deceiving the public, and destroying the reputations of Kimmel and Short. Stinnett himself was of two minds.

On the one hand, he wrote: "As a veteran of the Pacific War, I felt a sense of outrage as I uncovered secrets that had been hidden from Americans for more than fifty years." Stinnett's sense of outrage is reflected throughout his book. On the other hand, speaking of "the agonizing dilemma faced by President Roosevelt," Stinnett said that "he was forced to find circuitous means to persuade an isolationist America to join in a fight for freedom," a fight that led to the "victory of allied forces over the Axis nations that threatened the liberties we all cherish."[77]

SACRIFICING AMERICANS II: OPERATION NORTHWOODS

After Fidel Castro in 1959 overthrew Fulgenicio Batista's corrupt, dictatorial, US-supported regime, the US government looked for ways to bring Cuba back under American control. Early in 1962, the Joint Chiefs of Staff presented President John F. Kennedy with a plan, called Operation Northwoods, describing "pretexts which would provide justification for US military intervention in Cuba." This document advocated "a period of heightened U.S.-Cuban tensions which place the United States in the position of suffering justifiable grievances." This plan would make the world ready for US intervention "by developing the international image of the Cuban government as rash and irresponsible, and as an alarming and unpredictable threat to the peace of the Western Hemisphere."[78]

The document then suggested several possible actions that would help create this image, such as a "Communist Cuban terror campaign in the Miami area . . . and even in Washington." One of the possibilities was what the Joint Chiefs called a "Remember the Maine" incident: "We could blow up a U.S. ship in Guantánamo Bay and blame Cuba." Accordingly, this false flag operation, devised by the Pentagon's military leaders, would have involved killing American citizens. President Kennedy did not approve this plan, but who can say that some other person in the oval office, such as Richard Nixon, would not have done so? In any case, the Joint Chiefs of Staff evidently had no hesitation to suggest that the US government would kill American citizens in order to further political aims.

SACRIFICING AMERICANS III: THE 9/11 ATTACKS

In light of the facts that (a) the United States, like other imperialist governments, has engaged in false flag attacks to achieve political goals; that (b) the US has engineered such attacks on citizens of allied countries as well as enemies; and that (c) US leaders were even willing to sacrifice Americans for political reasons, one should not exclude *a priori* the possibility that the 9/11 attack on the World Trade Center and the Pentagon was a false flag operation. A decision about this question should be based not on the belief that American leaders simply "would have not done such a thing," but on evidence about relevant facts. Judging what is relevant requires considering the context in which the attacks occurred.

A central fact about the context was the unexpected disappearance, only 10 years prior to the 9/11 attacks, of the Soviet Union, which had for decades provided a pretext for America's imperialistic forays. Each American overthrow of a government could be justified as a defensive move in response to the "evil empire." American imperialists were suddenly faced with the need for a substitute.

Since the 1980s, when the "Soviet threat" had begun to lose its power, some thinkers had proposed replacing it with the "Islamic threat." But "it was not until the events of 9/11," said Deepa Kumar in her book *Islamophobia and the Politics of Empire,* "that this rhetoric became the United States' dominant means of justifying its imperialism."[79]

Of course, the 9/11 attacks could be used to justify war on Muslims only if Muslims were believed to have carried out the attacks. And that, of course, was the claim of the Bush-Cheney administration. But there is overwhelming evidence that this claim is false, in spite of a largely successful campaign by the government and the media to dissuade citizens from studying the evidence provided by credible scholars and organizations.

This evidence need not be rehearsed here; it has been provided at length in several publications.[80] But just to give one example: The Mohamed Atta who grew up in Egypt and studied in Hamburg was a very gentle and pious Muslim, who never touched alcohol or women. He was also very small, being under 5'4" tall. But the man who used this name in America drank alcohol heavily, snorted cocaine, frequented strip joints and prostitutes, and was described as 5'8" and even 5'10" tall.[81]

CONCLUSION

False flag events are evil: They blame groups and individuals for events for which they are innocent; they allow evil-doers to escape punishment for their crimes; and they can result in extremely deadly wars. As stated earlier, WW II, started by false flag attacks by Japan and Germany, killed about 70 million people. The wars derived from the 9/11 attacks resulted in about 5.6 million Afghan deaths (counting both violent deaths and deaths resulting from war-imposed deprivation);[82] about 2.7 million Iraqi deaths;[83] and close to 500,000 deaths in Syria.[84] By 2018, moreover, 76 countries were involved in the so-called "war on terror" that resulted from the 9/11 false flag attacks.[85]

Many countries have resorted to false flag events. But the American Empire has been based on false flag events so much that it could be called the *false flag empire*—a label that has been especially appropriate since 9/11, which apparently issued in an America, in Tom Engelhardt's words, of "never-ending wars" and thereby "an empire of madness."[86]

CHAPTER THIRTEEN

Nuclear Weapons

IN CHAPTER 6, we saw that Jesus and early Christians, especially as represented by the final book of the New Testament, considered the Roman Empire demonic. Chapter 9 stated this book's non-mythical conception of the demonic: Besides being diametrically opposed to divine purposes, it is creaturely power that is strong enough to threaten those purposes. Creaturely power became this strong only after human beings created civilization.

The present chapter adds the idea of *extremely* demonic power, meaning creaturely power that, besides being diametrically opposed to divine purposes, is strong enough to destroy human civilization. This extremely demonic power did not arise until the twentieth century, when America created nuclear weapons and because it, having ignored multiple warnings, began the process of destroying the planet's climate. Chapter 14 will deal with climate destruction; the present chapter discusses nuclear weapons. The first section of this chapter discusses the creation and use of nuclear weapons; the second section discusses consequences of the bombings.

THE CREATION AND USE OF NUCLEAR WEAPONS

There are two kinds of nuclear weapons: atomic bombs and hydrogen bombs. Atomic bombs, which were created first, were of two types: uranium-based and plutonium-based. The first type was dropped on Hiroshima on August 6, 1945; the second type on Nagasaki three days later.

Getting Started

The decision to create an atomic bomb was motivated by the fear that Nazi Germany was making one. After German scientists split the uranium atom in 1938, two European physicists, Leo Szilard and Eugene Wigner, wrote a letter the following year, with Einstein's signature added, to President Roosevelt. A committee to study uranium chain reactions was quickly formed.[1] By 1942, the Manhattan Project to create an atomic bomb, under the leadership of General Leslie Groves, was up and running.[2] All the Manhattan Project scientists assumed that the bomb would be used on Germany:

> Émigré scientists from Europe . . . played pivotal roles in the Manhattan Project. To a man, they—along with their American and British colleagues—got involved for one overarching reason:. . . They were convinced that German science was fully capable of producing a terrible new weapon that Hitler would use to enslave the world.[3]

Until Germany surrendered, virtually all the scientists continued to believe that Germany was the target. However, in May 1943, having decided that Germany was not creating an atomic bomb, Groves and the political leaders switched the target to Japan. But Groves kept the scientists in the dark, in order to use the "fear of a German bomb to drive his team onward."[4]

Why Bomb Japan?

But why did the government decide to use the bomb on Japan? The government knew that it could defeat Japan without the bomb, partly because it knew that, if necessary, the United States could call on the Soviet Union for help. So why did the American government not simply cancel the idea of dropping an atomic bomb on *any* country?

Part of the reason, said nuclear engineer Arjun Makhijani, was that "the all-out U.S. effort had created its own momentum." A large part of this momentum was based on the fact that "a host of war-related projects were in fierce competition for industrial and intellectual resources," so "officials connected with [the Manhattan Project] were compelled to demonstrate that it would have a decisive effect on the outcome of the war." Some historians argued thus:

> It was simply not reasonable to believe that after spending so much money and swallowing up so much of the nation's scarce wartime resources that such a decisive new weapon would be put on the shelf.[5]

Roosevelt's director of the Office of War Mobilization, James F. ("Jimmy") Byrnes, was "acutely aware of the potential for intense political problems if atom bombs were not produced and used in the war." After Roosevelt died and Byrnes became President Harry Truman's secretary of state, he said that he wanted the atomic bomb used "as quickly as possible in order to 'show results.'"[6]

It appears, therefore, that the United States chose to use atomic bombs on Japan for political and bureaucratic, not military, reasons. But American citizens were led to believe that dropping atomic bombs on Japan was the only way to defeat it without the loss of an unacceptable number of American lives.

Was the Use of Atomic Bombs Necessary?

On August 9, 1945—the day the bomb was dropped on Nagasaki—President Truman said:

> We have used [the atomic bomb] in order to shorten the agony of war, in order to save the lives of thousands of young Americans.[7]

But was this claim true? In the year following Truman's statement, many authorities said that it was not. For example:

- At the Potsdam conference in July 1945, General Dwight Eisenhower, the supreme commander of the Allied Forces, told Truman that "there was no question but that Japan was already thoroughly beaten." Eisenhower later said that "the Japanese were ready to surrender and it wasn't necessary to hit them with that awful thing."[8]

- Only 11 days after the attack on Hiroshima, Henry "Hap" Arnold, the commanding general of the US Army Air Forces, told the *New York Times* that "the Japanese position was hopeless even before the first atomic bomb fell, because the Japanese had lost control of their own air."[9]

- Two months after the bombings, Admiral Chester Nimitz, Commander in Chief of the Pacific Fleet, stated: "The atomic bomb played no decisive part, from a purely military standpoint, in the defeat of Japan."[10]

- Admiral William "Bull" Halsey Jr., Commander of the US Third Fleet, stated in 1946 that "the first atomic bomb was an unnecessary experiment.... It was a mistake to ever drop it."[11]

Accordingly, Truman's claim—that the bombings were necessary to save a large number of American lives—was contradicted by many people in position to know.

The Hiroshima Myth

In February 1947, Secretary of War Henry Stimson published an article entitled "The Decision to Use the Atomic Bomb," in which he said:

> We estimated that if we should be forced to carry this plan to its conclusion, the major fighting would not end until the latter part of 1946, at the earliest. I was informed that such operations might be expected to cost over a million casualties, to American forces alone.[12]

Besides supporting Truman's claim, Stimson's article greatly increased the estimate of the number of American lives that were saved by the atomic bombs—from Truman's "thousands" to Stimson's "over a million."

In an essay entitled, "The Hiroshima Myth," John V. Denson explained that the Stimson article was the idea of James B. Conant, a prominent scientist who was the president of Harvard University from 1933 to 1953, and who, during the war, had been one of the central figures overseeing the Manhattan Project.

> Conant [said Denson] became concerned about his future academic career, as well as his positions in private industry, because various people began to speak out concerning why the bombs were dropped.[13]

Denson mentioned Admiral Halsey, whose statement was quoted above; and Einstein, who said that the use of the bombs was a "political-diplomatic decision rather than a military or scientific decision."[14] Einstein's statement then gave rise to a front-page *New York Times* story entitled "Einstein Deplores Use of Atom Bomb."[15] In light of these developments, wrote Denson,

> Conant came to the conclusion that some important person in the administration must go public to show that the dropping of the bombs was a military necessity, thereby saving the lives of hundreds of thousands of American soldiers, so he approached Harvey Bundy and his son, McGeorge Bundy. It was agreed by them that the most important person to create this myth was Secretary of War, Henry Stimson. It was decided that Stimson would write a long article to be widely circulated in a prominent national magazine. This article was revised repeatedly by McGeorge Bundy and Conant before it was published in *Harper's* magazine in February of 1947. The article became the subject of a front-page editorial in *The New York Times...*, which stated: "There can be no doubt that the president and Mr. Stimson are right when they mention that the bomb caused the Japanese to surrender."[16]

With regard to the origin of the estimate of "over a million American casualties," Truman, who later endorsed this figure, claimed that he got it from General George Marshall; but Marshall had estimated that an invasion of Japan would result in 31,000 US casualties.[17] As to the real source of the over-a-million-casualties claim, "McGeorge Bundy, the man who first popularized this figure, later confessed that he had pulled it out of thin air in order to justify the bombings."[18] Nevertheless, Stimson's article became the most influential defense of the dropping of the bombs.[19]

But the question still remained: Why did the United States drop bombs on Japan?

Unconditional Surrender

The common answer is that, even after Hiroshima was bombed, Japan refused to surrender, and it was still ready to refuse after the bombing of Nagasaki. That was true, but why was Japan not willing to surrender?

This was because the Truman administration insisted that Japan surrender *unconditionally,* which was understood by Japanese leaders to mean that Japan's emperor would be removed and even be subject to prosecution for war crimes. To the Japanese, that was completely unacceptable, partly because they believed their Emperor to be a god (a direct descendant of the sun goddess, Amaterasu; the reigning emperor, Hirohito, was the 124th in the direct line of descent).[20]

> The stark fact [wrote Denson] is that the Japanese leaders, both military and civilian, including the Emperor, were willing to surrender in May of 1945 if the Emperor could remain in place and not be subjected to a war crimes trial after the war. This fact became known to President Truman as early as May of 1945.[21]

For example, Under-Secretary of State Joseph Grew, the US government official considered most knowledgeable about Japan, told Truman:

> The greatest obstacle to unconditional surrender by the Japanese is their belief that this would entail the destruction or permanent removal of the Emperor and the institution of the throne.[22]

Moreover, Truman was repeatedly told that he should clarify the meaning of the "unconditional surrender" he demanded—that it did not mean the loss of the throne. This was the issue most discussed in the huge 1995 book, *The Decision to Use the Atomic Bomb,* by political economist Gar Alperovitz.[23]

In advance of the Potsdam conference, the last of the conferences of Truman, Churchill, and Stalin to achieve agreement about various matters after the war, Stimson and the assistant secretary of war, John McCloy, prepared a draft for Truman's talk that included explicit assurances about the Emperor's status.[24]

Nevertheless, when the Potsdam Proclamation was made public, it demanded "the unconditional surrender of all the Japanese armed forces," without saying anything about the retention of the Emperor's position. The Proclamation even contained assertions that seemed threatening to the Emperor.[25] As a result, Japan refused to surrender, so America dropped an atomic bomb on Hiroshima and then, three days later, on Nagasaki.

The Truman administration's retention of the unconditional surrender policy was described as the "biggest political mistake of the war."[26]

However, whether the policy was a "mistake" depends on what the Truman administration wanted to achieve. And, contrary to what most Americans believed, its goal was *not* to bring the war to an end without using atomic weapons. Rather, the goal of Byrnes and Truman was the opposite. Alperovitz explained:

> [I]n making the decision to excise the recommended language concerning the Emperor, American officials understood that the warning to Japan ... almost certainly could not be accepted—and that therefore the atomic bomb would be used.[27]

In 2005, historian Tsuyoshi Hasegawa, who taught at the University of California at Santa Barbara, published a major study entitled *Racing the Enemy*, which stated the point even more bluntly:

> Truman knew that the unconditional surrender demand

without any promise to preserve a constitutional monarchy would be rejected by the Japanese. He needed Japan's refusal to justify the use of the atomic bomb.[28]

But why did Truman and Byrnes want to use the bomb? Truman and Byrnes made a demand that would not be accepted, said Denson, "so that the bombs could actually be dropped thereby demonstrating to the Russians that America had a new forceful leader in place."[29] In fact, Byrnes told Truman, the atomic bomb might put the United States in position to "dictate" terms to the Soviets at the end of the war.[30]

The Soviets as the Real Target

This idea, that the American government wanted to use the bombs not to defeat Japan but to impress and control the Soviets, has been accepted by many scholars. For example:

- Kai Bird and Martin J. Sherwin said: "Truman and his closest advisor, Secretary of State James Byrnes, quite plainly used it primarily to prevent the Soviets from sharing in the occupation of Japan."[31]

- Peter Kuznick, director of the Nuclear Studies Institute at American University, wrote: "Japanese and Soviet diplomatic archives suggest that Truman's main motive was to limit Soviet expansion in Asia."[32]

- Mark Selden, a historian in Cornell University's East Asia Program, said: "Impressing Russia was more important than ending the war in Japan."[33]

The Claim that the Bombs Ended the War

The use of atomic bombs on Japan was, and has remained, controversial because of the simple question: Was it morally justified? If it was not, then the American government was guilty of one of history's major crimes. And if the dropping of the bombs was a major war crime, then those political and military leaders who supported it, such as James Conant, could be charged with complicity.

In arguing that the use of the bomb was justified, the Truman administration, besides claiming (i) that it was needed to save over a million American lives, also claimed, with the help of the US press, (ii) that the bombing of Japan actually brought the war to an end. This second claim undergirded the first one: If the bombs had actually brought the war to an end, that provided good reason to believe that the bombs were used *in order to* end the war.

It had not been difficult for the government to make this claim, because Americans were predisposed to believe the bombs won the war, given the sequence of events: Just five days after the Nagasaki bombing, it was announced that the Japanese emperor had accepted the US terms for surrender. Cause and effect seemed so clear that most Americans took it as self-evident that the two atomic bombs caused Japan to surrender. Most of the stories one finds on the Internet still make this claim.[34]

The View that the Bombs Did Not End the War

But in recent decades, scholarship has shifted to the view that the bombs were *not* responsible for ending the war. For example, in a 1995 *New Yorker* essay asking "Did the Bomb End the War?" legendary writer Murray Sayle wrote:

> Once, like everyone else, I thought that the atomic bombs had caused the surrender. Now I know that they did not.... [T]he Soviet invasion of Manchuria was what eventually led to the sudden unexpected surrender offer to the U.S. in the days following Hiroshima and Nagasaki.[35]

Both Gar Alperovitz and Tsuyoshi Hasegawa argued forcibly for this view.[36] In fact, Hasegawa's argument was so persuasive that Richard Rhodes—author of the Pulitzer Prize-winning book *The Making of the Atomic Bomb*—said: "Hasegawa has changed my mind: The Japanese decision to surrender was not driven by the two bombings."[37]

Contrary to the belief that Japan was willing to surrender because of the shock caused by the bombs, Hasegawa maintained:

> The two bombs alone would most likely not have prompted the Japanese to surrender.... The Hiroshima bombing did

not significantly change Japan's policy.... Without the Soviet entry, it is not likely that the Nagasaki bomb would have changed the situation.... [Whereas] the atomic bombs were not sufficient to change the direction of Japanese diplomacy. The Soviet invasion was.[38]

Here is what happened: After learning that the Soviet army had attacked Manchuria at midnight of August 8, Japan's Supreme Council discussed in the morning of August 9 how to surrender in the terms most favorable to it. The Council did not hear about the bombing of Nagasaki until the afternoon. So Japan had made the decision to surrender after the Soviet invasion and prior to learning about the Nagasaki bombing.[39]

When the Japanese learned about the Soviet invasion, Prime Minister Suzuki said that Japan needed to surrender immediately, or else,

> the Soviet Union will take not only Manchuria, Korea, Karafuto, but also Hokkaido. This would destroy the foundation of Japan. We must end the war when we can deal with the United States.[40]

Japan preferred to surrender to America because "[the] Japanese were deathly afraid of Communism," so they chose to surrender to a fellow capitalist country.[41]

Conditional Unconditional Surrender

However, there was yet another step that had to be taken before Japan would surrender. When it submitted its surrender proposal, Japan insisted on one condition, saying it was "ready to accept the terms" of the Potsdam Declaration, on the understanding that it "does not comprise any demand which prejudices the prerogatives of His Majesty as a Sovereign Ruler."[42] But the Truman administration would not accept a surrender labeled "conditional." How could this impasse be overcome? Navy Secretary James Forrestal suggested a solution:

> [W]e might indicate willingness to accept yet define the terms
> of surrender in such a manner that the intents and purposes
> of the Potsdam Declaration would be clearly accomplished.[43]

Agreeing, Truman had a reply drafted by Byrnes, who had to figure out, in Paul Ham's words, "how to impose a 'conditional unconditional surrender.'" Byrnes's solution was to draft "a compromise that read as an ultimatum." While accepting the continuation of the emperor implicitly, the Byrnes Note declared that "the authority of the Emperor shall be subject to the Supreme Commander of the Allied Powers." Ham commented: "Not for nothing had Stalin called Byrnes the most honest horse thief he had ever met."[44]

Accordingly, it is doubly erroneous to say that the atomic bombs forced the Japanese to surrender unconditionally. Rather, "They surrendered only *after* the Russians invaded and *after* the Byrnes [draft] effectively met Tokyo's condition."[45]

In any case, although Byrnes and Truman had long insisted that Japan had to surrender unconditionally, which was generally assumed to mean that Japan would not be able to retain its emperor, the bombing of Hiroshima and Nagasaki left them happy to retain the emperor. As Alperovitz pointed out, "Truman did not hesitate to modify the 'unconditional surrender' policy after the atomic bomb was used."[46] In other words, the insistence on unconditional surrender was simply a ploy to give Truman and Byrnes a pretext to use the bombs.

CONSEQUENCES OF THE BOMBINGS

The Physical Effects

The bombs on Hiroshima and Nagasaki killed many more than expected. Although Oppenheimer had predicted that the Hiroshima bomb would kill 20,000 people, it actually killed 80,000 immediately and another 60,000 by the end of 1945. By 2016, the bomb had taken 300,000 lives (including people who died from radiation-related cancer). The Nagasaki bomb killed about two-thirds as many.[47]

Moreover, the bombs had other terrible effects. In 2015, the *Los Angeles Times* published an essay entitled "What U.S. Citizens Weren't Told about the Atomic Bombings of Japan." Following are some excerpts:

> With searing heat and annihilating force, the nuclear blasts tore through factories, shops and homes in both cities. Huge portions of Hiroshima and Nagasaki vanished. . . . Within a week of each nuclear attack, thousands who had escaped death began to experience inexplicable combinations of symptoms: high fever, dizziness, nausea, headaches, diarrhea, bloody stools, nosebleeds and whole-body weakness. Their hair fell out in large clumps, their wounds secreted extreme amounts of pus, and their gums swelled and bled. Purple spots appeared on their bodies, signs of hemorrhaging beneath the skin. Infections ravaged their internal organs. Within a few days of the onset of symptoms, many people lost consciousness, mumbled deliriously and died in extreme pain; others languished for weeks before either dying or slowly recovering. Even those who had suffered no external injuries fell sick and died. . . . A second wave of radiation illnesses and deaths swept through Nagasaki in late August through early October. . . . [H]igh-level U.S. officials . . . rebuffed news reports about the bombs' horrific aftereffects. Gen. Leslie Groves . . . dismissed these reports as propaganda. . . . Groves testified before the U.S. Senate that death from high-dose radiation exposure is "without undue suffering" and "a very pleasant way to die."[48]

Criticisms of the Bombings

Thanks to the effective propaganda, such as the articles by Stimson and Compton, the American public never staged a major moral protest against the use of the atomic bombs. Nevertheless, some very serious criticisms were published. For example:

- Although Truman described the atomic bomb as the "most powerful weapon in the arsenal of righteousness,"[49] the Federal Council of Churches (the predecessor to the

National Council of Churches) called the bombings *morally indefensible,* adding: "We have sinned grievously against the laws of God and against the people of Japan."[50]

- The bombings, said an article in the *Christian Century* entitled "America's Atomic Atrocity," put the United States in "an indefensible moral position." Moreover, it said: "The Churches of America must dissociate themselves from this inhuman and reckless act of the American government."[51]

- Writing in *The Freeman,* a conservative magazine, Forrest Davis—an influential journalist associated with the *Saturday Evening* Post—observed that Truman's refusal to change the terms of "unconditional surrender" came "little short of being a high crime."[52]

- Felix Morley, editor of the conservative magazine *Human Events*, asked: "If December 7, 1941, is a 'day to live in infamy,' what will impartial history say of August 6, 1945?"[53]

- Raymond Swing, a popular broadcaster on ABC, said: "The decision to drop the bomb was perhaps the most fateful of our time. . . . [I]n using the bomb we became the most ruthless nation in warfare on earth."[54]

- George Kennan, one of the six "wise men" of that era,[55] wrote: "[T]he readiness to use nuclear weapons against other human beings. . . and, in doing so, to place in jeopardy the natural structure upon which all civilization rests, . . . this is nothing less than a presumption, a blasphemy, an indignity— an indignity of monstrous dimensions."[56]

- Leo Szilard became concerned that "by demonstrating the bomb and using it in the war against Japan, we might start an atomic arms race between America and Russia which might end with the destruction of both countries."[57]

- Whereas most of those criticisms deplored the immorality of the atomic bombing, the final two criticisms warned that America's use of the nuclear weapons could lead to the destruction of civilization. But the US government ignored these warnings, demonstrating that—as documented in Chomsky's 2004 book—it considers hegemony more important than survival.[58]

For example, the United States, in the heat of the Cold War, created a thermonuclear (hydrogen) bomb, which is many times more powerful than an atomic bomb. It was detonated in 1952 but—illustrating the dynamics of the Parable of the Tribes—the US leadership in the arms race provided by this creation was short-lived: By 1953, the Soviets developed their own thermonuclear bomb. The nuclear arms race was on.[59]

CONCLUSION

The creation and use of nuclear weapons by the United States show the American Empire to be demonic, and even *extremely* demonic, because (a) it acts in ways that are diametrically opposed to divine purposes and (b) it has created and maintained a nuclear arsenal that threatens the divine purpose to support the flourishing of human as well as other forms of life on this planet.

Although the original decision to create an atomic bomb was arguably justified, because it seemed that Nazi Germany was working on one, it was no longer justified after American leaders knew that they did not need any atomic bombs to defeat either Germany or Japan. These leaders were aware that creating and using an atomic bomb would start a nuclear arms race and might even lead to a war that could destroy civilization. What would justify these risks?

US leaders decided to go ahead and create nuclear weapons partly to avoid criticism for wasting Manhattan Project money (even though this would be a pittance compared with the tax dollars that would later be wasted on the nuclear arms race). More importantly, they did it to give the United States an edge on the Soviet Union. In other words, *there was no justification for this fateful decision whatsoever.* Sociologist Edward Curtin discussed this issue in an essay entitled "The Satanic Nature of the Atomic Bombings of Hiroshima and Nagasaki."[60]

The second great sin was to use the "unconditional surrender" ruse to prevent Japan from surrendering before the two bombs could be dropped. The American deceitfulness was then continued by falsely telling the world that there was no acceptable alternative to the use of the bombs.

Finally, US behavior since the bombing of Japan has further illustrated the extremely demonic nature of the American Empire: It has increasingly risked the destruction of civilization by continuing to increase the nuclear arsenal for the sake of flexing its muscles, making money for the country's arms makers, and working towards the creation of a universal *Pax Americana*.

Saying that demonic possession is to be "captive to the power of death in one or another of the manifestations which death assumes in history," William Stringfellow said that a nation is possessed when it is "governed by the power of death." Having cited Nazi Germany as an example, he said: "The biblical story of such a realm is the saga of Babylon. The extraordinary instance in the present time," Stringfellow added, "is the United States of America."[61]

And yet most Christians in America have referred to their country, as did the "German Christians,"[62] as a "Christian nation."

CHAPTER FOURTEEN

Climate Destruction

THE WORLD has long known that civilization could be destroyed by nuclear weapons. It is not yet as widely known that climate change could be equally fatal. But this fact is now recognized by people who know the facts about both threats. For example:

- Reporting on an interview she had in 2016 with Noam Chomsky, Amy Goodman entitled her report "Climate Change & Nuclear Proliferation Pose the Worst Threat Ever Faced by Humans."[1]

- Pointing out that, several decades ago, the "two superpowers made 'end times' a human possession for the first time in history," Tom Engelhardt in 2015 observed that "while an instant apocalypse loomed, a slow-motion version of the same, also human-made, was approaching, unrecognized by anyone."[2]

- In 2018, the climate website Grist published an essay with a self-explanatory title: "If Nuclear War Doesn't Get Us, Runaway Climate Change Will."[3]

MASS EXTINCTION

In 2014, *New Yorker* writer Elizabeth Kolbert published *The Sixth Extinction.* The title alludes to the fact that, between 444 million to 66 million years ago, there were five mass extinctions. The worst of these was the Permian mass extinction, which occurred about 252 million years ago and wiped out 95 percent of all life on Earth. We are now in the midst of a sixth mass extinction, in which 150–200 living things go extinct each day.[4] In 2018, the World Wildlife Fund reported that humanity has wiped out 60% of animal populations since 1970.[5]

In 2010, the Center for Biological Diversity wrote:

> We're currently experiencing the worst spate of species die-offs since the loss of the dinosaurs 65 million years ago.... Scientists estimate we're now losing species at 1,000 to 10,000 times the background rate, with literally dozens going extinct every day.[6]

Besides going much faster than previous mass extinctions, the present one is unique in being created by human civilization. In 2018, the World Wildlife Fund reported that humanity has wiped out 60% of animal populations since 1970.[7]

Mass extinctions result from many causes, including habitat loss, over-exploitation, pollution, and climate change. But the cause that is now most responsible for mass extinctions is climate change, which in recent times has been brought about by global warming produced from greenhouse gases. The most important of the greenhouse gases has been carbon dioxide (CO_2), which has been responsible for 70 percent of the warming. Methane (CH_4) pollution has become increasingly dangerous, but this situation was created by CO_2.

In 1750, prior to the industrial age, CO_2 constituted only 275 parts per million (ppm) of the atmosphere. By 1958, CO_2 had risen to 280 parts per million. But then, the increase in the atmosphere's content started speeding up. By 2013, it passed 400 ppm, which was considered a really big deal. But by 2017, it had reached 410, showing an alarming increase in the rate of its acceleration.[8]

These increases in the atmosphere's CO_2 have led to increases in the global temperature. Since the late nineteenth century, global surface temperatures have risen about 2 degrees Fahrenheit (1.1 degrees Celsius). Because of global warming, the oceans are rising, glaciers are melting, rainfall and snowfall are increasing, hurricanes are more destructive, wildfires are getting more dangerous, and so on.

THE HOLOCENE

To understand fully the threat from global warming, it is necessary to realize that, since the beginning of civilization, we were in an epoch called the Holocene.

About 19,000 years ago, the Earth, having been in a glacial period ("ice age") that had begun about 110,000 years ago, started to warm up, because of changes in the Earth's orbit around the sun. By 11,700 years ago, the changes brought about a transition from the glacial to an "interglacial."

This interglacial period, which was named the Holocene, brought the partial melting of glaciers, the formation of lakes, and the spreading of forests across much of the planet. It was in this context that civilization emerged about 10,000 years ago.

The Holocene climate was remarkably stable. It never become warm enough or cold enough to bring human civilization to an end. In most places, it was even suited for human thriving. The Holocene thereby "enabled the development of modern civilization, global agriculture, and a world that could sustain a vast population."[9]

About 5,000 years ago, however, the climate started cooling, due primarily to decreased solar radiation. It continued to cool until the end of the 19th century, at which time this long-term cooling "ended abruptly with the rapid warming of the 20th Century." Physicist Stefan Rahmstorf of the Potsdam Institute for Climate Impact Research said: "Within a hundred years, the cooling of the previous 5000 years was undone."[10]

In fact, the planet's temperature has been getting so warm, said Rahmstorf, "We are catapulting ourselves way out of the Holocene."[11] To mark this transition, climate scientists are preparing to announce that civilization has initiated a new epoch, called the "Anthropocene," signifying "the human-dominated geological epoch."[12] In biblical terms, the Holocene can be thought of as the Garden of Eden, in which the conditions for life were (relatively) ideal.

With regard to banishment from the Garden of Eden, the details of the biblical myth—according to which humanity was banished because of its violation of an arbitrary divine command—cannot be endorsed today. But the general notion applies: We had been given ideal conditions for existence, but now we are in a process of being banished—that is, banishing ourselves—from the garden, because we are violating divinely grounded laws of nature that, rather than being arbitrary, are laws we understand: ecological laws that are rooted in the laws of physics, chemistry, and biology. These violations have resulted in the transition from the Holocene to the Anthropocene.

GLOBAL WARMING'S THREAT TO HUMANITY

Given the fact that civilization had existed in the Holocene from the beginning, there is no evidence that it could long exist outside of it.[13] Many informed commentators have suggested that it could not:

- Asking why climatologists are speaking out about the dangers of global warming, National Medal of Science recipient Lonnie Thompson said: "The answer is that virtually all of us are now convinced that global warming poses a clear and present danger to civilization."[14]

- Noam Chomsky and Andre Vitchek wrote that "we are moving toward what may in fact be the ultimate genocide— the destruction of the environment."[15]

- In Elizabeth Kolbert's earlier book, *Field Notes from a Catastrophe*, she wrote: "It may seem impossible to imagine that a technologically advanced society could choose, in essence, to destroy itself, but that is what we are now in the process of doing."[16]

In *The Sixth Extinction,* Kolbert asked: "In an extinction event of our own making, what happens to us?" Many people, she observed, seem to think that we self-named *Homo sapiens* are so wise and powerful that nothing could drive us to extinction. However, she pointed out, "When a mass extinction occurs, it takes out the weak and also lays low the strong."[17] In other words, by leaving the Holocene, we are on a path leading to human extinction.

Another first-rate journalist, Dahr Jamail, said in 2018. "I've spoken to prestigious scientists both on and off the record who believe that sooner rather than later, global population will be reduced to around 1 billion humans."[18]

By making possible the emergence of civilization, the Holocene had allowed for:

- the development of philosophy (as exemplified by Plato, Aristotle, Kant, and Whitehead);

- modern science (as exemplified by Newton, Darwin, and Einstein);

- modern medicine (as exemplified by Curie, Pasteur, Salk, and Sabin);

- liberation and human rights activists (such as Gandhi, Mandela, Elizabeth Cady Stanton, Harriet Tubman, Sojourner Truth, and Martin Luther King, Jr.);

- and for the flourishing of the arts, such as:

    +playwrights (as exemplified by Aeschylus, Sophocles, Shakespeare, and Ibsen);

    +novelists (as exemplified by Austen, Dickens, Eliot, Melville, and Tolstoy);

    +painters (as exemplified by Leonardo, Van Gogh, and Monet);

+sculptors (as exemplified by Donatello, Bernini, Michelangelo, and Rodin);

+composers (as exemplified by Vivaldi, Bach, Mozart, and Beethoven).

Prematurely destroying human civilization and all of its achievements—by ignoring the ecological laws—would surely be one of the greatest tragedies in God's universe. Indeed, the prophet Isaiah gave us an idea of the divine reaction:

> The earth lies polluted
> under its inhabitants;
> for they have transgressed laws,
> violated the statutes,
> broken the everlasting covenant.
> Therefore a curse devours the earth,
> and its inhabitants suffer for their guilt.[19]

HOW THE CARBON THREAT COULD LEAD TO HUMAN DESTRUCTION, EVEN EXTINCTION

Heat

According to the National Weather Service, "Heat is the number one weather-related killer in the United States."[20] If the global temperature continues to rise, scientists say, temperatures will exceed livable limits.[21] And it *has* continued to rise: "On July 30 [2018], a Norwegian town 350 miles into the Arctic Circle saw the temperature reach 90°F."[22]

Climate scientists have given much attention to the question of what the world will be like if it reaches 4°C above pre-industrial temperatures.[23] In 2012, Kevin Anderson of England's Tyndall Centre for Climate Change Research said: "I think it's extremely unlikely that we wouldn't have mass death at 4°C.... [Y]ou might have half a billion people surviving."[24]

More recently, moreover, researchers from the Carnegie Institution for Science have determined that, if business as usual continues, "There is a 93 per cent chance that global warming will exceed 4°C by the end of this century."[25]

Anderson, as we saw, said that in a 4°C world, only a half billion people would survive. And that is the optimistic view: Other climate scientists believe that soon there would be no people whatsoever.[26]

Sea-Level Rise

Some scientists believe that "sea level rise will likely be the first to produce a human catastrophe on a global scale."[27] Shanghai, China's largest city with its more than 24 million people, is less than 2 meters (7 feet) above sea level. In 2010, some experts said the sea level might rise that much by the end of the century. They were considered extremists, but by 2016, this had become the consensus view.[28] Because a rise of seven feet will deluge cities on the coasts of China, the United States, and other countries, a significant portion of the human race will need to move. Moreover, a 2017 study said that the ocean may rise 10 feet by 2100.[29]

Moreover, this will be only the start, if global warming continues. The Greenland and Antarctic ice sheets, long considered stable, are now melting rapidly. The complete melting of the Greenland and Antartica ice sheets would raise the ocean by about 220 feet. This would leave relatively little land left for some 9 billion people, who are already too crowded in many places.[30]

Food Shortage

Lester Brown wrote an article in *Scientific American* asking, "Could Food Shortages Bring Down Civilization?"[31] Answering yes, he wrote a book entitled *Full Planet, Empty Plates*, in which he said:

> Food is the weak link in our modern civilization—just as it was for the Sumerians, Mayans, and many other civilizations that have come and gone. They could not separate their fate from that of their food supply. Nor can we.[32]

Already a billion people a year are going hungry or even starving to death. But the situation is fated to become much worse if global warming continues. The amount of food produced can be reduced by many dimensions of global warming-caused climate change besides sea-level rise, including heat and drought, wildfires, fresh-water shortage, hurricanes, tornadoes, and extreme rain with flooding.[33]

According to an Oxfam report, "the food security outlook in a future of unchecked climate change is bleak."[34]

Ocean Acidification

Besides the fact that too much CO_2 in the atmosphere causes global warming, it also produces ocean acidification. It has reached a crisis stage because about 30 percent of civilization's CO_2 emissions have been absorbed by the ocean.[35]

Ocean acidification involves a decrease in the ocean's pH, which had held steady for at least the past 600,000 years. But since the industrial revolution, there has been a whopping 30 percent increase in acidity.[36]

The absorption of increasingly more CO_2 is destructive because, when it is combined with sea water, it produces carbonic acid, which destroys animals with chalky skeletons—animals that calcify, such as corals, sea butterflies, molluscs, crabs, clams, mussels, oysters, and snails—"which make up more than a third of the planet's marine life."[37]

Most important for the cycle of life, however, is plankton—especially phytoplankton (as distinct from zooplankton), consisting of tiny plants. Being capable of photosynthesis, phytoplankton are at the base of the marine food web. Besides providing about half of the biosphere's oxygen, phytoplankton also "account for about half of the total organic matter on Earth." They "ultimately support all of our fishes." Therefore, a reduction in the ocean's phytoplankton is extremely serious. Marine ecologist Boris Worm said he could not think of a bigger biological change.[38]

As pointed out earlier, the CO_2 in the atmosphere climbed from 280 parts per million in 1958 to 410 ppm in 2017.[39] If CO_2 reaches roughly 500 ppm, thereby driving the pH down still more, said Danish marine biologist Ove Hoegh-Guldberg, "you put calcification out of business in the oceans."[40] This would mean the death of the type of phytoplankton that calcifies—coccolithophorid phyto-plankton (of which there are 200 species).[41]

The calcification crisis is central to the world's food problem. Besides being the world's largest source of protein, with over 2.6 billion people depending on it as their main source of protein, the ocean also serves as the primary source of food for 3.5 billion people.[42] How would we survive if three and a half-billion people can no longer rely upon what had always been their primary source of food? "Global warming is incredibly serious," said Ove Hoegh-Guldberg, "but ocean acidification could be even more so."[43]

Ecosystem Collapse

Global warming and ocean acidification could conspire to produce a global ecosystem collapse.

An ecosystem (ecological system) is a network of living organisms (plants, animals, microbes) interacting with nonliving things (including air, water, soil, and minerals), and functioning as a unit. An ecosystem can be very small, such as a small lake, or very large, such as the ocean. The planet as a whole is the ultimate ecosystem.[44]

Small local ecosystems can collapse, so that they no longer provide support for animals. For example, the Dead Sea is dead because it became so salty that nothing other than microbes can live in it. Because of ocean acidification, the oceanic ecosystem as a whole might collapse.[45]

The Methane Threat

Natural gas is primarily methane (CH_4), which is a greenhouse gas dozens of times more potent than CO_2. Methane has increasingly been released into the atmosphere. Many scientists consider this increase the greatest threat to the global ecosystem and hence to human survival, primarily because of the recent thawing of permafrost.[46]

Permafrost (perennially frozen soil) was formed in the Arctic during the most recent glacial period, popularly called an "ice age" (from 2.6 million years ago to 11,700 years ago). It contains an enormous amount of carbon from dead plants and animals that were prevented from thawing by the Arctic's extremely cold climate. It appears the Arctic has more carbon in frozen form than the carbon that has been emitted by fossil fuels since 1750.[47]

One of the most serious effects of CO_2-caused global warming is the creation of the methane threat: When permafrost thaws, it releases its carbon. And now the Arctic is warming up twice as fast as the rest of the planet except for Antarctica. If business as usual continues, the thawing of permafrost will dump 100 billion tons of carbon equivalents into the atmosphere, in the form of CO_2 and methane, by 2100.[48] Highly regarded glaciologist Jason Box has expressed the danger graphically, saying: "Even if a small fraction of the Arctic carbon were released to the atmosphere, we're fucked."[49]

As the above pages show, there are many ways in which the elevated CO_2 in the environment, by producing global warming and ocean acidification, could destroy civilization, and perhaps even bring about human extinction.

But why did the modern world, the United States of America in particular, allow these deadly threats to civilization to occur? Central to this explanation could be Christian complacency, the mainstream media, neoliberal economics, and the American government.

CHRISTIAN CLIMATE COMPLACENCY

According to the headline of a 2013 *Washington Post* article, "Americans Are Less Worried about Climate Change than Almost Anyone Else." One of the main reasons has been the climate complacency of American Christians.

This complacency exists most fully among supernaturalists who, as discussed in Chapters 2 and 3, hold that the divine creator of the world is omnipotent. To give three examples:

- In a book called *The Greatest Hoax*, Republican Senator James Inhofe explained why people should not be worried about climate change by citing Genesis 8:22: "As long as the earth remains there will be seedtime and harvest, cold and heat, winter and summer, day and night." Saying that this passage shows that God promised that "cold and heat should not cease," Inhofe declared: "This is what a lot of alarmists forget. God is still up there, and He promised to maintain the seasons." It is arrogant, added Inhofe, to "think that we, human beings, would be able to change what He is doing in the climate."[50]

- Talk-show host Rush Limbaugh declared: "If you believe in God, then intellectually you cannot believe in manmade global warming." To worry about it, Limbaugh said, is to imply that "we are so . . . omnipotent that we can . . . destroy the climate."[51]

- In response to the question of why Hurricane Katrina occurred, David Crowe, the executive director of Restore America, said: "The answer is found in understanding that man is not in control. God is! Everything in the sky, the sea and on earth is subject to His control." Saying that Katrina was "God's judgment on America," Crowe referred to the upcoming "gay, lesbian and transgender 'Southern Decadence' Labor Day gala."[52]

THE FAILURE OF THE AMERICAN MEDIA

Whereas the beliefs of Christian supernaturalists tend to make them complacent about climate change, the convictions of Americans in general tend to be most heavily shaped by the mass media. The media, moreover, have not led most Americans, including politicians, to be worried about the climate.

Americans are not sufficiently concerned about climate change, said America's most well-known climate scientist, James Hansen, because there is "a huge gap between the public's understanding of the situation and the scientific understanding."[53]

This gap is largely due to the existence of a carbon lobby, which uses—in the words of journalist Mark Hertsgaard—"a deceptive campaign to put its financial interests ahead of the future of our children and civilization." However, Hertsgaard continued, "the [carbon] lobby could never have succeeded without the assistance of the media."[54]

The failure of the media to resist the carbon lobby's propaganda was expressed by Eric Pooley, one of America's leading journalists, by means of a parable:

> Suppose our leading scientists discovered that a meteor, hurtling toward the earth, was set to strike later this century; the governments of the world had less than ten years to divert or destroy it. How would news organizations cover this story? Even in an era of financial distress, they would throw teams of reporters at it and give them the resources needed to follow it in extraordinary depth and detail. After all, the race to stop the meteor would be the story of the century.[55]

In this parable, carbon-using humanity is, of course, the meteor, which is threatening to destroy civilization. This threat is, Pooley continued, "the great test, and the great story, of our time. But news organizations have not been treating it that way."[56]

We cannot imagine that, if we knew that we had only 10 years to divert or destroy a humanity-destroying meteor heading straight at us, the governments and media would work together day and night to figure out the best approach, then provide all the needed resources—many trillions of dollars, if necessary—to prevent the destruction of human civilization.

The US media would, as they did in World War II, explain the nature of the threat and why citizens will need to make sacrifices— perhaps enormous ones, because no sacrifice would be too great. But the American media have done nothing like this in response to the climate threat. Talk-show host Thom Hartmann spoke of "The Mainstream Media's Criminal Climate Coverage."[57]

Likewise, Wen Stephenson, who had worked at NPR, PBS, and the *Boston Globe*, wrote an open letter to his former journalism colleagues, saying:

> [Y]ou are failing . . . to tell the most urgent truth we've ever faced. What's needed now is crisis-level coverage. . . . In

crisis coverage, you "flood the zone." The climate crisis is the biggest story of this, or any, generation—so why the hell aren't you flooding the climate "zone," putting it on the front pages and leading newscasts with it every day?[58]

The failure to treat climate change as the biggest story of our time has even been true of the *New York Times*. Although the evidence of the destructiveness of fossil fuels had become ever stronger, the *Times* in 2013 began cutting its coverage of climate change. It eliminated its climate desk, which had had two editors and seven reporters. The number of stories mentioning either "global warming" or "climate change" plummeted more than 40 percent.[59]

The *Times* also eliminated its Green blog, which had a dozen contributors in addition to its two editors. The editors who made this decision, wrote Curtis Brainard, the editor of the *Columbia Journalism Review*,

> should be ashamed of themselves. They've made a horrible decision that ensures the deterioration of the *Times*'s environmental coverage at a time when debates about climate change, energy, natural resources, and sustainability have never been more important to public welfare.[60]

Similarly, Drexel University's Robert Brulle, whom the *Times* had called "an expert on environmental communications," said: "The NY Times coverage of the environment has continued its journey from bad to worse."[61]

A Parallel to the Pooley's Parable

This chapter summarized a parable by Eric Pooley. The point was that if "we had only 10 years to divert or destroy a humanity-destroying meteor heading straight at us, the governments and media would work together day and night to figure out the best approach." This seems likely. But we now have been presented a similar situation in real life: The Intergovernmental Panel on Climate Change urgently warned the world in October 2018 that it had only 12 years left to "limit the climate change catastrophe."[62]

Television devoted some time to this story, and the major newspapers a little more. But this report from the IPCC did not stimulate a qualitative transformation in the presentations of the newspapers and the TV networks. In Kolbert's most cited statement, which was quoted above, she said:

> It may seem impossible to imagine that a technologically advanced society could choose, in essence, to destroy itself, but that is what we are now in the process of doing.[63]

Another quotation alluding to our failure was by Nobel Prize-winning scientist F. Sherwood Rowland, who asked in 1995:

> What's the use of having developed a science well enough to make predictions if, in the end, all we're willing to do is stand around and wait for them to come true?[64]

Neo-Liberalism

In August 2018, the *New York Times*, appearing to try to make up for its dereliction of duty during the previous decade, published a piece on climate change so long that it filled the entire *York Times Magazine*. Written by Nathaniel Rich, this article, entitled "Losing Earth," dealt with the world's failure to confront the global climate crisis in the 1980s.[65]

Naomi Klein, while saying that it was exciting "to see the *Times* throw the full force of its editorial machine behind Rich's opus," added that it was "enraging that the piece is spectacularly wrong in its central thesis." Klein wrote:

> According to Rich, between the years of 1979 and 1989, the basic science of climate change was understood and accepted, the partisan divide over the issue had yet to cleave, the fossil fuel companies hadn't started their misinformation campaign in earnest, and there was a great deal of global political momentum toward a bold and binding international emissions-reduction agreement. Writing of the key period at the end of the 1980s, Rich says, "The conditions for success could not have been more favorable."[66]

"And yet," Rich said, "we blew it." As to why, Rich said: "All the facts were known, and nothing stood in our way (except ourselves)."[67]

By contrast, Klein argued, the late 1980s did *not* provide an opportune moment for bold climate action, because,

> the late '80s was the absolute zenith of the neoliberal crusade, a moment of peak ideological ascendency for the economic and social project that deliberately set out to vilify collective action in the name of liberating "free markets" in every aspect of life.[68]

In abstraction from the ascendancy of neoliberalism, world momentum in the late 1980s—1988 in particular—seemed to be "building toward a tough, science-based global agreement." Klein wrote:

> James Hansen ... testified before Congress that he had "99 percent confidence" in "a real warming trend" linked to human activity. Later that same month, hundreds of scientists and policymakers held the historic World Conference on the Changing Atmosphere in Toronto, where the first emission reduction targets were discussed. By the end of that same year, ... the United Nations' Intergovernmental Panel on Climate Change, the premier scientific body advising governments on the climate threat, held its first session.... [W]hen the editors of *Time* magazine announced their 1988 "Man of the Year," they went for "Planet of the Year: Endangered Earth." ... [I]t really did seem like a profound shift was within grasp.

But then it all slipped away, said Klein, because of an epic case of historical bad timing:

> Just as governments were getting together to get serious about reigning in the fossil fuel sector, the global neoliberal revolution went supernova, and that project of economic and social reengineering clashed with the imperatives of both climate science and corporate regulation at every turn. ... 1988-89 was *the worst possible moment* for humanity to decide that it was going to get serious about putting planetary health ahead of profits.

. . . It was this convergence of historical trends—the emergence of a global architecture that was supposed to tackle climate change *and* the emergence of a much more powerful global architecture to liberate capital from all constraints—that derailed the momentum.[69]

Having no awareness of this convergence, Rich tried to explain the loss of climate momentum by reference to "human nature," as if human beings always and everywhere, in Rich's words, "are incapable of sacrificing present convenience to forestall a penalty imposed on future generations."[70]

THE AMERICAN GOVERNMENT

Christian supernaturalists, the carbon lobby, the media, and neoliberalism all played a role in preventing Americans thus far from being sufficiently concerned about climate change, given its threat to destroy civilization and even the human race. But the ultimate responsibility is that of the US government. For example, the government should be exerting the kind of leadership that the Roosevelt administration had provided in WW II.

Joe Romm, speaking of the need for industry to switch to clean energy, wrote: "This national (and global) re-industrialization effort would be on the scale of what we did during World War II, except it would last far longer."[71]

Whereas most people have imagined a World War III as involving a nuclear war involving the United States and Russia and/or China, Bill McKibben argued that we should think of WW III as our battle with climate change, which we are now losing. The burning of carbon and methane, wrote McKibben, has

fueled a global threat as lethal as the mushroom-shaped nuclear explosions we long feared. Carbon and methane now represent the deadliest enemy of all time, the first force fully capable of harrying, scattering, and impoverishing our entire civilization.[72]

Although we commonly use "war" as a metaphor—the war on poverty, on drugs, on cancer—the war on climate change is no metaphor, argued McKibben.

> By most of the ways we measure wars, climate change is the real deal: Carbon and methane are seizing physical territory, sowing havoc and panic, racking up casualties, and even destabilizing governments....It's not that global warming is *like* a world war. It *is* a world war. Its first victims, ironically, are those who have done the least to cause the crisis. But it's a world war aimed at us all. And if we lose, we will be as decimated and helpless as the losers in every conflict—except that this time, there will be no winners, and no end to the planetwide occupation that follows.[73]

The only hope for saving civilization, McKibben maintained, would be if we "mobilize for World War III on the same scale as we did for the last world war." Just as FDR was able to do quickly much of what was required, through executive action, concluded McKibben, we will lose WW III "without immediate executive action."[74]

But none of the presidents have grasped the fact that climate change is our World War III. For example, the aim of the Earth Summit in Rio de Janeiro was to stabilize atmospheric greenhouse gas concentrations at levels that would prevent dangerous changes in the global climate system, but the United States played the leading role in making the Summit a failure. In response to critics of the US role, the first President Bush said: "The American way of life is not up for negotiation."[75]

Even the best of our recent presidents did not get it. In an interview by David Remnick of the *New Yorker*, President Obama said: "I think we are fortunate at the moment, that we do not face a crisis of the scale and scope that Lincoln or F.D.R. faced."[76] Obama did not seem to understand that we now face a crisis far more difficult and fateful—not simply saving the Union or saving us from Fascism, but saving human civilization and even the human race. "The stakes, for all life on the planet," said James Hansen, "surpass those of any previous crisis."[77]

CONCLUSION

The failure of political leaders to rise to challenge climate change, *Guardian* journalist George Monbiot rightly said, is "the greatest political failure the world has ever seen."[78]

It is also the civilization's greatest religious failure. It seems, as argued in Chapter 2, that our universe was created by a Divine Reality that wanted to promote life. And our planet allowed for the emergence of very complex forms of life—forms of life with capacities for logic, mathematics, science, philosophy, religion, art, music, and literature.

The creation of such beings took many billions of years of cosmic and then geological evolution. The creation of human civilization then required the existence of a period that has been named the Holocene. Would it not be an unspeakable crime to destroy this work of divine art prematurely?

As terrible as were the holocausts caused by the Nazis and the Communists, these holocausts do not compare with a destruction of the human race and higher forms of life in general.

The American Empire is *extremely* demonic because it, for the sake of power and money, is in the process of prematurely destroying the Holocene, all the forms of life that depend on it, and all the creativity made possible by the development of civilization.

This empire is extremely demonic because its present leaders, seemingly interested only in themselves and their immediate descendants, are destroying the possibility that countless generations of human beings could be nurtured by the Garden of Eden known as the Holocene.

The American Empire is extremely demonic because its leaders have been too preoccupied with military projects to devote time and money to the evidently boring task of saving humanity and civilization. In 2018, Noam Chomsky said that America's Republican government is "the most dangerous organization in human history. Nobody, not even the Nazis, was dedicated to destroying the possibility of organized human life."[79]

Saying that there is a competition for the title of the worst empire of all time, Tom Engelhardt said that the USA has "a shot at taking the number one spot for all eternity."[80]

Most Americans today who believe in God were brought up assuming that America is at least basically on God's side, perhaps even the chief instrument of divine purposes in our world. To have to switch to the view that our country is instead the chief embodiment of demonic power, hence the primary threat to divine purposes on our planet, is not an enjoyable transformation for American Christians to make. But it is a transformation that is necessary if our beliefs are to correspond to reality, and if we are to be in a position to repent: to turn our churches, our country, and hence hopefully our civilization, in a different direction, before the human race becomes extinct.

Salvation and the Reign of God

CHAPTER FIFTEEN

Salvation

GIVEN THE FACT that Americans live in an evil, even demonic, empire, Americans need hope for salvation. Bumper stickers and billboards in America often say "Jesus saves." The question of the present chapter is how Jesus could mediate salvation to us.

Chapter 7, dealing with Christology proper, presented Jesus as a special incarnation of God. The present chapter deals with the "work" of Jesus Christ: How does Jesus as the Christ bring salvation to people? There were four dimensions of salvation as presupposed by Jesus. They can be labeled Salvation$_1$, Salvation$_2$, Salvation$_3$, and Salvation$_4$.

The chapter begins, however, with a discussion of what Christian salvation is *not*.

WHAT SALVATION IS NOT

The standard Christian doctrine of salvation has been one of the main reasons that Christian belief has fallen into disrepute. The basic problem has been the idea that God decided to save people by sending Jesus to earth to die. In the early Christian centuries, the dominant idea was that God sent Jesus to die to save us from the dominion of Satan. (Calling it the "classic doctrine of atonement," Swedish theologian Gustaf Aulén reinvigorated this idea in his 1931 book *Christus Victor.*[1])

The Anselmian Doctrine of Atonement

But then in the eleventh century, Anselm, the archbishop of Canterbury, articulated an alternative view in a little book titled *Cur Deus Homo* ("Why God Became Human"). Anselm's answer to that question was that human sin offended the divine justice, making all people deserving of hell, and so unless the divine justice is satisfied, God cannot save us. His argument ran:

> (i) The satisfaction needs to be rendered by a human being, because it is humanity that is guilty of the offence. (ii) An ordinary human being cannot pay the penalty, because the offence, being against God, was infinite, so only God could pay the price. (iii) Accordingly, the sacrifice had to be made by the God-man.[2]

This Anselmian theory came to be called the "sacrificial" or "substitutionary" atonement.

This idea was presupposed in Ingmar Bergman's film *Winter Light,* which was centered around Pastor Tomas Ericsson, who was having trouble with his faith because he could not reconcile the atrocities in the world with a loving God. In a crucial scene, looking at the crucifix in his church, the pastor said "absurd."

In any case, the Anselmian view—according to which Jesus "came down to earth" to die as a *sacrifice* to pay for our sin, to die as a *substitute* for us—became dominant in American Christianity. It became so central that when, in reaction to theological modernism, evangelical Protestants formulated a list of five fundamental Christian doctrines, one of which was "the substitutionary atonement of Christ."[3]

As Marcus Borg pointed out, this understanding of salvation is multiply problematic: It makes Jesus's death God's plan. It makes

Jesus's death more important than his life and teachings. And "it obscures and even renders invisible the historical reasons for [Jesus's] crucifixion"—the fact that "Jesus was killed because he challenged the powers that ruled his world."[4]

Salvation from Hell

Traditional thinking about salvation has thought of salvation as being given eternal life: Jesus saved us by dying on the cross for our sins, thereby saving us *from* hell and *for* heaven. Marcus Borg as a young man had begun questioning the idea that one can avoid hell only by faith in Jesus. He began by raising the question of fairness: "Was it fair that only Christians could go to heaven? What about people who had never heard of Jesus or Christianity?"[5]

Rejecting the view that salvation is "about going to heaven and avoiding hell," Borg argued—as the title of a chapter by him put it—"Salvation Is More About This Life than an Afterlife." As shown by his discussion of the appearances of Jesus in Chapter 7, Borg by no means rejected the idea of the reality of continued life beyond bodily death. However, he said, "Christianity and salvation are mostly about *this* life, not the next."[6] Although Borg was a liberal Protestant, among whom this idea has long been commonplace, there are also Evangelicals and Roman Catholics who share his rejection of hell.

In 2011, an Evangelical pastor named Rob Bell published a bestselling book entitled *Love Wins: A Book About Heaven, Hell, and the Fate of Every Person Who Ever Lived*. The title "Love Wins" means that salvation is universal, so that no matter how long we resist God's love, this love will always win out in the end.[7]

Bell's book created so much controversy in Evangelical circles that *Time* magazine put it on the cover and had famous historian Jon Meacham write a long article, which he entitled, "What if Hell Doesn't Exist?"[8] Like Borg, Bell used the issue of fairness to challenge the idea that hell is the destiny of everyone except those who confess faith in Jesus and get baptized. With regard to people who, through no fault of their own, die before knowing about the Gospel, Bell asked, "What if the missionary got a flat tire?"[9]

Meacham reported that Bell's book "has Evangelicals in a fury."[10] Much of this fury resulted from misunderstandings of Bell's book, as if he denied the reality of hell. But Julie Clawson, offering a more accurate summary of his position, wrote:

> Does Bell believe in hell? Yes. . . . Hell is real, but it is a place we create for ourselves as we reject the gift of life God offers to us. But . . . God's essence is love and . . . God can never stop being God which means that in the end, love has to win.[11]

However, some of the fury produced by Bell's book was because of its rejection of a particular conception of hell. In response to the book, the Southern Baptist Convention issued a resolution "On The Reality Of Hell," which affirmed its "belief in the biblical teaching on eternal, conscious punishment of the unregenerate in Hell."[12]

Strongly rejecting this kind of theology, Carol Meyer, an author for the *National Catholic Reporter,* wrote an article entitled "Debunking the Myth of Hell," in which she called it "an unthinkable, horrible, destructive concept that can't possibly be true." She continued:

> Could any wrong merit the terrible pain of burning in fire, while fully conscious, for a week or a year, much less eternity? What kind of a monster would inflict that on anyone? How could such cruelty and sadism be consistent with a God of love?[13]

Illustrating the point that theologians should never—as discussed above in the Introduction—let the Gospel's primary doctrines be undermined by secondary or tertiary doctrines, Carol Meyer wrote:

> It is an insult of the highest degree to think God could ever be so mean and evil as to create hell. . . . And we don't need the concept to justify the need for Christ. All arguments for hell, however reasonable they once sounded, are debunked by one single truth—God is *Love.* The end of the story.[14]

The gist of the various Evangelical criticisms of Bell's book was, said Borg, "If there is no hell [in the traditional sense], why be a

Christian?" Saying that thinking like that leads to a distorted view of Christianity, Borg explained why:

- It turns Christianity into "a religion of self-preservation" and "a religion of requirements and rewards."

- "[I]t produces a contractual understanding of the Christian life. Namely, if we fulfill our part of the contract, God will fulfill God's part."

- "Finally, an emphasis on the afterlife focuses attention on the next life to the detriment of attention to this life. Working to change the conditions of life in this world [such as human destructiveness to the environment] becomes relatively unimportant except insofar as it might be a requirement for salvation [after death]."[15]

As to what salvation really is, Borg said that it is about "transformation—to be saved from one way of life to another."[16] This transformation, which is implicit in Jesus's message, can be described as four dimensions of Christian salvation: Salvation$_1$, Salvation$_2$, Salvation$_3$, and Salvation$_4$.

SALVATION$_1$

Similar to Borg's description of salvation as transformation, John Cobb was quoted in Chapter 8 as saying that we should think of "salvation as something we participate in here and now rather than, or in addition to, life beyond."[17]

The idea that we "participate in salvation here and now" has been described as "realized eschatology." If eschatology is the doctrine of the last things (*eschaton* being the Greek word for "last"), *realized* eschatology is the idea that those last things have already happened, or are now happening. This idea gets the most scriptural support from the passage in which Jesus said that "the kingdom of God is within you" (Luke 17:21). (By contrast, the Gospel of Mark said that "the kingdom of God is at hand" [1:15]; the Gospel of Matthew said "the kingdom of heaven has come near" [4:17].) According to the view that the Reign of God is within us, salvation is a reign of God in individual hearts and social relations.

The term "realized eschatology" was associated primarily with New Testament scholar C. H. Dodd (1884–1973), who argued that Jesus's references to the Kingdom of God meant a present reality rather than a future apocalypse. However, although Dodd at first tried to interpret all passages about the Kingdom of God in this way, most scholars called this attempt a failure. In fact, Dodd himself eventually agreed that not all passages were consistent with the idea of realized eschatology.[18]

There is now consensus among New Testament scholars that the kingdom of God should be understood as both future and present (with the meaning of "future" often left vague by liberals).

However, for much modern liberal theology, Salvation$_1$ is the only type of salvation of which we can today speak. By denying, or at least ignoring, the other dimensions of salvation, modern liberal theology has provided little, if any, support for other dimensions. Salvation$_1$ is central. But if all the other dimensions of salvation are removed, it is unclear what is supposed to generate a reign of God in human hearts and social relations.

SALVATION$_2$

In his book *The Meaning of Revelation,* H. Richard Niebuhr (Reinhold Niebuhr's brother) said that the Christian belief in God overcomes the idea that we live in "a great impersonal cosmos, which does not know that we exist and does not care for us."[19] Niebuhr here was referring to Salvation$_2$: freedom from the threat of meaninglessness through confidence that we are known and loved by the creator of the universe. This is crucial because "the culminating fact of rational life," wrote Alfred North Whitehead, "refuses to conceive of itself as a transient enjoyment, transiently useful."[20] Atheism is a serious problem, because it implies that the universe will eventually be as if we had never existed. This nihilism sometimes contributes to the fact that some people become addicted to alcohol or drugs.

By contrast, Jesus and others whose beliefs were nurtured by the Hebrew Scriptures did not face this problem, because they had confidence that they were known and valued. For example, Psalm 139:1–3 said:

> O Lord, you have searched me and known me.
> You know when I sit down and when I rise up;
> you discern my thoughts from far away.
> You search out my path and my lying down,
> and are acquainted with all my ways.

Likewise, Isaiah 49:15 assured readers that God would never forget them.

> Can a woman forget her nursing child, or show no compassion for the child of her womb? Even these may forget, yet I will not forget you.

Inheriting and passing on this vision of reality, Jesus taught his followers that they were known and valued by God:

> Are not two sparrows sold for a penny? Yet not one of them will fall to the ground apart from your Father. And even the hairs of your head are all counted. So do not be afraid; you are of more value than many sparrows. (Matthew 10:29–31)

Objective Immortality

In language very different from the biblical language, both Whitehead and Charles Hartshorne affirmed a view similar on this issue to the biblical view absorbed and transmitted by Jesus. Hartshorne said:

> Infallibly and with unrivaled adequacy aware of all others, God includes others—not, as we do, in a mostly indistinct or largely unconscious manner, but with full clarity. ... Since God forgets nothing, loses no value once acquired, our entire worth is imperishable in the divine life.[21]

This doctrine is called "objective immortality," according to which one exists forever by virtue of being permanently an object of God's knowledge and love.

Social Immortality?

To be sure, some people believe that we do not need objective immortality in God. They believe that it is sufficient to recognize that we will have "social immortality," according to which we are objectively immortal in the hearts, minds, and memories of other people—that we will live on through their memories.

However, despite the name, so-called social immortality does not really provide immortality. Memory fades, and we are aware that, for most of us anyway, our contributions will become less and less significant as time passes. Most of us are consciously remembered for only a few decades, if that. Of course, a few very famous people, such as Moses and Plato, are remembered for a few thousand years. But being remembered for thousands of years is considerably less than being remembered forever.

The fact that so-called social immortality is not really immortality raises in the strongest possible terms the question of the meaning of our lives. We may have struggled mightily to realize certain aims, but reflection upon the impermanence of all finite structures raises the question of whether our struggles really make any ultimate difference. Hartshorne wrote:

> Be the aim Nirvana, the Classless Society, the Welfare State, Self-realization, the query is never silenced, what good is it, from the cosmic and everlasting perspective, that one or the other or all of these aims be attained for a time on this ball of rock?[22]

Reflection tells us that the human race will eventually perish. If so-called social immortality is the only kind of immortality we have, then our lives make no permanent contribution to anything, so the universe will eventually be as if we had never been. Being remembered by God alone provides genuine objective immortality.

This idea was so central to Hartshorne's spirituality that he spoke of his "religion of contributionism," according to which: "We contribute our feelings to others, and above all to the Universal Recipient of feeling, the One 'to Whom all hearts are open.'"[23]

Sufficient as Well as Necessary?

Belief in our objective immortality in God can provide a basis for a type of realized eschatology—for experiencing the reign of God here and now. Hartshorne makes a good case, moreover, for his view that belief in some kind of objective immortality in the universe is a necessary ingredient in a fulfilled life.

But if belief in objective immortality is a necessary condition for experiencing salvation here and now, is it also sufficient? Hartshorne himself clearly found it to be so. On that basis, he and some other process theologians have said that, therefore, the question of life after death is a matter of indifference.

But many theologians from other schools of thought have strongly disagreed. For example, Anglican theologian Austin Farrer, referring to criticism of process theology he wrote after examining the writings of Hartshorne and Schubert Ogden,[24] reported that "he wrote it in a rage."[25]

However, the position Farrer was criticizing is only one of the positions held by process theologians; other process theologians have said that the question of life after death should not be treated as a matter of indifference.

SALVATION₃

For example, in an essay entitled "The Resurrection of the Soul," John Cobb pointed to the widespread tendency of liberal theologians to limit their discussion of the resurrection to its "symbolic value" or "existential meaning." By contrast, Cobb said,

> the question of what, if anything, happens after we die has not disappeared from the range of human concerns. It has simply moved out of professional theology into other hands. Our sophisticated equivocations on this topic have contributed to our general irrelevance to the religious interests of our contemporaries.[26]

Although Borg was right to say that salvation in an afterlife is not what Christian salvation is primarily about, this does not mean that it is unimportant. The next section, which deals with this issue, is quite lengthy, constituting the remainder of this chapter.

The third dimension of salvation presupposed by Jesus involves an ultimate salvation in a resurrected life beyond bodily death. This formulation emphasizes the fact that salvation should not simply be equated with being given continued life after physical death. Rather, life after bodily death would be important primarily because it provides the possibility for attaining salvation, to experience the transformation understood as "sanctification."

Salvation by Fidelity

The Kingdom of God as proclaimed by Jesus was understood as an alternative to the Roman Empire, with its supposedly divine Caesars. Just as the Caesars demanded fidelity (fides) from their subjects (see Chapter 6), worship of the God of Jesus and Israel requires fidelity:

> You shall love the Lord your God with all your heart, and with all your soul, and with all your strength, and with all your mind; and your neighbor as yourself. (Luke 10:26, based on Deuteronomy 6:5: "You shall love the Lord your God with all your heart, and with all your soul, and with all your might.")

Accordingly, "salvation by faith" should be understood as *salvation by fidelity*. This fidelity—with all it entails—can be considered the sole requirement for becoming saved in the sense of sanctified. But such fidelity is seldom, if ever, a virtue that is developed suddenly.

Given their belief in purgatory, Roman Catholics have generally not thought in terms of sudden salvation, holding instead that one must go through a long process, though which one's sins are purged. By contrast, Protestants in the sixteenth century rejected the idea of purgatory. And so, insofar as they have accepted a supernaturalist idea of the God-human relation, they have been able to hold that God could transform you into a saint in a twinkling of an eye—perhaps if on your deathbed you sincerely said (to use a common formula):

"I believe Jesus is the Christ, the son of the living God, and I accept him as my personal savior."

As mentioned in Chapter 8, holding that salvation can no longer credibly be understood in supernatural terms, John Hick said that salvation should *not* be understood as conforming to an arbitrary divine decision, such as "being forgiven and accepted by God because of the atoning death of Jesus." Rather, we should understand salvation "as an actual change in human beings," which involves "a long process," not a sudden, supernaturally effected transformation.[27]

Eastern Orthodoxy especially emphasizes salvation in this sense. Patriarch Philaret of Moscow wrote:

> Every Christian should find for himself the imperative and incentive to become holy. If you live without struggle and without hope of becoming holy, then you are Christians only in name and not in essence.... It is a trustworthy saying that Jesus Christ came into the world to save sinners (I Tim. 1:15). But we deceive ourselves if we think that we are saved while remaining sinners. Christ saves those sinners by giving them the means to become saints.[28]

Life after death could provide us with time to engage in this long process—time in which we might come to love God with all our hearts, souls, and minds, and other persons as ourselves—time to develop fidelity to God. Being divinely influenced to reach this state would be the sanctification of the soul. But is life after death philosophically possible?

Modern Philosophy against Life after Death

Few liberal theologians in our time affirm the reality of life after death straightforwardly (rather than only symbolically or metaphorically). The reason for this is the widespread belief that our continuation as experiencing subjects after bodily death is impossible. This is so because of the rejection of supernaturalism combined with the acceptance of a view of the mind-body relation—either materialism or epiphenomenalism—that makes the mind's existence apart from the brain seem impossible. As was discussed in Chapter 4:

- Materialists say that what we call the soul or mind—with its experience—is not some entity distinct from the brain. Rather, it is in some sense identical with it. Materialists, in fact, have often called their position "identism."

- Epiphenomenalists, not seeing how experiences can be properties of a material object—even one as complex as a human brain—regard the mind as a nonefficacious byproduct of the brain's functioning. Although the mind is distinct from the brain, it has no power of its own.

Neither materialists nor epiphenomenalists, accordingly, regard the soul or mind as an entity that could conceivably exist apart from the physical body. Given this view, life beyond bodily death would be possible only if the physical body were to be resurrected.[29] But such a resurrection, which would require the agency of an omnipotent deity, is ruled out by the rejection of supernaturalism. From the point of view of modern thought, therefore, the idea of life after death cannot be taken seriously.

Life after Death and Panexperientialism

However, from the point of view of Whitehead's postmodern philosophy, with its panexperientialism, the possibility of life after death is not ruled out *a priori*. Although Whitehead in his writings never explicitly affirmed life after death, he did acknowledge that his philosophical position made it *possible*. In 1926, he wrote that his philosophy was "neutral on the question of immortality, or on the existence of purely spiritual beings other than God."[30] Being neutral meant that his doctrine of the human soul did not, like those of Plato and Descartes, entail that the soul would necessarily survive the death of the body, and also that it did not, like materialism and epiphenomenalism, make it impossible.

Whitehead's philosophy does not entail its impossibility, because it does not hold, with materialism, that the mind or soul is identical with the brain or, with epiphenomenalism, that it is real but has no power of its own. Rather, it holds the position known as "interactionism," according to which the brain acts on the mind and the mind in turn acts on the brain.

As explained in Chapter 2, interactionism should not be called "dualism," because that term almost inevitably suggests *ontological* dualism, which makes interaction impossible (apart from supernatural aid).

No Souls without Brains?

However, even without affirming materialism, epiphenomenalism, or ontological dualism, one might argue that a mind or soul could not exist in a disembodied state—that is, without a brain. This might even be thought to be supported by Whitehead's position, according to which human souls could not evolutionarily have arisen apart from human brains.

In other words, just as the living occasions of experience in the eukaryotic cell could not have arisen apart from a structured society something like the eukaryotic cell as a whole, with its macromolecules and organelles (see Chapter 2), a high-level enduring individual like a chimpanzee or human soul could not have arisen apart from some structured society with the complexity of a chimpanzee or human brain. In the same way, one could argue, the dominant occasions constituting the human soul could not exist apart from the environment provided by a brain.

Whitehead himself, however, evidently did not draw this conclusion. In *Adventures of Ideas*—one of his last writings—he again left open the possibility (as he had in *Religion in the Making*) that the human soul might exist apart from the body. Having defined the human soul as "a personal living society of high-grade occasions," he added:

> How far this soul finds a support for its existence beyond the body is:—another question. The everlasting nature of God, which in a sense is non-temporal and in another sense is temporal, may establish with the soul a peculiarly intense relationship of mutual immanence. Thus in some important sense the existence of the soul may be freed from its complete dependence upon the bodily organization.[31]

It should be noted that Whitehead's openness to this possibility did not contradict his doctrine that every occasion of experience must have a physical pole. He was only suggesting here that the physical prehensions required by each occasion of the soul's existence might not necessarily need to include prehensions of a brain.

To explain: A physical prehension has nothing to do with "physical" in the ordinary (Cartesian) sense. Rather, a prehension is "physical" (rather than conceptual) if its object is an actuality, not a mere possibility. For example, whereas the prehension of the number 2 is a *conceptual* prehension, a direct prehension of another human mind (telepathy) is a physical prehension, as is a direct experience of God.

Whitehead's openness to the possibility that human experience may be freed from ongoing information from one's brain may have reflected the influence of J. M. E. McTaggart, who was one of Whitehead's closest philosophical friends.[32]

McTaggart provided an answer to the argument that the entirely brain-dependent nature of the mind is proved by empirical facts. This supposed proof appealed to the fact that damage to the brain results in derangement, loss of various cognitive abilities, or even complete loss of consciousness. These consequences, McTaggart argued, support only the proposition that "*while a self has a body,* that body is essentially connected with the self's mental life." For example, "the fact that an abnormal state of the brain may affect our thoughts does not prove that the normal states of the brain are necessary for thought."[33]

Although Whitehead did not explicitly endorse McTaggart's position on this issue, at least in print, this position is consistent with the above-quoted statement from *Adventures of Ideas.* To repeat: Having defined the human mind or soul as "a personal living society of high-grade occasions," Whitehead added:

> How far this soul finds a support for its existence beyond the body is:—another question. . . . [I]n some important sense the existence of the soul may be freed from its complete dependence upon the bodily organization.[34]

Whitehead could say this, while rejecting supernaturalism, because of his position on the mind-body relation, according to which (i) the mind or soul is numerically distinct from the brain—the brain is one entity, the mind another—and (ii) the mind has power of its own (contra-epiphenomenalism). Therefore, the idea that the soul could survive apart from the brain is ontologically possible.

Resurrection of the Soul

Given Whitehead's ontology, life after death does not require super-naturalism. The fact that supernatural intervention is unnecessary, however, does not imply the unimportance of divine influence. If the human soul now has the natural capacity to survive bodily death, it has this capacity because of billions of years of previous divine activity during which it brought the evolutionary process to the point at which human-like beings could emerge. Also, even if the soul now has the capacity to survive the death of its bodily organism, it would actually do so only because it is continually receiving fresh divine aims from God. (This is Whitehead's dynamic version of what has traditionally been called the "sustaining activity of God.")

To express this point, John Cobb spoke (as mentioned earlier) of the "resurrection of the soul," a phrase that combines the points made by each of the two traditional phrases for life after death. Like "immortality of the soul," this phrase implies that the power to survive death is now inherent in the soul, so that no supernatural intervention is needed. But like "resurrection of the body," this phrase points to the idea that this power is not *simply* inherent, but was, and still is, dependent on divine influence.[35]

Process theologians can, in any case, think of salvation as the sanctification of the soul within the framework of a fully naturalistic theism, according to which divine influence is by persuasion alone.

Therefore, one could not appeal to Whitehead's authority to support the contention that process philosophy makes life after death impossible. However, to say that life after death is not metaphysically ruled out does not by itself provide sufficient reason to affirm its plausibility. This issue is discussed next.

Empirical Evidence vs. Resurrection of the Soul?

Central to this issue is the fact that—to review—by virtue of its doctrine of the human being as a compound individual, process philosophy provides the primary necessary condition for the possibility of life after death within a naturalistic framework, namely, the numerical distinction between mind and brain, because this distinction means that the death of the brain does not logically entail the death of the mind.

However, even many philosophers who accept the brain-mind distinction would claim that empirical evidence rules out the idea that the mind might exist apart from the brain. For example:

- In *The Illusion of Immortality*, Corliss Lamont said that modern philosophy has shown the mind to be wholly dependent on the brain.[36]

- J.J.C. Smart said that "the empirical evidence in favor of an invariable correlation between mental states and brain states is extremely strong," so "it is hard to believe that after the dissolution of the brain there could be any thought or conscious experience whatever."[37]

- "All the evidence," claimed Bertrand Russell, "goes to show that what we regard as our mental life is bound up with brain structure and organized bodily energy."[38]

However, when Russell spoke of "all the evidence" (and Lamont and Smart saw things the same way), he meant *the evidence read from a materialist perspective*. For example Canadian philosopher Kai Nielsen said that no amount of empirical evidence could lead him to believe in life after death. If "we think that the concept of disembodied existence makes no sense," said Nielsen, "then we will interpret the data differently." That is:

[W]e will say, and reasonably so, even if we do not have a good alternative explanation for [certain kinds of happenings], that [disembodied existence] cannot be the correct description of what went on.[39]

However, as pointed out in Chapter 4, process philosophy's position on the reality of nonsensory perception is supported by a massive amount of empirical evidence. On the basis of a more open-minded reading of "all the evidence," therefore, the mind's dependence on the brain for its perceptions is not as complete as materialists assume. It is not so clear that, "after the dissolution of the brain," in Smart's words, there could not be "any thought or conscious experience whatever."

Evolution vs. Resurrection of the Soul?

Even if life after bodily death cannot be shown to be impossible, one might argue that it is too implausible to be taken seriously. One somewhat widespread objection to the belief that human beings survive bodily death can be expressed in terms of a *reductio ad absurdum:* Given an evolutionary worldview, in which ontological dualism must be rejected, then if we posit life after death for humans, argued Corliss Lamont, we must do the same for Neanderthals, chimpanzees, rats, and even fleas. And we certainly cannot believe this.[40]

That attempted *reductio* would work, however, only on the assumption that—in the language of process philosophy—the soul or dominant member of a compound individual, purely by virtue of being a soul, has the capacity to exist apart from the body that was originally necessary to bring it forth. Accordingly, every creature with a soul would continue after bodily death. However, Whitehead explicitly rejected this all-or-none view, saying (in a statement quoted in Chapter 4):

> [T]he personality of an animal organism may be more or less. It is not a mere question of having a soul or of not having a soul. The question is, How much, if any?[41]

Whitehead thereby implied a third possibility, which is that the human capacity to survive apart from the body might be a historical emergent.

Within an evolutionary perspective, the idea of historical emergents is not an unusual idea, even within a panexperientialist perspective. Although all actual entities are occasions of experience, so that experience as such does not emerge, there are many capacities that do. *Conscious* experience, for example, emerged at some stage of the evolutionary process, and *self*-consciousness at a still later stage. The capacity to use symbolic language also emerged at a rather late stage of the evolutionary process, bringing about a mode of existence that is virtually different in kind from that which went before. This emergence, in fact, was surely part and parcel of the emergence of self-consciousness.

In saying that the personality of an animal organism "may be more or less," Whitehead was speaking of *degrees of soul*. As we saw in Chapter 4, this idea was developed by John Cobb in a discussion of the rise of human existence, with its distinctive capacities. This rise, Cobb argued, was fueled by a great increase in "surplus psychic energy," meaning energy beyond that needed for the well-being of the body. The threshold dividing humans from other primates occurred, he suggested, when "the surplus psychic energy became sufficient in quantity to enable the psychic life to become its own end rather than primarily a means to the survival and health of the body." This surplus psychic energy was the precondition for religion and all those other activities in which the mind treats itself as an end in itself, not simply as the director of its bodily activities.[42]

According to this account, although all animals have soul, human beings have enormously more soul than others: more creative energy, more power to engage in symbolizing activities, and more social order through time, so that people's concern for their past and future experiences may become stronger than their concerns for their bodily welfare.

Perhaps another emergent is the capacity of the human soul, once it has emerged, to survive separation from the body. If so, it might well have been simply one of the effects of that great increase in power involved in the human soul's development of symbolic language and self-consciousness. In other words, the capacity to ask, "When we die, will we live again?" (Job 14:14), may be one of the expressions of the power to do just that.

THE IMPORTANCE OF LIFE AFTER DEATH

Because of its position on the mind-body relation, process philosophy makes life after death possible within a fully naturalistic framework. Some people would reply, however, that establishing this possibility is irrelevant, because life after death is not important. Even some Whiteheadians have argued for this view. But the existence of uniquely human problems shows that they are mistaken.

In the world's various religions, the doctrine of human destiny has usually involved some mode of existence beyond bodily death. It has widely been held that, if some of the uniquely human problems are to be resolved, such a resolution could occur only in a life after death.

The distinctive nature of human consciousness, with its element of *self*-consciousness, makes death a special problem for human beings. Besides the fact that we, like all other animals, will die sooner or later, we can *consciously anticipate* this fact. The usual assumption that this anticipation is unique to us on this planet is probably correct, at least largely. Even if some of the other higher animals have an inchoate anticipation of their own deaths, we appear to be the only ones with elaborate rituals and meaning-systems connected with death. In any case, because we do anticipate our own death and that of others, death is a problem, which seems to have four distinguishable aspects.

Ultimate Meaning?

First, our awareness that we will die raises the question of whether our lives have any ultimate meaning. Although this issue was mentioned earlier, there is a need here to explore more fully the nature of the problem that arises from the fact that, in the words of Whitehead quoted there, "rational life refuses to conceive of itself as a transient enjoyment, transiently useful."[43] The problem is that, if we come to believe that we make no permanent contribution—that our lives *are* merely "transiently useful" at best—the resulting disappointment can empty our "transient enjoyment" of most of its enjoyment. Such a result that would mean that the evolutionary process had brought about a self-defeating result.

That is, the purpose behind the evolutionary process is, by hypothesis, the development of creatures with increasingly greater capacity for intrinsic value. Human beings appear to be the apex of this development on our planet. And yet human existence, by virtue of its capacity to ask the question of ultimate meaning, could end up being less, rather than more, enjoyable than the other forms of animal existence.

Ultimate Justice?

The second aspect of the problem created by our awareness that we all die is the issue of ultimate justice. We are aware that human life is terribly unfair, that some people, through no merit of their own, are extremely fortunate, whereas others, through no fault of their own, are extremely unfortunate. Many are, for example, born into situations of abject poverty, from which there is no escape, or with terrible deformities. Many others are born with great potential, but die young, before having had much chance to develop this potential.

Beyond these obvious facts, there is also the problem, emphasized by Immanuel Kant, that a gap between virtue and happiness often exists, with immoral people often having happier lives than truly good people. The resulting intellectual problem, as Kant pointed out, is that these discrepancies throw into doubt the validity of our sense that there is a moral order to the universe. That is, the universe seems to call us to be moral; most of the religions of the world agree, Whitehead pointed out, on the existence of a "character of rightness" inherent in the nature of things.[44] But if the universe itself is not just, then our confidence that it really contains objective moral principles is undermined, with the result that we are led toward moral nihilism. Kant believed that we could prevent this undermining only by postulating a life after death in which the gap between virtue and happiness would be progressively overcome.[45]

Longing for More Life

The third aspect of the problem raised by our anticipation of death is the fact that most people evidently have a longing for more life. Even apart from questions of ultimate meaning and justice, they are simply not ready to have their personal stream of experience extinguished. Much modern thought has, to be sure, portrayed this longing as a sign of immaturity or simply a lingering after-effect of the traditional religions, which had created unrealistic expectations. The hope for continued life after death, in either case, has been treated as a problem that we can "get over."

This assumption, however, has not been borne out, including in the United States. Most Americans still believe in a life after death, and at least most of the rest evidently find their lack of belief a problem.[46] Some philosophers who completely reject this belief candidly admit, in fact, that they wish that they could accept it.

In any case, if this longing is a permanent feature of human existence as such, as it seems, then it raises a problem about the goodness of the universe: If there is no continued life beyond bodily death, as most modern thought assumes, then the universe has created an ineradicable desire in us that it will not fulfill—a conclusion that implies a form of Manichaeism.

Salvation as Integrity or Wholeness

A fourth aspect of the problem created by our conscious anticipation of death involves the human religious desire for salvation in the sense of integrity or wholeness. Religious beliefs and practices are largely oriented around the sense that there is an ideal mode (or some ideal modes) of existence and that, through proper relation to the Holy Reality, we can realize this mode (or one of these modes) of existence. Most people, however, also have the sense of now being far from the goal, much too far for the gap to be traversed within the present life. The sense of this gap—between what we now *are* and what we *ought* to be—has been closely connected to ideas of a life beyond the present one, in which this gap may be overcome. For strongly religious people, in other words, the desire for *more* life, discussed above, has been intimately related to a desire for a *sanctified* life.

If we believe that there is no life after death, however, then we seem forced to the conclusion that it is impossible for the ideal to be realized, at least for most people, because of insufficient time, which produces a dilemma: On the one hand, if we hold to the religious ideal, we in effect accept a form of Jean-Paul Sartre's view that the human being is a "futile passion," called to an ideal that cannot possibly be realized.[47] On the other hand, in light of the widespread intuition that *ought* implies *can*, we may simply give up the religious ideal of wholeness, concluding that the old idea that human beings are called to realize such an ideal is a colossal mistake.

The divine *modus operandi,* using solely persuasion, only occasionally creates saints within the span of an earthly life. However, given a return to the medieval view, according to which the divine persuasion works on us during a lengthy process of purgation and sanctification after bodily death, hope for universal Salvation$_3$ is intelligible.

EVIDENCE FOR LIFE AFTER DEATH

Just as Christian faith in our time can no longer presuppose a super-naturalistic worldview, belief in life after death cannot be based on faith—in the sense of believing without evidence. It must be based on evidence that can be tested.

This was Whitehead's view. After pointing out that his philosophy allows for the possibility that a soul might survive bodily death, he said that the question of whether the soul does in fact survive should "be decided on more special evidence, religious or otherwise, provided that it is trustworthy."[48]

In speaking of evidence "religious or otherwise," Whitehead meant events associated with religions, such as the post-crucifixion appearances of Jesus, and the evidence from psychical research (now often called *parapsychology*). After all, Whitehead's career at Cambridge University overlapped with that of Henry Sidgwick, the first president of the Society for Psychical Research, whose autobiography Whitehead quoted.[49] Also, Whitehead was heavily influenced by the writings of William James, whom he called "that adorable genius,"[50] and James was the intellectual leader and co-founder of the American Society for Psychical Research.[51]

Direct evidence for life after death can be provided by apparitions, mediums, apparent reincarnation, apparent possession, and out-of-body experiences.[52] Apparitions were discussed in Chapter 7. The present chapter focuses on out-of-body experiences (OBEs).

Out-of-Body Experiences

There are two major types of OBEs: (1) ones that come about in ordinary circumstances and (2) ones that come about when people are physically near death, called near-death out-of-body experiences (ND OBEs).

Near-death experiences (NDEs) typically have two phases: a *mundane* phase, in which one is experiencing this-worldly things, such as the patient's hospital room, followed by a *transcendental* phase, in which one has other-worldly experiences (such as going through a tunnel, moving up towards a bright light, seeing deceased relatives, having a life review, and being told that one's time is not up and hence must go back to his or her body).

To refer to an "out-of-body experience" does not necessarily imply that one's mind or soul was literally out of the body. Rather, an OBE is "an experience in which a person seems to perceive the world from a location outside his [or her] body."[53] Whether people's minds or souls are literally outside their bodies is at the center of the critical discussion of these experiences.

The view that one's mind is really outside the body is the *extra-somatic hypothesis*. The view that one's soul or mind, while having an OBE, remains in the body is known as the *intrasomatic hypothesis*. The scientific question is: Which hypothesis can better account for the various features of OBEs?

In addition to the feeling of being out of the body, other common features of OBEs are: (1) Strong conviction that the experience is *real;* (2) absence of pain; (3) normal or better-than-normal hearing; (4) normal or better-than-normal visual perception; and (5) exceptionally positive emotional state.

However, these features cannot be used for definitely preferring the extrasomatic hypothesis. Advocates of the intrasomatic hypothesis can just dismiss all of these features as fantasies.

Veridical OBE's: Discussion

However, OBEs sometimes have one more feature, which does support the extrasomatic hypothesis. When people have OBEs, they afterwards are sometimes able to report events that can be corroborated by others. This is especially the case with regard to ND OBEs, given the typical circumstances.

For example, one who has a near-death OBE is typically on a hospital bed after having a heart attack. The OBE occurs when one is not breathing, one's heart is not beating, and one's eyes are closed. Nevertheless, a person may report having heard and seen the doctor and nurses working on him or her. If the person's reported perceptions are corroborated by one of the doctors or nurses or some other reliable witness, researchers speak of *veridical perceptions* (which are analogous to the veridical apparitions discussed in Chapter 7).

Persons normally cannot see without their brains receiving information from their eyes. Of course, we have visual experiences in dreams, without receiving information from our eyes. But such visual experiences do not constitute *seeing* unless they provide us with accurate information about the world beyond our minds.

Reports of veridical perceptions during OBEs have serious implications for the mind-body relation. Accordingly, some people interested in the possibility of life after bodily death have become very interested in the study of OBEs with veridical perceptions.

To be sure, OBEs are fascinating even apart from the issue of veridical perceptions. Having an OBE often leads one who had the experience to conclude that his or her mind can exist apart from the body. And ND OBEs, whether or not they are preceded by a mundane OBE, often contain transcendental experiences that seem utterly real. Persons who have had these experiences often take them as foretastes of their life after death. Moreover, Kenneth Ring, one of the giants of NDE studies, reported that the NDE tends to bring about lasting changes in personal values and beliefs—[people who have these experiences] appreciate life more fully, experience increased feelings of self-worth, have a more compassionate regard for others and indeed for all life, develop a heightened ecological sensitivity, and report a decrease in purely materialistic and self-seeking values. Their religious orientation tends to change, too, and becomes more universalistic, inclusive and spiritual in its expression. In most instances, moreover, the fear of death is completely extinguished.[54]

Nevertheless, neither a transcendental near-death experience, nor a mundane OBE without veridical perceptions, can be taken as evidence that the experience was extrasomatic, certainly not evidence that can be considered scientific: Both types of experience can simply be dismissed as fantasies, hallucinations.

An article entitled "The Science of Near-Death Experiences," published in the *Atlantic,* explained why scientists have increasingly become interested in near-death experiences:

> [M]any NDEs happen when a person is surrounded by an arsenal of devices designed to measure every single thing about the body that human ingenuity has made us capable of measuring. ... [A]s medical technology continues to improve, it's bringing people back from ever closer to the brink of death. A small, lucky handful of people have made full or nearly full recoveries after spending hours with no breath or pulse, buried in snow or submerged in very cold water....All of this makes NDEs perhaps the only spiritual experience that we have a chance of investigating in a truly thorough, scientific way.[55]

Although this statement referred simply to NDEs, the author clearly meant ND *OBEs*, as he added:

> As the only stage in an NDE that involves perceiving the physical rather than the spiritual world, an out-of-body experience has the most potential to convince skeptics.[56]

To emphasize this point: Reports of NDEs and OBEs simply cannot be seriously presented as evidence for anything, or even as unquestionably authentic, unless they contain veridical perceptions.[57]

Veridical OBEs: Examples

A most remarkable feature of OBEs—whether they occurred in ordinary circumstances or as the mundane phases of NDEs—is that their perceptions are remarkably accurate. In a chapter of *The Handbook of Near-Death Experiences* (2009), Janice Miner Holden wrote:

> Of the 111 cases of apparently nonphysical perception [that I studied], I found that 92 percent contained absolutely no errors, 6 percent contained minor errors, and 2 percent were completely erroneous. Thus, the vast majority of these apparently nonphysical perceptions were veridical.[58]

Given this introduction, the rest of this section looks at six examples of people who had ND OBEs with veridical perceptions.

Maria: When a migrant worker named Maria was visiting friends in Seattle in 1977, she had a heart attack. She was rushed to Harborview Hospital and placed in the coronary care unit. A few days later, she had a cardiac arrest, from which she was resuscitated rather quickly. The following day, she was visited by her critical care social worker, Kimberly Clark, a professor at the University of Washington's School of Medicine.

Anxious to tell Clark "the strangest thing," Maria told her that during her cardiac arrest, she was able to look down from the ceiling and watch the medical team working on her body. At one point in this experience, Maria said, she found herself outside the hospital, where she spotted a blue tennis shoe on the ledge of the north side of the third floor. Maria added that one of its laces was stuck underneath the heel and that the little toe area was worn. Wanting to know whether she had actually seen that shoe, she begged Clark to try to locate it, and Clark, who years before had herself had an NDE,[59] agreed. Describing her effort, Kimberly Clark said:

I went up to the third floor and began going in and out of the patients' rooms and looking out their windows, which were so narrow I had to press my face to the screen just to see the ledge at all. Finally, I found a room where I pressed my face to the glass and looked down and saw the tennis shoe!

Having retrieved the shoe, Clark confirmed Maria's observations about the shoelace and the worn little toe area. "The only way she could have had such a perspective," Clark said, "was if she had been floating right outside."[60] The shoe, she said, "was very concrete evidence for me."[61]

Al Sullivan: On January 18, 1988, a 56-year-old van driver named Al Sullivan had emergency quadruple bypass surgery at Hartford Hospital in Connecticut. After being given an anesthetic, he had an NDE, with both mundane and transcendental experiences (in which he saw his deceased brother and mother). After regaining consciousness, he told his cardiologist, Dr. Anthony LaSala, about his mundane experience. While observing his body in the operating room from above, he reported, he saw the cardiac surgeon, Dr. Hiroyoshi Takata, flapping his elbows as if he were trying to fly. Realizing that Sullivan's experiences were not simply based on the drugs he had been given, Dr. LaSala explained that this was a peculiar habit of Dr. Takata's.[62]

In 1997, Bruce Gerson (one of the authors of this account) spoke with Drs. LaSala and Takata. Dr. Takata confirmed that what Sullivan called "flapping" was a regular practice: After he has scrubbed in, he does not wish his hands to touch anything until he is actually ready to do the surgery, so he flattens his palms against his chest and gives instructions to his assistants by pointing with his elbows. Dr. LaSala added that he had never seen any other surgeons using their elbows like this.[63]

When Gerson asked Sullivan if he remembered any more details about what he had observed, Sullivan said that he had seen Dr. Takata standing alone over his opened chest, which was being held open by metal clamps. He also saw two other surgeons working over one of his legs. He was puzzled why they were working on a leg when his heart was the problem. Sullivan later learned that the surgeons were stripping the vein out of his leg to create the bypass graft for his heart.[64]

Pam Reynolds: The story about Maria has long been the best-known example of veridical perception; close behind is now the account of singer-songwriter Pam Reynolds, who in 1991, at age 35, underwent surgery to remove an aneurysm at the base of her brain. If it were to burst, it would kill her; but the standard surgery to drain and repair it might also kill her. So her surgeon—in a procedure known as "hypothermic cardiac arrest"—chilled her body to 60 degrees F., which stopped her heart, and then drained the blood from her head. (The cooling would prevent her cells from dying while deprived of oxygen.)[65]

After Pam's eyes were lubricated (to prevent them from drying) and then taped shut, the surgeon—in order to make certain that her brain was completely inactive during the operation—had her ears fitted with small speakers that made continuous clicks at 100 decibels. If any part of her mind was working, the clicking would cause electrical signals in the brain stem.[66] The surgeon, Dr. Robert Spetzler, then began cutting through Pam's skull with a Midas Rex bone saw, which produces a noise similar to a dental drill.

Following the surgery, Pam said that, after the surgeon had begun cutting her skull, she felt herself "pop" out of her body and hover above it, watching as doctors worked on her body. She was able to report several details about what had happened.

- Saying that she hated the dental-drill sound of the bone saw, she said that the saw "looked like an electric toothbrush"—an accurate description of a Midas Rex bone saw.

- When a female cardiac surgeon was attempting to locate the femoral artery in Pam's right groin, Pam heard a male voice saying, "Try the other side." She also heard a female voice say, "We have a problem. Her arteries are too small."[67]

- Finally, Pam reported hearing the song "Hotel California" (by the Eagles), to which the staff was listening.[68]

After the operation, and before any of her perceptions had been shown to be veridical, Pam assumed she had been hallucinating. But a year later, she told some of her experiences to Dr. Spetzler.

Spetzler did not check out the details, but this task was performed by cardiologist Michael Sabom (whose 1981 book, *Recollections of Death,*[69] began the study of veridical perceptions in near-death experiences). The records from her surgery, reported Sabom, matched her memories, including the conversation about her arteries, the electric-toothbrush-appearing bone saw, and the playing of "Hotel California."[70]

57-Year-Old Man: In 2014, a multi-hospital project known as AWARE studied the awareness of 140 patients who had survived cardiac arrest. The study, led by Dr. Sam Parnia of Stony Brook University, focused on the accuracy of reports of visual and auditory perception during cardiac arrest. Especially noteworthy was the account of a 57-year-old man who had had an ND OBE.[71] According to a summary of the patient's statements:

- He felt quite euphoric during the experience.

- The patient heard an automated voice saying "Shock the patient, shock the patient."

- The patient said: "I was on the ceiling looking down. I saw a nurse that I did not know beforehand who I saw after the event. I could see my body and saw everything at once. I saw my blood pressure being taken whilst the doctor was putting something down my throat. I saw a nurse pumping on my chest."

- The patient also said that there was a man—bald and "quite a chunky fella"—who wore blue scrubs and a blue hat. ("I could tell he didn't have any hair, because of where the hat was.")

- The next day, the patient recognized the bald man, who had attended him during the resuscitation.

- The medical record confirmed the use of an Automated

External Defibrillator, which would give the automated instructions the patient heard and the role that the identified man played during the resuscitation.[72]

Dr. Parnia told the *Independent:* "The man described everything that had happened in the room, but importantly, he heard two bleeps from a machine that makes a noise at three minute intervals. So we could time how long the experience lasted for."

This patient's testimony changed the opinion of the doctor, who "previously thought that patients who described near-death experiences were only relating hallucinatory events."[73]

44-Year-Old Man: In 2001, *The Lancet*, a highly respected medical journal, published a large study of NDEs directed by Dr. Pim van Lommel of Rijnstate Hospital (Netherlands). The study included 344 survivors of cardiac arrest from 10 hospitals, 18 percent of whom reported having had an NDE.[74]

One of the patients was a 44-year-old man, who had arrived at the hospital in a comatose state. While the nurse attempted to resuscitate him, she found he was wearing dentures, which she removed and placed in her cart. A week later, when the man regained consciousness, this nurse came to his room to administer drugs. Upon seeing her, the man exclaimed:

> Oh, yes, but you know where my dentures are. Yes, you were there when they brought me into the hospital, and you took the dentures out of my mouth and put them into that cart. It had all these bottles on it, and there was a sliding drawer underneath, and you put my teeth there.[75]

The nurse and the staff learned that the man had had an OBE. He said that during it, he watched his resuscitation, trying to make those present aware that he was still alive, so that they should keep trying to save him. Dr. van Lommel wrote: "The facts of the case were later verified down to the descriptions the man gave of the doctors and nurses present at the time."[76]

Vicki Umipeg: As researchers became increasingly aware of

OBEs and NDEs, they began wondering whether blind persons ever have them and, if so, whether they differ from the experiences of sighted people. Having found that blind persons do have NDEs and OBEs, Kenneth Ring and Sharon Cooper carried out a study of 31 such persons, 21 of whom had had ND OBEs and 10 of whom had had OBEs only.

Another question was whether the NDEs and OBEs of people who had been blind from birth were different from those who had been able to see in the past. Ring and Cooper found that they did not differ. The only difference was that those who were blind from birth did not have visual perceptions in their dreams.[77]

Here is an example provided by Ring and Cooper. Having been born prematurely, weighing only 3 pounds, Vicki Umipeg was born blind, because an excess of oxygen in the incubator had destroyed her optic nerve. When Vicki was 22, she was working as a singer at a nightclub in Seattle. One night, she couldn't get a taxi after work, so she accepted a ride from some patrons, who turned out to be intoxicated. The car crashed, and she suffered serious injuries, including a fractured skull.

After she was taken to a room in Harborview Hospital, she felt that she had left her body and floated up toward the ceiling. She heard a male doctor talking about the possibility that damage to her eardrum could make her deaf as well.

Looking down, she saw a body, at first not being certain it was hers (she, of course, had never seen her own body). But then she realized it was, because she recognized her wedding ring, which was very distinctive, and her hair, which was very long; she was upset that some of it had been shaved off. She also saw that her head was cut, and there was a lot of blood (although she could not tell that it was red, because thus far she had no concept of color).

She then "went up through the roof"; it seemed like the roof had "just melted." She then started feeling a tremendous sense of freedom, which gave her joy. "It was wonderful to be out there and be free, to not worry about bumping into anything." She then had a rather classic transcendental NDE, which she found overwhelming, but she was soon told that she had to go back to take care of her children. When she returned to her body, she said, "It was excruciatingly painful."[78]

Veridical OBEs and Life after Death

The modern denial of life after death is based primarily on two claims: (1) Life after death is impossible, because there can be no conscious experience without information from a functioning brain. (2) Even if one thought that life after death might be possible, there could be no good evidence for it. For example, the feeling in OBEs that one is really out the body proves nothing, because OBEs can be understood as intrasomatic.

However, if OBEs include veridical perceptions, they show that the experiencers have seen and/or heard things that suggest that their minds or souls were really, as they seemed to be, outside their bodies. Near-death OBEs of people who have been blind from birth show that minds or souls can have visual perceptions that are not at all rooted in the brain. Accordingly, near-death OBEs confirm J. M. E. McTaggart's hypothesis, that when the soul is freed from its body, it can continue to have experiences.

Veridical Apparitions and Veridical OBEs

Evidence for life after death is strengthened by taking veridical apparitions and OBEs together, because what is an apparition from one perspective may be an OBE from another. This was the main point of a study of apparitions by Hornell Hart. He argued that veridical OBEs "provide an internal view of the phenomena observed externally in connection with apparitions of the living." He then marshaled data to show that knowledge about the living acquired in OBEs "are in most respects essentially indistinguishable from apparitions of the [dead and] and dying."[79] If Hart is right, then the appearances of Jesus discussed in Chapter 7, insofar as they are authentic, can be taken as out-of-body experiences of Jesus. This line of thought supports the view of B. F. Streeter, quoted in Chapter 7, that the appearances of Jesus were "directly caused by the Lord himself, veritably alive."

CONCLUSION

People who have had near-death OBEs typically report them to be wonderful experiences that transform their lives.[80] However, this existence outside the body, assuming that it continues beyond bodily death, should not be equated with ultimate salvation. Insofar as ND OBEs are accepted as foretastes of life after bodily death, they should be valued because they free people from the fear of death and provide promise that that they will have time to be sanctified.

Also, salvation should not be understood as being saved from an everlasting hell (as if there were such a place). This does not mean that life beyond bodily death is either impossible or unimportant. But there is much more to salvation than continuing to live after bodily death. Rather, it involves transformation into people who love God with all their heart, soul, and might and their neighbors as themselves. For Americans as for Jesus, salvation is ultimate fidelity to God instead of to one's empire and/or other idols, such as fame and riches.

Besides providing time for souls to be sanctified by developing fidelity to God, life after death would also give us more time to make greater contributions to God. These dimensions of salvation also free people to work for another dimension of salvation, Salvation$_4$, as understood by Jesus, to which the following chapter is devoted.

CHAPTER SIXTEEN

The Reign of God and Global Democracy

A FOURTH DIMENSION of salvation in Jesus's worldview is the dimension around which his message was centered: a coming kingdom (or reign) of God, as stated in the Lord's Prayer: "Your kingdom come, your will be done, on earth as it is in heaven" (Matthew 6:10). This new era would be one in which the present order, which is now ruled by demonic values, would be replaced by a religious-social-political-economic order based on divine values.

This Salvation$_4$ was central to the "social gospel," as articulated in the early decades of the 20th century. It's most famous advocate, Walter Rauschenbusch, contrasted the "kingdom of God" with the "kingdom of evil."[1] Although most non-fundamentalist Christian theology turned away from this approach in later decades in favor of some version of neo-orthodoxy, theologians started coming back to Salvation$_4$ in the latter decades of the twentieth century through the influence of liberation and political theologies, along with the new search for the historical Jesus, as exemplified in Chapter 6.

CHRISTIAN FAITH AND A REIGN OF DIVINE VALUES

The reorientation of the Christian gospel around Jesus's message of the reign of God has been affirmed by many process thinkers, including John Cobb. Describing the teaching of Jesus as "contra-imperial," Cobb wrote that "the clearest and most accurate way of presenting Jesus' contra-imperial vision is by focusing on his teaching about what he called the *basileia theou.*"[2]

However, the terms "kingdom of God" and "reign of God" are problematic. Besides the fact that "kingdom of God" implies that God is male, this term and "reign of God" have been widely understood to mean a state of absolute perfection, which could never be realized in our world. But as pointed out in Chapters 5 and 6, Jesus, like Isaiah, meant a world ruled on the basis of justice and compassion—a world in which the economic system would not be used to impoverish people and take their land, in which all families had their daily bread so that babies did not die for want of food, in which people's homes were not taken for excessive taxes or destroyed by armies on the rampage. This is not an impossible vision.

In speaking about a reign of God, Jesus was referring to a social-political-order based on divine values. It would be best, accordingly, to say that Jesus was looking forward to a reign of divine values.

Global Anarchy

At the root of the present reign of demonic values is the system of global anarchy, which was preliminarily discussed in Chapter 10.

In political discussions, "anarchy" refers to a realm in which there is no political authority. To speak of the "global anarchy" is simply to say that there is no global government over and above the governments of the various countries. In other words, there is no central authority capable of making and enforcing rules of behavior on the international system's units (states).[3] It is a system that allows for, and even encourages, wars.

In a 1926 book entitled *The International Anarchy*,[4] Goldsworthy Lowes ("Goldie") Dickenson said that, without a global institution that can prevent war,

> civilisation is doomed. For modern war, equipped by modern science, is incompatible with the continuance of an industrial

civilisation. A change has taken place in the last century which cuts us off absolutely from all the preceding history of mankind. We have learned how to use or misuse nature, and we hold in our hands the powers of life and death.[5]

International anarchy, said Dickenson, could be overcome only by means of a global government. As pointed out in Chapter 10, most advocates of Political Realism have believed that anarchy could not be overcome. But a few Political Realists have thought otherwise—that we do not forever have to put up with the perils of anarchy. There have been, in fact, some major Realists who have advocated the creation of a global government.

Anarchy and Political Realism

Although the term "anarchy," with the meaning described above, is widespread among theorists of international politics, the fact and the implications of international anarchy are especially emphasized by Political Realism.

In the preface to *The Perils of Anarchy*, a book that is oriented around the Realist approach to international politics, we read:

> [R]ealists regard anarchy—the absence of any common sovereign—as the distinguishing feature of international life. Without a central authority to enforce agreements or to guarantee security, states must rely on their own means to protect their interests.[6]

One of the contributors to that volume, University of Chicago's John Mearsheimer, wrote:

> [T]he international system is anarchic. This does not mean that it is chaotic or riven by disorder. It is easy to draw that conclusion, since realism depicts a world characterized by security competition and war. However, "anarchy" as employed by realists has nothing to do with conflict; rather, it is an ordering principle, which says that the system comprises independent political units (states) that have no central authority over them. Sovereignty, in other words, inheres in

states, because there is no higher ruling body in the international system. There is no "government over governments."[7]

However, although most Realists have assumed that this situation could not be transcended, so that we must forever more put up with "the perils of anarchy," this assumption is not part of the definition of Political Realism. There have been, in fact, some Realists who have advocated the creation of a global government.

One example was Frederick Schuman (1904–1981), who taught international relations at the University of Chicago and who became the Carter Administration's leading expert on the Soviet Union. In 1933, Schuman published the first edition of his well-received textbook *International Politics,* in which he argued that the only way to overcome war was to overcome "the Western state system" through the political unification of the world by means of a world federation.[8]

Another major Realist who argued this case was the prolific author Georg Schwarzenberger, who was born in Germany but became a British citizen and a professor at the University of London. Being one of the world's leading writers about international relations, his *Manual of International Law* (1952)[9] went through six editions. But he had already made his argument for the need to overcome international anarchy in his 1941 book, *Power Politics,* in which he wrote: "Power politics, international anarchy and war are inseparable," so the "antidote [to war] is international government." By an *international government,* he meant a "world State," preferably of the federal type.[10]

Global Democracy

A global government could be created in one of two ways. One would be for an imperialist country to subdue the rest (as Rome did, controlling much of the known world at the time). This has long, of course, been the goal of the US government, especially since the demise of the Soviet Union, which seemed to make a global *Pax Americana* possible.[11]

The other way would be for the various nations to create a global *democratic* government, which would obviously be the only morally acceptable way, and which would provide a realistic chance for the ancient dream of a world order based on divine values to be realized.

The early Reinhold Niebuhr said (in the language of the time): "Man's capacity for justice makes democracy possible; but man's inclination to injustice makes democracy necessary."[12] In other words, because human beings have some capacity to adopt the moral point of view, which is the impartial point of view, human communities can rule themselves democratically.[13] But in spite of this capacity, human being also have an inclination to act unjustly, so that democracy, with its checks and balances, is necessary.

Because of that inclination, said Niebuhr, we do not dare give absolute power to any individual or nation. From this perspective, Niebuhr criticized Plato's idea of the philosopher-king, according to which the political ideal would be to give all power to a philosopher. As a philosopher (a lover of wisdom), such a king, Plato thought, could be trusted to use his power wisely, for the benefit of all his subjects.

But Niebuhr, holding that "only God can perfectly combine power and goodness," argued that the expectation of an ideal king "hopes for an impossible combination of the divine and the historical."[14] Partly on this basis, Niebuhr concluded that there will never be a "reign of peace," so that the biblical tradition's Messianic hope must be rejected. The solution to the problem of human history, Niebuhr concluded, can lie only "beyond history."[15]

However, although only God can *perfectly* combine power and goodness, this insight is compatible with the suggestion that a global democratic government could at least *approximate* the divine combination of power and goodness, thereby bringing about a far closer approximation to a reign of divine values than what we have now.

A global democracy could achieve such an approximation, because the collective body, being from all regions of the world, could partly make up for the defects in each individual country. That is, the ignorance of the leaders of each nation about most of the world except for their own regions would be corrected by the knowledge of the representatives from those other regions. The indifference that each representative has toward the welfare of peoples from most parts of the world would be corrected by the sympathy expressed by the representatives from these other parts. The partisan biases of each representative could be balanced by the biases of the others.

The collective body could, therefore, embody first-hand knowledge of the facts, along with real sympathy for, and benevolence toward, the affected peoples in the various regions.[16]

A global government of this type would not, therefore, fit the image that is often conjured up by talk of a "world state," in which all power is concentrated at the top. This global federation would not, furthermore, be imposed by one part of the world on the rest. Rather, it would be based on a global constitution, complete with a global bill of rights and responsibilities that would be worked out by representatives from all peoples, then ratified by these peoples themselves. It would have a legislature, through which the representatives of the world's people could finally becoming self-legislating, and an executive branch to enforce these laws.[17]

There would also be a world judiciary system with mandatory jurisdiction, through which the constitution would be interpreted and applied and through which disputes between countries would be settled peacefully—rather than, as now, through war, whether military or economic. There would also be a global police force to enforce the orders from the executive and judicial branches.

But there would be no global military force. This would be unneeded because the nations will have disarmed. In the absence of a global democratic government, disarmament is impossible, because there is no organization that could protect the various nations. The United Nations (as now structured) is not such an organization, but it could become such if some major modifications would be made, as suggested in *Transforming the United Nations System,* by Joseph E. Schwartzberg.[18]

But once we have a global democratic government, war would be unnecessary and even unthinkable, just as war is not thinkable between, say, California and Colorado, in spite of their disputes about water. The global democratic government would need only a police force to enforce the laws enacted by the global legislature.

Global Democracy and a Reign of Divine Values

Global democracy is a precondition for a reign of divine values on earth. A reign of divine values, in which all people have sufficient food, water, and housing, and in which they are treated with justice and compassion, is a realistic vision. It is simply a vision of a world ordered in terms of moral principles. Such a vision could not be realized, to be sure, under an anarchic world order, which is based on competition rather than cooperation, on promoting one's own good by defeating the good of others, and on using force to intimidate and even destroy those who get in one's way. The vision of a world ordered in terms of divine values could be realized through the creation of a global democracy.

To see why a moral order would simultaneously be a divine order, one can reflect on what is meant by speaking of something as morally right. According to what at least many moral philosophers consider the best analysis, what is right in any situation is that which an *ideal observer* would prefer, with an "ideal observer" meaning one who is *fully informed* as to all the relevant facts, *impartially benevolent* to all affected parties, and *impartially sympathetic* to the feelings of all such parties. "When we make moral judgments," said Charles Taliaferro, "we implicitly commit ourselves to hold that if there were an ideal observer. . . , then the [ideal observer] would make the same judgment."[19]

But this means, as Taliaferro knew, that which is morally right is that which God wills, because the perspective of the ideal observer would be identical with the divine perspective as understood by Christian faith. God, who as omniscient is fully informed, is also impartially sympathetic to all creatures, hence impartially benevolent to all, wishing all creatures the best that is possible for them. To the extent that a social-political-economic order is based on basic moral principles, reflecting this benevolence, it could be called a reign of God.

Why a Pax Americana *Will Not Do*

Given this point, the next question is why a global democracy would provide a precondition for such a reign. We can begin negatively, by asking why the other route for overcoming global anarchy, a global *Pax Americana*, cannot be expected to overcome the reign of demonic power.

Those who think that a *Pax Americana* might have this effect may well agree with Andrew Bacevich, according to whom the history of American imperialism thus far has been anything but benign, so that the expectation of a benign *Pax Americana* cannot be based on past history.[20] They might say, nevertheless, that once America overcomes all its opponents so that a global *Pax Americana* finally exists, American leaders would likely institute a form of rule that is benign, even divine.

One problem with this expectation is that besides having no support in American history,[21] it goes against a very widespread generalization about human nature, which has been summarized in Lord Acton's famous axiom: "Power tends to corrupt, and absolute power corrupts absolutely."[22] Notice the careful wording, which is often misquoted. Acton did not say that all power corrupts, only that it *tends to*. But when he spoke of *absolute* power, he dropped the "tends to." Absolute power corrupts absolutely—period.

Acton's saying can, of course, be considered simply a secular version of the Christian doctrine of original sin, which (correctly interpreted) says that people of all races, religions, genders, ideologies, nations, and classes, without exception, tend to be self-centered. The central heresy of Marxism was its doctrine that there was one class, the proletariat, that was unaffected by sinful tendencies, so that it could be trusted with absolute power during a temporary "dictatorship of the proletariat." It was the resulting failure of many Marxist governments to build in checks and balances that lay behind their worst excesses. In the case of Stalin, absolute power within the Soviet Union clearly corrupted absolutely.[23] And yet now the US government is seeking absolute power at the global level.

Why a Global Democracy Could Be Different

At first glance, it would seem that the idea of giving supreme power to a global government would also run afoul of Acton's dictum. If a global government had sufficient power to enforce its rulings on the various states, would this not be at least *virtually* absolute power? And if Acton's dictum is correct, should we not expect the global government to become absolutely corrupt, at least virtually so?

To see why this does not follow, we need to see a qualification that was implicit in Acton's dictum. Acton would not have believed that absolute power would *always* corrupt because, as a traditional Catholic, he surely believed that God has absolute power without believing that God is made corrupt by such power.

The difference between God and any creature, including any creaturely institution,[24] is that creatures have limited sympathies, so that their interests in the welfare of the rest of the world are quite limited. God's sympathy, by contrast, is all-inclusive, so that God's "self-interest," if we wish to put it this way, is identical with God's interest in the welfare of the whole world and all its creatures.

This is, in any case, the idea of God presupposed in the present work. In God, and in God alone, self-interest (promoting one's own interests) and altruism (promoting the interests of others) is identical. This is because the world exists *within* God. By analogy, suggested Charles Hartshorne,

> [S]uppose all "others" were within the body, as its members; then, since the need of the body is for the flourishing of its own parts or members, bodily desire and altruism would be coincident.[25]

As it is, however, our self-interest is very exclusive and hence, as we put it, selfish. Promoting our own self-interest usually means acting in a way that involves indifference to, or even active opposition to, the welfare of other creatures.

With this distinction between God and human beings in mind, we can see that Acton's dictum, spelled out more fully, should read: "Human beings, because of their limited sympathies and hence selfish interests, tend to be corrupted by power; and they are corrupted absolutely by absolute power." Although this statement is not as pithy as Acton's, it states the point more fully by bringing out the crucial fact: that it is because of our limited sympathies that we cannot be trusted with unlimited power.

Based on this same reasoning, there is one kind of human institution—a global democratic government—in which supreme power would not necessarily corrupt. This is the case because a global democratic government's interests would by definition be all-inclusive. It would be mandated by charter to serve the good of human civilization as a whole. It would have a bill of rights and responsibilities in which the rights of all human individuals and also all nations are protected. And it would have representatives from all peoples in its legislative, executive, and judicial branches, and in its police forces.

Although such a government would have *supreme* power, the issue of *absolute* power would not arise, because we are speaking of a *federated* government, not a unitary state. In a unitary state, all power exists at the top. But in a federated government, sovereign power is divided between the central authority and a number of regions having authority over most of their internal affairs.

In any case, insofar as we think of God's central feature as impartial love for all creatures and hence active good will towards all creatures, a global democratic government would provide at least the necessary condition for fulfilling the basic religious urge to live in terms of an *imitatio dei*, because in global democracy at its best, self-interest and altruism would be identical. Insofar as that is actually the case, a global government's power would be used to heal rather than to destroy, because it, being impartially concerned for the welfare of all its peoples, would always be working for the general good.

Such a government could, therefore, meet the need, seen by Niebuhr, to transcend our anarchical world order, in which disputes based on conflicting perspectives are settled by brute force. "There must be an organizing centre," Niebuhr said, that can "arbitrate conflicts from a more impartial perspective than is available to any party of a given conflict."[26] If force is to be redemptive rather than destructive, he added, "it is an absolute prerequisite that it be exerted by an agency that is impartial."[27]

Niebuhr in these passages did not demand perfection, only a

power that is exercised with far greater impartiality than possessed by any of the competing parties. We could hope for such impartiality from a global democratic government.

American Exceptionalism?

As discussed above, God is the one exception to the general principle that power tends to corrupt. It is the coincidence of self-interest and altruism in God that lies behind divine exceptionalism. And there could in principle be a human organization that could approximate that coincidence. But advocates of the position known as American Exceptionalism absurdly claim that America embodies that approximation. For example:

- In an essay entitled "The Benevolent Empire," neocon Robert Kagan said that "the identification of the interests of others with its own has been the most striking quality of American foreign and defense policy."[28]

- According to Samuel Huntington, "The conflict between American power and American principles virtually disappears when it is applied to the American impact on other societies."[29]

- "To the extent that interests [have] figured at all," wrote Andrew Bacevich in summarizing the claim of American Exceptionalists, "American interests and American ideals were congruent."[30]

- The claim of American Exceptionalism, said Stephen Kinzer, is "the view that the United States has a right to impose its will because it knows more, sees farther, and lives on a higher moral plane than other nations."[31]

American Exceptionalism has been this country's primal intellectual sin. The extreme advocates of it suggest that human nature, simply by being stamped "made in America," becomes transformed into a finite version of the divine coincidence between self-interest and universal altruism.

If the good, as Niebuhr said, is "always the harmony of the whole on various levels," whereas "evil is always the assertion of some self-interest without regard to the whole,"[32] American foreign policy has been evil, not good. The American Empire neither has been, nor will be, the exception to Acton's dictum.

Contemplation, Action, and a Global Constitution

But if human nature is so self-interested, how can we hope that human beings could create a constitution for universal self-rule that would embody justice? Here we need to return to the first part of Niebuhr's dictum, which speaks of our "capacity for justice." The contrast between this and our "inclination to injustice" depends upon a distinction between two contrasting stances: contemplation and action.

In contemplation, Niebuhr said, it is possible for us to rise to a high level of disinterested impartiality, in which we can see, with regard to some particular issue, what would be just for all affected parties. But the self *in action*—one that is actually participating in the historical process, with its claims and counterclaims—will almost inevitably lose this impartiality, becoming one egoistic combatant among others.

The fact that our practical reason is intertwined with our "vitality," including our will to power, Niebuhr said, "guarantees that egoistic purposes will be pursued with all vital resources which an individual or collective will may control."[33]

This has been true of America as it has been a participant in the parable of the tribes. But this fact about the self in action is compatible with the recognition that the self in contemplation can rise to a high level of disinterested impartiality. In speaking of "contemplation," Niebuhr did not refer only to the activity commonly called contemplation (as distinct from prayer), such as Buddhist meditation. Rather prayer in the sense of attempting to align oneself with the divine will is a type of meditation.

The ideological bias that would still remain could, furthermore, be overcome in "contemplative conferences," conferences designed for people from various regions to contemplate the needs for the world as a whole. In such conferences, the biases in each perspective would tend to cancel each other out. We can, therefore, have a realistic hope that a global constitutional convention, based on numerous preparatory conferences and documents, could construct a constitution that would truly embody the principles of justice.

Patriotism and Morality

Through the creation of global democracy, the perennial conflict between patriotism and morality could be overcome. Morality demands that we work impartially for the good of all, whereas patriotism, within our anarchical, tribalistic world, demands that leaders work for the good of their own citizens, which often means, as we have seen, working *against* the good of the peoples of the rest of the world.

When some citizens criticize these self-centered policies as immoral, they are often accused of being unpatriotic, a fact showing that "patriotism" is widely understood to demand uncritical acceptance of the policies of one's country, at least as long as those policies are seen as promoting the welfare of its citizens. As a result, in those circles in which there is a larger sense of morality, the word "patriot," especially "super-patriot," tends to become a word of derision.

With the creation of a global federation, however, this conflict between morality and patriotism could be largely overcome. The global government would establish and enforce general policies aimed at the general and long-term good of human civilization as a whole. The policies of each country would, therefore, have to be such as to be compatible with this general and long-term good. In this situation, the citizens of a country could be patriots without being immoral.

CHRISTIAN FAITH AND HUMAN RIGHTS

One of the major moral problems of the present world order is that, although the UN's acceptance of the Universal Declaration of Human Rights has enshrined human rights in international law, these rights are as widely violated now as they were earlier. In the words of Michael Perry, "there is little reason to believe that many basic human rights are really any more secure now than they were before 1945."[34]

This violation cannot, of course, be a matter of indifference to Christians, because what we now call "human rights" were implicitly implied by the reign of God preached by Jesus. One of the main reasons global democracy is needed is that this would be the only way that the human rights of most people could be protected.

Genocide

The extent to which people are still unprotected, unless they happen to live in a state that guarantees human rights, was shown by the massacre in Rwanda in 1994. Although it was widely known in advance that the massacre of the Tutsis by the Hutus was going to occur, a million unarmed people, including 300,000 children, were slaughtered over a period of three months, while the world's leaders, knowing full well what was going on, did nothing. This was no spontaneous outbreak of "ethnic violence" but a systematic slaughter, based on lists of names and carried out in broad daylight. Each group of killers had been "trained to kill 1,000 human beings every twenty minutes," and garbage trucks had been organized to haul away the bodies.[35]

Although a modest UN force with the authority to stop it could have done so, authorization was never given, primarily because of the United States. As Linda Melvern, whose book *A People Betrayed* reports the sickening details, says: "The Rwandan genocide should be the defining scandal of the presidency of Bill Clinton."[36]

Especially important was the observation by moral philosopher Henry Shue: "Any system of global governance" that allows such an event to occur, said Shue, "is ridiculous."[37] The revealing nature of the Rwanda massacre is even more telling when it is recalled that the construction of the new world order after World War II, especially the creation of the United Nations and its adoption of the Genocide Convention, was "guided by the principle: Never again." That is, the UN was to prevent genocide, such as that perpetrated by the Nazis against European Jews, from ever happening again. Nevertheless, "the world failed to react to the first indisputable genocide since that perpetrated against the Jews."[38]

Why are human rights still so unprotected, even to the point that genocide can still occur? The problem can be summarized in terms of a distinction, made by Richard Falk, between three logics: universalist logic, statist logic, and imperialist logic.[39] According to universalist logic, the rights of human beings in all places should be given equal protection.

According to statist logic, states protect or violate human rights insofar as they believe that such behavior furthers their interests. The imperialist logic is the same except that the state in question rules an empire, which gives it not only a lot more interests but also distinctive interests, such as maintaining its "credibility," which can lead it to terrorize disobedient peoples to warn other peoples not to disobey. This practice, as stated in Chapter 6, goes back at least to Roman crucifixions.

Human rights have been so unprotected because they are at the mercy of the interests of very self-interested states. In the case of Rwanda, America had no material or geopolitical interests in the region, so the ridiculousness of the present world order, from the point of view of the universalist logic of human rights, was fully revealed. The massacre in Rwanda, furthermore, was simply an especially appalling exemplification of the fact that the rights enumerated in the Universal Declaration of Human Rights are massively violated in many parts of the world, as the annual reports of Amnesty International and Human Rights Watch make all too clear.

The basic problem is that the imperialist and statist logics are firmly embodied in the present world order, but the universalist logic is still disembodied. Although it is supposedly embodied in the UN, it is embodied there only rhetorically, because the UN was given no autonomy.[40] Accordingly, the UN intervenes only when its Security Council authorizes an intervention, and the five permanent members of the Security Council, each of which has veto power, are all imperial powers.

There is a history behind the fact that the United Nations is so impotent. In revulsion to the carnage of World War I, Europeans and Americans created the League of Nations to prevent any such wars in the future. The assumption was that the revulsion was great enough to persuade the Great Powers to give up what Jean Jacques Rousseau had mockingly called their "precious right to be unjust when they please."[41] But the revulsion was not great or long-lasting enough. George Bernard Shaw, a member of the Fabian Society, said that solving the disputes between nations could be resolved without war would require a "supernational sheriff" to "adjust the disputes of nations." What is needed, Shaw argued, is "a Supernational Legislature, a Supernational Tribunal, and a Supernational Board of Conciliation."[42]

But Great Britain, speaking of the "sacredness of the independence and the sovereignty of independent and sovereign States," according to which "every state must remain absolute master of its own destiny," would not authorize an organization with supernational powers.[43] As for the United States, it would not even join the League. Twenty years after the formation of the League of Nations, World War II began.

At the end of that war, the United Nations was created in order "to save succeeding generations from the scourge of war."[44] The idea that inspired its creators was that "the League had failed *because* it was not a super-state, and that something like a super-state would have to be created if aggressor states as strong as Nazi Germany were going to be halted in their tracks."[45] However, wrote F. S. Northedge, "the United Nations is almost as much a lost cause [with regard to the maintenance of peace] as the League was in the late 1930s."[46] This occurred because the founders gave up their original ideas. Why? Because, wrote Stephen Hilderbrand,

> the United States, Great Britain, and the Soviet Union decided that their own, individual interests were too important to entrust to a world body, that the wartime dream of an international peacekeeping agency might interfere with their own nationalistic dreams of hegemony. . . . [T]he protection of

their own sovereignty and freedom of action seemed more important to them than permanent peace.[47]

We can only hope that national leaders will soon realize that war is now so dangerous that they must give up their "precious right to be unjust when they please." Only with the creation of a global democratic government, based on a global bill of rights and responsibilities, will the universalist logic of human rights finally be embodied in such a way that it can trump the logics of statism and imperialism. Preventing human rights violations is one of the reasons why global democracy is needed.

Global Apartheid and the Right to Life

The phenomenon of Global Apartheid was introduced in Chapter 11, which pointed out that human rights could probably be protected only by global democracy. The present chapter discusses the fact that Global Democracy would also be needed if global apartheid is to be overcome.

In human civilization as a whole, just as it was in apartheid South Africa, one-sixth of the population, consisting primarily of white people, owns over three-fourths of the planet's resources and exercises military, political, economic, and cultural hegemony. There is democracy, affluence, leisure time, and consumer choice for the few, but there is oppression, poverty, long hours, and a struggle for subsistence for the many.

The United Nations condemned the South African regime as a "crime against humanity."[48] But global apartheid is even worse, having greater inequality in income, health care, education, and mortality rate.[49] How could we not call it a crime against humanity?

Although it is widely assumed that the division between rich and poor countries is natural, it actually originated in the colonial period, during which the European imperial powers restructured the economies of its colonies. The imposed trading arrangements involved what is called "asymmetrical interdependence," through which the European powers were enriched and their colonies impoverished. In the twentieth century, the United States took primary control of this system in the disguised form of neo-colonialism.

Despite all the talk of "development," the asymmetry persists. Much more money flows from the poor to the rich countries than flows in the opposite direction, so the gap between rich and poor countries continues to increase.[50] For example, the disparity in per capita income between America and the undeveloped nations in 1947 was about 13 to 1; by 1989 it was 60 to 1,[51] and in later decades the disparity became even greater.[52]

As a result of this systemic creation of poverty, over half of the world's human beings now live in poverty, with many of them in *abject* poverty, which is the world's leading cause of death. We are right to be horrified by the Nazi's murder of 11-12 million people and the several million people murdered by the Stalinist regime. But we should be even more horrified by the fact that the global economy, over which the US has long presided, is responsible for approximately 56 million deaths *every year* because of the lack of adequate food, clean water, and elementary health care.[53] Becoming aware of this fact is so staggering, or at least should be, that even if there were no other reason, the need to overcome global apartheid, which is a result of the present world order, should provide us with sufficient motivation for devoting ourselves wholeheartedly to the cause of global democracy. Over 50 million preventable deaths a year is not acceptable "collateral damage."

The issue of adequate food and water is central to the issue of human rights. The unifying idea in the Universal Declaration of Human Rights is "the idea of a decent or minimally good life for all people."[54] Article 3 of the Universal Declaration specifically says that "everyone has the right to life." The right to a minimally decent life obviously involves the rights not to be murdered and not to be arbitrarily imprisoned, which we call *civil and political rights*. But it also includes *economic* rights: the rights to adequate food, drinking water, and basic health care.

Both kinds of rights belong to what Henry Shue calls "basic rights," because they are implicit in the very right to life. The most basic economic rights are known as "subsistence rights," because they constitute the right to have enough simply to subsist, to stay alive. Basic rights, said Shue, constitute "the morality of the depths," because they specify "the line beneath which no one is to be allowed to sink."⁵⁵ In the present global economy, however, at least a billion people are allowed to slip below this line every year. Most of them are, in fact, *pushed* under.

In pointing at other countries, such as China and Cuba, for violating human rights, the US Government arbitrarily limits the idea of human rights to civil and political rights. But the United States, like most other countries, signed the UN's Covenant on Economic, Social and Cultural Rights, which is legally binding. Article 11 of this Covenant says:

> The States Parties to the present Covenant recognize the right of everyone to an adequate standard of living for himself and his family, including adequate food, clothing, and housing.⁵⁶

So the United States is legally committed to honoring subsistence rights, which would require a radical change in the global economic system. But in the present world order, the United States can force other countries to live up to their commitments or punish them if they do not, but no one has been able to force the United States to live up to its commitments and no one can punish it when it refuses.

In the global economy that is part and parcel of the American Empire, the economic rights of hundreds of millions of poor people are regularly denied food and water in the name of the economic "rights" of the rich, which means that subsistence rights are trumped by "luxury rights." As David Korten said, "property rights are too often used to legitimate denying others the right to live."⁵⁷

In this economic system, the "right" of the owners and CEOs of banks and corporations to have luxury automobiles, yachts, and several villas around the world trump the rights of poor people to have food, clean water, and even minimal health care. The ethical system embodied in the present global economy, Canadian philosopher John McMurtry observed, "simply recognizes no right to live."⁵⁸ Even the quite conservative writer John Vincent said that "the whole international economic system in which we are all implicated" is morally illegitimate because of its "failure to provide subsistence rights."[59]

Besides being outraged by this morally illegitimate economic system, we should also be outraged that the global apartheid created by colonialism has been deliberately perpetuated by the neocolonial policies of the United States. George Kennan's notorious State Department memo of 1947 cannot be too often repeated. In this top secret memo, Kennan said:

> We have about 50% of the world's wealth, but only 6.3% of its population.... Our real task in the coming period is to devise a pattern of relationships which will permit us to maintain this position of disparity without positive detriment to our national security.[60]

Although Kennan considered himself a Christian, he was certainly not advocating the Golden or Silver Rule. He was, instead, observing the Golden Rule practiced by plutocrats: Those with the gold make the rules.

We need a global economic system that does not implicate us in crimes against humanity. For this change to occur, the global economy needs to be regulated in terms of guidelines established by a global democratic government, which needs to include a global bill of rights and responsibilities that gives the subsistence rights of the poor priority over the "luxury rights" of the rich.

We need an economic system that, rather than increasing global apartheid, begins overcoming it. This would mean reversing the direction taken by the global economy over the previous five centuries—the age of European imperialism—and especially the past century—the age of America's neocolonial empire. The only realistic basis for hope that this massive change of direction—this massive repentance—might occur is through the establishment of a global democratic government, through which the global economy can be regulated by principles promoting life for all rather than, as in Palestine at the time of Jesus, obscene wealth for the few and misery and death for the many.

WHY GLOBAL DEMOCRACY IS ABSOLUTELY NECESSARY

Thus far, this chapter has addressed how the creation of a global democratic government would allow an approximation to the reign of divine values that Jesus envisaged. But today the creation of global democracy is necessary not simply for Christians, but for civilization as such.

Moreover, global democracy is now necessary in the strictest sense of the term: necessary for the very survival of human civilization. Political leaders have always given highest priority to *raison d'État* ("reasons of state"), meaning things necessary for the very survival of the state. Now the highest priority should be given to "reasons of civilization."

Prevention of Nuclear War

As mentioned above,[61] G. Lowes Dickenson, in his 1926 book *The International Anarchy*, argued that without an institution that can prevent war, "civilisation is doomed." However it was only after the creation of atomic weapons that this sentiment became widespread.

The most famous person who came to work passionately for global government because of the development of nuclear weapons was Albert Einstein, who had been partly responsible for this development. As pointed out in Chapter 13, Einstein added his signature to a letter to FDR encouraging him to authorize the creation of atom bombs—an act he later called his "one great mistake."[62]

Einstein came to call world government "the most important goal of our time."[63] In making his famous statement that everything has changed except our way of thinking, Einstein had in mind our thinking about world order. "As long as the present condition of international anarchy prevails," he said, "all of us will continue to live under the constant threat of sudden annihilation."[64]

Einstein felt so strongly about this issue that he refused to lend his name to half-way measures. For example, having been asked to sign the resolutions of a peace conference in which Thomas Mann had participated, Einstein declined, saying:

[T]he resolutions are not far-reaching enough to solve the problem of international security. That goal can be attained only by creating a world government with authority to settle conflicts on the basis of law.... No less radical a measure will call a halt to the arms race and prevent war.[65]

In response to a fellow pacifist who thought it was inconsistent of Einstein to support the war against Nazi Germany while calling himself a pacifist, Einstein replied:

I am indeed a pacifist, but ... I am of the conviction that realization of the goal of pacifism is possible only through supranational organization. To stand unconditionally for this cause is, in my opinion, the criterion of true pacifism.[66]

Many others have argued that nuclear weapons have made global government necessary. For example, the eminent historian William McNeill, whose 1980 study *The Pursuit of Power* traces the development of the technology of warfare over the past 1000 years, concluded this study by saying:

To halt the arms race, ... [n]othing less radical than [a global sovereign power] seems in the least likely to suffice. ... The alternative appears to be the sudden and total annihilation of the human species.[67]

Ronald Glossop, a professor of philosophy and peace studies, wrote in a 1982 book entitled *Confronting War*: "Either the war problem gets solved or humanity risks extinction," adding that the world has been much too optimistic about the continued nonuse of nuclear weapons.[68]

Likewise Sydney Lens said: "World government is an idea whose time has come. ... In the past it was simply considered desirable by certain philosophers.... Now, however, it has become indispensable to the survival of civilization."[69]

Prevention of Climate Destruction

Chapter 14 laid out the threat of climate destruction and discussed several ways in which it could lead to the end of civilization. The question here is why the world has not been able stop the trajectory toward ecocide. The basic answer is that global anarchy has made it impossible for global environmental laws to be passed.

In her book on *The Global Politics of the Environment*, Lorraine Elliott distinguished between a *reformist* approach, according to which "it is possible to mitigate environmental problems without changing the underlying political and economic factors responsible for environmental degradation," and a *critical* approach, which finds such reformism inadequate, calling instead for radical transformation, meaning the creation of a global authority to deal with the environment. Elliott published this statement back in 1988, but still no steps have been taken in this direction.[70]

CLAIM THAT GLOBAL GOVERNMENT IS UNDESIRABLE AND IMPOSSIBLE

Proposals for global government are commonly confronted with the claim that it would be unnecessary, undesirable, and impossible. Having treated the issue of necessity, this chapter concludes by addressing, briefly, the issues of desirability and possibility.

A Global Government Would Not Be Undesirable

A common objection to a global government is that, even if it would allow us to solve various problems, it would nevertheless be undesirable. For example, in an important 1959 book entitled *Man, the State, and War*, neorealist Kenneth Waltz warned of the possibility that "a world state would be a world tyranny" in which "we might find ourselves . . . living a life worse than death."[71]

This danger is almost always the principal one used to justify the claim that a world government would be undesirable. But this argument was answered long ago by Thomas Hobbes, who said that although people tend to fear the possible consequences of a single supreme power,

> yet the consequences of the want of it, which is perpetual war. . . , are much worse. The condition of man in this life shall never be without inconveniences.[72]

As David Gauthier said in his study of Hobbes's political theory:

> Hobbes states a fundamentally important principle in this argument...: the alternative to an intolerable situation is never an ideal situation, but rather a barely tolerable situation. We must replace presently intolerable risks by tolerable ones.[73]

Hobbes, to be sure, was talking only about the need for a supreme power in a localized region. Moreover, he even specifically argued against the need for a global government. His argument was that, as Waltz put it, although anarchy breeds war, it "so far has not made life itself impossible." Waltz accordingly quoted with approval Hobbes' statement that the logic showing world government to be the solution to war "does not carry men ... to the founding of a world state."[74]

But that was 300 years ago, and in the meantime, as Gauthier argued, the changed situation, especially the creation of nuclear weapons, has made the international anarchy as threatening to our security as local anarchy would be, so that today Hobbes would consider world government necessary.[75] Einstein made a similar reply, saying:

> I agree . . . with respect to the dangers which would be involved in the creation of a world government. But I believe that these dangers are less significant than the dangers of the international anarchy which, in fact, involves the perpetual threat of war.[76]

Creating a Global Government Would Not Be Impossible

Although it has widely been claimed that it would be impossible to create a viable global government, Joseph Schwartzberg has shown, in a book entitled *Transforming the United Nations System,* how this could be done. By means of many changes in the UN, global anarchy could be replaced by a "democratic, federal world government."[77] Here are most important changes he suggested:

1. Reform the General Assembly so that it can pass binding law, by removing the one-nation-one-vote system, according to

which China, with 1.3 billion citizens, gets the same vote as Nauru, with a population of 9,300.

2. Reform the Security Council by (a) abolishing the present system, according to which five members are permanent and can veto any suggestion; and (b) correcting the power distribution by having members from various regions of the world.

3. Create a credible human rights system, by (a) elevating the Human Rights Council so that it is on par with the Security Council and the General Assembly, giving it decision-making authority; (b) choosing members on the basis of their merits, not as representatives of their countries; (c) having a mandatory gender balance; and (d) having members from indigenous peoples.

4. Strengthen the judicial system by (a) giving the International Court of Justice the power of judicial review; (b) expanding the jurisdiction of the International Criminal Court to include aggression, terrorism, and illicit arms trade; (c) giving the Security Council authority to mandate compulsory mediation or arbitration; and (d) creating a World Court of Human Rights, with the power to deal with issues such as arms trade, international financial fraud, and crimes against the environment.

5. Make the executive plural, consisting of perhaps 12 members, with the honorific title "president" rotating every two years.

With these and some additional changes—such as strengthening the capacity for peacekeeping and putting the budget on a solid basis—the organization would be structurally capable of exercising global governance.

CONCLUSION

The creation of a global democracy could finally overcome the reign of demonic power. The present world order is demonic because it is based on principles that are diametrically opposed to divine purposes and powerful enough to defeat them, and because it is idolatrous, giving primary devotion to wealth and power instead of the creator and lover of life.

Because the American Empire is the organizing center of the present world order, it must, from a Christian point of view, be judged to be demonic—indeed, the most dangerous embodiment of demonic power ever. Simply overcoming this empire would not, however, cure the basic problem, if the world order remains otherwise the same. Replacing the American Empire with, for example, a Chinese hegemon would probably not make for a much better world. Only the creation of global democracy can put an end to the system of warfare, empire, apartheid, and pollution, thereby making possible a form of global governance incorporating divine rather than demonic values.

Morality and the
Christian Community

CHAPTER SEVENTEEN

Morality:
The Golden and Silver Rules

THE MORAL PRINCIPLES discussed in this theology obviously must be Christian. At the same time, however, we live in a pluralistic world, and even an increasingly pluralistic country, in which there is growing interaction between peoples from different religious traditions. For Christians in America to evaluate their country's foreign and domestic policies in a way that can be received as relevant by peoples of other traditions, both inside and outside the United States, we need a moral position that, while being Christian, is also shared by peoples of other religious traditions.

Also, as pointed out in the previous chapter, a global democratic government would need to have a constitution, complete with a bill of rights and responsibilities. Such a bill would require agreement on basic moral principles; it would require, in other words, a global ethic.

CHRISTIAN AND UNIVERSAL MORAL PRINCIPLES

Some moral philosophers believe that a global ethic would be unattainable, on the grounds that there is no "natural law," in the sense of a set of moral principles rooted in the nature of things that can be endorsed by peoples in various traditions. Christianity, Judaism, and Islam are theistic, all being Abrahamic religions. But—so goes the argument—most other religions are not theistic, so they lead either to relativism or to moral principles very different from Christian principles.

However, that argument is based on a too-narrow conception of theism. It is true that most other religions do not hold Abrahamic theism, especially when it is understood to affirm divine omnipotence. But natural law could be based on an affirmation of *theism in a broad sense,* according to which moral norms are inherent in the nature of the universe. Philosophers who deny the objectivity of moral norms do so on the basis of *atheism in the broad sense,* according to which moral norms are not "part of the fabric of the world."[1]

But few, if any, religions affirm atheism in this broad sense, which would be denying that moral norms belong to the fabric of the universe. For example, it is commonly said that Buddhism is not theistic. It is true that it does not affirm Abrahamic theism; it certainly does not affirm *creatio ex nihilo.* But Gene Reeves, an expert on the Lotus Sutra (which is the most important sutra for most Buddhists in East Asia), wrote:

> Certainly if by "God" is meant a literally all-powerful being who is the only Creator of the universe, then the Lotus Sutra has no God. But if by "God" is meant something more like what is taught by Whitehead and Hartshorne, there can be little question but that the Sutra's "Eternal Buddha" is indeed God.[2]

Likewise, it is often said that Confucianism is not theistic. But Confucianism strongly affirms that moral norms are inherent in the nature of things.[3]

Religious Pluralism and Moral Universalism

A second argument against the possibility of a Christian-and-global ethic points to the fact that all the religious traditions are different from each other, some of them radically so. This view was endorsed above in Chapter 8. From this fact, some thinkers argue that a search for an ethic that is simultaneously Christian and universal would be futile.

However, philosophers and theologians actually involved in interreligious dialogue have concluded that this is not true. A book entitled *Prospects for a Common Morality* argued that, although some people in the world of theoretical philosophy have lost confidence in the possibility of any universal moral consensus, there is now in the practical world of international relations "a remarkable kind of cross-cultural moral agreement about human rights."[4]

This agreement came about through dialogue. Although members of each tradition tend to begin with the assumption that their own moral code should be accepted as the universal code, they soon realize that they need to distinguish between those elements in their tradition that are truly universal, shared with all the other traditions, and those that are not. Through this process, Christians, for example, can articulate a set of moral principles that is both Christian and universal. Muslims can articulate an ethic is that is both Islamic and universal. The same with Judaism, Buddhism, Hinduism, and other traditions.

Through this process we can, even in our pluralistic world, develop a set of moral criteria that can be universally recognized as valid for judging matters of public policy, such as US foreign policy.

COSMOPOLITANS AND COMMUNITARIANS

A third argument that has been made against the idea of a universal ethic appeals to the existence of a school of thought known as "communitarianism," which emphasizes the importance of the particular community to which a moral philosopher belongs.

According to a common understanding, the leading communitarian philosophers reject the position known as "cosmopolitanism," which affirms universal moral principles. Whereas "cosmopolitans" insist on universal principles, they are (it is often held), completely at odds with communitarians, who insist on local differences. The existence of the communitarian school of thought, the argument seems to go, provides strong evidence against the view that the various communities, each with their different traditions, share any common moral principles. Accordingly, one is forced to accept relativism.

However, this argument is based on a false premise. At least most of the leading communitarian philosophers are *not* relativists. They instead affirm the reality of basic moral principles that *are* universal. They are, in other words, *cosmopolitan* communitarians.

Michael Walzer: Thick and Thin Morality

This position was developed at some length by Michael Walzer in a book called *Thick and Thin*. In earlier writings, Walzer's concern with difference and particularity had seemed to lead him to a relativistic position. But in this later book, he wrote that difference was still his "major theme and abiding interest," but he also wanted to "defend a certain sort of universalism."

This universalism consists of the idea that, although every concrete morality in terms of which some society lives is always a particularist, "thick" morality, "locked into a locally established symbolic system," there are, nevertheless, "the makings of a thin and universalist morality inside every thick and particularist morality."[5] This thin morality, said Walzer,

> consists in principles and rules that are reiterated in different times and places, and that are seen to be similar even though they are expressed in different idioms and reflect different histories and different visions of the world.[6]

Walzer even said that it is possible, "by abstracting from social practices reiterated in many countries and cultures," to offer "some substantial account of the moral minimum."[7]

Whereas a thick morality is "maximalist," consisting of everything a particular tradition wants to say, the thin morality is "minimalist," being the absolute minimum that must be insisted on always and everywhere.

However, Walzer emphasized, to call the universal element "thin" and "minimalist" is *not* to say that it is unimportant. To the contrary, he said:

> The opposite is more likely true: this is morality close to the bone. There isn't much that is more important than "truth" and "justice," minimally understood. The minimal demands that we make on one another are, when denied, repeated with passionate insistence. In moral discourse, thinness and intensity go together.[8]

Every attempt to formulate this universal moral minimum, Walzer suggested, will probably be stated in terms of negative injunctions, such as "rules against murder, deceit, torture, oppression, and tyranny." In the West, Walzer suggested, "these standards will probably be expressed in the language of rights, which is the language of our own moral maximalism." However, he quickly added, "that is not a bad way of talking about injuries and wrongs that no one should have to endure."[9]

Accordingly, although Walzer is a communitarianism, he is a *cosmopolitan* communitarianism. The same is true of the other best-known communitarians: Amitai Etzioni, Michael Sandel, and Charles Taylor.

Other Communitarians

In a book entitled *The New Golden Rule,* Amitai Etzioni, after explaining why he is a communitarian, criticized the cultural relativism of some communitarians, saying:

> It is not only possible but highly necessary *to combine some universal principles with particularistic ones to form a full communitarian normative account.* Like many other dichotomies, that between universalism and particularism stands in the way of developing a solid paradigm, and recognizing the merit of combination moves us forward.[10]

In a book entitled *Democracy's Discontent,* Michael Sandel said that "the cosmopolitan ideal is flawed" by virtue of holding that "our encompassing loyalties should always take precedence over more local ones."[11] But he also said:

> The cosmopolitan ideal rightly emphasizes the humanity we share and directs our attention to the moral consequences that flow from it. It offers a corrective to the narrow, sometimes murderous chauvinism into which ethnic and national identities can descend. It reminds wealthy nations that their obligations do not end at the water's edge.... All this makes the cosmopolitan ideal an attractive ethic, especially now that the global aspect of political life requires forms of allegiance that go beyond nations.[12]

Charles Taylor also expressed a both-and position. Having argued the communitarian point that governments should help cultures "defend themselves," he added this proviso: "within reasonable bounds." What those bounds are is indicated by his statement that there should be an "invariant defense" of "fundamental rights," such as the "rights to life, liberty, due process, free speech, free practice of religion."[13]

THE GOLDEN AND SILVER RULES

The previous section shows that the existence of communitarian philosophers provides no basis for considering impossible the goal of Christians to develop a global ethic—one that could be simultaneously Christian and universal.

The Golden Rule

Could the Golden Rule fill the bill? Catholic theologian Hans Küng, who led the way toward the articulation of a global ethic, pointed out that at least most religious traditions affirm some version of what Christians have called the *Golden Rule*:

- Jesus of Nazareth: "So in everything, do to others what you would have them do to you, for this sums up the Law and the Prophets" (Matthew 7:12).

- Islam: "None of you is a believer as long as he does not

wish his brother what he wishes himself" (Forty Hadith of an-Nawawi, 13).

- Jainism: "Human beings should . . . treat all creatures in the world as they would want to be treated themselves" (Sutrakritanga I, 11,33).

The Golden/Silver Rule

The Golden Rule, however, has often been criticized, usually on the grounds that what we like is not necessarily evidence of what others would like. For example, George Bernard Shaw famously quipped: "Do not do unto others as you would that they should do unto you. Their tastes may be different."[14] But this criticism can be answered. For example, Walter Stace wrote:

> Mr. Bernard Shaw's remark "Do not do unto others as you would that they should do unto you. Their tastes may be different" is no doubt a smart saying. But it seems to overlook the fact that "doing as you would be done by" includes taking into account your neighbor's tastes as you would that he should take yours into account. Thus the "golden rule" might still express the essence of a universal morality.[15]

Stace's answer is well taken. However, there is still a problem with using the Golden Rule as a universal ethical principle. It works well within a family and between good friends, and perhaps even within a small village. But the Golden Rule cannot provide a moral principle that could be followed in relation to strangers and hence most of the world. Shaw's objection is correct.

Moreover, there is the problem of infinity: There may be no end to the things that some people would like us to do for them.

But these problems are avoided by the negative formulation of the principle, sometimes called the *silver rule*:

> Judaism: Rabbi Hillel, who probably influenced Jesus, gave this formulation: "That which is hateful to you, do not unto another: This is the whole Torah. The rest is commentary." (Shabbat 31a)

Combining the positive and negative formulations of the principle by Jesus and Hillel, respectively, we could speak of "the Golden/Silver Rule," understood as suggested above: the Golden Rule (along with the Silver Rule) is for relations to family and very good friends, whereas the Silver Rule is for our relations to people in general. To be sure, the Golden Rule could be considered universal, given the fact that the Silver Rule is implicit in it (you could not "do to others what you would have them do to you" while doing things to them that you would find hateful if done to you). However, explaining this would be needlessly complex. It is simplest to say that the Silver Rule, which is endorsed by most traditions, is a universal principle, whereas some traditions (such as Christianity, Islam, and Jainism) recommend the Golden Rule for intimates.

In any case, it is rather surprising that all discussions of Christian ethics are not oriented around the Golden Rule (understood as the Golden/Silver Rule), given the fact that Jesus in the Gospel of Matthew said that this principle "sums up the Law and the Prophets." This is especially the case in light of the fact that Rabbi Hillel said of the Silver Rule: "This is the whole Torah. The rest is commentary." Because both Jesus and Hillel made this point central, Jews and Christians should be able to agree about the essence of morality.

But the main point here is that the Golden/Silver Rule gives Christians a moral principle that is universal as well as Christian. Christians can simply call it the Golden Rule, given the fact that the Silver Rule is implicit in it.

The Silver Rule

The fact that the silver rule is universal, at least virtually, is shown by the following examples of statements in various religious traditions:

- Confucianism: "What you yourself do not want, do not do to another person" (Analects of Confucius 15:23).

- Buddhism: "Hurt not others in ways that you yourself would find hurtful" (Udana-Varga 5:18).

- Hinduism: One should not behave towards others in a

way which is unpleasant for oneself: that is the essence of morality" (Mahabharata XIII, 114,8). (As can be seen, this Hindu dictum, like the dicta of Jesus and Hillel, added that the Silver Rule is the essence of morality.)

- Zoroastrianism: "Whatever is disagreeable to yourself do not do unto others" (Shayast-na-Shayast 13:29).[16]

- The Incas: "Do not to another what you would not yourself experience" (Manco Capoc, founder of the Peruvian empire).

This principle is also, said philosopher Simon Blackburn, contained in virtually every ethical tradition.[17] Here are three examples in Greek philosophy:

- Thales: "Avoid doing what you would blame others for doing."[18]

- Isocrates: "Do not do to others that which angers you when they do it to you."[19]

- Sextus the Pythagorean: "What you do not want to happen to you, do not do it yourself either."[20]

Although an ethical position based on the Silver Rule (or Golden/Silver Rule) seems at first glance too narrow, it actually is not, as all ethical issues can be stated in terms of it.

BASIC RIGHTS

This rights-based approach to morality is especially natural for Americans, since it is rooted in the American Declaration of Independence, which speaks of entitlements founded on "the laws of nature and of nature's God" and says that all people "are endowed by their Creator with certain unalienable rights."

One American philosopher who developed the rights-based position in great detail, and specifically in relation to US foreign policy, was Henry Shue of the University of Oxford. In his book *Basic Rights*, Shue focused on those rights that are most basic in the sense that they are common to all human beings. Rights are basic, said Shue, if the "enjoyment of them is essential to the enjoyment of all other rights."[21] Such rights, Shue says, constitute "the morality of the depths," because they specify "the line beneath which no one is to be allowed to sink."[22]

The basic rights approach is reflected in the United Nations' Universal Declaration of Human Rights, which says in Article 3 that "everyone has the right to life" and in Article 25 that "every man, woman and child has the inalienable right to be free from hunger and malnutrition."[23] As United Nations scholar James Nickel wrote, the unifying idea behind the Universal Declaration is "the idea of a decent or minimally good life for all people."[24]

Besides the right to life and adequate food, Shue pointed out that a minimally good life also requires "minimal economic security, or subsistence," "unpolluted air, unpolluted water ..., adequate clothes, adequate shelter, and minimal preventive public health care."[25]

Thanks in large part to the UN's Declaration of Rights, the human-rights approach to morality has become increasingly universal. This approach can easily be phrased in terms of the Silver Rule: I would not want to be deprived of any of these things to which all people have a right, so I should not deprive any other people of any of these things.

Moreover, the Silver Rule should not be stated in simply individualist terms. To say that we should not deprive other people of adequate food entails that we do not want our government to deprive any people around the world of any of these rights, so our voting should be guided by the Silver Rule.

The distinction between basic and nonbasic rights has vast implications. Basic rights, by virtue of being basic, should trump all nonbasic rights. Rights that are essential to life are people's *vital interests* in the most literal sense of the term. The vital interests of people should always take precedence over the non-vital interests of others. Even if these non-vital interests be considered *rights*, they are not *basic* rights and hence can be trumped.

A society can be just, therefore, only if its laws and institutions are such as to guarantee that the non-vital rights and preferences of some are not protected at the expense of the vital interests of others.

Some people hold that an interest in having an unlimited amount of money gives one a right to make it, along with a right to have all the luxury items one desires. But insofar as a right to such riches and luxuries exists—it is really a desire, not a right—it would be immoral to allow this "right" to trump the vital necessities, and hence basic rights, of others. Shue noted that John Locke, whose writings inspired much in early American thought, "had taken for granted that the right to accumulate private property was limited by a universal right to subsistence."[26]

In light of these moral principles, the "right" of ExxonMobil, Chevron, and the Koch brothers to accumulate more and more money would, in a moral system of national and global governance, be trumped by the basic rights of people around the world to have non-toxic air, non-polluted water to drink, adequate water for agriculture, thriving marine life, and a sea-level that will not force them to move.

Another major implication: Rights entail demands. Basic rights are, in Shue's words, "everyone's minimum reasonable demands upon the rest of humanity."[27] The truth of this point can be easily seen: If everyone has a right to adequate food, then everyone else has the duty not to violate this right.

In addition, the basic rights of human beings imply duties beyond this merely negative duty not to violate them. They also imply positive duties to *protect* the rights of people to have, for example, adequate food and then, if this protection fails, to *provide aid* to those who fall victim to social failures or natural disasters. This means that we in America have a duty not only to prevent our government from violating the rights of people in other countries to have adequate food but also, because we are a wealthy country, to aid peoples in poor countries.

Aiding all the poor people in the world to have adequate food is obviously not something that we as individuals or even America as a whole could do. But a global government could organize the world and its economy so that no one would starve.

Also, the requirement to protect people's rights can be phrased in terms of the Silver Rule: We want our basic rights to be protected, so we should work toward a global community in which the basic rights of all people are protected.

THE GOLDEN / SILVER RULE AND US FOREIGN POLICY

The USA likes to see itself as a basically Christian country. There is still a sense in which this is true, in terms of nominal identification with Christianity. But to be *substantively* Christian, America's policies would need to reflect Christianity's most basic moral principle, the Golden/Silver Rule. Because the Golden Rule is much more demanding than the Silver Rule—in fact, no country's foreign policy could be expected to follow this principle, given the present anarchical global order—so we should judge US foreign policy in terms of the Silver Rule. Even here, we should not expect too much as long as the anarchical world order persists.

However, for America in the present world order to be considered a Christian country, its foreign policies should not flagrantly violate the Silver Rule. But it does. Here are examples derived from Chapters 11, 13, and 14.

- The United States has sought to create a universal empire that could dictate the political and economic policies, and perhaps even cultural policies, of other countries. But Americans would not like to have our country's political and economic policies determined by another country, such as Russia or China.

- The United States overthrew 30 governments during the Cold War alone, and continued this practice afterwards. But Americans would not want its government to be overthrown. Indeed, Americans became very upset by the idea that Russia influenced the US presidential election in 2016.

- Policies dictated by the United States caused the standard of living in many countries to be lowered, leaving many of their citizens with inadequate food, water, and health care. But Americans would be very upset if China, after becoming stronger than the US, adopted policies that decreased Americans' food, drinking water, and available medical care.

- America used nuclear weapons on Japan, even though there was no military necessity for this use. In spite of this, Americans would be outraged if China or Russia, or angry terrorists used nuclear weapons on us.

- If the fossil-fuel usage of the present generation means that a future generation finds itself in the midst of an unstoppable ecological holocaust, that generation will certainly wish that we had followed the Golden/Silver Rule with regard to our usage of fossil fuels.

More generally, US foreign policy could be judged in terms of an updated list of "ten commandments," such as:

1. Don't murder people.

2. Don't deprive people of food and water.

3. Don't steal people's oil and other natural resources.

4. Don't steal people's personal property.

5. Don't deprive people of their freedom.

6. Don't cause people needless pain.

7. Don't terrorize people.

8. Don't rape people.

9. Don't humiliate people.

10. Don't treat people as mere means to your ends.

These commandments can be reworded in terms of the Silver Rule. For example: "I would not like my family members to be murdered, so neither I nor my government should murder other people." Likewise, I would not like to be terrorized, so I should try to prevent my government from terrorizing other people.

Many would say that the moral teachings of Jesus were intended only for personal relations, not for the political and economic policies of the governing power. But that certainly was not the view of Jesus, who in the Lord's Prayer lifted up the problems of chronic debt and inadequate food and who, more generally, preached an anti-imperial gospel.

CONCLUSION

The Silver Rule, which has been advocated by virtually all religious and philosophical traditions, can provide an ethic that is simultaneously Christian and global. Being global, this ethic can provide the moral basis for a global democracy. If America were part of a global democracy, it would not be able to violate the Silver Rule so fully and flagrantly. Christians may prefer to speak of the Golden Rule, with its ethic being applied to close friends and intimates, and with the Silver Rule understood to be implicit in relation to everyone else. In a statement advocating a revival of the Golden Rule, Karen Armstrong explained why she felt urgency about this:

> If we don't manage to implement the Golden Rule globally, so that we treat all peoples, wherever and whoever they may be, as though they were as important as ourselves, I doubt that we'll have a viable world to hand on to the next generation. The task of our time, one of the great tasks of our time, is to build a global society, as I said, where people can live together in peace.[28]

To this task, she added, the religions "should be making a major contribution."[29]

CHAPTER EIGHTEEN

The Christian Community

No man can serve two masters: for either he will hate the one, and love the other; or else he will hold to the one, and despise the other. Ye cannot serve God and Mammon. ~Matthew 6:24 (NKJV)

THE PREVIOUS CHAPTER goes far toward enunciating moral principles that should be exemplified by the Christian Community worldwide as well as in local congregations. Those principles are ones that are ideally shared by all religions and ethical systems. The present chapter enlarges the discussion by focusing on ideas and principles of the Christian Community in particular. However, this discussion does not attempt to deal with all such ideas and principles. Rather, this discussion focuses, like this volume as a whole, on American foreign policy.

THE CHRISTIAN COMMUNITY'S MISSION

The Christian Community should base itself, all of its activities, on the Christian Community's mission. Its basic mission is to lead the way in God's battle against demonic power on Earth. The church is meant to serve as a counterforce to the demonic dimension of the symbolic structure in which human beings live. God's incarnational activity in Jesus should be understood as a divine offensive against the power of the demonic.

The Christian Community should, of course, engage in ethical and political activity as usually understood. But this activity should be carried out in the context of a *spiritual* offensive, in which the power of prayer is used to reinforce the divine influence upon the individuals and institutions involved. Praying for those who are especially enslaved to demonic power, and who are incarnating it in especially destructive ways, will not only serve to remind us that they are essentially good creatures who are loved by God, but also that our battle is not with them but with the demonic power to which they are enslaved.

Individual Christians

The Christian Community is comprised of individuals and communities who seek to imitate Jesus's own fidelity to God. One role of the Christian Community is to help individuals and churches to overcome, as fully as possible, their subjugation to demonic influences.

Through preaching, sacraments, prayer, meditation, study, and fellowship, members help each other focus on the workings of the Holy Spirit in their souls. St. Paul described the Spirit's effects on us in terms of various values, such as love, joy, peace, patience, kindness, goodness, faithfulness, gentleness, and self-control (Galatians 5:22–23). The Divine Spirit whets our appetites to incarnate these values.

Part of the value of the Christian Community results from the fact that we directly influence other souls for good or for ill. Insofar as our influence is for ill, we thereby contribute to the demonic power on our planet, adding to the demonic aspect of the general psychic matrix into which other souls are born and by which they are influenced willy-nilly. In a healthy community, we influence each other for good, not simply willy-nilly, but also intentionally.

By sharing reasons to believe in continued life after physical death (as in Chapters 7 and 15), the Christian Community encourages people to consider our present life to be part of a larger journey. When they do, they tend to begin seeing spiritual development as centrally important. Some sort of spiritual discipline becomes more important than the search for pleasure, power, fame, or riches (Chapter 15). St. Paul said:

> [T]hose who live according to the flesh set their minds on the things of the flesh, but those who live according to the Spirit set their minds on the things of the Spirit.... [Y]ou are not in the flesh; you are in the Spirit, since the Spirit of God dwells in you. (Romans 8:5–9)

The Public Sphere

A second role of the Christian Community is to seek to lead the way in overcoming the power of the demonic in the public sphere. William Stringfellow, who is featured in this section, wrote much about Ephesians 6:12, which says:

> [O]ur struggle is not against enemies of blood and flesh, but against the rulers, against the authorities, against the cosmic powers of this present darkness, against the spiritual forces of evil in the heavenly places.

There are many ways, Stringfellow said, in which spiritual forces of evil can lead people to embody and transmit the demonic.

> If the powers and principalities be legion, so are the means by which they assault, captivate, enslave, and dominate human beings.[1]

With regard to powers and principles that dominate and enslave human beings, Stringfellow judged that

> the State has a particular eminence.... Those human beings and communities of humans who persevere in fidelity to God, do so under the condemnation of the State in one way or another, be it in ridicule and ostracism, in poverty or imprisonment, as sojourners or fugitives, in clandestine existence, as a confessing movement [see below], or, otherwise, in resistance.[2]

In many cases, resistance is demanded:

> [T]he act of resistance to the power of death incarnate in
> Nazism was the only means of retaining sanity and conscience.
> In the circumstances of the Nazi tyranny, *resistance became*
> *the only human way to live.* ... Not to resist, on the other hand,
> involved the certitude of death—of moral death, of the death
> of one's humanity, of death to sanity and conscience.[3]

The Christian Community, living out its Christian vocation,
Stringfellow concluded, is often "an alien in a hostile land."[4]

Christians in America might assume that, although Christians
in Nazi Germany were living in an alien land, so that resistance was
demanded, the only obligation placed on us is to thank God that we
do not live in such a land. However, Stringfellow said:

> [M]orally the demonic spirit incarnate in the Axis powers
> won the war. The illusion has been that, in the aftermath
> of the Second World War, America succeeded British
> imperialism. ... But the truth is that America succeeded Nazi
> Germany, ... having the same moral identity as Nazism—
> which can be symbolized and summarized in three words:
> *war, racism, genocide.*[5]

Crucifixion and Resurrection

"That Jesus was *crucified* by the Roman governor," summarized
Richard Horsley, "stands as a vivid symbol of his historical relationship with the Roman imperial order."[6]

The Q speeches in the Synoptic Gospels depict Jesus as the latest
and most important in a long line of Israelite prophets. At points, the
speeches present him as killed by the rulers—as many of the prophets
had been (Luke/Q 7:18–35; 11:47–51; 13:34).

In meditating on the cross and taking communion, we should
always remind ourselves of the centrality of the symbol of Jesus's
death on a Roman cross. Truly following Jesus, this symbol reminds
us, includes willingness to challenge imperialism today.

Remembering that we will, like Jesus, be resurrected can help empower us and fellow Christians to battle valiantly against demonic powers in high places. It can empower us insofar as we remember that we are not subject to the state's coercive power. As St. Paul said:

> If God is for us, who is against us?. . . . For I am convinced that neither death, nor life, nor angels, nor rulers, nor things present, nor things to come, nor powers, nor height, nor depth, nor anything else in all creation, will be able to separate us from the love of God in Christ Jesus our Lord. (Romans 8:31–39)

Divine Power

Belief in God's power to give us continuing life beyond bodily death does not, however, require the traditional view of divine omnipotence. In fact, it is important to reject the image of God as the omnipotent male warrior, which has provided a prime stimulant for warfare in Christian civilization.

Given humanity's religious drive to imitate deity, the image of God as a mighty warrior gave warfare a religious aura. Alfred North Whitehead said:

> Th[e] worship of glory arising from power is not only dangerous: it arises from a barbaric conception of God. I suppose that even the world itself could not contain the bones of those slaughtered because of men intoxicated by its attraction.[7]

God's ultimate victory over evil will come about through love, not coercive power. The resurrection of Jesus symbolizes the efficacy of God's persuasive power.

CONFESSING CHURCH

In Germany in 1934, a year after the rise to power of the National Socialist (Nazi) Party, the movement known as the *Deutsche Christen*—"German Christians"—was created. The German Christians believed the program of the National Socialists would bring Germany the greatness it deserved. So they supported the Nazis, even though the latter wanted to make the church subservient to the state. "The German Christians accepted Adolf Hitler as a 'German prophet' and preached that racial consciousness was a source of revelation alongside the Bible."[8] Besides accepting the Nazi doctrine of the racial superiority of so-called Aryans, the German Christians also said that, among the Aryans, Germans were superior and hence called to rule the world.[9]

But a number of pastors and theologians, led by Martin Niemöller, Dietrich Bonhoeffer, and Karl Barth, among others, began a movement of Confessing Christians who said, in their famous Barmen Declaration of 1934, that the support for National Socialism violated basic principles of the Christian faith, thereby creating a *status confessionis* (confessional situation), meaning a binding doctrinal stance on sociopolitical questions. The Barmen declaration, which was written primarily by Barth (Reformed) and Hans Asmussen (Lutheran),[10] rejected the attempt to make the church "an organ of the state."[11]

Later in the century, some Christian bodies decided that the system of apartheid in South Africa could not remain a matter of indifference. One such body was the Lutheran World Federation. "Under normal circumstances," it declared in 1977, "Christians may have different opinions in political questions." But the system of apartheid in South Africa, it declared, is "so perverted and oppressive" that this situation "constitutes a *status confessionis*." The Christian faith required, therefore, that "churches would publicly and unequivocally reject the existing apartheid system."[12]

It is now time for Christians in America—actually, long past time—to engage in an extensive examination of the nature of the American Empire to see if it is "so perverted and oppressive" that Christians, individually and as churches, should "publicly and unequivocally" reject it. Chapters 9–13 of this book have argued that this is indeed the case.

If the apartheid system in South Africa was "so perverted and oppressive" as to require churches and individual Christians to renounce this system publicly and unequivocally, nothing less can be required in relation to the system of *global* apartheid, which by every measure is worse than the apartheid in South Africa (see Chapter 10). Global apartheid should be a *status confessionis* for the Christian Community worldwide.

Moreover, there can be no meaningful renunciation of this system without rejecting the imperialistic policies that have produced it. More generally, American political, economic, and military leaders have long been engaged, since at least the end of the Cold War, in a "global domination project," similar to the Nazi project. Like the Germans, America has used its power toward bringing the whole world under its control. How could we fail to regard the American Empire's domination project—like the Nazi project—as wholly antithetical to Christian faith?

Our Christian faith at its best would lead us, both as individual Christians and as churches, to oppose the American Empire in the name of God. As long as the church does not explicitly oppose this empire, it is, by its silence, a *de facto* supporter.

In addition, a book entitled *Facing the Nuclear Heresy* was published in 1986 by G. Clarke Chapman, who taught religion at Moravian College. As suggested by his book's title, Chapman argued that Christians should declare nuclear weapons a *status confessionis* (see note 8). His cause did not evoke much response, but this was probably because of the success of the propaganda, as discussed in Chapter 13, that the atomic bombs dropped on Hiroshima and Nagasaki were necessary to end the war with Japan.

However the facts discussed in that chapter show America's creation and use of nuclear weapons to be one of the reasons to classify the American Empire as *extremely* demonic. As such, nuclear weapons should be declared a *status confessionis*.

Finally, climate destruction, also extremely demonic, is even more certain than nuclear weapons to destroy civilization. The continued burning of fossil fuels should be declared a *status confessionis* by the worldwide Christian Community while there is still time to prevent complete human extinction.

Notes

INTRODUCTION

1   A particularly good example is Delwin Brown, *What Does a Progressive Christian Believe? A Guide for the Searching, the Open, and the Curious* (Seabury, 2008).

2   William Stringfellow, *An Ethic for Christians and Other Aliens in a Strange Land* (Word Books, 1973), 13.

3   Dick Cheney and Liz Cheney, *Exceptional: Why the World Needs a Powerful America* (Threshold Editions, 2015), 1.

4   Thomas Jay Oord, *God Can't: How to Believe in God and Love after Tragedy, Abuse, and Other Evils* (SacraSage Press, 2019).

5   Stringfellow, *An Ethic for Christians and Other Aliens in a Strange Land*, 14.

6   Saint Anselm, *Proslogium; Monologium; An Appendix in Behalf of the Fool by Gaunilon; and Cur Deus Homo*, trans. S. N. Deane (Open Court, 1903), 11, 13.

7   Rudolf Bultmann, *Theology of the New Testament*, vol. 1 (Charles Scribner's Sons, 1951), 36.

8 Hans Werner Bartsch, ed., *Kerygma and Myth* (SPCK, 1953), 197.

9 Bartsch, ed., Bultmann, *Kerygma and Myth,* 197.

10 Gregory W. Dawes, *The Historical Jesus Question: The Challenge of History to Religious Authority* (Westminster John Knox Press, 2001).

11 Immanuel Kant, *Religion Within the Limits of Reason Alone,* trans. Theodore M. Greene and Hoyt H. Hudson (Harper & Row, 1960), 163.

12 David Ray Griffin et al. *Founders of Constructive Postmodern Philosophy: Peirce, James, Bergson, Whitehead, and Hartshorne* (State University Press of New York, 1992).

13 David Ray Griffin, "Reconstructive [Postmodern] Theology," in *The Cambridge Companion to Postmodern Theology,* ed. Kevin J. Vanhoozer (Cambridge University Press, 2003), 92–108.

14 Alfred North Whitehead, *Process and Reality: An Essay in Cosmology,* corrected edition, ed. David Ray Griffin and Donald W. Sherburne (Free Press, 1978), 151.

15 Whitehead, *Process and Reality,* 13.

16 Martin Jay, "The Debate over Performative Contradiction: Habermas versus the Poststructuralists," *Force Fields: Between Intellectual History and Cultural Critique,* 25–37 (Routledge, 1993), 25–37, at 29.

CHAPTER ONE: THE BIBLE AND THEOLOGICAL METHOD

1 Scripture and Tradition," Catholic Answers, https://www.catholic.com/tract/scripture-and-tradition.

2 Fr. Francis J. Connell, "Are All Revealed Truths in Sacred Scripture?" Catholic Culture.org. According to a newer view, Connell explained, "new dogmas defined by the magisterium [teaching authority of the Church] are not new revelations, but rather explanations of the revelation given to the apostles." Connell argued, however, that this view, according to which all revealed truths are in the Bible, is in serious tension with the heretofore unanimous acceptance of the traditional view—according to which tradition contains some revealed truths not found in Scripture.

3 Chuck Collins, "Throw Away the Three-Legged Stool," *The Living Church,* 26 July 1998.

4 Albert Outler, "The Wesleyan Quadrilateral—in John Wesley," in *The Wesleyan Theological Heritage: Essays of Albert C. Outler,* ed. Thomas C. Oden and Leicester R. Longden (Zondervan, 1991). For an extensive discussion, see Donald A.D. Thorsen, *The Wesleyan Quadrilateral: Scripture, Tradition, Experience & Reason as Model of Evangelical Theology* (Zondervan, 1990).

5 Edward Farley and Peter Hodgson, "Scripture and Tradition," in *Christian Theology: An Introduction to Its Traditions and Tasks,* ed. Peter C. Hodgson and Robert H. King, 2nd ed. (Fortress, 1985), 61–87.

6 Farley and Hodgson, "Scripture and Tradition," 61–87.

7 To be more precise, this basic idea stood for many decades, but recently some scholars have started challenging it. See Jan C. Gertz, et al., eds., *The Formation of the Pentateuch: Bridging the Academic Cultures of Europe, Israel, and North America* (Mohr Siebeck, 2016).

8 Farley and Hodgson, "Scripture and Tradition," 69.

9 "What Is Wrong with the Allegorical Interpretation Method?" GotQuestions, https://www.gotquestions.org/allegorical-interpretation.html.

10 Dan G. McCartney, "Literal and Allegorical Interpretation in Origen's Contra Celsum," *Westminster Theological Journal* 48.2 (Fall 1986): 281–301.

CHAPTER TWO: GOD AS CREATOR OF HEAVEN AND EARTH

1 Bertrand Russell, "A Free Man's Worship" (1903), *The Collected Papers of Bertrand Russell, Volume 12: Contemplation and Action, 1902–14* (Routledge, 1988).

2 E.O. Wilson, *On Human Nature* (Bantam Books, 1979), 179, 200.

3 William R. Uttal, *The Psychobiology of Mind* (L. Erlbaum Associates, 1978), 10, 82, 5, 28.

4 Peter W. Atkins, *The Creation* (W.H. Freeman & Co., 1981).

5   Peter W. Atkins, "Professor Says Science Rules out Belief in God," *Electronic Telegraph*, 11 September 1996.

6   "The Meaning of El Shaddai," Knowing the Bible, https://www .knowingthebible.net/topics/the-meaning-of-el-shaddai.

7   Thomas Jay Oord, *The Uncontrolling Love of God: An Open and Relational Account of Providence* (IVP Academic, 2015).

8   Mary Daly, *Beyond God the Father: Toward a Philosophy of Women's Liberation* (Houghton Mifflin, 1973), 19.

9   Mary Daly, "After the Death of God the Father: Women's Liberation and the Transformation of Christian Consciousness," in *Womanspirit Rising: A Feminist Reader in Religion,* ed. Carol P. Christ and Judith Plaskow (Harper & Row, 1979), 53–62 (originally published in *Commonweal,* 12 March 1971).

10 Merlin Stone, *When God Was a Woman* (Mariner Books, 1978), 1.

11 Carol P. Christ, *Rebirth of the Goddess: Finding Meaning in Feminist Spirituality* (Addison-Wesley, 1997), 50.

12 "The Great Goddess," Museum of Ancient and Modern Art.

13 Christ, *Rebirth of the Goddess,* 47.

14 Carol P. Christ and Judith Plaskow, *Goddess and God in the World: Conversations in Embodied Theology* (Fortress, 2016), 259.

15 Christ, *Rebirth of the Goddess,* 104.

16 Christ and Plaskow, *Goddess and God in the World,* passim.

17 Alfred North Whitehead, *Process and Reality: An Essay in Cosmology,* corrected edition, ed. David Ray Griffin and Donald W. Sherburne (Free Press, 1978), 96.

18 Whitehead, *Process and Reality,* 115.

19 Virginia Ramey Mollenkott, *The Divine Feminine: The Biblical Imagery of God as Female* (Crossroad, 1983), 119. For a discussion of Mollenkott's position, see Pamela D. H. Cochran, *Evangelical Feminism: A History* (New York University Press, 2005), 59–60.

20 Vernard Eller, *The Language of Canaan and the Grammar of Feminism* (Eerdmans, 1982), 12–14.

21 Mollenkott, *The Divine Feminine,* 3.

22 Eller, *The Language of Canaan and the Grammar of Feminism*, 14.

23 David Ray Griffin, *God Exists but Gawd Does Not: From Evil to New Atheism to Fine-Tuning* (Process Century Press, 2016).

24 A movement that came to be called the New Atheism has been discussed primarily in terms of books by three men: Richard Dawkins (*The God Delusion*, 2006); Sam Harris (*The End of Faith*, 2005, and *Letter to a Christian Nation*, 2008); and Christopher Hitchens (*God is Not Great: How Religion Poisons Everything*, 2007). Some critics have considered the term New Atheism a misnomer because, in the words of one writer, it is "difficult to identify anything philosophically unprecedented in their positions and arguments" (James E. Taylor, "The New Atheists," *Internet Encyclopedia of Philosophy*, 2010).

25 The non-existence of Gawd is shown by (a) the contradiction of Gawd—as an omniscient, omnipotent, and perfectly good being—with horrendous evil; (b) the contradiction between science's most fundamental presupposition, that there can be no violations of the laws of nature, with Gawd, who can violate such laws at will, as in miracles; (c) the contradiction of the evolutionary worldview, according to which our universe could have come about only through slow evolutionary developments, and Gawd, who could have created the present universe in an instant. (For the arguments for these claims, see Part I of Griffin, *God Exists but Gawd Does Not*.) The existence of God is shown by the reality of mathematics, morality, logic and rationality, truth, religious experience, and the teleological order of the universe. (The arguments for these claims are contained in see Part II of *God Exists but Gawd Does Not*.)

26 John D. Barrow and Frank J. Tipler, *The Anthropic Cosmological Principle* (Oxford University Press, 1986), 336.

27 Martin Rees, *Just Six Numbers: The Deep Forces that Shape the Universe* (Basic Books, 2000), 54–57.

28 John Leslie, *Universes* (1989; Routledge, 1996), 34 (quoting Freeman Dyson, "Energy in the Universe," *Scientific American*, September 1971: 51–59).

29 Paul Davies, *Cosmic Jackpot: Why Our Universe is Just Right for Life* (Houghton Mifflin Co., 2007), 143.

30 Leslie, *Universes*, 34.

31 "Gravity is Really Weak?" Stanford Solar Center.

32 "The Strength of the Force of Gravity as an Example of Cosmic Fine Tuning," God: New Evidence; "What If Gravity Was Weaker or Stronger?" Science Bits.

33 Stephen Hawking, *A Brief History of Time* (Bantam, 1998), 129.

34 Oliver Sacks, "My Periodic Table," *New York Times*, 24 July 2015; Paul Davies, *The Goldilocks Enigma: Why Is the Universe Just Right for Life?* (Mariner Books, 2006), 141–43.

35 Ethan Siegel, "It Takes 26 Fundamental Constants to Give Us Our Universe, But They Still Don't Give Everything," *Forbes*, 22 August 2015.

36 Paul Davies, "How Bio-Friendly is the Universe?" *International Journal of Astrobiology*, 2 (2003).

37 Many people assumed that Hawking was not an atheist because he had spoken about the possibility of knowing "the mind of God." In 2014, however, Hawking said: "Before we understand science, it is natural to believe that God created the universe. But now science offers a more convincing explanation. What I meant by 'we would know the mind of God' is that we would know everything that God would know, if there were a God, which there isn't. I'm an atheist." Alan Boyle, "'I'm an Atheist': Stephen Hawking on God and Space Travel," NBC, 23 September 2014.

38 Stephen Hawking, *A Brief History of Time*, 125.

39 Paul Davies, *The Cosmic Blueprint* (Simon & Schuster, 1988), 203.

40 Antony Flew with Roy Varghese, *There is a God: How The World's Most Notorious Atheist Changed His Mind* (Harper Collins, 2007), 121.

41 Sir Fred Hoyle, "The Universe: Past and Present Reflections," *Engineering and Science*, November 1981.

42 John C. Lennox, *God's Undertaker: Has Science Buried God?* (Lion Hudson, 2007), 68.

43 Roberto Mangabeira Unger and Lee Smolin, *The Singular Universe and the Reality of Time* (Cambridge University Press, 2015), 353–54, 360.

44 Sean Carroll, "Does the Universe Need God?" *The Blackwell Companion to Science and Christianity,* ed. James B. Stump and Alan G. Padgett (Wiley-Blackwell, 2012).

45 Denis Brian, *Genius Talk: Conversations with Nobel Scientists and Other Luminaries* (Plenum Press, 1995), 164.

46 Carroll, "Does the Universe Need God?"

47 Martin Rees, *Our Cosmic Habitat* (Phoenix, 2003), 164.

48 Stephen Hawking and Leonard Mlodinow, *The Grand Design* (Bantam, 2012), 153, 165.

49 Thomas Nagel, *Mind and Cosmos: Why the Materialist Neo-Darwinian Conception of Nature Is Almost Certainly False* (Oxford University Press, 2012), 131.

50 Unger and Smolin, *The Singular Universe,* 117–19, 160.

51 Paul Davies, *Cosmic Jackpot: Why Our Universe is Just Right for Life* (Houghton Mifflin Co., 2007), 179–85.

52 Luke Barnes, "The Fine-Tuning of the Universe for Intelligent Life," *Publications of the Astronomical Society of Australia* 29/4 (2012): 529–64.

53 Maggie McKee, "Ingenious: Paul J. Steinhardt," *Nautilus* 25 (September 2014).

54 Brian Greene, *The Elegant Universe: Superstrings, Hidden Dimensions, and the Quest for the Ultimate Theory* (W. W. Norton, 2010) and *The Hidden Reality: Parallel Universes and the Deep Laws of the Cosmos* (Vintage, 2011).

55 Brian Greene, "The Multiverse," in *What Is Your Dangerous Idea? Today's Leading Thinkers on the Unthinkable,* ed. John Brockman (Harper Perennial, 2007), 120–21.

56 Davies, *The Goldilocks Enigma,* 204; Davies, "Stephen Hawking's Big Bang Gaps," *Guardian,* 4 September 2010.

57 "Science's Alternative to an Intelligent Creator: the Multiverse Theory," *Discover,* December 2008.

58 See Griffin, *God Exists but Gawd Does Not: From Evil to New Atheism to Fine-Tuning.*

59 Nagel, *Mind and Cosmos,* 131.

60   Nagel, *Mind and Cosmos*, 130.

61   Carroll, "Does the Universe Need God?"; Hawking and Mlodinow, *The Grand Design*, 34; Stephen Hawking, interviewed by Pablo Jáuregui, "No hay ningún dios. Soy ateo," *El Mundo*, 26 October 2014.

62   Richard Lewontin, "Billions and Billions of Demons," New York Review of Books, 9 January 1997: 28–32, at 31.

63   Unger and Smolin suggested that they had a third position, which allows them to reject theism as well as the multiverse theory. But their argument for this third position does not work (see Griffin, *God Exists but Gawd Does Not*, 297–98).

64   Robert J. Richards, "Moral Foundations of the Idea of Evolutionary Progress," in *Evolutionary Progress*, ed. Matthew H. Nitecki (University of Chicago Press, 1988), 129–48, at 131, 142.

65   Stephen Jay Gould, *Ever Since Darwin* (W. W. Norton, 1977), 36, 45.

66   Whitehead, *Process and Reality*, 244; *Religion in the Making* (Fordham University Press, 1996), 100.

67   Whitehead, *Process and Reality*, 88.

68   Nagel, *Mind and Cosmos*, 7.

69   William Provine, "Progress in Evolution and Meaning in Life," in *Evolutionary Progress*, ed. Matthew H. Nitecki (University of Chicago Press, 1988), 64–66.

CHAPTER THREE: GOD'S LOVE AND THE WORLD'S EVIL

1   Richard Swinburne, *The Evolution of the Soul* (Clarendon, 1986), 198–99.

2   See "The Denial of Spirit" in Chapter 4.

3   Bart D. Ehrman, *God's Problem: How the Bible Fails to Answer Our Most Important Question—Why We Suffer* (HarperOne, 2008), 3.

4   Ehrman, *God's Problem*, 26.

5   Jon D. Levenson, *Creation and the Persistence of Evil: The Jewish Drama of Divine Omnipotence* (Harper & Row, 1988).

6   Levenson, *Creation and the Persistence of Evil*, 12, 26, 122–23.

7   Gerhard May, *Creatio Ex Nihilo: The Doctrine of "Creation out of Nothing" in Early Christian Thought*, trans. AS. Worrall (T. & T. Clark, 1994), xi, 27.

8   May, *Creatio Ex Nihilo*, xiii, 61, 74, 122.

9   May, *Creatio Ex Nihilo*, 140–42.

10 May, *Creatio Ex Nihilo*, 40, 43, 56.

11 May, *Creatio Ex Nihilo*, 147, 159, 178.

12 May, *Creatio Ex Nihilo*, 161.

13 May, *Creatio Ex Nihilo*, 167–68, 174.

14 St. Augustine, *Enchiridion,* trans. J.F. Shaw, in *Basic Writings of St. Augustine,* ed. Whitney J. Oates (Random House, 1948), XIV. 95–96; XVI.102; St. Augustine, *The City of God,* trans. Marcus Dods, X.14

15 St. Augustine, *Enchiridion,* X.14.

16 John Calvin, *Institutes of the Christian Religion,* ed. John T. McNeill, trans. Ford Lewis Battles (Westminster Press, 1960), Vol. III, xxiii. 7.

17 Calvin, *Institutes of the Christian Religion*, Vol. III: xxiii.1; xiv.15.

18 Millard J. Erickson, *Christian Theology* (Baker Book House, 1985), 277.

19 St. Augustine, *The City of God,* trans. Edward Bouverie Pusey, in *Basic Writings of St. Augustine,* ed. Whitney J. Oates (Random House, 1948),, XI.18; XI.23.

20 St. Augustine, *Enchiridion,* VIII.27 and XX14.96.

21 For a more complete summary of Augustine's theodicy, see Chapter 6 of my *God, Power, and Evil: A Process Theodicy* (1976); reprinted with a new preface (Westminster John Knox Press, 2004), Chapter 6.

22 This argument is made at length in David Ray Griffin, *Reenchantment Without Supernaturalism: A Process Philosophy of Religion* (Cornell University Press, 2000), Ch. 6.

23 *Mark Twain and Philosophy,* ed. Alan Goldman (Rowman and Littlefield, 2017), 90.

24 Richard Swinburne, *Is There a God?* (Oxford University Press, 2010), 86.

25 Dale Aukerman, *Darkening Valley: A Biblical Perspective on Nuclear War* (Seabury, 1981), 160–61.

26 Alvin Plantinga, "Reply to the Basingers on Divine Omnipotence," *Process Studies* 11/1 (Spring, 1981), 25–29, at 28.

27 Plantinga, "Reply to the Basingers on Divine Omnipotence," 26-27.

28 David Ray Griffin, *Evil Revisited: Responses and Reconsiderations* (State University of New York Press, 1991), Chap. 2.

29 Griffin, *Evil Revisited*, Chap. 5.

30 See "Introduction: The Reenchantment of Science," in *The Reenchantment of Science: Postmodern Proposals,* ed. David Ray Griffin (State University of New York Press, 1988); John B. Cobb, Jr., and David Ray Griffin, "Lynn Margulis on Spirituality and Process Philosophy," in *Lynn Margulis: The Life and Legacy of a Scientific Rebel,* ed. Dorion Sagan (Chelsea Green, 2012).

31 Charles Hartshorne, *Omnipotence and Other Theological Mistakes* (State University of New York Press, 1984), 52–62.

32 May, *Creatio Ex Nihilo*, 141.

33 May, *Creatio Ex Nihilo*, 3–4.

34 We do not have any of Hermogenes' writings, because when he was declared a heretic, his writings were destroyed. But scholars have been able to reconstruct his position by studying the polemics against him, especially Tertullian's *Adversus Hermogenes*. The best study in English is J. H. Waszink, *Tertullian: The Treatise against Hermogenes*.

35 Charles Hartshorne, *Man's Vision of God and the Logic of Theism* (Harper & Row, 1941), 207.

36 Charles Hartshorne, *The Divine Relativity: A Social Conception of God,* 2nd ed. (1948; Yale University Press, 1964), 138.

37 See Griffin, *God, Power, and Evil*, Chapter 18.

CHAPTER FOUR: HUMANITY—THE CROWN OF GOD'S CREATION

1 Gordon Baker and Katherine J. Morris, *Descartes' Dualism*

(Routledge, 1996), 167–70.

2   Richard Swinburne, *Is There a God?* (Oxford University Press, 1996), 7.

3   Colin McGinn, *The Problem of Consciousness: Essays Toward a Resolution* (Basil Blackwell, 1991), 29.

4   McGinn, *The Problem of Consciousness*, 45.

5   Geoffrey Madell, *Mind and Materialism* (The Edinburgh University Press, 1988), 140.

6   Madell, *Mind and Materialism*, 9.

7   McGinn, *The Problem of Consciousness*, 45.

8   Thomas Nagel, *Mortal Questions* (Cambridge University Press, 1979), 189.

9   Michelle A. Gonzalez, *Created in God's Image: An Introduction to Feminist Theological Anthropology* (Orbis Books, 2007), 8.

10 The claim that all living creatures have equal value is defensible if one is considering extrinsic value—especially ecological value—as well as intrinsic value. See David Ray Griffin, "Whitehead's Deeply Ecological Worldview: Egalitarianism without Irrelevance," in Griffin, *Whitehead's Radically Different Postmodern Philosophy: An Argument for Its Contemporary Relevance* (SUNY Press, 2007).

11 Alfred North Whitehead, *Adventures of Ideas* (1933; Free Press, 1967), 208. In saying that some beings do not have *any* soul, Whitehead was referring to the fact that beings such as rocks and typewriters have no central experience. They are mere *aggregational* societies, which by definition have no central experience. In saying that some beings have souls, he meant that animals, while they are still alive, have souls, because they are "compound individuals," in which the experiences at one level—the brain cells—give rise to a society of dominant occasions of experience, the mind or soul. In saying "How much, if any?", he was referring to the fact that low-grade animals, such as beetles, cannot have the kinds of experiences that can be enjoyed by high-grade animals, such as gorillas, elephants, and humans.

12 Francis Crick, *The Astonishing Hypothesis: The Scientific Search for the Soul* (Simon & Schuster, 1994), 3, 7.

13 Crick, *The Astonishing Hypothesis*, 3, 7.

14 John R. Searle, *Minds, Brains, and Science: The 1984 Reith Lectures* (British Broadcasting Corporation, 1984), 117.

15 Nagel, *Mortal Questions*, 189.

16 McGinn, *The Problem of Consciousness*, 45.

17 William James, *Some Problems of Philosophy* (Longmans, Green, and Co., 1911), 195.

18 William Provine, "Progress in Evolution and Meaning in Life," in *Evolutionary Progress*, ed. Matthew H. Nitecki (University of Chicago Press, 1988), 66.

19 Searle, *Minds, Brains, and Science*, 92.

20 Searle, *Minds, Brains, and Science*, 13.

21 Searle, *Minds, Brains, and Science*, 92, 97.

22 Alfred North Whitehead, *Process and Reality,* corrected edition, ed. David Ray Griffin and Donald W. Sherburne (Free Press, 1978), 151.

23 John R. Searle, "The Mind-Body Problem," in *John Searle and His Critics,* ed. Ernest Lepore and Robert van Gulick (Basil Blackwell, 1991), 141–46, at 145.

24 Robert J. Richards, "Moral Foundations of the Idea of Evolutionary Progress," in *Evolutionary Progress*, ed. Matthew Nitecki (University of Chicago Press, 1988), 129–48.

25 Charles Darwin, *The Descent of Man* (John Murray, 1871), Vol. I, 70.

26 Provine, "Progress in Evolution and Meaning in Life," 65.

27 John Mackie, *Ethics: Inventing Right and Wrong* (Penguin, 1977), 15, 24.

28 Mackie, *Ethics*, 79–80.

29 Mackie, *Ethics*, 48.

30 John Mackie, *The Miracle of Theism: Arguments For and Against the Existence of God* (Clarendon, 1982), 1.

31 Immanuel Kant, *Religion within the Limits of Reason Alone*, trans. Theodore M. Greene and Hoyt H. Hudson (Harper & Row, 1960), 163.

32 Émile Durkheim, *The Elementary Forms of the Religious Life*, trans. Joseph Ward Swain (Free Press, 1963), 57.

33 Preus, *Explaining Religion: Criticism and Theory from Bodin to Freud*, (Yale University Press), xiii, xiv.

34 Robert A. Segal, *Religion and the Social Sciences: Essays on the Confrontation* (Atlanta: Scholars Press, 1989), 71.

35 Gordon D. Kaufman, *In Face of Mystery: A Constructive Theology* (Harvard University Press, 1993), 415, 323.

36 Whitehead, *Adventures of Ideas,* 177.

37 Whitehead, *Adventures of Ideas*, 204.

38 Whitehead referred to these enduring individuals as "personally ordered societies."

39 William G. Lycan, *Consciousness* (MIT Press, 1987), 113–14.

40 Whitehead, *Adventures of Ideas*, 207.

41 Alfred North Whitehead, *Modes of Thought* (1938; Free Press, 1968), 157.

42 Ted Honderich, "Mind, Brain, and Self-Conscious Mind," in *Mindwaves: Thoughts on Intelligence, Identity, and Consciousness*, ed. Colin Blakemore and Susan Greenfield (Basil Blackwell, 1987), 445–58, at 447.

43 Charles Hartshorne, *Creative Synthesis and Philosophical Method* (Open Court, 1970), 9, 27.

44 Jaegwon Kim, *Supervenience and Mind: Selected Philosophical Essays* (Cambridge University Press, 1993), 104, 367. For a critique, see David Ray Griffin, "Materialist and Panexperientialist Physicalism: A Critique of Jaegwon Kim's *Supervenience and Mind*," *Process Studies* 28/1-2 (Spring-Summer 1999): 4–27.

45 Charles Hartshorne, *The Logic of Perfection and Other Essays in Neoclassical Metaphysics* (Open Court, 1962), 229.

46 Albert Einstein, "Maxwell's Influence on the Development of the Conception of Physical Reality," in *James Clerk Maxwell: A Commemorative Volume,* ed. J. J. Thomson et al. (Cambridge University Press, 1931), 66–73, at 66.

47 David Hume, *A Treatise of Human Nature, The Philosophical Works*

of David Hume (1739), Bk. III, Sect. II.

48 Whitehead, *Process and Reality*, 151.

49 Hume, *A Treatise of Human Nature,* Bk. I, Sect. VI; quoted by Whitehead in *Symbolism: Its Meaning and Effect* (1927; Capricorn, 1959), 3–34.

50 Whitehead, *Symbolism*, 51.

51 Whitehead, *Process and Reality*, 171.

52 George Santayana, *Scepticism and Animal Faith* (Dover, 1955), 14–15.

53 Whitehead, *Adventures of Ideas*, 181.

54 Whitehead, *Modes of Thought*, 154.

55 Whitehead, *Modes of Thought*, 103.

56 Mircea Eliade, *The Sacred and the Profane: The Nature of Religion* (Harvest Books, 1959).

57 Alfred North Whitehead, *Modes of Thought*, 120.

58 Preus, *Explaining Religion*, xv.

59 See "Scientific Naturalism and Religious Experience," chapter 5 of David Ray Griffin, *Panentheism and Scientific Naturalism: Rethinking Evil, Morality, Religious Experience, Religious Pluralism, and the Academic Study of Religion* (Process Century Press, 2014).

60 William James, *The Varieties of Religious Experience*, Postscript.

61 Reuben Hersh, *What is Mathematics, Really?* (Oxford University Press, 1997), 11.

62 Hilary Putnam, *Words and Life*, ed. James Conant (Harvard University Press, 1994), 503. The quotation comes from an essay originally published in 1979, when Putnam still held a materialist worldview, with a functionalist, cybernetic view of the mind, according to which there could be no nonsensory perception.

63 Hartry Field, *Science without Numbers* (Princeton University Press, 1980); G. Hellman, *Mathematics without Numbers* (Oxford University Press, 1989).

64 Y. N. Moschovakis, *Descriptive Set Theory* (North Holland, 1980), 605–06.

65 For quotations from several other philosophers and mathematicians

who agree, see Hersh, *What is Mathematics, Really?* 7, and Penelope Maddy, *Realism in Mathematics* (Clarendon Press, 1990), 2–3.

66 Roger Penrose, *The Emperor's New Mind: Concerning Computers, Minds, and the Laws of Physics* (Oxford University Press, 1989), 123.

67 Kurt Gödel, "What is Cantor's Continuum Problem? Supplement to the Second [1964] Edition," in *Collected Works*, Vol. II, ed. Solomon Feferman et al. (Oxford University Press, 1990): 266–69, at 268.

68 Hersh, *What is Mathematics, Really?* 11, 12.

69 Richard Hooker, "Renaissance Neo-Platonism," The Hermetic Library.

70 Hersh, *What is Mathematics, Really?* 12.

71 Whitehead, *Process and Reality*, 40.

72 Whitehead, *Process and Reality*, 46.

73 Roger Penrose, "Interview with Jane Clark," *Journal of Consciousness Studies* 1/1 (1994): 17–24, at 23.

74 Richard Feynman, *The Meaning of It All: Thoughts of a Citizen-Scientist* (Basic Books, 1998), 43.

75 Mario Livio, *Is God a Mathematician?* (Simon & Schuster, 2009), 218.

76 James Trefil, *Reading the Mind of God: In Search of the Principle of Universality* (New York: Scribner's, 1989), 1.

77 Whitehead, *Adventures of Ideas*, 147.

78 Whitehead, *Process and Reality*, 257.

79 Whitehead, *Process and Reality*, 26, 192.

80 Thomas Nagel, *The Last Word* (Oxford University Press, 1997), 37-38.

81 Hilary Putnam, *Words and Life*, ed. James Conant, 500.

82 Putnam himself would not have asked these questions, given his view that ethics should be discussed apart from ontology; see Hilary Putnam, *Ethics without Ontology* (Harvard University Press, 2005). But how can a realistic philosophy of morality be advocated apart from a philosophy of what exists?

83 Colin McGinn, *The Problem of Consciousness: Essays Toward a Resolution* (Basil Blackwell, 1991), 23n.

84 Charles Larmore, *The Morals of Modernity* (Cambridge University Press, 1966), 86, 87, 99.

85 To clarify: As pointed out in the section above entitled "The Denial of Soul," efficient causation should not be equated with mechanistic, billiard-ball causation—except within a materialistic worldview.

86 Hilary Putnam, *Realism and Reason* (Cambridge University Press, 1985), 191.

87 Jaegwon Kim, *Supervenience and Mind*, 215.

88 Nagel, *The Last Word*, 70.

89 Nagel, *The Last Word*, 132.

90 Whitehead, *Adventures of Ideas*, 147.

91 Julius Adler and Wung-Wai Tso, "Decision-Making in Bacteria," *Science* 184 (1974): 1292–94.

92 For a few examples, see Kim McDonald, "Bacteria Provide New Insights into Human Decision Making," UC San Diego, 8 December 2009; James A. Shapiro, *Evolution: A View from the 21st Century* (FT Press, 2011); "Bacteria Use Chat to Play the 'Prisoner's Dilemma' Game in Deciding Their Fate," *American Chemical Society*, 27 May 2012); Matthew Russell, "How Do Bacteria Make Decisions?" *Frontiers*, 23 January 2014. The final of these articles began: "Decision making is not limited to animals like humans or birds. Bacteria also make decisions with intricate precision."

93 Widely recognized as the most gifted evolutionary biologist of her generation, Margulis was a Distinguished University Professor at the University of Massachusetts, Amherst, before her untimely death.

94 Lynn Margulis, "Gaia and Machines," in *Back to Darwin: A Richer Account of Evolution*, ed. John B. Cobb, Jr. (Eerdmans, 2007), 167–75, at 172.

95 Dick Teresi, "Lynn Margulis Says She's Not Controversial, She's Right," *Discover Magazine*, April 2011.

96 Teresi, "Lynn Margulis Says She's Not Controversial, She's Right," 1.

97 Lynn Margulis, "Gaia Is a Tough Bitch," in *The Third Culture: Beyond the Scientific Revolution*, ed. John Brockman (Simon & Schuster, 1995), Chapter 7.

98 James A. Shapiro, "Transposable Elements as the Key to a 21st Century View of Evolution," *Genetica* 107 (1999): 171-70.

99 Lanying Zeng, et al., "Decision Making at a Subcellular Level Determines the Outcome of Bacteriophage Infection," *Cell*, 13 May 2010.

100 Clement Aussignargues, "Not Just a Pouch of Enzymes: Bacteria also Have Organelles," Nature Research Microbiology Community, 12 March 2018, discussing Cheryl A. Kerfeld et al., "Bacterial Microcompartments," *Nature Reviews Microbiology,* March 2018.

101 On James, see Marcus Peter Ford, *William James's Philosophy: A New Perspective* (University of Massachusetts Press, 1982); "William James," in *Founders of Constructive Postmodern Philosophy: Peirce, James, Bergson, Whitehead, and Hartshorne*, David Ray Griffin, et al. (State University of New York Press, 1993), 89–132. On Whitehead, see David Ray Griffin, *Unsnarling the World-Knot: Consciousness, Freedom, and the Mind-Body Problem* (University of California Press, 1998; Wipf and Stock, 2008). On Hartshorne, see "Physics and Psychics: The Place of Mind in Nature," in *Mind in Nature: Essays on the Interface of Science and Philosophy,* ed. John B. Cobb, Jr., and David Ray Griffin (University Press of America, 1977), 89–96. On Peirce, see Peter Ochs, "Charles Sanders Peirce," in *Founders of Constructive Postmodern Philosophy: Peirce, James, Bergson, Whitehead, and Hartshorne*, David Ray Griffin, et al. (State University of New York Press, 1993), 43–88.

102 Thomas Nagel, "What Is It Like to Be a Bat?" *Mortal Questions* (Cambridge University Press, 1979), and Nagel's *Mind and Cosmos: Why the Materialist Neo-Darwinian Conception of Nature Is Almost Certainly False* (Oxford University Press, 2012), 33, where he endorsed Hartshorne's "Physics and Psychics: The Place of Mind in Nature." On Strawson, see his *Mental Reality* (MIT Press, 1994) and his "Mind and Being: The Primacy of Panpsychism," in *Panpsychism: Philosophical Essays*, ed. G. Brunstup and L. Jaskolla (Oxford University Press, 2015).

103 See, for example, Michael Blamauer, ed., *The Mental as Fundamental: New Perspectives on Panpsychism* (Ontos Verlag, 2013); David Chalmers, *The Character of Consciousness* (Oxford University Press, 2010); D. S. Clarke, *Panpsychism and the Religious Attitude* (State University of New York Press, 2003); Freya Matthews, *For Love of*

Matter: A Contemporary Panpsychism (State University of New York Press, 2003); David Skrbina, *Panpsychism in the West* (Bradford Books, 2007); *Mind That Abides: Panpsychism in the New Millennium* (John Benjamins, 2009); and G. Brunstup and L. Jaskolla, eds.,*Panpsychism: Philosophical Essays* (Oxford University Press, 2015).

104 Lyell's statements are quoted in R. Hooykaas, *Natural Law and Divine Miracle: A Historical-Critical Study of the Principle of Uniformity in Geology, Biology, and Theology* (E. J. Brill, 1959), 114.

105 *The Life and Letters of Charles Darwin*, ed. Francis Darwin, Vol. 2: 6–7.

106 John B. Cobb, Jr., *The Structure of Christian Existence* (Westminster Press, 1967), 39.

107 Cobb, *The Structure of Christian Existence*, 39, 41.

108 "Anatomically Modern Humans," Wikipedia; "Modern Human Behavior," Wikipedia.

CHAPTER FIVE: THE HEBREW PROPHETS

1 For example, Louis Berkhof, *Systematic Theology* (GLH Publishing Reprint, 2917); Wayne Grudem, *Systematic Theology: An Introduction to Biblical Doctrine* (InterVarsity Press, 1994); Thomas C. Oden, *A Systematic Theology: Classic Christianity* (HarperCollins 1992).

2 John B. Cobb, Jr., *The Structure of Christian Existence* (Westminster Press, 1967), 94–95.

3 Karl Jaspers, *The Origin and Goal of History* (Yale University Press, 1953).

4 Cobb, *The Structure of Christian Existence*, 52, n. 13.

5 Cobb, *The Structure of Christian Existence*, 94.

6 Cobb, *The Structure of Christian Existence*, 95.

7 Marcus J. Borg, *Reading the Bible Again for the First Time* (HarperCollins, 2002), 111.

8 For the other prophets, see Victor H. Matthews, *The Hebrew Prophets and Their Social World: An Introduction* (Baker Academic, 2012).

9 Borg, *Reading the Bible Again for the First Time*, 127.

10   Borg, *Reading the Bible Again for the First Time*, 127.

11   Borg, *Reading the Bible Again for the First Time*, 128.

12   Borg, *Reading the Bible Again for the First Time*, 128.

13   Walter Brueggemann, *Money and Possessions: Interpretation* (Westminster John Knox Press, 2016), 140.

14   Brueggemann, *Money and Possessions*, 141.

15   Richard Horsley, *Covenant Economics: A Biblical Vision of Justice for All* (Westminster John Knox, 2009), 68.

16   Horsley, *Covenant Economics, 68.*

17   Horsley, *Covenant Economics*, 59.

18   Brueggemann, *Money and Possessions,* 142.

19   The New Revised Standard Version (NRSV) is always used for biblical passages unless indicated otherwise.

20   Matthews, *The Hebrew Prophets and Their Social World*, 99.

21   Matthews, *The Hebrew Prophets and Their Social World*, 99.

22   Thanks to the collapse of the Assyrian empire (due to pressure from the rising of Babylonian empire), Josiah, the king of Judah, was able to become independent from Assyria and to institute religious reform. The occasion for the reform was the discovery of the Book of the Law while the temple was being renovated (II Kings 23). Josiah's reform (623 BCE) was an attempt to renew the worship of God according to the teachings of Moses. The reforms included the centralization of worship in the temple in Jerusalem, the adoption of the legislation in Deuteronomy, the reestablishment of the Passover and the Passover celebration, and the elimination of child sacrifice, magic, Baal and astral worship—in fact, of everything pagan. However, the reform died out after Josiah was killed in battle in 609 BCE. (Ferdinand O. Regaldo, "Josiah's Reform," *Spectrum*, 19 November 2015; Chester Morton, "The Religious Reforms of King Josiah," Virtual Kollage, 22 February 2016.)

23   Matthews, *The Hebrew Prophets and Their Social World,* 141.

24   Borg, *Reading the Bible Again for the First Time,* 125. For more detail, see Matthews, *The Hebrew Prophets,* Chapter 12.

25   Matthews, *The Hebrew Prophets and Their Social World,* 158.

26 James A. Sanders, *The Monotheizing Process: The Origins and Development* (Cascade Books, 2004), 36–37.

27 Abraham Joshua Heschel, *The Prophets* (Jewish Publication Society of America, 1962), Vol. I: 309, 102.

28 Heschel, *The Prophets*, 26, 224, 231, 314.

29 Alfred North Whitehead, *Adventures of Ideas* (1933; Free Press, 1967), 233.

30 Whitehead, *Adventures of Ideas*, 183; Whitehead, *Process and Reality: An Essay in Cosmology* (1929), corrected edition, ed. David Ray Griffin and Donald W. Sherburne (Free Press, 1978), 237–38.

31 Whitehead, *Process and Reality*, 162.

32 Kazoh Kitamori, *Theology of the Pain of God*, 5th edition (1946 John Knox, 1965), Preface to the third edition.

33 Kitamori, *Theology of the Pain of God*, Preface to the English edition.

34 Kitamori, *Theology of the Pain of God*, 13.

35 Sanders, *The Monotheizing Process*, 1.

36 Sanders, *The Monotheizing Process*, page 1

37 Sanders, *The Monotheizing Process*, 8.

38 Sanders, *The Monotheizing Process*, 30-31.

39 Amos 9:7.

40 Sanders, *The Monotheizing Process*, 31.

41 Sanders, *The Monotheizing Process*, 40, 44.

42 Sanders, *The Monotheizing Process*, 36, 37.

43 Sanders, *The Monotheizing Process*, 36-37.

44 Sanders, *The Monotheizing Process*, 72.

CHAPTER SIX: JESUS AND THE ROMAN EMPIRE

1 Chalmers Johnson, *Blowback: The Costs and Consequences of American Empire* (Henry Holt, 2000), 8.

2 Andrew J. Bacevich, *American Empire: The Realities and Consequences of U.S. Diplomacy* (Harvard University Press, 2002), 244.

3 Richard A. Horsley, *Jesus and Empire: The Kingdom of God and the New World Disorder* (Fortress, 2003), 13.

4 Susan P. Mattern, *Rome and the Enemy: Imperial Strategy in the Principate* (University of California Press, 1999), 90.

5 See Mattern, *Rome and the Enemy,* and Edward N. Luttwak, *The Grand Strategy of the Roman Empire: From the First Century A.D. to the Third* (Johns Hopkins University Press, 1976).

6 Klaus Wengst, *Pax Romana and the Peace of Jesus Christ* (Fortress, 1987), 9.

7 Horace, *Odes* III, 5, 1–3; quoted in Wengst, *Pax Romana and the Peace of Jesus Christ,* 14.

8 Horsley, *Jesus and Empire,* 20–23.

9 Quoted in Horsley, *Jesus and Empire,* 23–24.

10 Quoted in Wengst, *Pax Romana,* 7.

11 Horsley, *Jesus and Empire,* 197.

12 Tacitus, *Agricola* 14.1; quoted in Horsley, *Jesus and Empire,* 31.

13 Mattern, *Rome,* 22, 117. The crucial nature of this perception was central to Luttwak's study, *The Grand Strategy of the Roman Empire,* which said of the empire in the early part of the first century A.D.: "Client states great and small are … kept in subjection by their own perceptions of Roman power. … [T]he sphere of imperial control is limited only by the range at which others perceive Roman power as compelling obedience" (192).

14 Polybius, 10.15–17; quoted in Horsley, *Jesus and Empire,* 27.

15 Horsley, *Jesus and Empire,* 108.

16 Horsley, *Jesus and Empire,* 117, 172.

17 Horsley, *Jesus and Empire,* 27; Marcus Borg, *Jesus: Uncovering the Life, Teachings, and Relevance of a Religious Revolutionary* (HarperSanFrancisco, 2006), 21.

18 "Under the Roman Empire, the victims were beaten before being crucified. Then they were required to carry the cross or the crossbeam to the place of execution, they were stripped naked, and their forearms were nailed or bound to the beam, which was raised up and affixed to the stake, or they were simply nailed to the stake. The body was

partly supported by being seated on a peg on the upright, and the feet were bound or nailed to the stake with an iron nail through the heals. Death would come slowly, by asphyxiation, often after several days of excruciating pain.... Crucifixion was thus a method of slowly torturing the victims to death." Richard Horsley, *Jesus and the Powers: Conflict, Covenant, and the Hope of the Poor* (Fortress Press, 2011), 180.

19 Horsley, *Jesus and Empire*, 27.

20 Pseudo-Quinteilian, *Declamations*, 274.

21 K. C. Hanson and Douglas E. Oakman, *Palestine in the Time of Jesus: Social Structures and Social Conflicts* (Augsburg Fortress, 1998), 92.

22 Horsley, *Jesus and Empire*, 22.

23 Wengst, *Pax Romana*, 14.

24 Mattern, *Rome*, 214–15; Horsley, *Jesus and Empire*, 24.

25 Mattern, *Rome*, 135.

26 Hanson and Oakman, *Palestine*, 67.

27 Borg, *Jesus: Uncovering the Life*, 87.

28 Horsley, *Jesus and Empire*, 29, 34.

29 Horsley, *Jesus and Empire*, 29.

30 Horsley, *Jesus and Empire*, 6, 15, 28; Richard A. Horsley and Neil Asher Silberman, *The Message and the Kingdom: How Jesus and Paul Ignited a Revolution and Transformed the Ancient World* (Grosset/Putnam, 1997), 84–86.

31 Horsley, *Jesus and Empire*, 31–32; Horsley and Silberman, *The Message*, 16–17.

32 Horsley and Silberman, *The Message*, 17; Horsley, *Jesus and Empire*, 32, 85.

34 Borg, *Jesus: Uncovering the Life*, 118.

35 Borg, *Jesus: Uncovering the Life*, 118.

36 Borg, *Jesus: Uncovering the Life*, 94.

37 Horsley, *Jesus and Empire*, 15, 20, 30, 33, 46, 85; Richard A. Horsley, *Jesus and the Spiral of Violence: Popular Jewish Resistance in Roman*

Palestine (Harper & Row, 1987), 286–87; Horsley and Silberman, *The Message*, 78–79.

38 Horsley and Silberman, *The Message*, 83.

39 Horsley, *Jesus and Empire*, 41, 99.

40 Horsley and Silberman, *The Message*, 4.

41 Horsley and Silberman, *The Message*, 17; Horsley, *Jesus and Empire*, 32.

42 Quoted in Hanson and Oakman, *Palestine*, 115.

43 Horsley, *Jesus and Empire*, 61; Horsley and Silberman, *The Message*, 26.

44 Marcus Borg, *Jesus: A New Vision* (HarperSanFrancisco, 1991), 95; Richard A. Horsley and John S. Hanson, *Bandits, Prophets, and Messiahs: Popular Movements in the Time of Jesus* (Harper & Row, 1987), 54–56.

45 According to the Holiness Code of Leviticus, debts were supposed to be forgiven and land returned every 50 years, called the Jubilee (Leviticus 8:8–55). Accordingly, the permanent loss of land would not occur. However, the Jubilee was only sporadically observed, if ever.

46 Horsley and Silberman, *The Message*, 26–29.

47 Horsley and Silberman, *The Message*, 129.

48 Paula Fredriksen, *From Jesus to Christ: The Origins of the New Testament Images of Jesus* (Yale University Press, 1988), 47.

49 Horsley, *Jesus and the Spiral of Violence*, 170.

50 Horsley, *Jesus and Empire*, 81; Horsley and Silberman, *The Message*, 53–54.

51 Marcus Borg, *Conflict, Holiness and Politics in the Teachings of Jesus* (Edwin Mellen, 1984), 216.

52 Borg, *Conflict, Holiness and Politics in the Teachings of Jesus*, 216–17.

53 Borg, *Conflict, Holiness and Politics in the Teachings of Jesus* , 177–96.

54 Borg, *Jesus: Uncovering the Life,* 89.

55 Horsley, *Jesus and Empire*, 174–75.

56 Horsley, *Jesus and the Spiral*, 170.

57 Horsley, *Jesus and the Spiral*, 189. Horsley also pointed to Mark 3:27, which indicates that Satan's goods (demons) can be plundered only because Satan had been bound (*Jesus and Empire*, 102).

58 Horsley, *Jesus and Empire*, 101.

59 Horsley, *Jesus and Empire*, 84.

60 Horsley, *Jesus and the Spiral*, 157.

61 Herman E. Daly made this point in *Beyond Growth: The Economics of Sustainable Development* (Beacon, 1996), 208.

62 One feature of the Reign of God envisaged by Jesus, emphasized by some Jesus scholars, was egalitarian relations between the sexes. See, for example, books by Elisabeth Schüssler Fiorenza, such as *In Memory of Her: A Feminist Theological Reconstruction of Christian Origins* (Crossroad Publishing Company, 10th edition, 1994), and *Wisdom Ways: Introducing Feminist Biblical Interpretation* (Orbis Books, 2011).

63 The more complete passage says: "For I am about to create new heavens and a new earth; the former things shall not be remembered or come to mind. . . . no more shall the sound of weeping be heard in it, or the cry of distress. No more shall there be in it an infant that lives but a few days" (Isaiah 65:18–19).

64 (Third) Isaiah 65:21–23, cited in Horsley and Silberman, *The Message*, 6, 14.

65 Matthew 21:33–46; Mark 12:1–12; Luke 20:9–19.

66 Horsley, *Jesus and the Spiral*, 307–14.

67 Mark 12:1-9 and parallels: Matthew 21:33–46, Luke 20:9–19; see Horsley, *Jesus and the Spiral*, 305–06.

68 Horsley, *Jesus and the Spiral*, 282.

69 Mark: 13:1–2, 14:57–58, 15:29; Matthew 26:60–61; John 2:18–22.

70 Horsley, *Jesus and the Spiral*, 299; E. P. Sanders, *Jesus and Judaism* (Fortress, 1985), 69–70, 302.

71 Fredriksen, *From Jesus to Christ*, 120, 79.

72 Horsley, *Jesus and Empire*, 132.

73 William Stringfellow, *An Ethic for Christians and Other Aliens in a Strange Land* (Word Books, 1973), 27.

74 On this point, Horsley (*Jesus and the Powers*, 228, n. 6) cited many studies, including Marianus de Jonge, "The Use of the Word 'Anointed' in the Time of Jesus," *Novum Testamentum* 8 (1966): 132–48, and James H. Charlesworth, ed., *The Messiah: Developments in Earliest Judaism and Christianity* (Fortress Press, 1992).

75 Horsley, *Jesus and the Powers*, 187.

76 Horsley, *Jesus and the Powers*, 189-90.

77 Horsley, *Jesus and the Powers*, 190.

78 Horsley, *Jesus and the Powers*, 191.

79 Horsley, *Jesus and the Powers*, 191 (see Mark 1:44; 9:4–6; 9:11–13; 15:34–36).

80 Marcus J. Borg and N. T. Wright, *The Meaning of Jesus: Two Visions* (HarperCollins, 1999), 89, 91.

81 Borg, *Jesus: Uncovering the Life*, 271.

82 Horsley and Silberman, *The Message*, 227.

83 Clark M. Williamson, *Has God Rejected His People?: Anti-Judaism in the Christian Church* (Abingdon, 1982).

84 Horsley and Silberman, *The Message*, 11.

85 Horsley and Silberman, *The Message*, 157–58, 148, 203.

86 Horsley, *Jesus and the Spiral*, 307–14.

87 See Conrad Cherry, ed., *God's New Israel: Religious Interpretations of American Destiny*, rev. & updated ed. (University of North Carolina Press, 1997).

CHAPTER SEVEN: CHRISTOLOGY, TRINITY, AND THE RESURRECTION

1 John B. Cobb, Jr., *Christ in a Pluralistic Age* (Westminster Press, 1975), 147.

2 C. S. Lewis, *Miracles: A Preliminary Study* (1947; HarperCollins, 1996), Chap. 14; Don Mears, "The Greatest Miracle," Grace Communion International.

3 Karen Armstrong, *A History of God: The 4,000-Year Quest of Judaism, Christianity and Islam* (Ballentine, 1993), 117.

4   Austin Farrer, "The Prior Actuality of God," in *Reflective Faith: Essays in Philosophical Theology*, ed. Charles C. Conti (SPCK, 1972), 191, 180.

5   These paintings drove home the fact that the Church portrayed an all-male trinity. But this way of imaging the trinity was a radical shift from traditional views, including the Hebrew tradition, which made Sophia central, and yet in Sophia and the Gospel of John, passages about Sophia became changed to passages about (the male) Word.

6   Arguably, the best attempt to defend the doctrine of the Trinity against the charge of incoherence is a book by David William Brown entitled *The Divine Trinity* (Open Court, 1985). Although Brown failed, he failed brilliantly.

7   Valerie A. Abrahamsen, "Trinities: Historical Alternatives to 'Father, Son and Holy Ghost,'" Wisdom Words, 15 July 2016.

8   Abrahamsen, "Trinities."

9   Pamela D. H. Cochran, *Evangelical Feminism: A History* (New York University Press, 2005), 113–14.

10 "Logos," *Encyclopaedia Britannica*, https://www.britannica.com/topic/logos.

11 Adam Davis, "The Logos of Philo and John: A Comparative Sketch," Blogos, 30 May 2017.

12 John 1:1–3.

13 Marcel Sarot, "The Ultimate Miracle? The Historicity of the Resurrection of Jesus," *HTS Teologiese Studies/Theological Studies*, 70, September 2014; citing John Anthony McGuckin, *The Westminster Handbook to Patristic Theology* (Westminster John Knox, 2004), 293.

14 Raymond E. Brown, *An Introduction to New Testament Christology* (Paulist Press, 1994), 162.

15 Alfred North Whitehead, *Religion in the Making* (MacMillan, 1926), 155–56.

16 Alfred North Whitehead, *Adventures of Ideas* (Free Press, 1967), 166, 167.

17 Marcus J. Borg, *Jesus: Uncovering the Life, Teachings, and Relevance of a Religious Revolutionary* (HarperSanFrancisco, 2006), 6.

18   Langdon Gilkey, "Cosmology, Ontology, and the Travail of Biblical Language," *Journal of Religion*, Vol. XLI (1961): 200.

19   Referring to Plato's final conviction, "that the divine element in the world is to be conceived as a persuasive agency and not as a coercive agency," Whitehead called this "one of the greatest intellectual discoveries in the history of religion" (Whitehead, *Adventures of Ideas*, 166). But some people have found this distinction unclear, because (they say) some forms of persuasion can be quite coercive—as when a robber uses a pistol—sometimes called a "persuader"—to get people to turn over their money. The source of the confusion is the fact that the distinction can be used in either a psychological sense (as in the "persuader" example), or a metaphysical sense (as in the Whitehead statement). "In the *metaphysical* sense, the distinction between coercion and persuasion is an absolute difference. Coercion and persuasion are the two types of efficient causation. In *coercion* the effect is completely determined by the efficient causation upon it. In *persuasion* the effect is not completely determined by the efficient causation upon it; the effect, meaning the causally influenced individual, partially determines itself. So understood, the difference [between coercion and persuasion] is absolute: it is the difference between *none* and *some*, which is an absolute difference. The being upon whom the efficient causation is exerted either exercises some self-determination, or it exercises none." Quoted from David Ray Griffin, *Evil Revisited: Responses and Reconsideration* (State University of New York Press, 1991), 102.

20   Cobb, *Christ in a Pluralistic Age*, 142.

21   Cobb, *Christ in a Pluralistic Age*, 76, 172

22   Cobb, *Christ in a Pluralistic Age*, 136–37.

23   Cobb, *Christ in a Pluralistic Age*, 139.

24   Whitehead, *Adventures of Ideas*, 214 (emphasis added). For more detail, see Matthews, *The Hebrew Prophets*.

25   Ranald Macaulay, "Review of *Nuclear Holocaust and Christian Hope*," in Jerram Barrs, *Who Are the Peacemakers: The Christian Case for Nuclear Deterrence* (Crossway Books, 1983), 55–61.

26   John E. Walvoord, *Armageddon: Oil and the Middle East Crisis* (Zondervan, 1976).

27 William Temple, York Diocesan Leaflet, 1973; discussed in Charles E. Raven, *The Theological Basis of Christian Pacifism* (Fellowship Publications, 1951), 51.

28 Raven, *The Theological Basis of Christian Pacifism.*

29 Charles E. Raven, *Is War Obsolete: A Study of the Conflicting Claims of Religion and Citizenship* (George Allen & Unwin, 1935), 182.

30 Raven, *The Theological Basis of Christian Pacifism,* 65.

31 Brian Easlea, *Witch Hunting, Magic, and the New Philosophy: An Introduction to the Debates of the Scientific Revolution 1450–1750* (Humanities Press, 1980), 94–95.

32 Easlea, *Witch Hunting, Magic, and the New Philosophy,* 89.

33 Robert Lenoble, *Mersenne ou la naissance du méchanisme* (Librairie Philosophique J. Vrin, 1943), 9, 120, 133, 157.

34 Lenoble, *Mersenne ou la naissance du méchanisme,* 133, 157–58, 210, 375, 381; Margaret Galitzin, "The Supernatural and the Preternatural," Tradition in Action, 14 November 2008. For more on Hermeticism, see David Ray Griffin, *Religion and Scientific Naturalism* (State University of New York Press, 2000), Chapter 5, "Religion and the Rise of the Modern Scientific Worldview."

35 Alan Gauld, *The Founders of Psychical Research* (Shocken Books, 1978), 138.

36 Gauld, *The Founders of Psychical Research,* 141–42.

37 William James, *Essays in Radical Empiricism* and *A Pluralistic Universe,* ed. Ralph Barton Perry; introduction by Richard J. Bernstein (E. P. Dutton, 1971), 270–71.

38 *William James on Psychical Research,* ed. Gardner Murphy and Robert O. Ballou (Viking Press, 1960), 42.

39 James, *Essays in Radical Empiricism,* 270.

40 On the credibility of psychical research, see "Parapsychology, Science, and Religion," which is Chap. 7 of David Ray Griffin, *Religion and Scientific Naturalism: Overcoming the Conflicts* (State University of New York Press, 2000); on both psychical research and life after death, see Griffin, *Parapsychology, Philosophy, and Spirituality: A Postmodern Exploration* (State University of New York Press, 1997).

41 Alan Richardson, ed., *A Theological Word-Book of the Bible* (SCM Press, 1950), 194.

42 Brown, *An Introduction to New Testament Christology*, 162; Austin Farrer, "Introduction" to Michael C. Perry, *The Easter Enigma: An Essay on the Resurrection with Special Reference to the Data of Psychical Research* (Faber & Faber, 1959), 11.

43 First Corinthians, 15:44; William G. Witt, "Against a Subjectivist Interpretation of 1 Cor. 15: Contemporary Discussions of the Resurrection of Christ and the Apostle Paul" (blog), 11 February 2009.

44 George Tyrrell, *Apparitions* (University Books, 1961), 22.

45 Frederick W. H. Myers, *Human Personality and Its Survival of Bodily Death*, abridged by Susy Smith (University Books, 1961), 228–31; Curt J. Ducasse, *A Critical Examination of the Belief in a Life After Death* (Charles C. Thomas, 1961), 157–58.

46 Tyrrell, *Apparitions,* 36.

47 On types of apparitions, see David Ray Griffin, *Parapsychology, Philosophy, and Spirituality: A Postmodern Exploration* (State University of New York Press, 1997), 211–22.

48 Kirsopp Lake, *The Historical Evidence for the Resurrection of Jesus Christ* (Williams & Norgate, 1907), 275–76.

49 B. H. Streeter, *Foundations: A Statement of Christian Belief in Terms of Modern Thought* (Macmillan, 1912), 136.

50 B. H. Streeter, *Immortality: An Essay in Discovery Coordinating Scientific Psychical and Biblical Research* (Macmillan, 1921).

51 C. J. Cadoux, *The Historic Mission of Jesus* (Lutterworth, 1941), 166.

52 Marcus J. Borg and N. T. Wright, *The Meaning of Jesus: Two Visions,* 2nd ed. (HarperOne, 2007), 132–33.

53 Pichas Lapide, *The Resurrection of Jesus* (Augsburg Fortress, 1983), 92.

CHAPTER EIGHT: THE CHRISTIAN WAY AND OTHER WAYS

1 For essays by representatives of each of these ways, see *Deep Religious Pluralism*, ed. David Ray Griffin (Westminster/John Knox, 2005). This book was based a conference that was organized by the Center for Process Studies in honor of Marjorie Suchocki's retirement from

the deanship of Claremont School of Theology.

2   The exclusivist-inclusivist-pluralist typology was evidently first articulated by Alan Race in his 1983 book, *Christians and Religious Pluralism: Patterns in the Christian Theology of Religions* (SCM Press, 1983).

3   John Hick, "The Non-Absoluteness of Christianity," in *The Myth of Christian Uniqueness: Toward a Pluralistic Theology of Religions*, ed. John Hick and Paul F. Knitter (Orbis, 1992), 16–17.

4   Hick, "The Non-Absoluteness of Christianity," 33.

5   John Hick, *A Christian Theology of Religions: The Rainbow of Faiths* (Westminster John Knox, 1995), 24, 87, 125.

6   Paul F. Knitter, *No Other Name? A Critical Survey of Christian Attitudes toward the World Religions* (Orbis, 1986), 5, 17.

7   Paul F. Knitter, "Preface," in *The Myth of Christian Uniqueness: Toward a Pluralistic Theology of Religions,* ed. John Hick and Paul F. Knitter (Orbis, 1992), viii.

8   Paul F. Knitter, in John B. Cobb, Jr., *Transforming Christianity and the World: A Way beyond Absolutism and Relativism*, ed. and introduction by Paul F. Knitter (Orbis, 1999), 3, 61.

9   Paul F. Knitter, *Jesus and the Other Names: Christian Mission and Global Responsibility* (Orbis, 1996), 28.

10   *Knitter, No Other Name?* 36; Knitter, *Jesus and the Other Names*, 29, 31.

11   Wilfred Cantwell Smith, *Towards a World Theology: Faith and the Comparative History of Religion* (Orbis, 1981), 61.

12   Wilfred Cantwell Smith, "Idolatry in Comparative Perspective," in *The Myth of Christian Uniqueness*, ed. Hick and Knitter, 53–68, at 63, 64–65.

13   Marjorie Hewitt Suchocki, *Divinity and Diversity: A Christian Affirmation of Religious Pluralism* (Abingdon Press, 2003), 29–35.

14   Suchocki, *Divinity and Diversity*, 86.

15   John B. Cobb, Jr., *Christ in a Pluralistic Age* (Westminster, 1975), 18.

16   John B. Cobb, Jr., *Beyond Dialogue: Toward a Mutual Transformation of Christianity and Buddhism* (Fortress, 1982), 14, 41.

17 Cobb, *Transforming Christianity and the World*, 35, 50.

18 Cobb, *Transforming Christianity and the World*, 35, 50.

19 John B. Cobb, Jr., "Dialogue," in *Death or Dialogue? From the Age of Monologue to the Age of Dialogue*, Leonard Swidler, John B. Cobb, Jr., Paul F. Knitter, and Monika K. Hellwig (SCM Press; Trinity Press, 1990), 1–18, at 10.

20 Cobb, *Transforming Christianity and the World*, 86.

21 John Hick, *Philosophy of Religion*, 3rd ed. (Prentice-Hall, 1983), 117–18.

22 Knitter, *No Other Name?*, 121, 125, 116–17, 140.

23 Mark S. Heim, *Salvations: Truth and Difference in Religion* (Orbis, 1995), 72.

24 Hick, "The Non-Absoluteness of Christianity," 18.

25 See Clark M. Williamson, *Has God Rejected His People?: Anti-Judaism in the Christian Church* (1982; Wipf and Stock, 2017).

26 Hick, *A Christian Theology of Religions*, 123.

27 Hick, *A Christian Theology of Religions*, 13.

28 Hick, *A Christian Theology of Religions,* 53.

29 Knitter, *No Other Name?* 25.

30 Smith, "Idolatry in Comparative Perspective," 59.

31 Hick, *A Christian Theology of Religions*, 15.

32 Cobb, *Christ in a Pluralistic Age*, 27, 163.

33 Hick, *A Christian Theology of Religions,* 16-18.

34 Cobb, "Dialogue," 1.

35 Knitter, *No Other Name?*, 36; Knitter, *Jesus and the Other Names*, 29, 31; David Lochhead, *The Dialogical Imperative: A Christian Reflection on Interfaith Encounter* (Orbis, 1988).

36 Knitter "Interreligious Dialogue: What? Why? How?" in *Death or Dialogue?* Swidler et al., 19–44, at 27.

37 Knitter, *No Other Name?* 36; *Jesus and the Other Names*, 29, 31.

38 Race, *Christian and Religious Pluralism*, 90, 78.

39 Race, *Christian and Religious Pluralism*, 90, 78.

40 Langdon Gilkey, "Plurality and Its Theological Implications," in *The Myth of Christian Uniqueness,* ed. Hick and Knitter, 37–53, at 44-46.

41 Cobb, *Beyond Dialogue,* 13.

42 When Hick's *A Christian Theology of Religions* was published in 1995, a bibliography of critiques of his position filled almost five pages.

43 Kevin Meeker and Philip L. Quinn, "Introduction: The Philosophical Challenge of Religious Diversity," in *The Philosophical Challenge of Religious Diversity,* ed. Philip L. Quinn and Kevin Meeker (Oxford University Press, 2000), 1–28, at 3.

44 Heim, *Salvations,* 8, 42.

45 Caroline Franks Davis, *The Evidential Force of Religious Experience* (Clarendon Press, 1989), 167.

46 Cobb, *Beyond Dialogue,* 96.

47 John Hick, *An Interpretation of Religion* (Yale University Press, 1989), 249.

48 Davis, *The Evidential Force,* 172–73.

49 Hick, *An Interpretation of Religion,* 245.

50 Hick, *An Interpretation of Religion,* 239.

51 Hick, *An Interpretation of Religion,* 300; emphasis added.

52 Hick, *An Interpretation of Religion,* 301.

53 For negative critiques of Hick's position, see Heim, *Salvations*; Quinn and Meeker, eds., *The Philosophical Challenge of Religious Diversity*; and Gavin D'Costa, ed., *Christian Uniqueness Reconsidered: The Myth of a Pluralistic Theology of Religions* (Orbis, 1990).

54 Heim, *Salvations,* 129, 7. Gavin D'Costa said that "'pluralistic theology' ironically often seems to hinder rather than aid a proper recognition of religious plurality," in *Christian Uniqueness Reconsidered,* ed. D'Costa, xi. Christoph Schwöbel wrote that Hick's version of pluralistic theology "seems in danger of undermining what it sets out to preserve, that is, the plurality of religions," in "Particularity, Universality, and the Religions," in *Christian Uniqueness Reconsidered,* ed. D'Costa, 32. Joseph DiNoia said that pluralist accounts "turn out upon examination to be markedly nonpluralistic," *The Diversity*

of Religions: A Christian Perspective (Catholic University Press, 1992), 194.

55   Heim, *Salvations*, 7.

56   Heim, *Salvations*, 23.

57   Heim, *Salvations.*, 125.

58   Heim, *Salvations*, 129–30.

59   Heim, *Salvations*, 16, 87, 88, 89, 90, 101, 103, 109, 125, 129, 130, 228.

60   Heim, *Salvations*, 226.

61   Paul J. Griffiths, "Beyond Pluralism," *First Things*, January 1996: 50–52.

62   D'Costa, having criticized the pluralist project as defined in Hick and Knitter's *Myth of Christian Uniqueness*, questioned "whether 'pluralistic theology' is an appropriate or even adequate interpretation of religious plurality" (*Christian Uniqueness Reconsidered*, x–xi). See also Paul Griffiths' review in the previous note.

63   Alfred North Whitehead, *Science and the Modern World* (New York: Free Press, 1967), 185.

64   Alfred North Whitehead, *Religion in the Making* (Macmillan, 1926; Fordham University Press, 1996), 146.

65   Whitehead, *Religion in the Making*, 145, 149.

66   Cobb, *Beyond Dialogue*, 124–28; Cobb, *Transforming Christianity and the World*, 184–85; Cobb, "Response II," in Swidler et al., *Death of Dialogue?* 116.

67   Cobb, *Beyond Dialogue*, 43.

68   Cobb, *Transforming Christianity and the World*, 79.

69   Cobb, "Dialogue," in Swidler et al., *Death or Dialogue?* 6.

70   David Tracy, "Kenosis, Sunyata, and Trinity," in *The Emptying God: A Buddhist-Jewish-Christian Conversation,* ed. John B. Cobb, Jr., and Christopher Ives (Orbis, 1990), 135–54, at 139.

71   David Tracy, *Plurality and Ambiguity: Hermeneutics, Religion, Hope* (University of Chicago Press, 1987), 85.

72   David Tracy, *Dialogue with the Other: The Inter-Religious Dialogue* (Peeters Press, 1990), 74, 90.

73   Tracy, *Dialogue with the Other*, 91, 103; "Kenosis, Sunyata, and Trinity," 141–42.

74   Tracy, *Dialogue with the Other*, 91; "Kenosis, Sunyata, and Trinity," 149 (the same sentence is in both writings).

75   Tracy, *Plurality and Ambiguity*, 85.

76   Cobb, *Transforming Christianity and the World*, 186.

77   Cobb, *Transforming Christianity and the World*, 74; Cobb, "Response II," in Swidler et al., *Death or Dialogue?* 120.

78   Cobb, "Dialogue," in Swidler et al., *Death or Dialogue?* 14.

79   Cobb, *Transforming Christianity and the World*, 140.

80   Cobb, *Transforming Christianity and the World*, 86–87.

81   Race, *Christians and Religious Pluralism*, 98.

82   Cobb, *Transforming Christianity and the World*, 137.

83   Cobb, *Transforming Christianity and the World*, 185; see John A. Hutchison, *Paths of Faith* (McGraw Hill, 1969).

84   Cobb, *Transforming Christianity and the World*, 120–23, 136–37, 140, 185.

85   Cobb, *Transforming Christianity and the World*, 121.

86   Alfred North Whitehead, *Process and Reality,* corrected edition, ed. David Ray Griffin and Donald W. Sherburne (Free Press, 1978), 225.

87   John B. Cobb, Jr., "Being Itself and the Existence of God," in *The Existence of God* , ed. John R. Jacobson and Robert Lloyd Mitchell, (Edwin Mellen, 1988), 5–19, at 19.

88   Cobb, *Transforming Christianity and the World*, 122.

89   Cobb, *Transforming Christianity and the World*, 121. Aurobindo's experiences and his attempt to understand them were discussed in a dissertation by Ernest Lee Simmons, Jr., "Process Pluralism and Integral Nondualism: A Comparative Study of the Nature of the Divine in the Thought of Alfred North Whitehead and Sri Aurobindo Ghose (Dissertation, Claremont Graduate School, 1981). Simmons summarized some of this dissertation in "Mystical Consciousness in a Process Perspective," *Process Studies* 14/1 (Spring 1984): 1–10.

90   Cobb, *Transforming Christianity and the World*, 185-86

91   Cobb, *Transforming Christianity and the World*, 124, 186.

92   Cobb, *Transforming Christianity and the World*, 124, 186.

93   Cobb, *Beyond Dialogue*, 127.

94   Cobb, *Transforming Christianity and the World*, 186.

95   Whitehead, *Process and Reality*, 21.

96   Marjorie Hewitt Suchocki, *God-Christ-Church: A Practical Guide to Process Theology*, rev. ed. (Crossroad, 1989), 172.

97   Heim, *Salvations*, 124.

98   Cobb, *Transforming Christianity and the World*, 186.

CHAPTER NINE: THE DIVINE AND THE DEMONIC

1   If we focus on annual carbon emissions by countries, China is now the leader. But if we measure emissions on a per capita basis, the United States has remained the leader by far; it is also the leader by far in cumulative emissions over the past 100 years.

2   Jeffrey Burton Russell, *The Devil: Perceptions of Evil from Antiquity to Primitive Christianity* (Cornell University Press, 1977), 228, 248.

3   St. Augustine, *Enchiridion*, trans. J. F. Shaw: XIV.96; XXIV.95, in Whitney J. Oates, ed., *Basic Writings of St. Augustine*, 2 vols. (Random House, 1978).

4   St. Augustine, *Grace and Free Will*, trans. P. Holmes: XLI, XLII, in Oates, *Basic Writings of St. Augustine*.

5   St. Augustine, *The Nature of the Good*, trans. John H. S. Burleigh, in *Augustine: Earlier Writings*, The Library of Christian Classics, Vol. VI (Westminster, 1953), 32.

6   Paul Tillich, *Systematic Theology*, Vol. III (University of Chicago Press, 1963), 102.

7   See Isaiah 64:8, Jeremiah 18:4, and Romans 9:20-21.

8   Some physical cosmologists, to be sure, believe in a Big Bang that was the very beginning of finite existence as such, so that prior to it there was no space or time. Most cosmologists, however, realize that this interpretation is simply a philosophical assumption, with no possible evidence to back it up. In any case, regardless of whether

these Big Bang cosmologists believe that time and space in some sense have always existed, they all seem to agree that there had to be energy.

9   Alan H. Guth can serve as a representative of this version of the mainstream view. Guth, who sometimes spoke of a "vacuum" and sometimes of "a repulsive-gravity material," wrote: "It may seem strange to see the words 'vacuum' and 'material' used to describe the same thing, but keep in mind that this stuff is *strange*. The word 'vacuum' is used to emphasize that it is different from ordinary matter, while I am calling it a material to emphasize that it is different from an ordinary vacuum!" He also, for this reason, sometimes called it a "false vacuum." Alan Guth, "Eternal Inflation," in James B. Miller, ed., *Cosmic Questions*, Annals of the New York Academy of Sciences, Vol. 950 (The New York Academy of Sciences, 2001), 66–82, at 81, n. 7.

10 Nicolas Berdyaev, *The Destiny of Man* (Harper & Row, 1960), 22–35; Berdyaev, *Truth and Revelation* (Collier Books, 1962), 124.

11 There are, to be sure, different ways to interpret the principle of indeterminacy. But one possible way, which cannot be ruled out experimentally, is that the indeterminacy is a reflection of *self*-determinacy.

12 Charles Hartshorne reported that he heard Mullikan say this. (Robert Mullikan should not be confused with Robert Millikan.)

13 For a much longer discussion of this point, see David Ray Griffin, *Unsnarling the World-Knot: Consciousness, Freedom, and the Mind-Body Problem* (University of California Press, 1998), Ch. 9: "Compound Individuals and Freedom."

14 Alfred North Whitehead, *Adventures of Ideas* (1933; Free Press, 1976), 166.

15 For a more extensive discussion of this point, see Griffin *God, Power, and Evil* (Westminster John Knox Press, 1976), 291–97; Griffin, *Evil Revisited* (Westminster John Knox Press, 1991), 26–29; or Griffin and John B. Cobb, Jr., *Process Theology: An Introductory Exposition* (Westminster John Knox Press, 1976), 69–75.

16 Assuming, at least, that life did not appear elsewhere much earlier than it appeared on our planet, which was almost 4 billion years ago.

17 This period, better known as the "Cambrian explosion," is discussed in Griffin, *Religion and Scientific Naturalism: Overcoming the Conflicts* (State University of New York Press, 2000), 280–81.

18 Alfred North Whitehead, *Process and Reality*, corrected edition, ed. David Ray Griffin and Donald W. Sherburne (Free Press, 1978), 225, 344.

19 For the way in which process theism affirms divine omniscience without denying the ultimate reality of time, see Griffin, *Reenchantment without Supernaturalism: A Process Philosophy of Religion* (Cornell University Press, 2001), 158–59.

20 Abraham Joshua Heschel, *The Prophets* (Jewish Publication Society of America, 1962), 26, 224, 231, 314.

21 Marcus Borg, *Jesus: A New Vision* (HarperSanFrancisco, 1991), 108–11.

22 See Charles Hartshorne, *Man's Vision of God and the Logic of Theism* (Harper & Row, 1941), 174–87, or *Omnipotence and Other Theological Mistakes* (State University of New York Press, 1984), 52–62. On God as soul of the universe, see Griffin, *Reenchantment without Supernaturalism*, 140–42.

23 Henry David Aiken, "God and Evil: A Study of Some Relations Between Faith and Morals," *Ethics* 68/2 (January, 1958): 77–97, at 82; P. H. Nowell-Smith, "Morality: Religious and Secular," in *Christian Ethics and Contemporary Philosophy*, ed. Ian T. Ramsey (SCM Press, 1966), 95–112, at 97.

24 J. Brenton Stearns, "The Naturalistic Fallacy and the Question of the Existence of God," *Religious Studies* 8/3 (September, 1972): 207–20, at 212–13.

25 Matthew Fox, *Original Blessing* (Bear & Co., 1983).

CHAPTER TEN: THE EMERGENCE OF THE DEMONIC

1 "History of Life on Earth," BBC, 2014; Evolution of Modern Humans: Early Modern Homo Sapiens," https://www2.palomar. edu/anthro/homo2/mod_homo_4.htm.

2 "What Does It Mean to Be Human? Homo Sapiens," Smithsonian Natural Museum of Natural History; "Modern Humans Emerged More Than 300,000 Years Ago, New Study Suggests," Phys.Org,

Uppsala University, 28 September 2017.

3 Hillary Mayell, "When Did 'Modern' Behavior Emerge in Humans?" *National Geographic News,* 20 February 2003; Kim Sterelny, "From Hominins to Humans: How *Sapiens* became Behaviorally Modern," *Philosophical Transactions of the Royal Society B,* 27 March 2011.

4 Andrew Bard Schmookler, *The Parable of the Tribes: The Problem of Power in Social Evolution* (Houghton Mifflin, 1986). The central importance of the war-system in shaping the direction taken by civilization was also articulated in *The Pursuit of Power: Technology, Armed Force, and Society since A.D. 1000* (University of Chicago Press, 1982), by the great historian William H. McNeill.

5 The question of whether the war-system was more of a cause or a result of the settled agricultural communities can here be left aside.

6 Schmookler, *The Parable of the Tribes,* 45.

7 Christopher Layne, "The Unipolar Illusion: Why New Great Powers Will Rise," in *The Perils of Anarchy: Contemporary Realism and International Security,* ed. Michael E. Brown et al. (MIT Press, 1995), 130–78, at 293.

8 The term "anarchy" has, of course, a quite different valence in the philosophical-political theory known as "anarchism." But I am here restricting the discussion to the way the term is used in the discourse of political realists.

9 David Held said: "Realism posits that the system of sovereign states is inescapably anarchic in character; and that this anarchy forces all states, in the inevitable absence of any supreme arbiter to enforce moral behaviour and agreed international codes, to pursue power politics in order to attain their vital interests" (*Democracy and the Global Order: From the Modern State to Cosmopolitan Governance* [Stanford University Press, 1995], 74–75).

10 These statements from Thucydides are quoted in Schmookler, *The Parable of the Tribes,* 70.

11 Brown, et al., *The Perils of Anarchy,* ix.

12 Gerda Lerner, *The Creation of Patriarchy* (Oxford University Press, 1986), 35.

13 Martin Woessner, "Reconsidering the Slaughter Bench of History: Genocide, Theodicy, and the Philosophy of History," *Journal of*

Genocide Research 13 (2011).

14   Arthur C. McGill, *Suffering: A Test of Theological Method* (Westminster, 1982), 51, 88, 99, 116, 129, 131.

15   Ernest Becker, "Buñuel and the Demonic," in *Angel in Armor: A Post-Freudian Perspective on the Nature of Man* (George Braziller, 1969), 111.

16   McGill, *Suffering*, 117.

17   See Daniel Chamovitz, *What A Plant Knows: A Field Guide to the Senses* (Oneworld Book, 2012).

18   C. G. Jung, "The Concept of the Collective Unconscious," *Collected Works* (1936/1980), Vol. 9, part 1, par. 99.

19   Schmookler suggests that the selection for power would have also operated with regard to religious ideologies (*The Parable of the Tribes,* 73, 80), but he does not develop this idea at length.

20   See Walter Rauschenbusch, *A Theology for the Social Gospel* (Macmillan, 1918), especially the chapters on "The Supra-Personal Forces of Evil" and "The Kingdom of Evil."

21   Marcus J. Borg, *Reading the Bible Again for the First Time* (Harper Collins, 2002), 277.

22   See David Ray Griffin, *The American Trajectory: Divine or Demonic?* (Clarity Press, 2019), Introduction, Conclusion.

23   See David Frum and Richard Perle, *An End to Evil: How to Win the War on Terror* (Random House, 2004).

CHAPTER ELEVEN: THE AMERICAN EMPIRE

1   See Conrad Cherry, ed., *God's New Israel: Religious Interpretations of American Destiny*, revised and updated edition (University of North Carolina Press, 1997).

2   Anders Stephanson, *Manifest Destiny: American Expansion and the Empire of Right* (Hill and Wang, 1995), xi.

3   Richard Van Alstyne, *The Rising American Empire* (1960; Norton, 1974), 159.

4   Stephanson, *Manifest Destiny*, 19.

5 Andrew J. Bacevich, *American Empire: The Realities and Consequences of U.S. Diplomacy* (Harvard University Press, 2002), 30.

6 Ronald Steel, *Pax Americana* (Viking Press, 1967), 15, 14.

7 Steel, *Pax Americana*, 16–17, 18, vii.

8 See Ronald Steel, *Temptations of a Superpower* (Harvard University Press, 1995).

9 Charles Krauthammer, "Tiananmen II," *Washington Post*, 5 April 1991.

10 Ben Wattenberg, *The First Universal Nation: Leading Indicators and Ideas about the Surge of America in the 1990s* (Free Press, 1991), 202.

11 William Kristol and Robert Kagan, "Toward a Neo-Reaganite Foreign Policy," *Foreign Affairs* 75 (July/August 1996): 18–32, at 20, 27.

12 Robert Kagan, "The Benevolent Empire," *Foreign Policy* (Summer 1998): 24–35.

13 Charles Krauthammer, "The Unipolar Moment Revisited: United States World Dominance," *The National Interest*, Winter, 2002; republished as "The Unipolar Era" in *The Imperial Tense: Prospects and Problems of American Empire,* ed. Andrew J. Bacevich (Ivan R. Dee, 2003), 47–65, esp. 59.

14 Dinesh D'Souza, "In Praise of an American Empire," *Christian Science Monitor*, 26 April 2002.

15 Max Boot, "What Next? The Foreign Policy Agenda beyond Iraq," *Weekly Standard*, 5 May 2003.

16 Boot, "What Next? The Foreign Policy Agenda beyond Iraq."

17 Joshua Muravchik, *Exporting Democracy: Fulfilling America's Mission* (American Enterprise Institute, 1991), 227; Wattenberg, *The First Universal Nation*, 196.

18 Gary Dorrien, *Imperial Designs: Neoconservatism and the New Pax Americana* (Routledge, 2004), 80.

19 George W. Bush, "Address of the President to the Nation," 7 September 2003.

20 Bush, "State of the Union Address," 28 January 2003.

21 Bush, "Second Inaugural Address," 20 January 2005.

22 Charles Krauthammer, "Tomorrow's Threat," *Washington Post,* 21 January 2005.

23 Daniel Bell, "The End of American Exceptionalism," *National Affairs* (Fall 1975): 4, 6, 16.

24 Hilde Eliassen Restad, "Are We Coming to the End of 'American Exceptionalism'?" *Newsweek,* 6 June 2016. (This essay was originally published in the *London School of Economics,* 4 March 2016, as "Donald Trump's Calls to 'Make America Great Again' Show that American Exceptionalism Is Still a Powerful Idea.")

25 See Andrew Kohut and Bruce Stokes, *America Against the World: How We Are Different and Why We Are Disliked* (Times Books, 2006).

26 See David Ray Griffin, *Bush and Cheney: How They Ruined America and the World* (Interlink Books, 2017). Chs. 2 and 4.

27 Dick Cheney and Liz Cheney, *Exceptional: Why the World Needs a Powerful America* (Threshold Editions, 2015), 1, 5.

28 Cheney and Cheney, *Exceptional,* 1, 5.

29 Cheney and Cheney, *Exceptional,* 257, 259.

30 Bacevich, *American Empire,* viii, 11.

31 Bacevich, *American Empire,* 46, 4.

32 Bacevich, *American Empire,* 133, 52.

33 Bacevich, *American Empire,* 115, 196.

34 Chalmers Johnson, *The Sorrows of Empire: Militarism, Secrecy, and the End of the Republic* (Henry Holt, 2004), 4.

35 Noam Chomsky, *Deterring Democracy,* 2nd ed. (Hill and Wang, 1992); Chomsky, *Hegemony or Survival: America's Quest for Global Dominance* (Metropolitan Books, 2003).

36 Richard Falk, "Will the Empire Be Fascist?" *Global Dialogues,* 2003; "Resisting the Global Domination Project: An Interview with Prof. Richard Falk," *Frontline* 20/8 (April 12–25, 2003); "Slouching toward a Fascist World Order," in *The American Empire and the Commonwealth of God,* David Ray Griffin et al. (Westminster John Knox, 2006).

37 Laurence H. Shoup and William Minter, *Imperial Brain Trust:*

The Council on Foreign Relations and United States Foreign Policy (Monthly Review Press, 1977), 135 (emphasis added).

38 Shoup and Minter, *Imperial Brain Trust*, 140, 142.

39 Shoup and Minter, *Imperial Brain Trust*, 145.

40 Shoup and Minter, *Imperial Brain Trust*, 146.

41 Walter LaFeber, Richard Polenberg, and Nancy Woloch, *The American Century: A History of the United States Since 1941*, 5th ed. (McGraw-Hill, 1998), 385.

42 William Blum, *Killing Hope: U.S. Military and CIA Interventions Since World War II* (Common Courage, 1995), 70.

43 Blum, *Killing Hope*, 71.

44 Audrey R. Kahin and George McT. Kahin, *Subversion as Foreign Policy: The Secret Eisenhower and Dulles Debacle in Indonesia* (University of Washington Press, 1995), 4.

45 Blum, *Killing Hope*, 69.

46 Walter LaFeber, *The American Age: U.S. Foreign Policy Since 1750*, 2nd ed. (Norton, 1993), 518.

47 Blum, *Killing Hope*, 70.

48 "The Iran Accord," *New York Times*, 6 August 1954, quoted in Noam Chomsky, *Deterring Democracy*, 2nd ed. (Hill and Wang, 1992), 50.

49 LaFeber, *The American Age*, 518.

50 Blum, *Killing Hope*, 72.

51 William Rivers Pitt, *War On Iraq* (Context Books, 2002), 17.

52 Pitt, *War On Iraq*.

53 Gareth Porter, "Yes, the Pentagon Did Want to Hit Iran," *Asia Times*, 7 May 2008; David Remnick, "War without End," *The New Yorker*, 21 April 2003.

54 Tom O'Connor, "Iran to U.S.: Don't Even Think about Overthrowing Our Government Again," *Newsweek*, 13 July 2017.

55 Robin Wright, "John ('Bomb Iran') Bolton, The New Warmonger in the White House," *The New Yorker*, 23 March 2018.

56 "State Department Publishes Formerly Expunged Documents on 1953 Iran Coup," Truthdig, 29 June 2017.

57 William Blum, "Overthrowing Other People's Governments: The Master List" (https://williamblum.org/essays/read /overthrowing-other-peoples-governments-the-master-list).

58 David Ray Griffin, *The American Trajectory: Divine or Demonic?* (Clarity, 2018), Chapter 9.

59 Griffin, *The American Trajectory*, Chapter 10.

60 Blum, *Killing Hope*, Chapter 21.

61 Blum, *Killing Hope*, Chapter 25.

62 Blum, *Killing Hope*, Chapter 26.

63 Blum, *Killing Hope*, Chapter 9.

64 Blum, *Killing Hope*, Chapter 9.

65 Blum, *Killing Hope*, Chapter 9.

66 Blum, *Killing Hope*, Chapter 24.

67 Blum, *Killing Hope*, Chapter 9.

68 Blum, *Killing Hope*, Chapter 50.

69 The success of the campaign was illustrated by ABC's Ted Koppel, who said: "Manuel Noriega belongs to that special fraternity of international villains, men like Qaddafi, Idi Amin, and the Ayatollah Khomeini, whom Americans just love to hate," so that "strong public support for a reprisal was all but guaranteed" (ABC TV, quoted in Chomsky, *Deterring Democracy*, 145).

70 Noam Chomsky, *Deterring Democracy*, 153, 180; William Blum, *Killing Hope*, 306–09.

71 Chomsky, *Deterring Democracy*, 153, 180; Blum, *Killing Hope*, 306–09.

72 Chomsky, *Deterring Democracy*, 168–69.

73 Chomsky, *Deterring Democracy*, 159–60.

74 Blum, *Killing Hope*, 305.

75 Chomsky, *Deterring Democracy*, 164–65 (quoting *Brecha*, CODEHUCA, "Report of Joint CODEHUCA-CONADEIP Delegation," January-February 1990, San José).

76 Chomsky, *Deterring Democracy*, 164; Blum, *Killing Hope*, 305.

77 Chomsky, *Deterring Democracy*, 169.

78 Chomsky, *Deterring Democracy*, 166.

79 Chomsky, *Deterring Democracy*, 166 (quoting *Aviation Week and Space Technology*, 1 January 1990).

80 Chomsky, *Deterring Democracy*, 166.

81 Blum, *Killing Hope*, 309.

82 Blum, *Killing Hope*, 305.

83 Andres Oppenheimer, *Miami Herald*, 20 June 1990.

84 *Washington Post*, 21 December 1989.

85 *El Tiempo*, 5 January 1990.

86 David Ray Griffin, *American Trajectory*, Chapter 12.

87 David Ray Griffin, *Bush and Cheney*, Chapter 2.

88 Griffin, *Bush and Cheney*, Chapter 4.

89 Michel Chossudovsky, "US Sponsored Coup d'Etat: The Destabilization of Haiti," Global Research, 29 February 2004.

90 Griffin, *Bush and Cheney*, Chapter 6: 92–97.

91 Griffin, *Bush and Cheney*, Chapter 6: 98–118.

92 Griffin, *Bush and Cheney*, Chapter 9: 189–96.

93 William Stringfellow, *An Ethic for Christians and Other Aliens in a Strange Land* (Word Books, 1973), 19–20.

94 Gernot Köhler, *Global Apartheid* (Institute for World Order, 1978).

95 Köhler, *Global Apartheid*, 4.

96 Köhler, *Global Apartheid*, 2.

97 Köhler, *Global Apartheid*, 6.

98 Köhler, *Global Apartheid*, 9.

99 Thomas C. Schelling, "The Global Dimension," in *Rethinking America's Security*, ed. Graham Allison and Gregory F. Treverton (Norton, 1992), 196–210, at 200.

100 Richard Falk, "Democratizing, Internationalizing, and Globalizing: A Collage of Blurred Images," *Third World Quarterly* 12/4 (1993): 627–40, at 629.

101 Schelling, "The Global Dimension," 200.

102 Titus Alexander, *Unraveling Global Apartheid: An Overview of World Politics* (Polity Press, 1996), 9, 246.

103 Alexander, *Unraveling Global Apartheid*, 257.

104 Alexander, *Unraveling Global Apartheid*, 176, 7.

105 Marie Clarke, "Is Rising Global Inequality a Form of Global Apartheid?" HuffPost, 24 September 2016.

106 Jason Hickel, "Global Inequality May Be Much Worse Than We Think," *Guardian,* 8 April 2016.

107 Matthew 25:40–45.

108 Quoted in Robert Heilbroner, *Twenty-First Century Capitalism* (W. W. Norton, 1993), 55–56.

109 Colin Parkins, "North-South Relations and Globalization after the Cold War," in *Global Politics: An Introduction,* ed. Charlotte Bretherton and Geoffrey Ponton (Blackwell, 1996), 49–73, at 50–51.

110 Parkins, "North-South Relations and Globalization after the Cold War," 51.

111 George F. Kennan, "PPS/23: Review of Current Trends in U.S. Foreign Policy," *Foreign Relations of the United States,* Vol. 1: 509–29 (1948); reprinted in *Documents on American Policy and Strategy, 1945–1950,* ed. Thomas H. Entzold and John Lewis Gaddis (Columbia University Press), 226–28.

112 John B. Cobb, Jr., *The Earthist Challenge to Economism: A Theological Critique of the World Bank* (Macmillan, 1999), 61.

113 David C. Korten, *When Corporations Rule the World* (Berrett-Koehler Publishers and Kumarian Press, 1995), 160.

114 Korten, *When Corporations Rule the World*, 172.

115 Korten, *When Corporations Rule the World*, 172.

116 Walden Bello, *Dark Victory: The United States, Structural Adjustment, and Global Poverty* (Pluto Press, 1994); John B. Cobb, Jr., "Imperialism in American Economic Policy," in Griffin et al., *The American Empire and the Commonwealth of God.*

117 John Perkins, *Confessions of an Economic Hit Man* (Berrett-Koehler, 2004).

118 Jason Hickel, "Global Inequality May Be Much Worse Than We

Think," *Guardian,* 8 April 2016.

119 *Human Development Report: International Cooperation at a Crossroads: Aid, Trade, and Security in an Unequal World,* United Nations Development Program.

120 Hickel, "Global Inequality May Be Much Worse Than We Think."

121 Reality of Aid 2004; Barry Mason, "World Hunger Report: 852 Million Starve in the Midst of Plenty," 19 December 2003.

122 "Vision for 2020," Global Security Institute, 1997.

123 Tim Weiner, "Air Force Seeks Bush's Approval for Space Weapons Programs," *New York Times,* 18 May 2005.

124 Robert Kagan, "The Benevolent Empire," *Foreign Policy* (Summer 1998): 24–35.

125 Timothy Snyder, "Hitler vs. Stalin: Who Killed More?" *New York Review of Books,* 10 March 2011.

126 Dorrien, *Imperial Designs,* 18.

127 Louise Ridley, "The Holocaust's Forgotten Victims: The 5 Million Non-Jewish People Killed by the Nazis," HuffPost UK, 15 February 2015.

128 Brandon Weber, "These Staggering Graphics Put the WWII Death Toll in Perspective," Upworthy, 10 August 2015.

129 Weber, "These Staggering Graphics."

130 Ben J. Wattenberg, "Neo-Manifest Destinarianism," *National Interest* 21 (Fall 1990), 54; quoted in Dorrien, *Imperial Designs,* 80.

131 Patrick Bond, *South Africa and Global Apartheid: Continental and International Policies and Politics, Discussion Paper 25,* Nordic Africa Institute, August 2004. This statement was made by Mbeki in his address to the Welcoming Ceremony for the World Summit on Sustainable Development in August 2002.

CHAPTER TWELVE: FALSE FLAG ATTACKS

1 Stephen Kinzer, "Hoisting the False Flag," *Boston Globe,* 27 April 2018. Kinzer mentions several examples not discussed in the present chapter.

2   On the Mukden incident, see Walter LaFeber, *The Clash: U.S.-Japanese Religions throughout History* (Norton, 1997), 164–66; or Louise Young, *Japan's Total Empire: Manchuria and the Culture of Wartime Imperialism* (University of California Press, 1999), 40.

3   The question of responsibility for the Reichstag fire had long remained controversial. The dominant view, that the fire was set by the Nazis themselves, was persuasively argued by William Shirer in *The Rise and Fall of the Third Reich* (Simon and Schuster, 1990), 191–93. This view was then confirmed in 2001 with the publication of *Der Reichstagbrand: Wie Geschichte Gemacht Wird*, by Alexander Bahar and Wilfried Kugel (Berlin, Edition Q, 2001). That book presented ample evidence of Nazi responsibility, including the testimony of a member of the SA, who said that he was in the subterranean passageway that night and saw other SA members bringing explosive liquids from one building to the other.

4   Wilhelm Klein, "The Reichstag Fire, 68 Years On" (review of Alexander Bahar and Wilfried Kugel, *Der Reichstagbrand*), World Socialist Website, 5 July 2001.

5   Klein, "The Reichstag Fire, 68 Years On."

6   See Ian Kershaw, *Hitler: 1936–45: Nemesis* (Norton, 2001), 221; Office of United States Chief of Counsel for Prosecution of Axis Criminality, *Nazi Conspiracy and Aggression, Vol. II: Criminality of Groups and Organizations* (United States Government Printing Office, 1946).

7   "Shelling of Mainila," Wikipedia.

8   "Lavon Affair, "Wikipedia."

9   Brandon Weber, "These Staggering Graphics Put the WWII Death Toll in Perspective," Upworthy, 10 August 2015.

10   Theodore Roosevelt, then the assistant secretary of the navy, accused Spain of "an act of dirty treachery" (Walter LaFeber, *The American Age: U.S. Foreign Policy Since 1750*, 2nd ed. [Norton, 1993], 11), although Washington knew that the last thing the Spanish would have wanted was for America to have an excuse to intervene). William Randolph Hearst used his newspapers to inflame the American public, using the slogan "Remember the *Maine,* to hell with Spain" (ibid., 237, 245–47). In 1976, a navy investigation concluded that the explosion was probably an accident resulting from ammunition stored too close

to the engine (Geoffrey Perret, *A Country Made by War: From the Revolution to Vietnam—the Story of America's Rise to Power* [Random House, 1989, 280n). However, Cubans have always maintained that the Americans blew up their own ship as a pretext to go to war ("USS *Maine*" (ACR-1), Wikipedia, accessed February 2017).

11　See Philip S. Foner's study, *The Spanish-Cuban-American War and the Birth of American Imperialism*, 2 vols. (Monthly Review, 1972), Vol. I: 304, 309; Richard Van Alstyne, *The Rising American Empire* (1960; Norton, 1974), 132, 188; and Thomas McCormick, *China Market: America's Quest for Informal Empire, 1893-1901* (Quadrangle Books, 1967).

12　Stuart Creighton Miller, *Benevolent Assimilation: The American Conquest of the Philippines, 1899–1903* (Yale University Press, 1982), 57–62.

13　Miller, *Benevolent Assimilation*, 57–62.

14　Quoted in Howard Zinn, *A People's History of the United States* (Harper, 1990), 307.

15　See Gabriel Kolko, *Anatomy of a War: Vietnam, the United States, and the Modern Historical Experience* (Pantheon Books, 1985), 124; and George McT. Kahin, *Intervention: How American Became Involved in Vietnam* (Anchor Press, 1987), 217-19.

16　Marilyn B. Young, *The Vietnam Wars 1945–1990* (HarperCollins, 1991), 116–17; Kahin, *Intervention*, 221.

17　Kahin, *Intervention*, 221.

18　Kahin, *Intervention*, 222–23; Young, *The Vietnam Wars*, 118-19.

19　Kahin, *Intervention*, 220.

20　Young, *The Vietnam Wars*, 119.

21　Young, *The Vietnam Wars*, 120–21.

22　"The Costs of the Vietnam War," Alpha History; Michael D. Yates, "Honor the Vietnamese, Not Those Who Killed Them," *Monthly Review*, 1 May 2015.

23　Paul Williams, *Operation Gladio: The Unholy Alliance between the Vatican, the CIA, and the Mafia* (Prometheus Books, 2015). An account of US false flag attacks in Europe based on both books is contained in David Ray Griffin, *The American Trajectory: Divine or*

Demonic? (Clarity, 2018).

24 Daniele Ganser, *NATO's Secret Armies: Operation Gladio and Terrorism in Western Europe* (Frank Cass, 2005), 53–54.

25 Ganser, *NATO's Secret Armies*, 27–29.

26 Ganser, *NATO's Secret Armies*, 16.

27 Ganser, *NATO's Secret Armies*, 119.

28 Ganser, *NATO's Secret Armies*, 5.

29 Ganser, *NATO's Secret Armies*, 3, 119-20.

30 Ganser, *NATO's Secret Armies*, 7 (quoting Judge Casson on *Newsnight*, BBC1, 4 April 1991).

31 Ganser, *NATO's Secret Armies* (quoting the *Observer*, 7 June 1992).

32 Ganser, *NATO's Secret Armies*, 9–11.

33 Ganser, *NATO's Secret Armies,* 82, 120. On the evidence linking NATO and the United States to the Bologna massacre, see ibid., 25, 81,

34 Ganser, *NATO's Secret Armies*, 138–39.

35 Ganser, *NATO's Secret Armies*, 144–47 (citing Allan Francovich, "Gladio: The Foot Soldiers," BBC2, 4 June 1992).

36 Ganser, *NATO's Secret Armies*, 142–43, 146.

37 Ganser, *NATO's Secret Armies*, 143 (quoting Phil Davison, "A Very Right-Wing Coup Plot Surfaces in Belgium," *Independent*, 24 January 1990).

38 Ganser, *NATO's Secret Armies*, 27, quoting the Portuguese newspaper *Expresso*, 24 November 1990. According to the Spanish newspaper *El Pais*, 26 November 1990, Wörner added that SHAPE's coordination of Gladio had been confirmed by US General John Galvin, who was then the Supreme Allied Commander Europe (ibid., 26).

39 Stephen J. Sniegoski, "The Case for Pearl Harbor Revisionism," *Occidental Quarterly*, Winter 2001.

40 "'A Date Which Will Live in Infamy': FDR Asks for a Declaration of War," History Matters.

41 Sniegoski, "The Case for Pearl Harbor Revisionism." In 1939, a Gallup Poll showed that 88 percent of Americans wanted this country

to stay out of the War (James Perloff, "Pearl Harbor: Hawaii Was Surprised; FDR Was Not," New American, 7 December 2016). Later polls put the opposition at 80 percent, or at least two-thirds, of the population ("America and the Second World War," America in the World Briefings).

42 David Greenberg, *Republic of Spin: An Inside History of the American Presidency* (W. W. Norton, 2016), 233.

43 James Perloff, "Pearl Harbor: Hawaii Was Surprised; FDR Was Not," New American, 7 December 2016.

44 Robert B. Stinnett, *Day of Deceit: The Truth About FDR and Pearl Harbor* (Touchstone, 2001). Although the book was originally published in 2000, the Afterword to the Touchstone (paperback) edition has additional information.

45 Sniegoski, "The Case for Pearl Harbor Revisionism."

46 Sniegoski, "The Case for Pearl Harbor Revisionism."

47 Stinnett, *Day of Deceit*, 275.

48 Stinnett, *Day of Deceit*, 321–22.

49 Robert Smith Thompson, *A Time for War: Franklin D. Roosevelt and the Path to Pearl Harbor* (Prentice Hall Press, 1991), 352, 379.

50 The occasion for Richardson's removal was the creation of a two-ocean navy, with Kimmel put in charge of the Pacific Fleet (Stinnett, *Day of Deceit*, 11).

51 Perloff, "Pearl Harbor: Hawaii Was Surprised; FDR Was Not."

52 Perloff, "Pearl Harbor: Hawaii Was Surprised; FDR Was Not"; Sniegoski, "The Case for Pearl Harbor Revisionism."

53 Perloff, "Pearl Harbor: Hawaii Was Surprised; FDR Was Not."

54 Stephen E. Ambrose, *Pearl Harbor Revisited* (St. Martin's, 1995), 99–100. Ambrose repeated this charge in an opinion piece in the *Wall Street Journal*, 27 May 1999 (both cited in Stinnett, 208, 374).

55 Walter Lafeber, *The Clash*, 197.

56 Stinnett, *Day of Deceit*, 23, 71.

57 LaFeber, *The Clash*, 211.

58 Stinnett, *Day of Deceit*, 196.

59 Stinnett, *Day of Deceit*, 47, 72, 154, 164, 269.

60 In November, FDR had asked to be given the raw intercepts, not simply the summaries that had previously been supplied (Stinnett, *Day of Deceit*, 47, 169).

61 Stinnett, *Day of Deceit*, 45, 72, 210, 219, 269.

62 Stinnett, *Day of Deceit*, 98–104.

63 Stinnett, *Day of Deceit*, 85.

64 Sniegoski, "The Case for Pearl Harbor Revisionism."

65 Consistent with these facts were reports about FDR's state of mind on the day of the attack—that upon receiving the report, he did not seem alarmed, and that his overriding concern about the attack seemed to be the public's reaction to it: whether it would unite Americans behind a declaration of war (Stinnett, *Day of Deceit*, 3, 233). Reflecting a similar attitude, FDR's secretary of war, Henry Stimson, wrote in his diary that his "first feeling" upon hearing the news "was relief that the indecision was over and that a crisis had come in a way which would unite all our people" (*The Diary of Henry Stimson,* available in the Sterling Library, Yale University), 7 December 1941; quoted by LaFeber, *The Clash*, 212.

66 Stinnett, *Day of Deceit*, 207.

67 Stinnett, *Day of Deceit*, 144–45, 150–51.

68 Stinnett, *Day of Deceit*, 171–72. On November 25, 1940, reported Henry Stimson in his diary, FDR and his "war cabinet" discussed the question "how we should maneuver them [the Japanese] into the position of firing the first shot without allowing too much danger to ourselves" (quoted by LaFeber, *The Clash,* 209). Part of their answer to the latter part of that question may be reflected in the fact that shortly thereafter the aircraft carriers, 30 fighter planes and all the modern warships were moved from Hawaii to other islands prior to the attack, so that "the warships remaining in Pearl Harbor were mostly 27-year-old relics of World War I" (Stinnett, *Day of Deceit*, 152).

69 Stinnett, *Day of Deceit*, 234–35.

70 Perloff, "Pearl Harbor: Hawaii Was Surprised; FDR Was Not."

71 Perloff, "Pearl Harbor: Hawaii Was Surprised; FDR Was Not."

72 Perloff, "Pearl Harbor: Hawaii Was Surprised; FDR Was Not."

73 Perloff, "Pearl Harbor: Hawaii Was Surprised; FDR Was Not."

74 Perloff, "Pearl Harbor: Hawaii Was Surprised; FDR Was Not."

75 Perloff, "Pearl Harbor: Hawaii Was Surprised; FDR Was Not."

76 Perloff, "Pearl Harbor: Hawaii Was Surprised; FDR Was Not."

77 Stinnett, *Day of Deceit*, xiii, xiv.

78 This memorandum can be found at the National Security Archive, 30 April 2001, http://www.gwu.edu/~nsarchiv/news/20010430. It was revealed to American readers by James Bamford in *Body of Secrets: Anatomy of the Ultra-secret National Security Agency* (2001; Anchor Books, 2002), 82–91.

79 Deepa Kumar, *Islamophobia and the Politics of Empire* (Haymaker Books, 2012), 135.

80 Architects and Engineers for 9/11 Truth, *Beyond Misinformation* (E-Book) and "Solving the Mystery of Building 7" (video); Enver Masud, *9/11 Unveiled*, 2nd ed. (Wisdom Fund, 2012); Arthur Naiman and Gregg Roberts, *9/11: The Simple Facts* (Soft Skull Press, 2011); David Ray Griffin, *The New Pearl Harbor Revisited* (Interlink Books, 2008); David Griffin, *9/11 Unmasked: An International Review Panel,* co-authored with Elizabeth Woodworth (Interlink Books, 2018).

81 Griffin and Woodworth, *9/11 Unmasked*, Chapter 44.

82 Dr. Gideon Polya, "US Afghanistan Invasion 10th Anniversary: 5.6 Million War-Related Deaths," *Countercurrents*, 10 October 2011.

83 Dr. Gideon Polya, "2.7 Million Iraqi Dead From Violence or War-imposed Deprivation," *Countercurrents*, 23 March 2015; Medea Benjamin and Nicolas J.S. Davies, "The Staggering Death Toll in Iraq," AlterNet, 15 March 2018.

84 Priyanka Boghani, "A Staggering New Death Toll for Syria's War—470,000," Frontline, 11 February 2016.

85 Tom Engelhardt, "Seventy-Six Countries Are Now Involved in Washington's War on Terror," TomDispatch, 4 January 2018.

86 Tom Engelhardt, *A Nation Unmade by War* (Haymarket, 2018), 162–63.

CHAPTER THIRTEEN: NUCLEAR WEAPONS

1   Doug Long, "Albert Einstein and the Atomic Bomb," http://www
    .doug-long.com/einstein.htm.

2   William J. Broad, "Why They Called It the Manhattan Project,"
    New York Times, 30 October 2007.

3   Broad, "Why They Called It the Manhattan Project." US and British
    scientists believed they were in a desperate winner-take-all race with
    German scientists. That was especially true of the émigré scientists
    who came to the Manhattan Project. They had experienced Nazism
    first-hand, and their fear and loathing of Hitler was intense.

4   Broad, "Why They Called It the Manhattan Project."

5   Arjun Makhijani, "'Always' the Target?" "Institute for Energy and
    Environmental Research," March 2013.

6   Makhijani, "'Always' the Target?"

7   "97. Radio Report to the American People on the Potsdam
    Conference," Public Papers: Harry S. Truman 1945–1953, Harry S.
    Truman Presidential Library & Museum.

8   John LaForge, "No One Saves Lives by Dropping Bombs on Cities,"
    Duluth Reader, 5 August 2015; "Ike on Ike," *Newsweek*, 11 November
    1963.

9   Gar Alperovitz, "The War Was Won Before Hiroshima—and the
    Generals Who Dropped the Bomb Knew It," *The Nation*, 6 August
    2015.

10 Daniel Russ, "Chester Nimitz Also Thought the Atom Bomb Was
    Not Why Japan Surrendered," Civilian Military Intelligence Group,
    28 February 2017.

11 Hew Strachan and Sibylle Scheipers, *The Changing Character of War*
    (Oxford University Press, 2011), 99.

12 Henry L. Stimson, "The Decision to Use the Atomic Bomb*," Harper's
    Magazine*, February 1947.

13 John V. Denson, "The Hiroshima Myth," MISES Institute, 2 August
    2006.

14 Denson, "The Hiroshima Myth."

15 *New York Times,* 19 August 1946.

16 Denson, "The Hiroshima Myth."

17 Paul Ham, *Hiroshima Nagasaki: The Real Stories of the Atomic Bombings and their Aftermath* (St. Martin's Press, 2011), 477.

18 Kai Bird and Martin J. Sherwin, "The Myths of Hiroshima," *Los Angeles Times,* 2 August 2005. Bundy would not be the last person to pull a big figure out the air to magnify the importance of the bombings: One writer claimed that the use of the bomb saved *ten* million lives! (Philip Jenkins, "Back to Hiroshima: Why Dropping the Bomb Saved Ten Million Lives," ABC Religion and Ethics, 19 May 2016.)

19 Sean L. Malloy, "Four Days in May: Henry L. Stimson and the Decision to Use the Atomic Bomb," *Asia-Pacific Journal,* 4 April 2009.

20 Malloy, "Four Days in May."

21 John V. Denson, "The Hiroshima Myth."

22 Joseph C. Grew, *Turbulent Era: A Diplomatic Record for Forty Years, 1904–1945* (2 Volume Set), ed. Walter Johnson (Houghton Mifflin, 1952), Vol. 2: 1428–29.

23 Gar Alperovitz, *The Decision to Use the Atomic Bomb* (Vintage Books, 1995), 228–32, 235, 243, 300–01.

24 Alperovitz, *The Decision to Use the Atomic Bomb,* 235.

25 Pacific War Research Society (with John Toland), *The Day Man Lost: Hiroshima, 6 August 1945* (Kodansha America, 1981), 212–14; The Potsdam Proclamation said: "There must be eliminated for all time the authority and influence of those who have deceived and misled the people of Japan into embarking on world conquest," and "stern justice shall be meted out to all war criminals."

26 Hanson W. Baldwin, *Great Mistakes of the War* (Harper and Brothers, 1950).

27 Alperovitz, *The Decision to Use the Atomic Bomb,* 302.

28 Tsuyoshi Hasegawa, *Racing the Enemy: Stalin, Truman, and the Surrender of Japan* (Harvard University Press, 2005), 292.

29 Denson, "The Hiroshima Myth."

30 Alperovitz, *The Decision to Use the Atomic Bomb,* 213.

31 Kai Bird and Martin J. Sherwin, "The Myths of Hiroshima."

32 Quoted in Rob Edwards, "Hiroshima Bomb May Have Carried Hidden Agenda," *New Scientist,* 1 July 2005.

33 Edwards, "Hiroshima Bomb May Have Carried Hidden Agenda."

34 See for example: G. V. Glines, "The Bomb that Ended the War," History Net, 12 June 2006 ("for all practical purposes, the Nagasaki mission had ended the war"); David Kaiser, "Why the United States Dropped Atomic Bombs in 1945," Time.com, 25 May 2016 ("The United States, then, dropped the bombs to end the war"); "Timeline: The Road to Hiroshima," NPR, 5 August 2005 ("Three days later, U.S. forces detonated a second atomic bomb over Nagasaki, Japan, forcing an end to World War II"); "The Manhattan Project and the Atomic Bomb," Khan Academy ("In 1945, the United States dropped two atomic bombs on Japan, ending World War II").

35 Murray Sayle, "Did the Bomb End the War?" *New Yorker,* 31 July 1995.

36 Gar Alperovitz, "The War Was Won Before Hiroshima—and the Generals Who Dropped the Bomb Knew It"; Tsuyoshi Hasegawa, *Racing the Enemy: Stalin, Truman, and the Surrender of Japan.*

37 Quoted in Gareth Cook, "Why Did Japan Surrender?" Boston.com, 7 August 2011. Hasegawa also influenced Ward Wilson, a senior fellow at the British American Security Information Council, who published an essay entitled "The Bomb Didn't Beat Japan ... Stalin Did" (*Foreign Policy,* 30 May 2013).

38 Hasegawa, *Racing the Enemy,* 296–98.

39 Wilson, "The Bomb Didn't Beat Japan . . . Stalin Did."

40 Wilson, "The Bomb Didn't Beat Japan . . . Stalin Did."

41 Denson, "The Hiroshima Myth."

42 Oliver Stone and Peter Kuznick, *The Untold History of the United States* (Gallery Books, 2012), 173.

43 Alperovitz, *The Decision to Use the Atomic Bomb,* 103.

44 Ham, *Hiroshima Nagasaki,* 386.

45 Ham, *Hiroshima Nagasaki,* 480.

46 Alperovitz, *The Decision to Use the Atomic Bomb,* 39.

47   Dan Listwa, "Hiroshima and Nagasaki: The Long Term Health Effects," Columbia Center for Nuclear Studies, 9 August 2012; Serina Sandhu, "Hiroshima: The Legacy of the Atomic Bombing in Numbers," inews, 27 May 2016.

48   Susan Southard, "What U.S. Citizens Weren't Told about the Atomic Bombings of Japan," *Los Angeles Times*, 7 August 2015.

49   Ham, *Hiroshima Nagasaki*, 461

50   *Atomic Warfare and Christian Faith*, 1946, republished as appendix to Harold L. Lunger, ed., *Facing War/Waging Peace: Findings of the American Church Study Conferences, 1940–1960* (Friendship Press, 1988), 299–312.

51   Ham, *Hiroshima Nagasaki*, 461.

52   Ham, *Hiroshima Nagasaki*, 484.

53   Alperovitz, *The Decision to Use the Atomic Bomb*, 439.

54   Alperovitz, *The Decision to Use the Atomic Bomb*,, 473.

55   See Walter Isaacson and Evan Thomas, *The Wise Men: Six Friends and the World They Made* (Simon & Schuster, 1986).

56   Alperovitz, *The Decision to Use the Atomic Bomb*, 627.

57   Alperovitz, *The Decision to Use the Atomic Bomb*, 186.

58   Noam Chomsky, *Hegemony or Survival: America's Quest for Global Dominance* (Henry Holt, 2004).

59   David Holloway, *Stalin and the Bomb: The Soviet Union and Atomic Energy, 1939–1956* (Yale University Press, 1996), Chapter 14; Ham, *Hiroshima Nagasaki*, 501–02; Swift, "The Soviet-American Arms Race."

60   Global Research, 6 August 2018.

61   William Stringfellow, *An Ethic for Christians and Other Aliens in a Strange Love* (Word Books, 1973), 32.

62   "German Christians," Wikipedia (https://en.wikipedia.org/wiki/German_Christians).

CHAPTER FOURTEEN: CLIMATE DESTRUCTION

1   Amy Goodman, "Noam Chomsky: Climate Change & Nuclear Proliferation Pose the Worst Threat Ever Faced by Humans,"

Democracy Now! 16 May 2016.

2   Tom Engelhardt, "Emperor Weather Turning Up the Heat on History: Planet of the Imperial Apocalypse," TomDispatch, 6 December 2015.

3   Zoya Teirstein, Grist, 25 January 2018.

4   Viviane Richter, "The Big Five Mass Extinctions," *Cosmos Magazine,* 31 May 2018; Dahr Jamail, "Sixth Mass Extinction Ushers in Record-Breaking Wildfires and Heat," Truthout, 20 August 2018.

5   Damian Carrington, "Humanity Has Wiped Out 60% of Animal Populations Since 1970, Report Finds," *Guardian,* 29 October 2018.

6   "The Extinction Crisis," Center for Biological Diversity, 2010.

7   Carrington, "Humanity Has Wiped Out 60%."

8   Brian Kahn, "We Just Breached the 410 PPM Threshold for CO_2," Climate Central, 21 April 2017.

9   Joe Romm, "Bombshell: Recent Warming Is 'Amazing and Atypical' and Poised to Destroy Stable Climate that Enabled Civilization," Climate Progress, 8 March 2013.

10 Stefan Rahmstorf, "Paleoclimate: The End of The Holocene," Realclimate, 22 September 2013.

11 Rahmstorf, "Paleoclimate: The End of The Holocene."

12 Elizabeth Kolbert, *Field Notes from a Catastrophe: Man, Nature, and Climate Change* (Bloomsbury, 2006), 107–10.

13 David Spratt, "NASA Climate Chief: Labor's Targets a 'Recipe for Disaster,'" Climate Code Red, 27 January 2011.

14 Lonnie G. Thompson, "Climate Change: The Evidence and Our Options," *Behavior Analyst* 33/2 (Fall 2010): 153–70.

15 Noam Chomsky and Andre Vitchek, *On Western Terrorism: From Hiroshima to Drone Warfare* (Pluto Press, 2013), 2.

16 Kolbert, *Field Notes from a Catastrophe,* 189.

17 Elizabeth Kolbert, *The Sixth Extinction: An Unnatural History* (Henry Holt, 2014), 267–68.

18 Dahr Jamail, "Sixth Mass Extinction Ushers in Record-Breaking Wildfires and Heat."

19 Isaiah 24:5–6.

20 NOAA National Weather Service, Office of Climate, Water, and Weather Services, 2012.

21 "Global Warming: Future Temperatures Could Exceed Livable Limits, Researchers Find," ScienceDaily, 4 May 2010.

22 Jamail, "Sixth Mass Extinction Ushers In Record-Breaking Wildfires and Heat."

23 Damian Carrington, "Climate Change Scientists Warn of 4C Global Temperature Rise," *Guardian*, 28 November 2010; Mark New et al., "Four Degrees and Beyond: The Potential for a Global Temperature Increase of Four Degrees and Its Implications," *Philosophical Transactions of the Royal Society* 369/1934 (November 2011).

24 "Tyndall Center: Global Warming Will Kill 90% of the Earth's Population," Real Science, 29 November 2009.

25 Tim Collins, "Shocking report reveals that there is a 93% chance that global warming will exceed 4°C by 2100 if greenhouse gas emissions continue at the current rate," Daily Mail, 6 December, 2017.

26 Cheryl Jones, "Frank Fenner Sees No Hope for Humans," *The Australian*, 16 June 2010; Guy R. McPherson, "Three Paths to Near-term Human Extinction," Canadians for Emergency Action on Climate Change, 9 November 2011; Malcolm Light, "Global Extinction within One Human Lifetime as a Result of a Spreading Atmospheric Arctic Methane Heat Wave and Surface Firestorm," Arctic News, 6 March 2012.

27 Orrin H. Pilkey and Rob Young, *The Rising Sea* (Shearwater, 2009).

28 Rob Young and Orrin Pilkey, "How High Will Seas Rise? Get Ready for Seven Feet," Environment 360, 14 January 2010; Brady Dennis and Chris Mooney, "Scientists Nearly Double Sea Level Rise Projections for 2100, because of Antarctica," *Washington Post*, 30 March 2016.

29 Le Bars et al., "A High-End Sea Level Rise Probabilistic Projection including Rapid Antarctic Ice Sheet Mass Loss," *Environmental Research Letters*, 3 April 2017.

30 "Quick Facts on Ice Sheets," National Snow & Ice Data Center (https://nsidc.org/cryosphere/quickfacts/icesheets.html).

31 Lester Brown, "Could Food Shortages Bring Down Civilization?" *Scientific American*, 22 April 2009.

32 Lester R. Brown, *Full Planet, Empty Plates: The New Geopolitics of Food Scarcity* (W.W. Norton, 2012), 122.

33 Max Frankel, "Intensifying Midwestern Drought Threatens Farmers, Water Supplies," Climate Progress, 6 July 2012; Jeff Wilson, "U.S. Corn Growers Farming in Hell as Midwest Heat Spreads," Bloomberg, 9 July 2012.

34 "Climate Change vs. Food Security: A Bleak Future for the Poor," Oxfam International, 5 September 2012.

35 "Ocean Acidification: Global Warming's Evil Twin," Skeptical Science, 2012.

36 Kathleen McAuliffe, "Ocean Acidification: A Global Case of Osteoporosis," *Discover*, July 2008; Alex Morales, "Oceans Acidifying Fastest in 300 Million Years Due to Emissions," Bloomberg News, 2 March 2012.

37 "Ocean Acidification: Global Warming's Evil Twin"; "Acid Oceans Warning," ARC Center of Excellence Coral Reef Studies, October 2007.

38 Seth Borenstein, "Plankton, Base of Ocean Food Web, in Big Decline," Associated Press, 28 July 2010; Steve Connor, "The Dead Sea: Global Warming Blamed for 40 Per Cent Decline in the Ocean's Phytoplankton," *Independent*, 29 July 2010. Daniel G. Boyce, Boris Worm, et al., "Global Phytoplankton Decline over the Past Century," *Nature*, 29 July 2010.

39 Brian Kahn, "We Just Breached the 410 PPM Threshold for CO2," Climate Central, 21 April 2017.

40 Julian Siddle, "Marine Life Faces 'Acid Threat,'" BBC News, 25 November 2008; "Acid Oceans Warning," ARC Center of Excellence Coral Reef Studies, October 2007.

41 Sean Anderson, *Tiny but Tough: Calcification in Marine Phytoplankton*, Oceanbites, 12 August 2016.

42 "Save the Sea"; "Oceans, Rio+20: The Future We Want," United Nations.

43 "Acid Oceans Warning," ARC Centre of Excellence in Coral Reef

Studies, 17 October 2007.

44 Charles J. Krebs, *Ecology: The Experimental Analysis of Distribution and Abundance*, 6th ed. (Benjamin Cummings, 2009), 572.

45 Krebs, *Ecology*.

46 Joe Romm, "Nature Bombshell: Climate Experts Warn Thawing Permafrost Could Cause 2.5 Times the Warming of Deforestation!" Climate Progress, 1 December 2011.

47 Alan Buis, "Is a Sleeping Climate Giant Stirring in the Arctic?" NASA, 10 June 2013.

48 Natalia Shakhova et al., "Extensive Methane Venting to the Atmosphere from Sediments of the East Siberian Arctic Shelf," *Science*, 5 March 2010.

49 Brian Merchant, "If We Release a Small Fraction of Arctic Carbon, 'We're Fucked': Climatologist," Motherboard, 1 August 2014.

50 Senator James Inhofe, *The Greatest Hoax: How the Global Warming Conspiracy Threatens Your Future* (WND Books, 2012), 70–71.

51 David Edwards, "Limbaugh: Christians 'Cannot Believe in Manmade Global Warming,'" Raw Story, 14 August 2013.

52 David Crowe, "Katrina: God's Judgment on America," Beliefnet, September 2005.

53 Richard Gray, "Climate Scientists Are Losing the Public Debate on Global Warming," *Telegraph*, 8 April 2012.

54 Mark Hertsgaard, *Hot: Living Through the Next Fifty Years on Earth* (Houghton Mifflin Harcourt, 2011), 263.

55 Eric Pooley, "How Much Would You Pay to Save the Planet? American Press and the Economics of Climate Change," Joan Shorenstein Center on the Press, Politics and Public Policy, John F. Kennedy School of Government, January 2009.

56 Pooley, "How Much Would You Pay to Save the Planet?"

57 Thom Hartmann, "The Mainstream Media's Criminal Climate Coverage," 26 February 2014; more recently, see Peter D. Carter and Elizabeth Woodworth, *Unprecedented Crime: Climate Science Denial and Game Changers for Survival*, with a foreword by Dr. James Hansen and a chapter called "Media Collusion" (Clarity

Press, 2018).

58 Wen Stephenson, "A Convenient Excuse," *The Phoenix*, 5 November 2012.

59 Joanna M. Foster, "Climate Coverage Drops at the *New York Times* after Paper Closed Its Environmental Desk," Climate Progress, 25 November 2013.

60 Curtis Brainard, "NYT Cancels Green Blog," *Columbia Journalism Review*, 1 March 2013.

61 Max Greenberg, "Two Big Climate Stories You Didn't Read About in *The New York Times: Times* Skips Stories Soon after Closing Environmental Desk and Green Blog," Media Matters, 7 August 2013.

62 Jonathan Watts, "We Have 12 Years to Limit Climate Change Catastrophe, Warns UN," *Guardian*, 8 October 2018.

63 Kolbert, *Field Notes from a Catastrophe*, 189.

64 Paul Brodeur, "Annals of Chemistry: In the Face of Doubt," *The New Yorker*, 9 June 1986. (On the history of the quoting of Rowland's statement, see "The New Yorker's Plagiarism Blunder," Edirin Oputu, *Columbia Journalism Review,* 28 April 2014.)

65 Nathaniel Rich, "Losing Earth," *New York Times Magazine,* 1 August 2018.

66 Naomi Klein, "Capitalism Killed Our Climate Momentum, Not 'Human Nature,'" The Intercept, 3 August 2018.

67 Klein, "Capitalism Killed Our Climate Momentum."

68 Klein, "Capitalism Killed Our Climate Momentum."

69 Klein, "Capitalism Killed Our Climate Momentum."

70 Rich, "Losing Earth."

71 Joe Romm, *Hell and High Water: The Global Warming Solution* (Harper, 2007), 235; Romm, "The Ghost of Climate Yet to Come," Climate Progress, 25 December 2012.

72 Bill McKibben, "A World at War," *New Republic,* 15 August 2015.

73 McKibben, "A World ar War."

74 McKibben, "A World at War."

75 "Transcript of President Bush's Address on the State of the Union," *New York Times*, 29 January 1992.

76 David Remnick, "Going the Distance: On and Off the Road with Barack Obama," *New Yorker*, 27 January 2014.

77 James Hansen et al., "Target Atmospheric CO_2: Where Should Humanity Aim?" *Open Atmospheric Science Journal* 2 (2008).

78 George Monbiot, "The Process Is Dead," *Guardian*, 21 September 2010.

79 Noam Chomksy, "Bernie Sanders Is the Most Popular Politician in the Country, but the Mainstream Media Is Ignoring Him," Interview by Lynn Parramore, Institute for New Economic Thinking, 25 March 2018.

80 Tom Engelhardt, *A Nation Unmade by War* (Haymarket, 2018), 162.

CHAPTER FIFTEEN: SALVATION

1 Gustav Aulén, *Christus Victor: An Historical Study of the Three Main Types of the Idea of Atonement* (SPCK, 1931).

2 "#205: Anselm on the Incarnation," Christian History Institute (https://christianhistoryinstitute.org/study/module/anselm).

3 The other four fundamentals were biblical inerrancy, the virgin birth, Christ's bodily resurrection, and the historicity of the biblical miracles. Actually, this list, which was formulated in about 1910 by the Northern Presbyterians, was simply the most popular of many lists of fundamentals. See Douglas A. Sweeney, "Who Were the 'Fundamentalists'?" *Christian History*, Issue 92, 2006.

4 Marcus J. Borg, *Convictions: How I Learned What Matters Most* (Harper One, 2014), 137–39, 142.

5 Borg, *Convictions*, 59.

6 Borg, *Convictions*, 60.

7 Rob Bell, *Love Wins: A Book About Heaven, Hell, and the Fate of Every Person Who Ever Lived* (HarperCollins, 2011).

8 Jon Meacham, "Pastor Rob Bell: What if Hell Doesn't Exist?" *Time*, 14 April 2011.

9   Meacham, "Pastor Rob Bell: What if Hell Doesn't Exist?"

10 Meacham, "Pastor Rob Bell: What if Hell Doesn't Exist?"

11 Julie Clawson, "What Does Rob Bell Really Say? (A Review of the Actual Book Itself)," *Sojourners*, 15 March 2011.

12 "On The Reality of Hell," Southern Baptist Convention (Phoenix, 2011).

13 Carol Meyer, "Debunking the Myth of Hell," *National Catholic Reporter*, 3 February 2011.

14 Meyer, "Debunking the Myth of Hell."

15 Borg, *Convictions,* 63-65.

16 Borg, *Convictions*, 62, 65.

17 John B. Cobb, Jr. "Dialogue," in *Death or Dialogue? From the Age of Monologue to the Age of Dialogue,* Leonard Swidler et al. (SCM Press; Trinity Press, 1990), 1–18, at 1.

18 Fred Sanders, "C. H. Dodd and Realized Eschatology," The Scriptorium Daily, 7 April 2009.

19 H. Richard Niebuhr, *The Meaning of Revelation* (Macmillan, 1960), 150.

20 Alfred North Whitehead, *Process and Reality*, corrected edition, ed. David Ray Griffin and Donald W. Sherburne (Free Press, 1978), 340.

21 Charles Hartshorne, *Omnipotence and Other Theological Mistakes* (State University of New York Press, 1984), 110.

22 Charles Hartshorne, *The Logic of Perfection and Other Essays in Neoclassical Metaphysics* (Open Court, 1962), 132.

23 Charles Hartshorne, *The Darkness and the Light: A Philosopher Reflects Upon His Fortunate Career and Those Who Made It Possible* (State University of New York Press, 1990), 379.

24 "The Prior Actuality of God," in Austin Farrer, *Reflective Faith: Essays in Philosophical Theism*, ed. Charles C. Conti (SPCK, 1972), 178–91.

25 Farrer's comment was made in a 1966 letter to Edward Henderson after Farrer had read some books by Charles Hartshorne and Schubert Ogden. Farer's comment was reported by Henderson in an unpublished ms., "Austin Farrer and Process Theology: Notes

on 'The Prior Actuality of God.'"

26 John B. Cobb, Jr., "The Resurrection of the Soul," *Harvard Theological Review* 80/2 (1987): 213–27. (Cobb's article was published before both of Gregory Riley's books discussing the "resurrection of the soul" appeared.)

27 John Hick, *A Christian Theology of Religions: The Rainbow of Faiths* (Westminster John Knox, 1995), 16–18.

28 St. Philaret of Moscow, Sermon of September 23, 1847, http://www .orthodoxchurchquotes.com/2013/07/10/st-philaret-of-moscow -every-christian-should-find-for-himself/.

29 Bruce R. Reichenbach pointed out that for those (like himself) who accept a deity with omnipotence in the traditional sense, materialism provides no obstacle to belief in life after bodily death (*Is Man the Phoenix? A Study of Immortality* [Christian University Press, 1978], 84–85).

30 *Religion in the Making* (1926; reprint by Fordham University Press, 1996), 111.

31 Alfred North Whitehead, *Adventures of Ideas* (Free Press, 1967), 208.

32 Alfred North Whitehead, *Essays in Science and Philosophy* (Philosophical Library, 1947), 116.

33 J. M. E. McTaggart, *Some Dogmas of Religion* (Edward Arnold, 1906), 105.

34 Whitehead, *Adventures of Ideas*, 208.

35 Cobb, "The Resurrection of the Soul," 213–27.

36 Corliss Lamont, *The Illusion of Immortality*, 4th ed. (Frederick Ungar, 1965), 86, 123.

37 J. J. C. Smart, "Religion and Science," in *Philosophy of Religion: A Global Approach*, ed. Stephen H. Phillips (Harcourt Brace, 1996), 217–24, at 221, reprinted from Paul Edwards, ed., *Encyclopedia of Philosophy* (New York: Macmillan Press, 1967], Vol. 7).

38 Bertrand Russell, *Why I Am Not a Christian and Other Essays on Religion and Related Subjects*, ed. by Paul Edwards (Simon & Schuster 1957), 51.

39 Kai Nielsen, *Philosophy and Atheism: In Defense of Atheism*

(Prometheus Books, 1985), 61.

40 Lamont, *The Illusion of Immortality,* 116–17.

41 Whitehead, *Adventures of Ideas,* 208.

42 John B. Cobb, Jr., *The Structure of Christian Existence* (Westminster Press, 1967), 39.

43 Whitehead, *Process and Reality,* 340.

44 Whitehead, *Religion in the Making,* 59–60.

45 Franco Cortese, "Immanuel Kant: Morality Necessitates Immortality," Humanity, 21 August 2013.

46 "Most Americans Believe in the Afterlife," Rasmussen Reports, 8 June 2017; Carlyle Murphy, "Most Americans Believe in Heaven … and Hell," Pew Research Center, 10 November 2015.

47 Jean-Paul Sartre, *Being and Nothingness,* trans. Hazel Barnes (Philosophical Library, 1956), 615. For commentary, see Jug Suraiya, "Our Thirst Is a 'Futile Passion,'" Speaking Tree, 19 August 2013, and Julian Young, *The Death of God and the Meaning of Life* (Routledge, 2003), 168.

48 Whitehead, *Religion in the Making,* 111.

49 *Henry Sidgwick: A Memoir* (London: Macmillan, 1906); cited in Alfred North Whitehead, *Science and the Modern World* (1925; Free Press, 1967), 142.

50 Whitehead, *Science and the Modern World,* 2.

51 "'Life Is in the Transitions': William James, 1842–1910" (a Web Version of an Exhibition Curated by Linda Simon), Houghton Library, Harvard College Library).

52 David Ray Griffin, *Parapsychology, Philosophy, and Spirituality: A Postmodern* Exploration (State University of New York Press, 1997), Chaps. 4–8.

53 Susan J. Blackmore, *Beyond the Body: An Investigation of the Out-of-the-Body Experience* (1982; Academy Chicago Publishers, 1992), 1.

54 Kenneth Ring and Evelyn Elsaesser Valarino, *Lessons from the Light* (Moment Point Press, 2006), 2–3.

55 Gideon Lichfield, "The Science of Near-Death Experiences," *Atlantic,* April 2015.

56   Lichfield, "The Science of Near-Death Experiences."

57   For example, a medical doctor named Eben Alexander published a best-selling book entitled *Proof of Heaven: A Neurosurgeon's Journey into the Afterlife* (Simon & Schuster, 2012). The book, which reportedly recounted near-death experiences he had while in a coma, made him rich and famous. But it also led to seemingly interminable debates, with some writers debunking his account and others defending it by debunking the debunkers. Because Alexander's book provides no reports of veridical perceptions, there is simply no way for the supporters of Alexander's book to refute the debunkers.

58   Janice Miner Holden, "Veridical Perception in Near-Death Experiences," in *The Handbook of Near-Death Experiences: Thirty Years of Investigation,* 2nd printing, ed. Janice Miner Holden, Bruce Greyson, and Debbie James (Praeger, 2009).

59   Kimberly Clark Sharp, *After the Life: What I Discovered on the Other Side of Life Can Change Your World* (William Morrow, 1995).

60   Kimberly Clark, "Clinical Interventions with Near-Death Experiences," in *The Near-Death Experience: Problems, Prospects, Perspectives,* ed. Bruce Grayson and Charles P. Flynn (Charles C. Thomas, 1982), 242–55, at 242–43.

61   Mario Beauregard, "Near Death, Explained," Salon, 21 April 2012.

62   Emily Williams Cook, Bruce Greyson, & Ian Stevenson, "Do Any Near-Death Experiences Provide Evidence for the Survival of Human Personality after Death?" *Journal of Scientific Exploration* 12/3 (1998).

63   Cook, et al., "Do Any Near-Death Experiences Provide Evidence for the Survival of Human Personality after Death?"

64   Cook, et al., "Do Any Near-Death Experiences Provide Evidence for the Survival of Human Personality after Death?"

65   Lichfield, "The Science of Near-Death Experiences."

66   Beauregard, "Near Death, Explained."

67   Beauregard, "Near Death, Explained."

68   Lichfield, "The Science of Near-Death Experiences."

69   Michael Sabom, *Recollections of Death: A Medical Investigation* (HarperCollins, 1981).

70   Barbara Bradley Hagerty, "Decoding The Mystery of Near-Death Experiences," NPR, 22 May 2009.

71   Sam Parnia et al., AWARE—AWAreness during REsuscitation: A Prospective Study," *Resuscitation* (a journal), 2014.

72   Parnia et al., AWARE—AWAreness during REsuscitation."

73   Adam Withnail, "Life after Death? Largest-Ever Study Provides Evidence that 'Out of Body' and 'Near-Death' Experiences May Be Real," *Independent,* 7 October 2014.

74   Graham Nichols, "Near Death and Out-of-Body Experiences: In Search of the Truth—Noetic Now" (blog), 9 August 2016.

75   Nichols, "Near Death and Out-of-Body Experiences."

76   Nichols, "Near Death and Out-of-Body Experiences."

77   Kenneth Ring and Sharon Cooper, "Near-Death and Out-of-Body Experiences in the Blind: A Study of Apparent Eyeless Vision," *Journal of Near-Death Studies,* December 1997.

78   Ring and Cooper, "Near-Death and Out-of-Body Experiences in the Blind." For more on experiences of the blind, see Kenneth Ring and Sharon Cooper, *Mindsight: Near-Death and Out-of-Body Experiences in the Blind,* 2nd ed. (iUniverse: 2008).

79   Hornell Hart, "Six Theories about Apparition," *Proceedings of the Society for Psychical Research* 50 (May 1956): 153–239, at 177, 235.

80   See, for example, Charles P. Flynn, *After the Beyond: Human Transformation and the Near-Death Experience* (Prentice-Hall, 1986); Phyllis M. H. Atwater, *Coming Back to Life* (Dodd, Mead, 1986); David Lorimer, *Whole in One: The Near-Death Experience and the Ethic of Interconnectedness* (Arkana, 1990); Cherie Sutherland, *Transformed by the Light: Life after Near-Death Experiences* (Bantam, 1992).

CHAPTER SIXTEEN: THE REIGN OF GOD AND GLOBAL DEMOCRACY

1   Walter Rauschenbusch, *A Theology for the Social Gospel* (1917; Abington, 1945).

2   John B. Cobb, Jr., "Commonwealth & Empire," in *The American Empire and the Commonwealth of God: A Political, Economic, Religious Statement,* David Ray Griffin, John B. Cobb Jr., Richard Falk, and

Catherine Keller (Westminster John Knox Press, 2006).

3   Christopher Layne, "Kant or Cant: The Myth of the Democratic Peace," in *The Perils of Anarchy: Contemporary Realism and International Security*, ed. Michael E. Brown et al. (MIT Press, 1995), 287–331, at 293.

4   G. Lowes Dickenson, *The International Anarchy, 1904–1915* (London: Allen and Unwin, 1926 [new edition 1937]). According to Hedley Bull, it was this book by Dickenson that made the phrase "international anarchy" commonplace (Hedley Bull, *The Anarchical Society: A Study of Order in World Politics* [Macmillan, 1977], 46).

5   This statement occurs in Dickenson's introduction to *A Project of Perpetual Peace: Rousseau's Essay*, trans. by Edith M. Nuttall, with an Introduction by G. Lowes Dickenson (Richard Cobden-Sanderson Press, 1917).

6   Michael E. Brown et al., eds., *The Perils of Anarchy: Contemporary Realism and International Security* (MIT Press, 1995), ix.

7   John Mearsheimer, "The False Promise of International Relations," in Brown et al., eds. *The Perils of Anarchy*, 332–76, at 333.

8   Frederick L. Schuman, *International Politics: An Introduction to the Western State System* (McGraw-Hill, 1933), 642, 661–63, 828–30.

9   Georg Schwarzenberger, A *Manual of International Law* (Stevens and Sons, 1952).

10 Georg Schwarzenberger, *Power Politics: An Introduction to the Study of International Relations and Post-War Planning* (J Cape, 1941), 399, 401–04, 430.

11 See David Ray Griffin, *The American Trajectory: Divine or Demonic?* (Clarity Press, 2018).

12 Reinhold Niebuhr, *The Children of Light and the Children of Darkness: A Vindication of Democracy and a Critique of Its Traditional Defense* (Scribner's, 1944), xiii.

13 In Niebuhr's words, "The capacity of communities to synthesize divergent approaches to a common problem and to arrive at a tolerably just solution proves man's capacity to consider interests other than his own" (*The Nature and Destiny of Man*, Vol. II: *Human Destiny* [Scribner's, 1943], 249).

14 Reinhold Niebuhr, *The Nature and Destiny of Man*, Vol. II, 19, 22, 27.

15 Niebuhr, *The Nature and Destiny of Man*, Vol. II, 29.

16 This statement reflects the democratic "all-affected principle," according to which all people affected by some policy should have been participants in creating it.

17 In accord with the principle of subsidiarity, this legislation would be "framework legislation," meaning "legislation which specifies the principles and objectives of cosmopolitan democratic law to be upheld, leaving the detailed implementation of these to those at 'lower' levels of governance" (David Held, *Democracy and the Global Order: From the Modern State to Cosmopolitan Governance* [Stanford University Press, 1995], 255).

18 Joseph E. Schwartzberg, *Transforming the United Nations System: Design for a Workable World* (United Nations University Press, 2013). Also promising is a series of Global Town Halls, sponsored by Global Voice, One Earth Future, and the Colorado European Union Center of Excellence, in support of a UN 2020 World Leaders' Summit on UN Renewal, Innovation and Reform. For background, see Griffin, *The American Trajectory*, Chapters 3 and 6.

19 Charles Taliaferro, "God's Natural Laws," in *Natural Law, Liberalism, and Morality: Contemporary Essays*, ed. Robert P. George (Clarendon, 1996), 283–301, at 293.

20 Andrew J. Bacevich, *American Empire: The Realities and Consequences of U.S. Diplomacy* (Harvard University Press, 2002), 4, 7, 46, 52, 80, 115, 133, 195–96, 242.

21 Griffin, *The American Trajectory*.

22 Lord Acton, *Essays*, ed. Rufus F. Fears (Liberty Classics, 1985), Vol. II: 383. as quoted in Garry Wills, *Papal Sin*: 2.

23 Sarah Le, "The Dystopian Principles of Real Communism," *Epoch Times*, 3 May 2017; Mark Aarons, *The Family File* (Black Inc., 2010), xiii; Roland Boer, *Stalin: From Theology to the Philosophy of Socialism in Power* (Springer, 2017).

24 Acton had in mind specifically the absolutism of the papacy, as Garry Wills pointed out in *Papal Sins: Structures of Deceit* (Doubleday, 2000), 1-2.

25 Charles Hartshorne, *Reality as Social Process* (Free Press, 1953), 141.

26 Hartshorne, *Reality as Social Process*, 266.

27 D. B. Robertson, ed., *Love and Justice: Selections from the Shorter Writings of Reinhold Niebuhr* (Westminster, 1957), 248.

28 Robert Kagan, "The Benevolent Empire," *Foreign Policy*, Summer 1998: 24–35.

29 Samuel Huntington, "American Ideals versus American Institutions," *Political Science Quarterly*, Spring, 1982.

30 Bacevich, *American Empire*, 46.

31 Stephen Kinzer, *The Brothers: John Foster Dulles, Allen Dulles, and Their Secret World War* (Times Books, 2013), 323.

32 Robert McAfee Brown, ed., *The Essential Reinhold Niebuhr: Essays and Addresses* (Yale University Press, 1986), 165.

33 Niebuhr, *The Nature and Destiny of Man*, Vol. II: 259.

34 Michael Perry, *The Idea of Human Rights: Four Inquiries* (Oxford University Press, 1998), 4.

35 Linda Melvern, *A People Betrayed: The Role of the West in Rwanda's Genocide* (Zed Books, 2000), 4–5, 219, 222–23, 233.

36 Melvern, *A People Betrayed*, 229.

37 Henry Shue, "Let Whatever Is Smoldering Erupt? Conditional Sovereignty, Reviewable Intervention and Rwanda 1994," *Between Sovereignty and Global Governance: The United Nations, the State, and Civil Society*, ed. Albert J. Paolini et al. (St. Martin's Press, 1998), 60–84, at 60–61.

38 Alain Destexhe, "The Shortcomings of the 'New Humanitarianism,'" in *Between Sovereignty and Global Governance*, ed. Paolini et al., at 85, 92, 110.

39 Richard A. Falk, *Human Rights and State Sovereignty* (New York and London: Holmes and Meier, 1981), 37–42. Although Falk lists seven "logics," they finally reduce to these three.

40 The UN is finally only an agent of the states—ultimately of the most powerful state. As Immanuel Wallerstein has said about the new world order that emerged in 1945: "We had in reality moved into the era of US hegemony in the world-system, in which US

economic strength was overwhelming and during which the United States was able to establish the set of rules for the world-system that best advanced its interests. . . . The United Nations was essentially assigned no role of any significance in the postwar geopolitical structure, except to be a sort of figleaf to all these arrangements" ("The New World Disorder: If the States Collapse, Can the Nations by United?" in *Between Sovereignty and Global Governance*, ed. Paolini et al., 171–85, at 174-75).

41 F. S. Northedge, *The League of Nations: Its Life and Times 1920–1946* (Holmes and Meier, 1986), 1.

42 Bernard Shaw, "Introduction," Leonard S. Woolf, *International Government: Two Reports* (Brentano's, 1916), xvi, xvii.

43 Woolf, *International Government*, 4–5, 111, 125.

44 It is important to emphasize that the focus here is on the UN's primary purpose, to prevent war, with brief attention to its secondary purpose, to protect human rights. In these areas it has largely been a failure. Some of the agencies of the United Nations, however, have done very good work.

45 Woolf, *International Government*, 51.

46 Northedge, *The League of Nations*, 1.

47 Robert C. Hilderbrand, *Dumbarton Oaks: The Origins of the United Nations and the Search for Postwar Security* (University of North Carolina Press, 1990), x, 3.

48 No. 14861, International Convention on the Suppression and Punishment of the Crime of Apartheid. Adopted by the General Assembly of the United Nations on 30 November 1973, https://treaties.un.org/doc/Publication/UNTS/Volume%201015/volume-1015-I-14861-English.pdf

49 Köhler, *Global Apartheid*, World Order Models Project, 2, 6.

50 Rajni Kothari argues that poverty in the non-Western world, far from being rectified by Western-financed development, is actually "a consequence of a certain model of development" because "the colonial outreach of world capitalism gave rise to structures where the new phenomenon of poverty was a necessary concomitant of the pursuit of wealth globally" (*Poverty: Human Consciousness and*

the *Amnesia of Development* [Zed Books, 1993], 2).

51 John B. Cobb, Jr., *The Earthist Challenge to Economism: A Theological Critique of the World Bank* (Macmillan, 1999), 83. These figures, which differ from those of some other authorities, were derived by Cobb from the World Bank's *World Development Report 1991* (Oxford University Press, 1991), 204–05.

52 Nicola Phillips, "Power and Inequality in the Global Political Economy," *International Affairs*, 1 March 2017.

53 "How Many People Die from Hunger Each Year?" The World Counts; Jonathan Parks-Ramage; "844 Million People Around the World Can't Access Clean Drinking Water," VICE Impact, 16 November 2017; "10 Million Children Die from Lack of Health Care," Associated Press, 5 June 2008.

54 James Nickel, *Making Sense of Human Rights: Philosophical Reflections on the Universal Declaration of Human Rights* (University of California Press, 1987), 51.

55 Nickel, *Making Sense of Human Rights*, 18.

56 See: https://www.ohchr.org/en/professionalinterest/pages/cescr.aspx.

57 David C. Korten, *Globalizing Civil Society: Reclaiming Our Right to Power* (Seven Stories Press, 1998), 25.

58 John McMurtry, *The Cancer Stage of Capitalism* (Pluto Press, 1999), 163.

59 R. J. Vincent, *Human Rights and International Relations* (Cambridge University Press, 1986), 127.

60 George F. Kennan, "Review of Current Trends: US Foreign Policy," Thomas H. Entzold and John Lewis Gaddis, eds., *Documents on American Policy and Strategy, 1945–1950* (Columbia University Press), 226–28, at 226–27.

61 G. Lowes Dickenson, *The International Anarchy, 1904–1915*, 46.

62 Albert Einstein, *Einstein on Peace*, ed. Otto Nathan and Heinz Norden (Random House, 1981), 589.

63 Einstein, *Einstein on Peace*, 405.

64 Einstein, *Einstein on Peace*, 415.

65 Einstein, *Einstein on Peace*, 513.

66 Einstein, *Einstein on Peace*, 564.

67 William McNeill, *The Pursuit of Power: Technology, Armed Forces, and Society Since AD 1000* (University of Chicago Press, 1980), 383–84.

68 Ronald Glossop, *Confronting War: An Examination of Humanity's Most Pressing Problem* (1982; McFarland, 1995), vii. Optimism about nonuse of nuclear weapons by major powers, he said, "overlooks the logic of war and the tremendous advantage which comes from using nuclear weapons first rather than second. The aim of war is to use military power to win, to impose one's will on the other side. In such a situation if either side were facing defeat, it would use nuclear weapons rather than surrender. At the same time the side which was winning the war would want to use its nuclear weapons before sustaining such an attack from a desperate opponent" (44).

69 Sydney Lens, "World Government Reconsidered," *The Nation*, 17 September 1983.

70 Lorraine Elliott, *The Global Politics of the Environment* (New York University Press, 1988), 97, 117.

71 Kenneth Waltz, *Man, the State, and War: A Theoretical Analysis* (Columbia University Press, 1959), 15, 228.

72 Quoted by David Gauthier, *The Logic of Leviathan: The Moral and Political Theory of Thomas Hobbes* (Clarendon, 1969), 211.

73 Gauthier, *The Logic of Leviathan*, 211.

74 Waltz, *Man, the State, and War*, 228.

75 Waltz, *Man, the State, and War*, 210–12.

76 Einstein, *Einstein on Peace*, 570.

77 Joseph E. Schwartzberg, *Transforming the United Nations System: Design for a Workable World* (United Nations University Press, 2013), xxxi, 1, 297.

CHAPTER SEVENTEEN: MORALITY: THE GOLDEN AND SILVER RULES

1 John Mackie, *Ethics: Inventing Right and Wrong* (Penguin, 1977), 24.

2 Gene Reeves, "The Lotus Sutra and Process Thought," *Process Studies* 23/2 (Summer 1994): 98–118, at 108.

3 See Tu Wei-Ming, *Centrality and Commonality: An Essay on Confucian Religiousness* (State University of New York Press, 1989).

4 Gene Outka and John P. Reeder, Jr., eds., *Prospects for a Common Morality* (Princeton University Press, 1993), 3.

5 Michael Walzer, *Thick and Thin: Moral Argument at Home and Abroad* (University of Notre Dame Press, 1994), 169.

6 Walzer, *Thick and Thin*, 17.

7 Walzer, *Thick and Thin*, 172.

8 Walzer, *Thick and Thin*, 6.

9 Walzer, *Thick and Thin*, 10.

10 Amitai Etzioni, *The New Golden Rule: Community and Morality in a Democratic Society* (Basic Books, 1996), 165–66.

11 Michael J. Sandel, *Democracy's Discontent: America in Search of a Public Philosophy* (Harvard University Press, 1996), 160.

12 Sandel, *Democracy's Discontent*, 164.

13 Charles Taylor, "The Politics of Recognition," in *Multiculturalism: Examining the Politics of Recognition*, Charles Taylor et al., edited and with an introduction by Amy Gutmann (Princeton University Press, 1994), 64.

14 George Bernard Shaw, *Man and Superman* (Archibald Constable & Co., 1903), 227.

15 Walter T. Stace, *The Concept of Morals* (The MacMillan Company, 1937), 136.

16 *Pahlavi Texts of Zoroastrianism, Part 2 of 5: The Dadistan-i Dinik and the Epistles of Manusckihar.*

17 Simon Blackburn, *Ethics: A Very Short Introduction* (Oxford University Press, 2001), 101.

18 Diogenes Laërtius, "The Lives and Opinions of Eminent Philosophers," 1:36.

19 Isocrates, *Nicocles or the Cyprians*, 3:61.

20 "The Sentences of Sextus."

21 Henry Shue, *Basic Rights: Subsistence, Affluence, and U.S. Foreign Policy*, 2nd ed. (Princeton University Press, 1996), 19.

22 Shue, *Basic Rights*, 18.

23 Available at http://www.un.org/en/universal-declaration-human-rights/index.html.

24 James Nickel, *Making Sense of Human Rights: Philosophical Reflections on the Universal Declaration of Human Rights* (University of California Press, 1987), 51.

25 Nickel, *Making Sense of Human Rights*, 23.

26 Shue, *Basic Rights*, 153, referring to John Locke, *Two Treatises of Government*, Book II, Ch. V.

27 Shue, *Basic Rights*, 19.

28 Karen Armstrong "Let's Revive the Golden Rule," TEDGlobal 2009.

29 Armstrong "Let's Revive the Golden Rule."

CHAPTER EIGHTEEN: THE CHRISTIAN COMMUNITY

1 William Stringfellow, *An Ethic for Christians and Other Aliens in a Strange Land* (Word Books, 1973), 97.

2 Stringfellow, *An Ethic for Christians and Other Aliens in a Strange Land*, 114.

3 Stringfellow, *An Ethic for Christians and Other Aliens in a Strange Land*, 114.

4 Stringfellow, *An Ethic for Christians and Other Aliens in a Strange Land*, 114.

5 Stringfellow, *An Ethic for Christians and Other Aliens in a Strange Land*, 125.

6 Horsley, *Jesus and Empire*, 132.

7 Alfred North Whitehead, *Religion in the Making* (1926; Fordham University Press, 1996), 59.

8 Robert McAfee Brown, "The Barmen Declaration," adapted from Brown, *Kairos: Three Prophetic Challenges to the Church* (Eerdmans, 1990).

9 "Confessing Church," Britannica (https://www.britannica.com/topic/Confessing-Church); Leonore Siegele-Wenschkewitz, "Christians

against Nazis: the German Confessing Church," *Christianity Today,* Issue 9 (1986).

10 Dale M. Coulter, "The Barmen Declaration after Eighty Years," *First Things* (blog), 3 June 2014, https://www.firstthings.com/blogs /firstthoughts/2014/06/the-barmen-declaration-after-eighty-years.

11 "The Theological Declaration of Barmen" (http://www.creeds.net /reformed/barmen.htm). "We publicly declare before all evangelical Churches in Germany that what they hold in common in this Confession is grievously imperiled, and with it the unity of the German Evangelical Church. It is threatened by the teaching methods and actions of the ruling Church party of the 'German Christians' and of the Church administration carried on by them. These have become more and more apparent during the first year of the existence of the German Evangelical Church. This threat consists in the fact that the theological basis, in which the German Evangelical Church is united, has been continually and systematically thwarted and rendered ineffective by alien principles, on the part of the leaders and spokesmen of the 'German Christians' as well as on the part of the Church administration. When these principles are held to be valid, then, according to all the Confessions in force among us, the Church ceases to be the Church and the German Evangelical Church, as a federation of Confessional Churches, becomes intrinsically impossible."

12 Quoted in G. Clarke Chapman, *Facing the Nuclear Heresy: A Call to Reformation* (Brethren Press, 1986), 50.

Index

Lightning Source UK Ltd.
Milton Keynes UK
UKHW021417250220
359295UK00009B/1779